FORENSICS!

Ayn Embar-Seddon
Allan D. Pass

Prentice Hall
Upper Saddle River, New Jersey
Columbus, Ohio

*This book is dedicated in loving memory
to Frederick B. Seddon (1974–2007)*

Library of Congress Cataloging-in-Publication Data

Becvar, Dorothy Stroh.
  Family therapy : a systemic integration/Dorothy Stroh Becvar, Raphael J. Becvar. — 7th ed.
    p. ; cm.
  Includes bibliographical references and indexes.
  ISBN 978-0-205-60923-9 (alk. paper)
  1. Systemic therapy (family therapy) I. Becvar, Raphael J., 1931- II. Title.
  [DNLM: 1. Family Therapy—methods. 2. Models, Psychological. WM 430.5.F2 B398f 2009]
  RC488.5.B388 2009
  616.89'156—dc22

                                                                    2008026097

Vice President and Executive Publisher: Vernon Anthony
Senior Acquisitions Editor: Tim Peyton
Editorial Assistant: Alicia Kelly
Media Project Manager: Karen Bretz
Director of Marketing: David Gesell
Marketing Manager: Adam Kloza
Marketing Coordinator: Alicia Dysert
Production Manager: Kathy Sleys
Creative Director/Cover Design: Jayne Conte
Cover Illustration/Photo: Jupiter Images
Image Permission Coordinator: Angelique Sharps
Full-Service Project Management/Composition: Yasmeen Neelofar/GGS Book Services PMG
Printer/Binder: Hamilton Printing Company
Cover Printer: Demand Production Center

Pearson Education Ltd., London
Pearson Education Singapore, Pte. Ltd
Pearson Education Canada, Inc.
Pearson Education–Japan
Pearson Education Australia PTY, Limited

Pearson Education North Asia, Ltd., Hong Kong
Pearson Educación de Mexico, S.A. de C.V.
Pearson Education Malaysia, Pte. Ltd.
Pearson Education Upper Saddle River, New Jersey

Prentice Hall
is an imprint of

www.pearsonhighered.com

10 9 8 7 6 5 4 3 2 1
ISBN-13: 978-0-205-49345-6
ISBN-10:   0-205-49345-9

CONTENTS

PREFACE

This preface can be viewed as a user's manual for this text and will introduce you to some of the key features of the book. There is no one right way to read this text—or any text for that matter, but there are some things that might make your reading easier and more profitable. Each chapter begins with an outline, which can be useful as a study guide and as an orientation to the chapter. Skim the outline first. See what interests you, and make note of which topics may present you with challenges—you may want to reread these sections several times. In each chapter sidebars on a variety of interesting topics are presented alongside the text to draw your attention to them. Some are unusual and some are just fascinating. Many of them highlight the more far-flung reaches of forensics.

At the end of each chapter, you will find five important learning tools: *Definitions*, a *Webliography*, a *Bibliography*, *Review Questions*, and *Some Things to Think About*. You may want to take a look at the definitions before you begin the chapter. These will define key terms in the chapter that you should know and be able to use by the end of the chapter. If there are words that you are not familiar with, take the time to learn them up front. The *Webliography* will refer you to web sites that may not be directly discussed in the chapter, but that can serve as valuable resources. Some of the sites will allow you to explore topics in much greater detail than could be included in the chapter. The bibliography contains the sources that were used in the research that went into the writing of each chapter. You are encouraged to explore these sources as well.

Finally, there are *Review Questions* and *Some Things to Think About*. The review questions reinforce the material from the chapter. You are encouraged to read through the questions before you begin each chapter and keep them in mind as you work your way through the chapter, so you will be able to answer them easily. The answers to all of these questions can be found in the chapter. There is also a second set of questions: *Some Things to Think About*. The answers to these questions will not necessarily be found in the chapter but are designed to get you to think beyond the material that is discussed in this chapter and take it a step further—to encourage you to think outside the box.

ACKNOWLEDGMENTS

The authors wish to thank the following individuals for their invaluable assistance during this lengthy project: Michael Golebieski for his assistance with copyediting and graphics throughout the process of getting this book together. Pam Matthews and David Holmes for providing proofreading and copyediting comments throughout the writing process. John Michelli for his assistance obtaining sketches and crime scene photographs. Chief Scott A. Slagle and the Washington Township Police Department for providing crime scene photographs.

Reviewers

Dan Moeser
East Tennessee State University
Criminal Justice & Criminology
Johnson City, TN

Deborah L. Laufersweiler-Dwyer
University of Arkansas-Little Rock
Criminal Justice
Little Rock, AR

Paul Boatwright
State University of West Georgia
Chemistry Department
Carrolton, GA

Barry Gordon Fookes
UCF University of Central Florida
Chemistry Department
Orlando, FL

Steven B. Lee
San Jose State University
Justice Studies/Forensic Science
San Jose, CA

Glenn Langenburg
Hamline University
Department of Criminal Justice &
*   Forensic Sciences*
St. Paul, MN

Susan F. Hornbuckle
Clayton College and State University
Department of Natural Science
Morrow, GA

Brian Baker
Central Penn College
Summerdale, PA

Robert W. Peetz
Midland College
Department of Criminal Justice
Midland, TX

Lisa Morris
Penn State Abington
Division of Social Studies
Abington, PA

Max M. Houck
West Virginia University
Forensic Science Research Center
Morgantown, WV

ABOUT THE AUTHORS

Ayn Embar-Seddon received her doctorate in Criminology from Indiana University of Pennsylvania. She has been an educator for over 20 years, teaching in criminal justice, criminology, human services, and psychology. She teaches wholly online for Capella University and Everest College. Her research interests include violent sexual offenders, minorities and crime, international criminology theory, and identity development. She has published extensively in journals, authored a chapter in a criminological theory text, and has served as editor for a forensics encyclopedia. She currently resides in Kamloops, British Columbia, Canada, with her husband, Dan O'Reilly, a professor of philosophy, and three children: Emma, Tarika, and Ravi.

Allan D. Pass is a licensed and board-certified mental health practitioner with a specialty in forensic mental health. He received his doctorate from the University of Pittsburgh and has been in practice for over 35 years. In 1986, he founded National Behavioral Science Consultants, a behavioral sciences consulting firm. He is a recognized expert in forensic mental health related matters and testifies for criminal defense attorneys, the prosecution, and under direct court order. Pass has served as a hostage negotiator and criminal personality profiler in murder and sexual crime investigations for various state and local law enforcement agencies; provided extensive training services in crisis management/intervention and hostage negotiations to mental health agencies, correctional facilities, and hospitals; guest lectured at a variety of health industry agencies, and colleges and universities. He has published numerous professional articles in various journals.

Background Material

Section I is comprised of Chapter 1, *Introduction to Forensics*, and Chapter 2, *The History of Forensics*. Together these two chapters will acquaint you with the broad and exciting field of forensics. They are very much like a road map that you will use on your journey through forensics, and as with any road map, you should return here often. Chapter 1 presents an overview of the broad field of forensics. It stresses how important it is for a criminal justice professional, as an end-user of forensic science services, to be knowledgeable about forensics. Chapter 2 covers a very brief history of forensics, examining the history of law, the history of legal medicine, and the history of criminalistics. Understanding the history of forensics not only helps us know where we have been, but also can help us predict where we are going.

CHAPTER 1

Introduction to Forensics

CHAPTER OUTLINE

WHY STUDY FORENSICS?

Without a doubt, forensic science is becoming increasingly popular; this popularity rise can be attributed, at least partially, to increased exposure in the media. Turning the television on any evening of the week will reveal a variety of shows that feature forensics—from dramas to movies to newcasts. This interest extends all the way to children in grade school! Not only does *Scholastic Book Club* offer a selection of mysteries that focus on forensics, but they also offer a "Spy University" that children can join. The welcome packet even contains fingerprint cards and instructions on how to fingerprint!

There has also been an increase in interest in the forensic sciences among academicians and professionals. This can be seen in the number and variety of academic departments that offer courses (many just like the one you are taking right now) dealing with forensic issues; the number of books and articles written on forensic topics; the variety of forensics-related conferences offered; and the number of professional positions open in forensics-related work (i.e., recent visit to the job postings on the web site for the American Academy of Forensic Sciences www.aafs.org revealed open positions for a variety of forensics jobs ranging from document examiner to fingerprint analyst, and from forensic pathologist to DNA technician).

Forensic science is a fascinating field. Few disciplines are as varied and encompass as many sub-areas as forensics, while offering as many different employment opportunities. Think of why you are taking this class. Unlike many other courses that you will take in college, most students take a forensics course because they *want* to, not because they *need* to. Common reasons why students take forensics include: desire to solve complicated crimes, want to get an interesting job, find crime scenes fascinating, want to help people, keen interest in criminal justice. Forensics is a fascinating field. One reason it is so fascinating is because it enables us to see things that can't be seen: forensics makes fingerprints visible; it unravels strands of DNA; it reconstructs the scene of the crime; it can even tell you how the killer held the knife, and in which hand it was wielded (Figures 1.1 and 1.2).

Much of the public's perception of forensics has been formed by the media. The O. J. Simpson trial brought courtroom forensics into the viewers' homes. Forensics comes into our homes from fictional portrayals on television programs such as *CSI* and reality-based shows like *Forensic Files*. And there is nothing wrong with having had your interest sparked by the media—but keep in mind, shows like *CSI* present a fictionalized view of forensics, not a realistic view. Students who come into a forensics class thinking it will be just like television might be better served majoring in drama. Even the view of forensics that we get from the evening news is strongly skewed. The news focuses on the medical examiner's 15-second sound-bite, not on the years of schooling it took to become a forensic pathologist. This is not to state that forensics isn't a fascinating field—it is, but it's not Hollywood. In fact one very interesting aspect of the field is to examine the differences that exist between how forensics is portrayed and how it is experienced by those who actually work in the field.

These are two of the major reasons why forensics should be studied. First, it is a very interesting field. It brings together a variety of disciplines, from accounting to nursing to psychology to chemistry. It quite literally has something for everyone. Second, this is an area in which there are many job opportunities, and these job opportunities are likely to increase. Few disciplines also offer as many different employment opportunities as forensics. Most college students choose a major because of a combination of these two factors—interest and job availability. If you choose your major solely on the first factor—interest—you may enter a field that you love, but after graduation you may be stunned to find out that you can't work in that area,

FIGURE 1.1 Fingerprints have long
been used to identify individuals.

DNA Double Helix

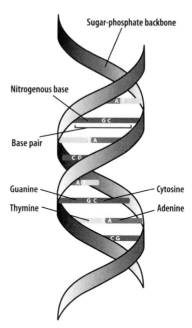

FIGURE 1.2 DNA has advanced the field of forensics.

or that jobs are very scarce—students who study philosophy or piano or rocket science often have difficulty finding a position in their field where they can make adequate money. On the other hand, if you focus solely on the second factor, you'll have no trouble finding a job, but it might be in an area that you really don't like and does not hold your interest for long. You may make adequate money, but you'll dread getting up each morning for work because you just don't like what you do—and that's a horrible way to live. As a student, it is best to keep both factors in mind. Yes, you want to do something that interests you, but you also want to be able to support yourself doing it!

WHY IS FORENSIC SCIENCE IMPORTANT?

Forensic science, a field related to criminal justice, has become increasingly important in recent years. There are at least four reasons why a student who is majoring in criminal justice should study the basics of forensic science:

1. The use of forensic evidence in the courtroom is increasing.
2. Many criminal justice students and professionals lack an understanding of what forensic science can and cannot do.
3. Forensic science services are often not used to their fullest potential.
4. Both students and professionals alike often have unrealistic expectations of forensics.

Prior to the 1960s, most cases were solved by direct admission of the suspect during questioning by law enforcement. The due-process revolution of the 1960s changed this. Once the rights of the accused were protected, and law enforcement could no longer rely on pressuring suspects to confess, physical evidence became increasingly important for the prosecution of cases.

Use of Forensic Evidence in the Courtroom Is Increasing

Scientific evidence has been used in courtrooms throughout recorded history, but during the past 100 years has evolved from being a fairly rare occurrence, usually limited to the medical profession— to becoming very routine. Scientific testimony has become increasingly important in criminal court, civil court, and in the classroom. Most criminal justice students are very surprised to learn that the bulk of the increase has been in the civil courts, in so-called toxic tort cases that involve product liability (Bjur and Richardson 1999). In criminal court, the increase in scientific testimony has been driven primarily by a decrease in reliance on confession of the suspect and secondarily by an increase in prosecutions that require statutory submission. In essence, criminal courts are *requiring* forensic evidence and testimony. The demand for scientific evidence—for understanding, collecting, and processing—has out-paced the knowledge of the hows and whys of forensic evidence possessed by many in the field. The overwhelming majority of forensic evidence presented in the criminal courts deals with drug evidence and DUI (driving under the influence) evidence, so-called "statutory submissions" because they are required to prove that a crime has occurred (DeForest et al. 1983). Because many criminal justice professionals do not have a good understanding of what forensic science *can* do, forensic laboratory services are often underutilized. Most laboratory time and effort is spent processing the statutory submissions, such as drug and alcohol evidence that must be submitted to the laboratory in order for the case to be prosecuted. Before a drug case can go to court, the laboratory must confirm that the substance that has been seized is, indeed, an illegal substance, and verify the amount of substance that has been seized (Figure 1.3). There has also been an increase in other types of forensic evidence presented in criminal court. DNA evidence has been used to exonerate individuals wrongly convicted and sitting on death row. Forensic psychologists and psychiatrists testify as to whether or not an individual is a violent sexual predator. In fact, many juries now have an expectation that forensic evidence will be presented to them and are often disappointed when very little actually is presented. When little or no forensic evidence is presented, the jurors may make unfounded assumptions based on the omission.

Lack of Understanding of Forensic Science's Capabilities

Even though forensic science is becoming more common in the criminal courtroom, the majority of criminal justice students and many criminal justice professionals lack a thorough understanding of what forensic science can and cannot do. This is not to imply that the education of the typical

FIGURE 1.3   Seized Marijuana plants.

criminal justice professional is lacking, but that there have been multiple difficulties in the delivery of forensic science education to criminal justice students. The forensic sciences are just that, sciences. Working in a laboratory with DNA or being a forensic entomologist requires years of specialized training in specific scientific disciplines. Most of this knowledge is far too specialized to be useful to the average criminal justice student who is not pursuing that particular area of study. Further, most of the forensic sciences develop and change at a rapid rate, requiring specialists to continually update their own education. (The same can be said for computer science.) If it is a challenge for the forensic biologist to remain up-to-date in forensic biology, it is unrealistic to expect that the patrol officer or detective would be able to stay current in the numerous areas that forensic science encompasses. Most police officers will receive on-the-job training that deals specifically with crime scene issues, however, some do not, or are not able to update their training often enough, and most other criminal justice professionals (lawyers and judges included) often receive no basic training in the forensic sciences. For many students, the extent of their knowledge may be limited to what they've seen on popular television shows like *CSI*, *Forensic Files*, or other similar shows, which would be like having all of your knowledge of the 1970s based on reruns of *Welcome Back, Kotter* and *The Brady Bunch*!

Acquiring knowledge about a particular area only through television is bound to give a rather skewed picture. While this may be only misleading for the general public, it is downright dangerous for forensic science consumers. Criminal justice professionals—especially those individuals in policing and the courts—are prime forensic science consumers on the criminal side of the law. Television, especially programs with a forensic theme, tends to present forensics as a cure-all—something that is capable of enabling criminal justice professionals to solve any case. Generally, these factors lead to unrealistically high expectations of forensics.

Forensic Services Underutilized

The lack of education and training amongst criminal justice professionals, especially those criminal justice professionals most likely to be forensics consumers, has led to an underutilization of forensic services. This is one reason why statutory submissions are the most frequent forensic evidence presented in the courtroom. Many law enforcement professionals submit only the forensic evidence they are required to. As a result, a considerable amount of forensic evidence never makes it into the courtroom and possibly valuable evidence, and valuable convictions may be lost. Proportionally, most forensic evidence is submitted for drug-related cases and not for serious felonies like rape and murder. Many of these non-drug cases still rely on eye-witness testimony to convict—which has often been found to be incorrect and has led to a considerable number of individuals going to prison for crimes they did not commit. Laboratory services other than those used for drug analysis are generally underutilized; conversely, the increasing need for analysis of drug submissions has driven an increase in these services at laboratories.

Unrealistic Expectations of Forensic Science

Even though forensic services are often underutilized, at the other extreme, many individuals have unrealistically high expectations of what forensics can do. This is seen among students, juries, and criminal justice professionals alike who may be influenced by what has been called the *CSI effect*. Although this term started as a clever way of referring to individuals who believed that all of the fancy forensics they see on television was true-to-life, researchers have begun to seriously look at the possible impact television might have on the outcome of court cases.

It is not uncommon to have beginning forensics students enter a classroom and expect things to be just like they are on television. They are stunned to find out that it may take hours to dust for fingerprints at a crime scene or that not all murder crime scenes have copious amounts of forensic evidence to analyze. They are surprised to discover that forensics has more to do with being in a laboratory than chasing criminals down the street. While forensics is very interesting, many areas of forensics require significant credit-hours in chemistry and numerous lab classes, which many students are not prepared for. The CSI effect can mislead college students as they choose a major that necessitates taking science courses they just can't handle. Students sometimes believe that forensics professionals are the ultimate jacks-of-all-trades—they respond to the crime scene, collect evidence at the scene, process evidence in the laboratory, and testify in court. In reality, forensic personnel are highly specialized. Some crime-scene technicians work solely on developing fingerprints. Some laboratories may have an individual who does nothing but processes DNA. But in no jurisdiction does the same person who develops fingerprints also process DNA!

The CSI effect may have created a heightened interest in forensics and this heightened interest has created a demand for universities to provide forensics classes. As incoming students clamor for forensics classes, many colleges and universities are adding classes to meet the demand. While some of these programs are rigorous and worthwhile, some offer courses that do little to prepare the student for working in the field. Employers are sometimes disappointed with new graduates—especially those who have degrees from programs that do not meet the American Academy of Forensic Sciences' accreditation standards.

While the CSI effect may mislead college students as they choose their majors, it is even more detrimental when a jury fails to convict a perpetrator because there is no forensic evidence or the forensic evidence was not exactly like it is on television. Juries are beginning to expect dramatic presentations of forensics—something that rarely occurs in criminal courts.

Criminal justice professionals are not immune to the CSI effect either. Some professionals also have unrealistically high expectations of forensic laboratories. They may erroneously believe that if there is forensic evidence in a case, good investigative work is not necessary, and forensic evidence alone guarantees a conviction. Even worse, they may labor under the premise that forensic evidence can make up for poor collection techniques or mishandling of the crime scene—when nothing could be further from the truth. This became a reality in the O. J. Simpson case.

If forensic science is to be used successfully in the criminal courts and to assist the judge and jury, criminal justice professionals need to know what forensic evidence should be collected, how forensic evidence should be collected, and what can realistically be expected from the analysis of this forensic evidence. A better understanding, through training, would lead to a broader use of forensic science services across the full spectrum of serious felonies. It is the aim of this text to provide such grounding for the student in the forensic sciences.

WHAT IS FORENSICS?

Before a study of any discipline can be undertaken it must first be defined. Forensic science can be defined either narrowly or broadly, and many different ways in between. The broad definition—the one that this text uses—defines forensic science as *the intersection of science and the law*. More narrowly, it can be defined as the application of the *natural sciences* to legal problems. This second definition would exclude areas like forensic psychology because psychology is a social science and not a natural science.

While defining the field to be studied is a great benefit, it can also be a drawback. Establishing boundaries for a discipline not only lets everyone involved know what is included, but it also states what is not included. It tells us what we should study to be knowledgeable about the field and in what areas the field is interested. It can also blind us to areas or research that is not contained within these boundaries that might be beneficial to the discipline. While we must define forensics, we should keep in mind that the boundaries of the discipline should be pliable enough to allow for new research and areas to be subsumed into the discipline.

Forensics—as the intersection of two disciplines, and sometimes several disciplines—is an interdisciplinary field. Forensics is not *one* discipline, but many that have come together to assist the finders of fact—the jury—in their search for the truth. Forensic science is also science in the service of the law. This does not imply that the law is *better than* or *more important* than science, but that forensics applies scientific knowledge to the legal arena.

WHAT IS CRIMINALISTICS?

A common error among beginning forensics students is to use the terms *forensics* and *criminalistics* interchangeably. While these terms are related, they are not interchangeable. Criminalistics is a subdivision of forensics that ". . . is concerned with the recognition, identification, individualization, and evaluation of physical evidence using the methods of the natural sciences in matters of legal significance" (DeForest et al. 1983, 4). The evidence must be examined with enough detail to be able to make a determination whether or not the evidence came from a particular source.

The American Board of Criminalistics defines criminalistics as "that profession and scientific discipline directed to the recognition, identification, individualization, and evaluation of physical evidence by application of the physical and natural sciences to law-science matters" (http://www.criminalistics.com/bylaws.cfm).

Forensics is the broader discipline; criminalistics is the narrower sub-section of forensics that includes the following areas: trace and transfer evidence (glass, soil, fibers, hairs, blood, and bodily fluids), accelerant and explosive residues, ballistics, document analysis, drug identification, and the interpretation of patterns and imprints (DeForest et al. 1983). Many of these areas, like fingerprint identification, developed out of good police and detective work—not inside academic laboratories.

ADVANCING THE FIELD OF FORENSICS

The field of forensics is advanced through the twin pillars of research and field experience—exactly the same way that any science advances. The testing and development of new forensic procedures in the academic arena is important, as is the testing and observation of what works in the field.

Research

Science is advanced through research. Research is a formal and controlled way of testing observations to learn about the nature of the world. We carry out informal research all the time through our observations. We may observe that we seem to get faster service in restaurants when we smile and make eye contact with the server. Because of this observation we may increase how often we smile and make eye contact with our server every time we visit a restaurant. We notice that we are always served promptly. Does this mean that smiling and making eye contact *actually* gets us better service? Maybe, then again, maybe not. While our perception may be that we are getting better service, it could be that because we are smiling, we feel more relaxed and happy, so even though we are waiting the same amount of time, we feel better during that wait. Or perhaps our server talks to us more frequently because we are smiling, but service actually isn't any faster. When we make these casual, everyday observations, there are many ways in which we could be wrong. Formal, controlled research seeks to eliminate many of the ways in which we can be wrong.

The formal way in which science learns about the world is through *the scientific method*, which is a process and consists of the following steps:

1. observing a phenomenon or identifying a problem
2. formulating a hypothesis that explains what has been observed; predicting results
3. choosing a procedure to investigate the phenomenon
4. conducting experiments—data collection
5. arriving at conclusions.

This procedure, with slight modifications, is the basis for all science. Although this is not a research text, let's discuss the process of research a little bit more.

OBSERVING   We can find our research question—that is the phenomenon we want to observe or the problem that we identify—in many ways. Some of our research questions come from what we observe in the field. Perhaps we observe that those interrogations that begin with several non-threatening questions are more likely to result in a confession than those interviews in which we begin by asking about the "instant offense"—the crime that has been committed. Research questions can also come from what we have observed in the laboratory. Advances in DNA technology have arisen because scientists who worked with DNA tried to find quicker, easier, and better ways of processing DNA.

Some research questions are designed to test a specific theory or portion of a theory. A theory is a broad set of statements that makes predictions about the way in which some aspect of the world behaves. For example, Gottfredson and Hirschi's (1990) version of Control theory states that the core reason why some individuals commit crime is that they lack adequate self-control.

FORMULATING   Once we have observed something that we want to investigate or arrived at a problem, we need to develop a hypothesis that explains the observation or problem. During this step, we predict our results from our hypotheses. We also need to determine if our hypothesis has already been investigated (from a thorough reading of the literature in our field), and whether or not our hypothesis can be investigated.

Our hypotheses may be written in the following ways:

Interrogations which begin with non-threatening questions are more likely to result in confessions.

DNA is processed better at higher temperatures.

Juveniles who commit crimes have lower levels of self-control than those who do not commit crimes.

CHOOSING   Perhaps the most important step in the research process and the one that presents the most problems to many beginning researchers is choosing how to investigate the phenomenon. The researcher faces many choices. First, the researcher must choose whether to investigate the phenomenon using a quantitative or a qualitative design. In the physical and biological sciences, quantitative designs are most frequently used. In the social and behavioral sciences, both quantitative and qualitative designs are conducted. Quantitative research seeks to make statements about a large number of subjects. It often collects data on many, many subjects. Qualitative research seeks mostly to describe phenomenon. It can be very useful when entering new areas of research that are not yet well defined; it is also useful to give a very detailed, in-depth picture of the research area.

The researcher may choose to use an experimental, quasi-experimental, or non-experimental design. Possible quantitative research options include experiments and surveys. Possible qualitative research options include case studies, focus groups, and surveys. This includes choosing what statistics to use. You can use descriptive statistics or inferential statistics (which make predictions).

CONDUCTING   The next step consists of conducting experiments. This is the process of data collection. Data may be collected in a laboratory, or it may be collected in the field. Some researchers will combine qualitative and quantitative methods in a mixed-method approach and collect data in several different ways—capitalizing on the strengths of each type of data collection and making up for the weaknesses.

ARRIVING   Finally the researcher will arrive at conclusions based upon the data that has been collected. During this final portion of the research, the researcher will write up and publish the results. This keeps the scientific community informed regarding what is happening. Researchers share their information with other researchers. This helps prevent duplication of effort—several researchers do not repeat the same research. It also encourages advancement. Other researchers can build upon what has been done and continue to advance the field.

Field Work

While modern forensics may seem to be driven by advances in DNA technology, it is also driven by the needs of the individuals who work in the field. Better fingerprint powders have been created because of the need to develop fingerprints on a wide range of surfaces and in a variety of environments. The area of criminalistics developed solely from those individuals who were working in the field and wanted to do things better. This will be discussed later in this chapter.

WHY THE INTERSECTION OF SCIENCE AND THE LAW CAN BE DIFFICULT

Forensics has been defined (broadly) as the intersection of science and the law. There are many reasons why this intersection can be especially difficult. Most of these difficulties stem from the very nature of interdisciplinary fields, and because the fields involved in forensic science have significant basic differences from each other.

Interdisciplinary fields are inherently difficult because we have traditionally separated academic disciplines into discrete departments. We have been trained to view separate disciplines as just that—separate, discrete, unrelated, unconnected. This traditional way of viewing academic disciplines as separate makes us believe, for example, that our knowledge of music is in no way related to our knowledge of math. Yet research has shown that the pattern recognition that makes someone good at music also may allow the person to excel at math.

It is difficult for such separate disciplines to come together in any fashion. Sometimes this is because a particular discipline fought long and hard for recognition as separate. Criminology, for example, arose primarily from sociology. There are still academicians who do not acknowledge it as a legitimate discipline. Many criminologists would dislike working in sociology for fear of losing their own identity.

Sometimes, there is resistance because being truly interdisciplinary requires knowledge of many areas (or at least several areas). The forensic psychologist not only must have good knowledge of psychology but of the law as well. Knowledge of one or the other is not enough. At a recent lecture, the speaker attempted to try to discuss a topic at the intersection of philosophy and criminal justice. While she was a well-known philosopher, her lack of criminal justice knowledge made her presentation much less relevant than if she also had a basic grounding in criminal justice.

Reluctantly, some closely related disciplines will come together, if necessary. Chemistry and biology form biochemistry, sociology and psychology form social psychology. In these two examples, like many other interdisciplinary fields, the two parent disciplines that come together are the same *type* of science. Chemistry and biology are natural sciences and sociology and psychology are social sciences. So, although the phenomena studied in each parent discipline differs and the knowledge base differs, the goals, methods, and *ways of knowing* are the same. In forensic science, the two parent disciplines are very dissimilar, having different goals, methods, ways of knowing, and different knowledge bases. This makes the intersection all the more difficult.

Considerable friction and difficulties occur when two or more unlike disciplines try to come together. Frequently, one discipline will try to be *dominant*, and impose its goals, methods, and ways of knowing on the others. Truly interdisciplinary fields should treat all disciplines as equal, respecting the contributions of each. Individuals in each discipline tend to know only their own discipline—lawyers know the law, scientists know science—and they tend to be territorial, not wanting to give up control of their own discipline and not wanting to admit outsiders (Meyer 1999).

Goals, Methods, and *Ways of Knowing* in Science and the Law

The goals of science and the law are inherently different. Science generally has as its goal the formulation of laws and theories that will reliably predict some sort of phenomenon. For example, Big Bang theory explains how the universe is constantly expanding from the instant of its creation. Science generally is future-oriented and seeks to make statements along the lines of: "If X happens, then Y will occur." The goals of the law, or at least the goal of the courtroom trial is to determine, as much as possible, how events occurred in the past. For example, the law may ask questions like "did this product cause an adverse reaction that lead to an individual's death?" or "did the defendant commit murder?" The law is less concerned with making future predictions. Only in limited ways does the court concern itself with the future. These areas often fall under the umbrella of forensic mental health (e.g., predictions of dangerousness), or in setting legal precedent for future prosecutions.

The interface of the goals of science and the goals of the law is further complicated because goals and methods vary considerably among types of sciences involved: medicine, the social sciences, and the physical sciences. We are not only trying to interface the goals and methods of one field of science with the law, but the various goals of several types of science with the goals of the law.

Science and the law also do not share similar methods. Science employs the scientific method; a process of formulating a hypothesis, testing that hypothesis through research, and formulating theories. Old theories are discarded as new ones are constructed that explain a phenomenon better. In the law, method consists of referring to past cases, decisions, and opinions and likening them to a current case. This is the case law method. By the very nature of how case law works, one case builds upon another. Later decisions build upon earlier decisions, with earlier decisions rarely overturned. (This is one reason why the *Brown v. Board of Education* decision was such a landmark case, not only did it pave the way for an end to segregation but it overturned years of previous Supreme Court decisions that had supported *Plessy v. Ferguson*.)

Beyond the differences between the goals and methods of science and the goals and methods of the law, there is a more basic difference in how individuals in these fields approach knowing (epistemology). These fields are vastly different from each other and they ask different types of questions. They view the world in different ways. Scientists—whether they are in medicine, physics, or psychology—are trained in vastly different ways than lawyers, judges, or police officers are trained.

Science in the Service of the Law

Although forensic science is the intersection of the discipline of science and the discipline of the law, in the context of the courtroom, science is in service of the law. Science becomes a tool of the law and the law takes precedence. This is an important point for anyone in forensics to keep in mind, especially the expert witness who will testify on the stand. The court wants the services of the expert to help the jury decide the facts of the case. The rules of evidence determine what sort of testimony the expert may give.

Media Presentation of Forensics

Much of the interest in forensics, or any area of criminal justice on the part of the student or the general public, is generated by the media and how criminal justice is portrayed therein. Many individuals who work in criminal justice today—whether they are police officers, professors, or forensic psychologists—initially became interested in criminal justice because of a television program, a movie, or a news story. In the early 1980s, *Hill Street Blues* made police work popular and *L.A. Law* made the legal field sexy. In the early 1990s, Jodie Foster in *The Silence of the Lambs* helped spur an interest in criminal personality profiling and forensic psychology among college-aged women. Of course, now we have shows like *CSI*, *Cold Case*, *Forensic Files*, and *The New Detectives* creating much of the current interest among students and the public.

Unfortunately, any representation of forensics in the media, even the news (some would say "especially the news"), is a misrepresentation. While the news may have historically been used primarily to inform the public, it now must compete for ratings and provide entertainment. There is an old saying in newscasting: "If it bleeds, it leads." While news professionals shudder to hear this, most acknowledge that in many markets, it is true. High profile criminal justice stories sell newspapers and increase television ratings. Also, in an economy where less money is being spent by media outlets on news, criminal justice stories require less time, effort, and money to produce; rather than having to do a lot of research on a story, the police blotter can be used to find an interesting case to be highlighted. These two factors have worked together to increase the overall percentage of crime and criminal justice stories in the media over the past 20 years. In fact, more than 20 percent of all media time is devoted to criminal justice-related news, programs, and movies.

The increased exposure of criminal justice in the media is a double-edged sword. On the positive side, there is an increased awareness of criminal justice and forensics, the public is better informed, an interest is created in the profession, and there is increased scrutiny of law enforcement, serving as yet another safeguard against abuse. On the negative side, the increased exposure of criminal justice in the media creates misperceptions regarding the types of crimes that occur and how the criminal justice system operates. The media create increased levels of fear of crime, pressure on law enforcement to resolve cases, and knee-jerk policy reactions. It also can create more clever criminals.

On a basic level, every newscast that focuses on criminal justice issues and every television show that deals with forensics helps create more awareness in the public of how criminal justice works. Even if this is your first criminal justice class, you already know the Miranda Warnings ("You have the right to remain silent . . ."). This has nothing to do with the criminal justice education you are currently receiving; it is a reflection of having watched television.

News broadcasts help to keep the public informed about crimes that may affect their daily lives. If there has been a rash of burglaries in your neighborhood, you can be advised to take extra precautions. When law enforcement is looking for a fugitive, his or her photo can be broadcast on local news and they may be located sooner. "Amber Alert" warnings inform a community that a child has been kidnapped and can mobilize the eyes and ears of an entire community to help find that child.

The increased media attention—especially when portrayed in an exciting light—creates an interest in the profession. We cannot help but be drawn toward interesting crime stories, whether those stories focus on the police, the courtroom, corrections, or the laboratory. Everyone wants to know "whodunit?"

Finally, the media helps the public scrutinize law enforcement. A hallmark of the policing system in the United States is that it does not operate in secret as many police organizations did in formerly Communist countries. Police operations can be observed by anyone. When the media shines its spotlight on law enforcement, it helps to keep law enforcement honest. Police officers know that at any time their actions could be observed and, therefore, are less likely to behave in an unscrupulous manner.

The increased exposure of criminal justice in the media has an equally negative side. Because the media concentrates on what sells, rather than the typical criminal justice stories, this creates misperceptions of the crime rate and severity, which in turn leads to a general misperception of what criminal justice is, and how it operates. Watch any newscast anywhere in the country and the top of the hour is usually filled with stories of homicides, rapes, robberies, and drug crimes; these stories are generally repeated for days. This ignores the fact that most crimes are non-violent, petty, and result in the loss of very little property or money.

Even though most viewers have a very low likelihood of victimization, fear of crime increases because of the way in which crimes are focused upon in the news. Constantly being bombarded with images of violent crime, the public feels increasingly vulnerable. It is a common perception that crime is increasing. In fact, crime has been decreasing at a fairly steady rate since the middle of the 1990s.

Media exposure can exacerbate pressures on law enforcement to quickly resolve cases. When law enforcement is pressured, mistakes can be made, or corners can be cut, resulting in the arrest of the innocent and the guilty going free. Media exposure can also impede the investigation of a case when key information is prematurely released to the public.

Overexposure to criminal justice issues also causes knee-jerk reactions and unwise policy creation as the public and government representatives react to criminal justice problems that either do not exist or that are being misrepresented.

THE REALITY OF FORENSIC SCIENCE'S USES

The reality of forensics and crime scene investigation is that only a small percentage of physical evidence is actually collected and submitted. The vast majority of effort expended by forensic personnel is concentrated upon the collection, submission, and analysis of drug and alcohol evidence. Finally, not all crimes will receive the same amount of investigative effort from law enforcement.

Small Percentage of Physical Evidence Actually Collected and Submitted

Although there have been many advances in forensics, we need to keep in mind that not all crimes yield the same types or amounts of forensic evidence and some evidence is better than other evidence. Also, even when there is forensic evidence, it may not be collected. Everyone has had the experience (or knows someone who has) of being the victim of a minor crime, such as theft, and when the police arrive at the scene, they do not dust for fingerprints, even though they may very well be present; in fact, little is done, other than taking an initial report. Many crimes are not deemed important enough to expend the effort to collect evidence. Many petty thefts would yield prints, but the cost of collecting the forensic evidence exceeds the dollar-value lost in the crime, so very little investigative effort and no forensic effort is devoted to these offenses (DeForest et al. 1983).

Most Laboratory Effort Spent on Drug and Alcohol Analysis

The types of cases that are most likely to have evidence submitted for forensic analysis are drug cases (DeForest et al. 1983), homicide, rape and sexual assault, arson, and burglary. By far, most evidence that is submitted to forensic laboratories for analysis are resultant from drug investigations and the samples must be submitted for identification and sometimes quantification before a case can be prosecuted. For DUI cases, blood-alcohol evidence must be submitted. These statutory cases comprise the vast majority of work of forensic laboratories across the country. The remaining evidence that is analyzed generally comes from serious felonies, index crimes like rapes and murders, however, these are a small minority of laboratory submissions.

Not All Crimes Receive the Same Amount of Investigative Attention

Because of the nature of certain crimes, some will create and (hopefully) leave behind significant amounts of forensic evidence. Crimes such as homicide, sexual assault, and arson tend to leave a lot more forensic evidence than theft or bribery. Other than drug and alcohol offenses which, by statute, must submit evidence for analysis, those crimes that leave more forensic evidence will receive more forensic attention.

It is true that not all crime scenes receive the same sort of treatment by law enforcement. The amount of investigative effort and law enforcement dollars spent on a crime varies with the type of crime that has been committed. This sometimes comes as a shock to the general public, especially when someone has been victimized, that law enforcement does not treat all crimes the same way.

Not all crimes are a priority. Crimes that are perceived as being more dangerous are given more attention. Crimes with certain types of victims may be given more attention. Law enforcement has been fairly bad at protecting children from those who cause them the most harm (parents). Unfortunately, crime that occurs in middle-class and wealthy neighborhoods may receive more attention than crimes that occur in lower-income areas. Generally felonious crimes are given high importance and misdemeanors are not. If a theft or burglary has occurred, law enforcement will only put substantial effort into a follow-up investigation when losses are in excess of a certain dollar-amount, generally $5,000.

High-profile crimes, such as the murder of JonBenét Ramsey, or Nicole Brown Simpson, received an inordinate amount of law enforcement attention. Oddly enough, neither crime has resulted in a successful prosecution. High-profile crimes are not just those that happen to the wealthy and famous; shocking and especially heinous crimes may also receive a significant amount of law enforcement attention.

The vast majority of crimes that are reported only receive an initial investigation, with its attendant paperwork, and nothing further is done. If the crime is a theft of books from an automobile, little more may be done by law enforcement than taking a report. The report can be useful for the tracking of crimes, perhaps to determine if there has been a series of similar crimes. For a simple theft like this, the vehicle will not be dusted for fingerprints. Nor should it be. If this was done, the damage to the vehicle from the fingerprint powders (which can be difficult to clean up), would generally exceed the total value of what was lost in the theft. For a victim, it can be disheartening to learn that law enforcement only pursues those investigations that reach a certain dollar value or dangerousness, but this is the reality of law enforcement. Like all other government agencies, law enforcement and what it can and cannot do, is driven by cost-concerns. Contrary to popular belief, law enforcement does not have a never-ending supply of money. Many state, county, and local agencies are barely getting by on the budget they have. This is especially the case in poorer counties and municipalities, many of which may not be able to even fund their own law enforcement agency and may rely on state law enforcement, or another larger agency to provide services. All of this stretches resources very thin and requires that difficult (or controversial) choices must be made as to which crimes will receive the greatest law enforcement expenditure of time and money. Law enforcement prioritizes the investigation of crimes based on what funding they have for operations; along with the severity of the crime, political pushes and pulls come into play along with other discretionary factors.

Sometimes criminal justice students—and more especially the general public—labor under the belief that all of the advances in the forensic sciences will lead to all cases being solved. There is also the perception that law enforcement investigates all crimes equally, giving all the same effort and devoting the same amount of resources to each case. Both of these perceptions are false.

Mishandling of Forensic Evidence

There have been a number of famous cases where forensic evidence was not handled properly. The O. J. Simpson trial drew considerable attention to the potential mishandling of forensic evidence. Proper evidence-handling boils down to proper procedure and proper processing. At the scene, on the way to the laboratory, and in the laboratory, evidence must be handled according to established guidelines to prevent contamination, which can lead to questions concerning the veracity of the evidence. There are copious opportunities for evidence to be mishandled, the first-responder may neglect to cordon off an area that contains evidence; an investigator may forget to sign the log and disrupt the chain of custody; evidence may be mislabeled at the laboratory or contaminated with another sample. Unfortunately, once that happens, the veracity of the evidence cannot be reestablished, and the evidence is lost. Everyone involved in the investigative process from the first-responder to the laboratory technician to the expert witness must follow established procedures.

WHAT THIS BOOK COVERS

This text will introduce the student to the sub-areas of forensics that are most likely to be encountered by criminal justice professionals in their daily work. It also presents topics that are not as frequently encountered but have special interest. The text is divided into six sections, each containing two or three chapters of related topics.

Section I, *Background Material* provides a foundation for your reading of the text and the study of forensic sciences. Chapter 1 begins with a discussion of the importance of forensic science not only to the student but to the field of criminal justice. Forensics is defined as the intersection of science and the law, an intersection that is sometimes difficult because the goals of science and the goals of the law are very different. There is also a discussion of the impact of how forensics is presented in the media. This presentation influences criminal justice policy in general and has been responsible for much of the current interest in forensics. Chapter 2 presents a history of forensic science. Because forensics is the intersection of numerous disciplines, it can be difficult to present a comprehensive history; this chapter will discuss several disciplines that have contributed to modern forensics, including the legal field, legal medicine, and criminalistics.

Section II, *Processing the Evidence*, acknowledges the importance of the crime scene and evidence processing in forensics. In a sense, Chapter 3, which discusses the crime scene, is the most important chapter of the book. It is at the crime scene that the practitioner must recognize what is forensic evidence and properly collect that evidence for processing. If the crime scene is not properly handled, all forensic evidence may be irrevocably lost or contaminated and therefore inadmissible in the courtroom. No amount of technical testimony or number of highly-qualified experts can make up for mistakes made at the crime scene. This chapter lists the crimes most likely to produce forensic evidence and discusses in detail how physical evidence is classified and what the prosecutor may establish with the forensic evidence. Chapter 4 introduces the student to the crime laboratory, including the history, organization, and services that crime laboratories provide. Not all laboratories are created equal. Laboratories in the United States may be run by state governments or county governments. Fewer laboratories are run privately at universities or private companies. The Federal Bureau of Investigation runs the only federal laboratory in the country.

Section III, *Drugs, Documents, and Doorjambs*, consists of Chapters 5 through 7. Chapter 5 presents a discussion of chemicals, poisons, drugs, chemical analysis, and statutory analysis. Drug and statutory analyses represent the largest volume of work for forensic laboratories. This chapter also discusses drug testing in the workplace, alcohol analysis, and toxicology. Chapter 6 looks at document analysis, computer forensics, and fraud. At first glance it may seem like these three areas are very diverse, but there is considerable overlap. Document analysis encompasses everything from the analysis of inks and papers, to verification of signatures, to analysis of faxes and copies. As computer technology and interconnectivity has advanced, computer forensics is becoming increasingly important. Computers can be used to assist in the commission of traditional crimes and they have spawned new crimes. Computers also present unique challenges to law enforcement because collection and processing of evidence from a computer is very different from the collection and processing of more traditional forms of evidence. Fraud is another very broad topic, ranging from identity theft to scams to insider trading. Chapter 7 looks at the forensic investigation of burglary and accidents, focusing on tool marks, tire and shoe impressions, soil examination, and paint and glass examination. It also discusses the oldest form of forensic evidence still in use—fingerprints.

Section IV, *Violent Felonies*, consists of Chapters 8 through 10. Chapter 8 focuses on the process of dying and death investigation. This includes many of the sub-areas of forensics that may be involved in conducting a death investigation; forensic pathology, forensic entomology, forensic anthropology, forensic odontology, bloodspatter analysis, and ballistics. This chapter also looks at the unique challenges of dealing with the "long" dead. While most homicide cases are quickly solved, the longer time that elapses from the commission of the crime and the discovery of the body, the more difficulties that may arise in successfully investigating the case. This chapter covers decomposition, buried bodies, forensic anthropology, forensic odontology, and forensic entomology. Chapter 9 is devoted to DNA analysis. DNA, first introduced to criminal justice in the mid-1980s has truly caused a revolution. DNA has been used to exonerate the wrongfully convicted and with the more recent advent of mitochondrial DNA, smaller samples can now be used for analysis—leading to the solving of many formerly unsolved cases. Chapter 10 presents assault, abuse, and sexual crimes, beginning with the area of victimology. Victimology is the "study of the victim" and focuses on how victims fit into the forensic investigation. Too often, the victim is discounted in the criminal justice system; in forensics, the victim is significant to the development of the case. This chapter examines rape and sexual crimes and many of the forensic sub-areas that may be involved in their investigation, including serology, DNA analysis, hair and fiber analysis, and fragment analysis. This chapter also discusses forensic aspects of domestic violence and child abuse investigation.

Section V, *Very Large Crime Scenes; Forensic Mental Health*, consists of Chapters 11 and 12. Chapter 11 covers fires, arsons, explosions, and mass casualties. These crime scenes are typically much larger than the *average* crime scene. Although an arson crime scene may be limited to a car or other small area, these scenes frequently encompass an entire building. Explosions create an even larger crime scene, with debris and evidence scattered far away from the center of the explosion. Mass casualties—airplane crashes, bombings, and explosions, involve many people and are often spread out over a significantly large area. These much larger crime scenes present unique problems to forensics teams. They are more difficult to secure and because evidence is located over a much larger geographic area, evidence may be harder to identify and collect. Chapter 12 presents forensic mental health. Not long ago, the only scientists who were routinely permitted to testify as experts in a court of law were medical doctors. If an expert opinion needed to be made regarding a person's mental state, perhaps while making out a will or during the commission of a crime, the individual who testified would be a forensic psychiatrist—a medical doctor who had specialized in psychiatry—although he (and it was almost always a he) would probably not have called himself a forensic psychiatrist but perhaps a criminal psychiatrist or simply a psychiatrist. The modern courtroom allows a variety of professionals with different types of training, education, and experience to now testify in court. Had this book been written just a few years ago, this chapter would have been entitled *Forensic Psychology*, but in the post-millennia courtroom, many individuals who testify regarding mental status do not hold degrees in psychology, they have degrees in social work or behavioral science or counseling. Forensic mental health deals with the interface of behavioral science and the law. Forensic mental health is a very broad discipline on its own. This chapter discusses topics ranging from police selection and training, to insanity and competency evaluations, to prediction of dangerousness, to treating offenders and mandated counseling. Unlike most forensic science professionals who do the majority of their work prior to a case going to court, the average forensic mental health professional can be involved in all aspects of the criminal justice process, from training police officers, to evaluating offenders prior to trial, to treating individuals in correctional settings and after they have been released back into society.

Section VI, *In the Courtroom and the Future of Forensics*, is comprised of Chapters 13 and 14. Chapter 13 moves away from the crime scene and into the courtroom, focusing on the functioning of the expert witness on the stand. All of the preparation from the previous chapters results in a case being ready to be presented in court. If forensic science is to be a useful tool within the criminal justice system, the expert witness must present findings to the jury in a clear, concise, and easily understandable manner. The forensic work that has taken place up until this point, from the crime scene to the laboratory, can be useless if the information is not presented well to the jury. Although many forensic scientists are reluctant to admit it, forensic science really is science in the service of the law. Chapter 14 presents forensics in an international light and also looks at the future of forensic science. The majority of this text has examined forensics from a U.S. point of view; but there is much to be gained from stepping back and using a more global perspective. Forensic techniques have been used to identify victims of genocide and mass disasters around the world. Any predictions that are made regarding the future, in any area, are likely to be more incorrect than correct; however, we can make some predictions about the future of forensics that are likely to be correct. DNA technology will continue to play an important role in forensics, as will computer technology. Technological advances touch all aspects of our lives, and forensics is no different. Yet there are many areas of forensics where future development is hard to predict. No doubt there will be many interesting developments in the future that we could not even begin to guess about right now. Science has a way of surprising even the experts.

Glossary

Criminalistics—a subdivision of forensics concerned with recognition, identification, individualization, and evaluation of physical evidence using the physical and natural sciences.

Interdisciplinary—the intersection of two or more fields or subfields of study.

Qualitative research—seeks mostly to describe phenomenon.

Quantitative research—seeks to make statements about a large number of subjects.

Scientific method—a formalized way of carrying out research.

Statutory submission—evidence that must be submitted for analysis to prosecute a case, drug or alcohol evidence, for example.

Webliography

American Board of Criminalistics
   http://www.criminalistics.com
Forensics on Television
   http://www.angelfire.com/jazz/jboze3131/forensicsontv
   .htm

http://www.science.ie/content/content.asp?id=734
http:// shop.store.yahoo.com/pomegranate/q125.html
Criminal Justice and the Media
   http://www.criminology.fsu.edu/cjlinks/media2.html

References

American Board of Criminalistics. Accesses on April 28, 2006, from http://www.criminalistics.com/bylaws.cfm

Bjur, R., and J. Richardson. "Expert Testimony Involving Chemists and Chemistry." In *Expert Witnessing: Explaining and Understanding Science.* Edited by Carl Meyer, 67–87, Chapter 5. Boca Raton, FL: CRC Press, 1999.

DeForest, P., R. Gaensslen, and H. Lee. *Forensic Science: An Introduction to Criminalistics.* NY: McGraw-Hill, 1983.

Eckert, W. ed., *Introduction to Forensic Sciences,* 3rd ed. Boca Raton, FL: CRC Press, 1997.

Gottfredson, M., and T. Hirschi. *A General Theory of Crime.* Standford: Stanford University Press, 1990.

Meyer, C. "Science, Medicine and the U.S. Common Law Courts." In *Expert Witnessing: Explaining and Understanding Science,* Edited by C. Meyer, 1–29, Chapter 1. Boca Raton, FL: CRC Press, 1999.

Review Questions

1. Why is the intersection of science and the law difficult?
2. Why don't all crimes receive the same amount of investigative effort?
3. What might contribute to the fact that drug and alcohol submissions comprise the bulk of the submissions to forensic laboratories?
4. Discuss some of the factors that have lead to an increased interest in forensic science.
5. Why is it important for criminal justice professionals to be acquainted with forensics?
6. Why are forensic services sometimes underutilized?
7. Why do interdisciplinary fields tend to be more difficult than those fields that are not interdisciplinary?
8. Explain how the increased exposure of criminal justice in the media is a "double-edged sword"
9. How does media exposure perpetuate misperceptions in the type and volume of crimes being committed?
10. Which crimes are most likely to yield a considerable amount of forensic evidence?

Some Things to Think About

1. Consider why you are taking this class right now. Why is it that you want to increase your knowledge of forensics? Is it because you are a fan of forensics shows and movies and find this area of study interesting? Do you plan on working within criminal justice and want to be an educated consumer of forensic science? Did you need an elective and this course fit your schedule? Or is it something else?

2. Should there be more restrictions on what sort of criminal justice stories can be shown on news broadcasts?

3. Take a look at the entire text. What area or areas do you think you will find most interesting? Why?

The History of Forensics

HISTORY OF FORENSICS—MANY THREADS

Forensic science is both complex and fascinating. Presenting a history of forensic science can be a complicated undertaking not only because of the diverse nature of the subdisciplines of forensics but also because forensics has a tendency to borrow only what it needs from a scientific discipline without necessarily embracing the entirety of that discipline. Forensic science is not one field but many disciplines that come together at the intersection of science and the law. This intersection makes for a highly diverse field, encompassing subdisciplines ranging from ballistics, fingerprinting, and document analysis to forensic anthropology, DNA analysis, and toxicology. The word *forensics*, after all means "having to do with the law." Placing the word "forensics" in front of any science or discipline denotes that we are now entering the area where that science or discipline deals with the law in some way.

It is not the goal of this text to present a comprehensive history of forensics that encompasses all of the unique histories of each forensic subdiscipline. An undertaking like that would necessitate thousands of pages and would be overwhelming. The history of forensics presented here is necessarily brief, highlighting the most important historical developments of many forensic subdisciplines, and providing you with a historical grounding for the remainder of the text. If you are asking yourself why we are bothering to look at the past in such detail, it is because what has happened in the past provided the groundwork for what is happening now and what will happen in the future.

This book will address four broad, key areas in the history and development of forensic science; the legal field, legal medicine, criminalistics, and forensic and police laboratories. This chapter discusses the history of the legal field and the history of legal medicine, both of which date back into antiquity. It also presents the history of the discipline of criminalistics, which has its origins in modern police work. Chapter 4 will present the historical development of forensic and police laboratories.

HISTORY OF THE LEGAL FIELD

The history of the law is a long history indeed. All societies, as they advance, develop systems of law and even less complex societies have tended to develop rudimentary legal systems. The laws that evolve develop to regulate interactions among human beings. In all societies, the powerful tend to have a disproportionate say in the laws that are created. Laws are also created by those in power to help them maintain their positions of power and to control the less powerful in society. In fact, until very recently, no attempt at any sort of equity in law making was made. Although modern democracy, in the United States and other nations, is far from perfect, it represents a very bold attempt at giving all adults a say in the laws and how they are governed.

The earliest complex legal systems appeared around 4000 B.C. in Egypt and Mesopotamia. The Ancient Greek and Roman legal systems significantly influenced not only our own legal system, but every legal system in the world. Scientific evidence has always had a place in courtrooms, especially evidence regarding cause of death. Other types of scientific evidence, in general, have not been welcomed into the courtroom until recently. This is largely due to the fact that science as we know it was only born a few hundred years ago. It has taken several centuries for science to make the advances that it has. Although medicine has been around for thousands of years, it too was very rudimentary until about 200 years ago.

Pre-History Law

Laws are written rules and regulations that govern behavior. Laws are established by a government or a ruler. Earlier societies that had not developed writing still had rules, but, of course, they were not written down. These rules are generally referred to as *mores*, which are the customs of the group. Mores are far more malleable than laws. Both mores and laws developed over time to regulate relations among human beings and to resolve conflict. Over time, as societies developed written ways of communicating some of these mores would become laws. They were written down, or codified. Others, those of lesser importance, remained mores.

The earliest laws developed around marital relations, not only regarding marriage specifically, but also pertaining to inheritance and property. These rules and laws became necessary as societies moved away from tribal and communal living, where everything (property and children) was shared, to familial living and individual ownership of property. And by saying *individual ownership*, we are really referring to male ownership of property (women and children were considered to be property).

Laws also developed governing contracts, sales, and agreements. The earliest laws that develop are civil laws. Criminal law has always been a rather late development in legal systems and some historical systems never developed a system of criminal law. This is not to say that actions like *murder* and *theft* were not considered to be wrong in these societies. These actions were wrong and punishments were attached to them, however, the laws punishing these sorts of behavior were not distinguished from the civil law.

Ancient History

Although certainly there are many ancient societies that developed complex legal systems, this section will briefly focus on the development of law in four significant ancient societies; the Egyptians, the Mesopotamians, the Greeks, and the Romans.

EGYPTIANS   The Egyptians had one of the earliest systems of law, dating back to at least 4000 B.C. (Figure 2.1). This was not a static system but became increasingly advanced over thousands of years. Scientific evidence was presented in Egyptian courts. Records exist indicating that high priests made determinations regarding cause of death. Interestingly, the Egyptians did not allow lawyers to represent the parties involved in a dispute. They felt that this would turn the court into a place where only argument mattered and not the truth. (Some critics of our own legal system would say that the court has become a place where the side that argues better wins.) Rather, the individual parties spoke directly to the judge (Wigmore 1936). The Egyptians also invented the concept of international law—making treaties and engaging in commerce with foreign nations.

MESOPOTAMIANS   The Mesopotamians developed a complex legal system, beginning at around the same time as the Ancient Egyptians, 4000 B.C. (Figure 2.2). Perhaps their greatest contribution to law was the Code of Hammurabi (2100 B.C.). This was not the first code of laws in Mesopotamia, but rather a compilation of laws assembled by King Hammurabi. The code of Hammurabi is inscribed on an eight-foot tall pillar, and obviously intended to be placed where it could be viewed. This is the first time in history that a ruler attempted to write down and display the laws so that everyone (who was literate) could read them. The Code was rediscovered in 1901 in what is now Iran. It currently resides in the Louvre Museum in Paris, France.

FIGURE 2.1   Ancient Egypt's system of law dates back to at least 4000 B.C.

FIGURE 2.2   The Mesopotamians developed a complex legal system around 4000 B.C.

Although the Code of Hammurabi addresses marital relations, inheritance, contracts, theft, kidnapping, harboring escaped slaves, assault, and murder, among other actions, it does not distinguish between civil and criminal law. So, although the Mesopotamians developed a highly complex legal system, they did not distinguish between civil law and criminal law. The Code describes the punishment to be enforced for all actions, which also makes it an early record of corrections. Interestingly sanctions for specific actions differ depending upon the status of the person committing the offense and the victim. More severe sanctions were reserved for cases in which the victim was of high status and the offender was of low status. In many cases, offenses committed by those of low status against those of high status were punished severely, even by death, whereas offenses committed by those of high status against those of low status were oftentimes not considered punishable. While the penalty of death was imposed for many actions, including adultery; fines were the most common penalty http://www.wsu.edu/~dee/MESO/CODE.HTM. This parallels our modern system, in which fines are also, by far, the most common penalty imposed. Some would also say that the differential treatment of rich and poor is also engrained in our own system.

GREEKS   The Ancient Greeks developed two early sets of written laws (Figure 2.3). The Code of Draco and the Code of Solon were both written around 600 B.C. The earlier Code of Draco was not so much a written code of laws, or a blueprint for change, but rather an accounting of the way things were. It described various offenses and their usual punishments—frequently death. It also proscribed slavery for those who could not repay loans. It is not a surprise that we use the word *draconian* to refer to a situation that is severe and oppressive. The Code of Solon replaced the Code of Draco and was much more humane.

The Greek philosopher Aristotle (384–322 B.C.) was influential in many disciplines; philosophy, science, metaphysics, ethics, law, and politics. He conceived of the concept of "a government of laws, not of men," where it is not a matter of who is the ruler but what the laws are and the laws are not as changeable and capricious as an individual. This concept was very influential in the formation of our early government.

FIGURE 2.3 The Ancient Greeks developed two sets of written laws.

ROMANS   Rome, founded in the eighth century B.C., was initially ruled by all-powerful kings, under whom most individuals had few rights, unless they were from the upper class, referred to as *the Patricians*. In the family, the father had absolute control and rights over his wife and children. As the church became more powerful, the absolute power of the father within the family lessened and women gained some freedom.

Eventually Rome became a republic and the laws began to favor the ruling class less (Figure 2.4). The Law of the Twelve Tables from 451 B.C. was a compilation of existing laws. It is important in the history of law because this was an early attempt to focus on procedure and due process of law. Each

FIGURE 2.4 The Romans also developed laws.

table dealt with a different type of law; civil lawsuits, bail and witnesses, debt, family, inheritance, ownership, and public law (Edmunds 1959).

During the sixth century A.D., Justinian I, the Byzantine Emperor, gathered together all proclamations and books of laws. These became the Code of Justinian in A.D. 529. It helped to cement the power of the Christian Church, while decreasing the rights of Jews. It also helped to advance anti-Semitism by not allowing Jews to testify against Christians, not allowing Jews to hold office, not allowing the Hebrew language to be used in worship. This compilation led to a revival of Roman Law, which remained a dominant legal system in Europe.

Medieval Law

During the Middle Ages there was significant development of canon law—law originating from the church. The Catholic Church had considerable power during the Middle Ages and the laws that were created tended to deal with church dogma—what the faith consisted of, and how to interact with others (others of the Catholic faith, along with others of different faiths) (Figure 2.5). Many popes would convene councils to discuss various issues that were of concern to the church and from these, canonical laws were created.

In England, common law developed quite early, beginning around the twelfth century. Along with the development of common law, English rulers, mostly kings, created laws as well. It was not as simple as it sounds, any land-owner, Lord, could also create laws of his own that were imposed upon those who lived on his lands. During this time a King would control a vast area of land, like England, and his most important nobles would control regions within England. Within each region that a particular noble controlled, lesser nobles would control even smaller areas and impose their own laws. Laws were not frequently written down, nor would the common peasant necessarily even be aware of what the laws were. For the common peasant, day to day existence consisted of working the land or tending to animals, these common people had very little contact with the law. Law in continental Europe was significantly influenced by the revival of Roman law but each European nation also developed its own set of laws, handed down by a monarch or another powerful figure.

FIGURE 2.5 The Catholic Church was a powerful influence on law during the Middle Ages.

Seventeenth and Eighteenth Century Developments in the United States

During the seventeenth century, each European power that attempted to colonize the New World brought their legal system with them and although the English eventually dominated, influences of the Spanish and French legal systems remain. The French legal system is especially evident in Louisiana and Quebec, Canada. Early colonists were not terribly concerned with creating significant bodies of laws. There was no need. In the early days, the population was small and laws were not necessary. Each colony created its own charter and was governed according to that charter. Laws were introduced slowly when the need arose.

Perhaps the single greatest achievement of the eighteenth century was the drafting of the U.S. Constitution. This single document can be looked at as the culmination of thousands of years of legal history. Although philosophers had spoken of freedom and individual rights for hundreds of years, the Constitution and the Bill of Rights were the first efforts by a government to assure these concepts for its population. To a very real extent, the assurance of individual rights was still theoretical. At the time of the ratification of the Constitution (1789) both women and African Americans had limited rights in many jurisdictions. It took many more years before what was spoken of in the Constitution became a very real possibility. Even today there are great disparities in our country.

During early U.S. history, most jurisdictions copied the English legal system and simplified it for their own use. As long as the population remained small, there was little need for the highly complex system of laws or courts that was in place in England. During the eighteenth century both laws and courts continued to be developed on an as-needed basis. Most citizens never had any interaction within a courtroom.

Nineteenth Century Developments

During the nineteenth century the world was rapidly changing. Many nations, especially Great Britain, that were great colonial powers, began to have significant problems with their colonial possessions, although the British Empire would not truly decline until after World War II. Slowly, many nations began to divest themselves of their possessions as they became more difficult to manage. Loss of colonies would continue to be a significant issue for all of the great European powers during the twentieth century.

The population in the United States grew rapidly during the second half of the nineteenth century. This was due to several factors. First, a steady stream of immigrants from Western and Eastern Europe entered cities like Boston and New York on the East Coast and later Chicago in the Midwest. This influx of immigrants caused the populations in cities to increase rapidly. Second, the medical advances developed during the Civil War era led to a longer life expectancy and the infant mortality rate declined dramatically during this same 50-year period.

The end of the Civil War also brought the end of slavery within the United States. Former slaves were granted citizenship with the ratification of the Thirteenth Amendment to the U.S. Constitution on December 6, 1865. While the Thirteenth Amendment guaranteed all former slaves full citizenship, this was not what happened in practice. Especially in the South, the rights of black Americans were not protected. Many Southern police forces that had been started to capture runaway slaves now would not protect the rights of black citizens when they were threatened or killed. On July 9, 1868, the Fourteenth Amendment was ratified. This amendment extended much of the Bill of Rights, which had applied only to the federal government, to the states.

In the countryside, where very few people lived and even those who lived there had very little contact with their neighbors, there was much less of a need for laws, courts, and judges. In the cities where there were many more people and many more opportunities for contact and conflict among people, the need for laws governing behavior increased. Courts and laws expanded to fit the needs of the expanding population.

While the eastern cities were growing larger, many individuals moved west seeking the promise of open land. The United States grew not only in population but in land mass. During this time, significant oppression of Native Americans occurred. Ancestral land that the various Native American nations had lived on for thousands of years was taken away from them and they were moved to reservations. Many Native Americans died of disease and exposure during the process. Although much was taken from the native peoples, this was all considered perfectly legal by the U.S. government. Members of the various native tribes were not considered to be U.S. citizens and were not protected by the Constitution and the Bill of Rights. They were not even granted the same rights that would have been afforded to an immigrant from Europe. Because they were not white and of European descent, they were not viewed as being equal, often, they were viewed as being less than human. Tribal leaders were forced to sign treaties with the U.S. government, giving up lands and rights.

Interestingly, Native Americans are considered to live within sovereign nations. The relationship among Native American peoples, Native American tribes, and the U.S. government is complex and has been evolving through Supreme Court decisions and laws. Tribal law exists as a separate legal system that operates both within and beside the federal system.

While the native people were driven from their lands, the Eastern population pushed into these new territories, creating western towns and cities. The completion of the transcontinental railroad in 1869 allowed individuals to travel to the Pacific Ocean. There were periods of considerable chaos and lawlessness in towns and cities in the west. The U.S. Marshals was created in 1789, and as the United States grew westward, Marshals were appointed to each territory to enforce the laws of the federal government.

Perhaps the most significant development of the nineteenth century occurred as that century was ending. Cook County established a separate juvenile court in 1899. Many other large cities followed suit. Prior to the inception of a separate juvenile court system, adult and juvenile offenders were treated the same. Children were subject to the same laws as adults. Children were arrested exactly the same as adults. Children were prosecuted as adults. Children were convicted and subjected to the same punishments as adults. Children were also incarcerated with adults. This made for a system in which young people were easily victimized by older offenders. It also created an environment where children who committed relatively petty offenses were housed with serious adult offenders and learned how to become serious adult offenders.

The Twentieth Century and Scientific Evidence

In the modern world there are three major legal systems: common law, Islamic sharia, and roman law. Common law is the system that originated in England and remains in use in many former English colonies (The United States, Canada, Australia, and India), Islamic sharia is practiced in some Muslim countries, although it is more of an influence than directly practiced in Muslim countries that have secular (nonreligion based) law. Roman Law, also referred to as civil law is used throughout most of Europe.

Common law has its basis in precedent. It is built upon the decisions that have been rendered by judges in previous cases. It is also based upon what has traditionally been done in a society. Islamic sharia law is based upon the Qur'an, the religious book of the Muslims. The Qur'an provides guidance for how to live life and Sharia law is the interpretation of the Qur'an. Roman law when it was revived was not law as it was practiced in Rome, but rather, a collection of legal concepts that arose from Rome. These concepts include; public law (which protects the interests of the state) and private law (which protects the interests of the individual); written law (from legislature) and unwritten law (arose from customary practice).

THE U.S. COURT SYSTEM

There is not one court system in the United States, but two major systems that work parallel to each other. There is a federal system of courts. Also, each state has its own state system. Within the state system, there are civil courts and criminal courts.

Within the federal system, the only court that was established by the U.S. Constitution is the Supreme Court. The Supreme Court was created by Article III, Section 1 of the Constitution. It states: "The judicial power of the United States, shall be vested in one Supreme Court, and in such inferior courts as the Congress may from time to time ordain and establish." The Supreme Court is the highest court in the United States, sitting over all federal and all state courts. There is a federal court in each state within the United States. Also, federal courts operate in all possessions and territories. The Judiciary Act of 1789 divided the United States into 12 regional circuits. Within the 12 circuits, there are 94 district courts within the United States. Each district has one court of appeals and one bankruptcy court. The federal court has a variety of special courts, including: U.S. Court of International Trade, U.S. Court of Federal Claims, Court of Appeals for Veterans' Claims, U.S. Court of Appeals for the Armed Forces, U.S. Tax Court. Although not considered to be courts of the United States, there are also tribal laws and courts that hold jurisdiction on tribal lands within the United States.

The court system in one state (for example, Florida) may vary considerably from the court system within another state (for example, Texas). Some state court systems are quite simple with a fairly linear set-up, with a state supreme or superior court functioning as the highest state court, an appellate court below the supreme court, the courts of general jurisdiction sit below that and courts of limited jurisdiction function at the lowest level. Each court has a different function. The supreme court functions as the court of last resorts for the state. Not all states have appellate courts—states with small populations do not have them—in that case, the state supreme court must hear all appeals. In other states, the appellate court will hear all appeals. Courts of limited jurisdiction are where all court cases begin. They also hold jurisdiction over all misdemeanor cases. Courts of general jurisdiction are the major trial courts of the states. They hold jurisdiction over all felony cases.

The Criminal Court Process

Although the criminal court is a state court and there is variance among the states as far as the names given to each part of the court process, the process remains relatively the same in all states. The defendant progresses from arrest, to initial appearance, to a Grand Jury appearance, to arraignment, to trial.

In the criminal court, the offender will generally enter the court system at the point of arrest. The defendant may also enter the system because of a summons or an indictment handed down by a grand jury.

The initial appearance may occur after an arrest, or after an individual has received a summons to appear in court. Bail will be set by the judge at this time. Bail is usually an amount of money (although in some jurisdictions it can be property) that is given to the court to guarantee that an individual will appear for the set court date. Bail is not guaranteed. In some cases, if the judge deems the individual to be highly dangerous or pose a significant flight risk, bail may be set very high, or denied. A date will be chosen for the preliminary hearing.

The preliminary hearing is conducted to determine if there is probable cause that a crime was committed and the defendant committed that crime. If there is not probable cause, the case may be dismissed here. Within the criminal justice system, the vast majority of cases are resolved through the use of a plea bargain. Approximately 90 percent of misdemeanor and 80 percent of felony charges are resolved in this manner.

Not all jurisdictions use a grand jury. When a grand jury is used, it will decide whether or not there is sufficient evidence to charge a person with an offence. This is an indictment. In a felony prosecution, the arraignment is the point at which the defendant appears and is formally notified of the charges. If no plea bargain has been accepted at this point, the case will proceed to trial. If the defendant is found guilty and it is a noncapital case, he or she will be sentenced at the end of the trial. (If it is a capital case, there is a separate sentencing phase.) For some crimes, there are specific guidelines for sentencing that must be followed and sentencing is carried out in an almost cookbook fashion. Certain drug crimes and crimes committed using a gun, for example, carry mandatory minimum prison terms. In other cases aggravating and mitigating factors may be taken into account during sentencing and the judge will have considerable discretion.

After conviction, the defendant's attorney may file postconviction motions. This is a request to have the sentence modified. Everyone who is convicted of a crime is also entitled to file one appeal.

The Civil Court Process

The process in civil court is very different from the process in criminal court. The civil court process begins with the plaintiff's complaint. The plaintiff states who is involved in the case, what happened, and what remedy is being sought, for example monetary damages. The defendant receives a copy of the complaint and a summons. The summons tells the defendant to respond to the complaint. Pretrial motions are filed. These may ask the court to void a summons, to clarify or strike the plaintiff's petition, or to dismiss the petition. It is then up to the defendant to respond in what is known as the defendant's answer. The next step in the civil court process is discovery. During discovery, each side reveals to the other the facts and information that it has. This is done through depositions (testimony taken from witnesses), interrogatories (questions that must be answered by the parties of the case), and documents that must be presented. Most civil cases do not go to trial. At least 90 percent of civil cases are settled at the settlement conference.

Science in the Courtroom

The Twentieth century also brought a change regarding how science was viewed in the courtroom; for the first time it was questioned whether a particular piece of science was good or bad. This was not a question when the only form of scientific evidence admitted into the courtroom was medical testimony. As the court began to admit different types of scientific evidence, the question arose: "what is good scientific evidence," and even more basic, "what is science." Even today, the discipline of the philosophy of science wrestles with the very basic question of defining what is science.

THE *FRYE* DECISION   Prior to 1923, questions about "bad science" and "good science" were not asked in the courtroom (Kiely 2001). Expert witnesses were called upon to testify whenever it was deemed that an ordinary person (juror) would not have sufficient knowledge of the topic under discussion. The *Frye* decision fundamentally changed the way in which science was viewed by the law. *Frye v. United States* dealt with admissibility of evidence from an early form of the lie detector. The issue at question was whether or not the results of the lie detector were reliable. In this Supreme Court decision, the Court held that only science that was of sound methodology and generally accepted by the relevant scientific community could be admitted into court; therefore the lie-detector results were not admissible because it was not accepted by the scientific community. In the Court's ruling, it set a new standard for the admissibility of scientific testimony. An expert could only be called upon to render testimony in areas in which the science was *generally accepted* by the scientific community.

DAUBERT AND FEDERAL RULES OF EVIDENCE   The *Frye* test was the acceptable standard until the *Daubert* decision of 1993. The *Daubert* decision placed more control over what types of scientific evidence are admitted into the courtroom and into the hands of judges. The issue in *Daubert v. Merrell Dow Pharmaceuticals* (509 U.S. 59, 113 Ct. 2786, 1993) was whether or not the drug Benedictin, manufactured by Merrell Dow, caused birth defects when taken by pregnant women.

Whereas, *Frye* had relied upon *general acceptance* as the standard for acceptable scientific methodology, *Daubert* was much more liberal and relied upon the Federal Rules of Evidence (Rule 401, 402, and 703) for instructions regarding what was acceptable scientific testimony. Rule 702 holds that scientific evidence is admissible if the trial judge feels that it is relevant and will assist the jury. In effect, *Daubert* has made the judge the *gatekeeper* for scientific testimony in his or her own courtroom. Unfortunately, this places a significant burden on the judge—a burden that many judges are still not prepared to handle. Although, within months of the *Daubert* decision, workshops and courses dealing with understanding and evaluating scientific evidence began to be offered to judges, Bjur and Richardson (1999) point out that most individuals, judges, lawyers, and jurors alike, do not understand the process of science. Very few judges have the scientific background necessary to make a good determination as to what is *good science*. The vast majority of judges were formerly attorneys and their training consists of having attended law school. Law students are trained in the various types of laws; administrative law, constitutional law, personal law, family law, property law, taxation, labor law, trade regulations, criminal law. Most schools do not offer classes covering the types of scientific evidence that may be encountered in a courtroom in their law school curriculum. There are some states that have recognized the need for both judges and attorneys to be educated consumers of scientific evidence and offer continuing education credits in this area. This is quite a daunting task. Evidence from a variety of scientific disciplines may be presented in the courtroom. It is difficult even for scientists to stay abreast of changes within their own discipline; even a judge or attorney who made a considerable effort to be trained in how to understand scientific evidence or who majored in a scientific discipline as an undergraduate would soon have an out-of-date bank of knowledge due to how rapidly science advances. So while the purpose of *Daubert* was to keep poor science out of the courtroom, it has instead functioned—and is continuing to function—in banning reliable science (Brickley 2003; Hileman 2003).

TOXIC TORTS   While many students automatically think of the criminal courts when forensic science is mentioned, it has been the civil court that has driven the increase of scientific testimony into the courtroom. These are the so-called *toxic torts* and product liability cases. These cases are common because a significant amount of money, in the form of *damages,* can be involved. Financially, the litigants (often corporations) have very *deep pockets*. If an individual does not have money, or attachable assets, very little (aside from personal satisfaction) can be obtained from taking him or her to court. Because of the amount of money that can be involved, there has been significant impetus to sue, and very large awards have arisen. Since very large amounts of money may be at stake, each side will obtain the assistance of one or more highly qualified experts to testify. In some instances this has led to the appearance of the courtroom being more a battle of expert witnesses rather than a search for the truth.

PERTINENT FEDERAL RULES OF EVIDENCE   In many jurisdictions, the Federal Rules of Evidence govern what may be presented in court and who may be an expert witness. Article IV of the Federal Rules of Evidence pertains to "relevancy and its limits."

FRE 401 Defines "Relevant Evidence"   This rule is fairly self-explanatory. Relevant evidence is any evidence that is valuable to the judge or jury in determining whether or not any fact that is pertinent to the case did, in fact, occur.

FRE 402 Relevant Evidence Generally Admissible; Irrelevant Evidence Inadmissible   This may seem like another fairly self-explanatory rule. Relevant evidence is admissible in court and irrelevant evidence is not. However, there are certain circumstances where other rules may supersede this and evidence that is not directly related to facts of the case may be admissible.

FRE 403 Exclusion of Relevant Evidence on Grounds of Prejudice, Confusion, or Waste of Time   Even if evidence is relevant, there are certain circumstances where it may be excluded. If a particular piece of evidence would cause prejudice, confusion, or be a waste of time it can be excluded. This is one of the reasons why crime scene photographs that contain copious amounts of blood are often submitted in black and white, rather than color. It is important that the jury see the photographs but it is also important that they are not prejudiced against the defendant because of all of the blood.

Article VII provides guidelines for opinions and expert testimony. This article addresses questions regarding: who may testify, what qualifies an expert to testify, and what expert testimony may be based upon.

FRE 702 Testimony by Experts FRE 702 addresses two separate issues, first how and why an expert is qualified, and second what expert testimony must be based upon. Expert witnesses may testify if they have scientific, technical, or specialized knowledge that will assist either the jury or the judge in their fact-finding at trial. This is in contrast to the early portion of the twentieth century when it was rare for anyone other than a medical doctor to testify in a court as a scientific expert witness. FRE 702 makes allowances for the testimony of a variety of professionals (for example: chemists, auto mechanics, and psychologists) who may have knowledge that is necessary for the judge or jury to understand all of the facts of the case. FRE 702 does not pertain just to scientists (chemists, physicists, and biologists), but also to individuals who have technical or specialized knowledge. An auto mechanic, engineer, or computer programmer might have technical knowledge and a finger print examiner or document examiner would have specialized knowledge.

FRE 702 stipulates that the expert witness must be qualified by knowledge, skill, experience, training, or education relative to the area in question. Some attorneys try to interpret this to mean that an expert must have knowledge, skill, experience, training, *and* education. However, any of these five factors can qualify an expert. This is important because for some areas of criminalistics, there are not specific educational programs—for example, document examiner. Document examiners do not attend a university and receive a degree in their specialty. Many of them will learn how to be a document examiner on the job and may attend training classes.

Qualifications of expert witnesses can be a particularly tricky area of the Federal Rules of Evidence for a judge to rule on. There are so many different types of specialties in forensics and the training is extremely varied. What qualifies a forensic botanist to testify in court is very different from what qualifies a latent fingerprint specialist to testify in court, and while this may be self-evident, it can be difficult to answer in exact terms—what exactly would qualify each individual expert. Ultimately it is the judge who decides who is and who is not qualified. The entire process is purposefully broad under the Federal Rules of Evidence because the judge must be able to enter in all possible information relative to the fact-finding process in order to find justice in accordance with applicable laws.

There are two ways in which experts can be qualified to testify in a courtroom. An expert may be qualified during the actual trial. An expert may also be prequalified by the court to testify; this latter method of qualification is covered by FRE 706. If the expert is testifying in the courtroom as an expert for either the defense or prosecution, the expert will be allowed to present his or her qualifications. During the cross-examination process the opposing counsel will be given the opportunity to discredit an alleged expert before he or she can be qualified by the court.

FRE 702 also states that the testimony that the expert gives must be based upon facts or data, as opposed to theories. The testimony must be the result of reliable principles and methods. The expert must apply those reliable principles and methods to the facts of the case.

FRE 703 Bases of Opinion Testimony by Experts FRE 703 emphasizes that the data that forms the basis for the expert's opinion does not have to also be admissible for the opinion to be admissible. However, this data must be derived from sources and methods that are considered to be reliable in that profession. Again, this stresses that it must be reliable science.

FRE 704 Opinion on Ultimate Issue

(a) Except as provided in subdivision (b), testimony in the form of an opinion or inference otherwise admissible is not objectionable because it embraces an ultimate issue to be decided by the trier of fact.

(b) No expert witness testifying with respect to the mental state or condition of a defendant in a criminal case may state an opinion or inference as to whether the defendant did or did not have the mental state or condition constituting an element of the crime charged or of a defense thereto. Such ultimate issues are matters for the trier of fact alone.

This second portion of FRE 704 becomes especially pertinent to forensic psychologists and psychiatrists who would be called upon to testify regarding the mental status of a defendant. The expert can give his or her opinion regarding the mental state of the defendant but can not tell the judge or jury that the individual was, in fact, sane or insane at any time. Ultimately this determination rests with the jury (or the judge in the case of a bench trial).

FRE 705 Disclosure of Facts or Data Underlying Expert Opinion FRE 705 states that the expert can testify based on underlying facts or data without first disclosing those underlying facts or data, unless the court requires it. The expert may also be required to disclose this information during cross-examination. For example, a forensic psychologist may testify about mental status based, in part, on the results of neurological testing. The actual test does not have to be admitted into court as evidence, but the psychologist may be required to state which tests were administered. The expert may testify regarding information that on its own would not be sufficient to be allowed into court. The expert may also testify regarding tests/surveys/measures that have not been admitted into court. This is similar to FRE 703.

FRE 706 Court Appointed Experts The court may appoint any expert that the parties agree upon. The court may also appoint its own experts. In some cases, having the court appoint an expert may be more favorable because attorneys can consume a considerable amount of court time trying to discredit one another's expert witnesses. And while, unqualified experts should not be testifying in court, often, both experts are well qualified. If the court has appointed an expert, this can save considerable time and energy in the courtroom. The courtroom proceedings can focus on fact finding.

A judge may also present both sides with a list of experts and have both sides mutually agree upon an expert to be used during the trial. This can help the expert to be impartial and circumvents the temptation for an expert to color testimony to favor the side that is paying for his or her bill. Conversely, the court or the parties involved in the case may also give reasons why an expert should not be appointed.

Rights of the Defendant

In the first half of the twentieth century, the majority of cases were solved by the direct admission of the suspect in the form of a confession. At times suspects were subjected to both physical and psychological pressure by law enforcement which may or may not have contributed to false confessions and adulterated the fact finding process. When Earl Warren was appointed as Chief Justice of the Supreme Court in 1953 (he retired in 1969) things began to change. During his tenure as justice, the court handed down many decisions that focused on the rights of the defendant, expanding the Fourth, Fifth, Sixth, and Fourteenth Amendment rights of the defendant.

The Warren court decisions radically altered the criminal justice system, from arrest procedures to how evidence is gathered to what could be presented as evidence in court. These greatly affected how cases could be investigated and solved. With these protections in place, it became less likely that suspects would confess and the importance of collecting forensic evidence grew.

Supreme Court Decisions That Influenced the Rights of the Defendant

Mapp v. Ohio, **367 U.S. 643 (1961).** This Supreme Court decision held that evidence that has been illegally seized, without a properly executed search warrant, in violation of the Fourth Amendment, could not be used at trial. This is also referred to as the "exclusionary rule" or the "Fruit of the Poisonous Tree Doctrine."

Gideon v. Wainwright, **372 U.S. 335 (1963).** This Supreme Court decision held that the right to counsel was a fundamental right. Prior to this time, several cases had underlined the importance of the right to counsel, but it was left up to individual states to determine how to protect this right. In many instances, lawyers were only provided to defendants who were being tried for capital crimes. After *Gideon v. Wainwright* the right to counsel was extended to all felony cases.

Escobedo v. Illinois, **378 U.S. 478 (1964).** This Supreme Court decision extended the exclusionary rule to illegally obtained confessions. It extended the right to counsel to individuals who are being interrogated.

Miranda v. Arizona, **384 U.S. 436 (1966).** This Supreme Court decision held that the accused must be advised of the right to counsel and right against self-incrimination prior to being questioned or any information obtained during that questioning will not be admissible in a courtroom.

Katz v. United States, **389 U.S. 347 (1967).** This Supreme Court decision extended protection against illegal searches, specifically wiretaps, to areas accessible to the public when there is an expectation of privacy. In the case of Katz, the public area was a telephone booth. A warrant is required before the government can execute a wiretap.

HISTORY OF LEGAL MEDICINE

Medicine and surgery are both very old disciplines, dating back into antiquity. Archeological evidence exists to indicate that surgeries were performed 7,000 years ago. During this same time period prehistoric humans were already using plants to bring on relief from a variety of ailments. Prior to recorded history, humans made attempts to use plant and mineral substances to cure illness and prolong life.

Legal medicine also has a very long history. The ancient Chinese had described procedures for investigating suspicious deaths. The code of Hammurabi, written around 2100 B.C., addresses what we would consider to be issues of medical malpractice. The penalties for performing an unsuccessful surgery ranged from payment of a fine (if the patient was a slave) to amputation of the surgeon's hand (if the patient was not a slave) (Hooker 1996). The ancient Egyptians developed a system to determine cause of death (Wecht 1997). In Rome, Antistius was asked to determine the cause of death of Julius Caesar (Meyer 1999). Lost writings from sixth-century China and published writings from thirteenth-century China detail the use of medicine in the courtroom (Eckert 1997).

Medical science has always had a place in U.S. courtrooms. Throughout much of history, science was used in the courtroom on an as-needed basis. Most frequently, medical science would be called upon during death investigations to make a determination regarding cause of death.

The dominant influence of the English in the colonies led to the adoption of the coroner system as the preferred system for dealing with death investigation in the United States. By 1635, the coroner system was already functioning in Maryland and by 1666, its coroners were appointed by county (Eckert 1997).

Because there was no medical training in the colonies, colonial physicians were usually trained in Europe. It would not be until the nineteenth century that any formalized medical training would be available in the United States. Prior to that time, midwives practiced in the United States, but were not formally trained. Also, in many immigrant communities there were individuals who provided medical care and advice but they too were untrained. In 1766, The Medical Society of New Jersey was founded. This organization was the first medical organization in the United States.

The first medical training program in the United States was founded in the early nineteenth century, although the first university-based medical program, founded at Johns Hopkins, did not open until 1893. During the intervening years, the amount and type of training that was required to become a medical doctor became increasingly complex. Medical jurisprudence was first taught to medical students during this time.

An important aspect of advancing the medical field in the United States was the establishment of both local and national medical associations. These groups serve to disseminate knowledge and provide opportunities for professionals to discuss issues in both formal and informal settings—such as medical training and the development of subdisciplines. The American Medical Association was established in 1847.

As medicine became a more advanced, cohesive discipline, legal medicine advanced as well. Modern legal medicine consists of three separate but often related fields: forensic pathology, forensic toxicology, and forensic psychiatry.

Forensic Pathology

Forensic pathology may be the oldest branch of the forensic sciences and the wellspring for the development of all other branches of forensics (Eckert and Wright, 1997). Death investigation or, at least, determination of cause of death and time of death has been significant in the development of forensic science. A significant portion of the scientific testimony that has been recovered in the historical record centers on determination of cause of death. As such, forensic pathology has played a key role, and the medical doctor has been the individual who most often presents forensic evidence in court. In fact, it has only been slowly over the past 60 years or so that other scientists have been allowed to present evidence.

In Europe, during the Middle Ages, two separate systems of death investigation arose. One system developed in continental Europe, the other in England. The continental system developed free from political influence; this led to departments of forensic medicine developing at European Universities. Death investigators were professors rather than elected officials.

In England, the death investigation system dates back to 1194 and coroners were elected officials (Dix and Calaluce 1999). The coroner system was very political, which led to individuals being elected who were not necessarily the most qualified for the position (Wecht 1997). These individuals were also frequently influenced by political colleagues.

In the nineteenth century, discontent with the coroner system began to grow and slowly, in many jurisdictions, the office of coroner was replaced with that of medical examiner. The two chief differences between these two systems are that the medical examiner is not elected and must also be a medical doctor. The first medical examiner was appointed in Boston in 1877. New York City developed an independent citywide system for death investigation in 1918. Maryland developed the first statewide system in 1939 (Dix & Calaluce 1999).

Forensic pathology, a subdivision of pathology, is the study of diagnosis of disease. This differs from all other branches of medicine that concern themselves with the treatment of disease. Forensic pathology is the application of scientific analysis to violent, sudden, and suspicious deaths. The forensic pathologist is concerned with establishing the cause, manner, mechanism, and time of death (Wright & Eckert 1997).

Forensic Toxicology

Toxicology is the study of poisons and toxins. Throughout history, poisons have been used to harm and kill. References are made to poisons and antidotes in ancient writings found in India, Egypt, Greece, and Rome. Writings suggest that the Roman emperor, Claudius may have been poisoned. Court histories throughout Europe are full of deaths by poisoning (Eckert 1997). "During the middle ages, professional poisoners sold their services to both royalty and the common populace. The most common poisons were of plant origin (such as hemlock, aconite, belladonna) and toxic metal (arsenic and mercury salts)" (Paklis in Eckert 1997, 109).

The Venetian Council of Ten, a powerful and secretive political group that existed between 1310 and 1797, was in charge of political stability within the Republic of Venice. This group used poisoning to kill off threatening controversial figures. There are numerous tales of poisoning involving the Borgia popes. Poisoning as a choice method of killing spread throughout Europe during the sixteenth, seventeenth, and eighteenth centuries. It was so common that it was universally feared by the nobility, and many of them employed food tasters.

It was not until the birth of modern chemistry at the close of the eighteenth century that toxicology developed (DeForest et al. 1983). It was Orfila (1787–1853), working in Paris in the mid-1800s, who was truly responsible for many of the early advances in toxicology. In 1814 he published *Traité des Poisons*—a study of poisons. Orfila also testified in court regarding poisoning and conducted early studies on blood and semen (DeForest et al. 1983). By the end of the 1800s, European toxicologists were able to isolate and detect alkaloids, heavy metals, and volatile poisons. Arsenic was the first poison that could be identified in body tissues and fluids (Paklis in Eckert 1997).

In 1911, the first forensic text was published in the United States: *Forensic Medicine and Toxicology* (Paklis in Eckert 1997). The New York medical examiner's office established the first toxicology laboratory in 1918, which predates the inception of the first forensic science laboratory in the 1920s. The American Board of Forensic Toxicology was founded in 1975.

Forensic Psychiatry

The third division of modern legal medicine is forensic psychiatry. Within the criminal court, forensic psychiatry has been mostly involved in dealing with issues of sanity, competency, medication and treatment. In the 1950s, forensic psychiatry developed the "psychological autopsy."

INSANITY   The question of insanity revolves around the individual's state of mind during the commission of the crime. Answering questions about a prior state of mind and proving this to the jury often prove difficult. The issue of insanity is tied to the defendant's behavior before, during, and after the crime and how this behavior illustrates the defendant's cognitive awareness of social reality, orchestration of planning, and avoidance of apprehension. The courts have wrestled with this issue for several centuries.

The *M'Naughten Rule*   In 1843, Daniel M'Naughten attempted to assassinate the prime minister of Britain, Sir Robert Peel—the same Peel who was responsible for significant policing reforms in that country. While his attempt on the prime minister's life was unsuccessful, he did succeed in killing the secretary to the prime minister, Edward Drummond. During trial, it was found that M'Naughten suffered from delusions, which included that the prime minister was responsible for the personal and financial troubles in M'Naughten's life. A number of witnesses testified that M'Naughten was, in fact, insane and he was acquitted.

The public was outraged. More importantly, Queen Victoria was outraged. Because of the general discontent with the verdict, the House of Lords established standards for the defense of insanity. The *M'Naughten Rule* states that in order to establish the defense of insanity it must be proved that at the time of the act the accused suffered from a "defect of reason, from disease of mind" that was such that he did not know the act he was doing or that it was wrong.

Irresistible Impulse   Because of dissatisfaction with *M'Naughten* and its focus on the cognitive aspect of right and wrong, the Alabama Supreme Court added the irresistible impulse test in 1887 in the case *Parsons v. State* (*Supreme Court of Alabama*, July 28, 1887). The irresistible impulse test adds to *M'Naughten* that it is possible for some individuals to know what they are doing is wrong but to still be unable to control their actions.

***Durham* Test**   The *Durham Rule*, also called the "product test," states that an individual is not "criminally responsible if his unlawful act is the product of a mental disease or defect." The purpose of *Durham* was to simplify *M'Naughten* and to make it easier to determine insanity by making it dependent upon a medical diagnosis rather than more subjective impressions. This change was pushed for by many in the psychiatric community, who would also benefit from being the ones who would be making the diagnoses. Unfortunately, this ruling did not solve the problem. One problem was that "mental disease or defect" was never adequately defined and the then-current standard of diagnosis was the DSM (*Diagnostic and Statistical Manual of Mental Disorders*) relied upon a psychodynamic approach and did not make clear distinctions between what was normal and what was abnormal. The *Durham Rule* was abandoned in 1972.

ALI (American Law Institute) Standard   In 1962 The ALI Standard also attempted to address the shortcomings of *M'Naughten*. While *M'Naughten* held that the individual must have no understanding of the nature of his acts, ALI states that an individual must lack a substantial capacity to distinguish between right and wrong. It combines *M'Naughten* and "irresistible impulse."

The Current Standard   There is not one established current standard across the U.S. criminal court systems for the insanity defense. About half of the states still employ the *M'Naughten Rule*, although several have added the irresistible impulse test, and half of the states use the ALI Standard. The majority of states place the burden of proof for the insanity defense on the defendant and a handful of states allow "guilty but mentally ill" (GBMI) verdicts. Montana and Utah have abolished the insanity defense but allow GBMI verdicts. Idaho and Kansas have abolished the insanity defense altogether.

Guilty But Mentally Ill   The verdict option of *guilty but mentally ill* arose from public dissatisfaction with offenders obtaining an insanity verdict and being released. In particular, the public was angered that John Hinckley was found not guilty by reason of insanity. Hinckley, in 1981, had attempted to assassinate President Reagan to impress actress Jodie Foster. The insanity verdict states that the defendant does not bear responsibility for his or her actions. In a GBMI verdict, the defendant assumes legal responsibility for the crime, and the individual is confined, but must receive mental health treatment. Often the confinement is in a forensic hospital. Unlike a verdict of insanity, in which the individual must be released if, at some point in time, he or she is determined to no longer be a danger, under the GBMI verdict the individual must serve out any remaining sentence in a correctional facility.

There is an inherent contradiction to GBMI. On the one hand, the court is saying that the individual is "mentally incompetent," yet still the court will hold the person responsible for a crime. The way in which public outrage pushed Congress to make changes in the insanity defense is a good illustration of how a celebrity case can present a skewed picture of the criminal justice system. In reality, the insanity defense has not allowed many guilty individuals to go free; the insanity defense is attempted only rarely, and generally when it is attempted, it is not successful.

Competency   Competency is the ability to knowingly engage in an action. Competency questions arise in both the civil and criminal courts. In civil courts, the question that most frequently arises is whether or not an individual is competent to make a will or engage in a contract. Generally, it is assumed that any individual is competent and the burden of proof rests on whomever raises the question. In criminal courts, questions may arise as to whether or not an individual is competent to bear witness in a criminal matter, enter a plea, competent to stand trial, or competent to be executed. The testimony of a child can be challenged based upon competency.

Credibility   The courts draw a distinction between competency and *credibility*. While competency is the ability to knowingly engage in an action, credibility boils down to whether or not an individual's testimony is believable. As amazing as it seems, an individual who has been deemed not to be competent can, at the same time, be deemed to be credible. An individual may not be able to distinguish right from wrong, engage in planning, but they may still be able to give an account of what they saw happen when a crime occurred.

PSYCHOLOGICAL AUTOPSY   The "psychological autopsy" was first developed in the 1950s. This tool is used during a death investigation when there is a question as to whether the death was an accident or a suicide. The psychiatrist, pathologist, social worker, friends, family, and police work together to determine the most likely cause of death.

HISTORY OF CRIMINALISTICS

Although there are forensic writers who argue convincingly that forensic science and criminalistics are not distinguishable (see, for example: Saferstein 2004), this text makes a distinction. Forensic science is the juxtaposition of science and the law, or, science in the service of the law. For the purposes of this text, criminalistics refers to those areas that originally developed from police investigative work. Therefore, criminalistics, is not necessarily science. At least not in the way we would tradition- ally think of science. For example, fingerprint analysis is not a science in the traditional sense. Another distinction can be made regarding how well an area can stand on its own. DNA, while it has application in the forensic arena, also has a much wider application in science for researching inher- ited diseases, or for the purposes of determining paternity, for instance.

Modern criminalistics includes the areas of trace and transfer evidence (glass and soil, fibers and hairs, blood and bodily fluids), accelerant and explosives residues, drug identification, interpre- tation of patterns and imprints, ballistics, document analysis, and fingerprint analysis.

European Developments–U.S. Developments

Criminalistics, like criminology, has its origins in Europe. The word *kriminalistic* (German for crimi- nalistics) was coined by an Austrian, Hans Gross (1847–1915). He defined criminalistics ". . . as the amalgamation of expert services of various specialists for the examination of physical evidence . . ." (DeForest et al. 1983, 12) Gross wrote the first criminalistics text in 1893 (*Handbuch fur Untersuchungsrichter, Polizeibeamte, Gendarmen, u.s.w.*), *Handbook for Examining Magistrates, Police Officials, Military Policemen, etc.*, which was translated into English in 1906 (Swanson et al. 2000).

ANTHROPOMETRY   Anthropometry was developed by Alphonse Bertillon (1853–1914) and earned him the distinction of being the "father of criminal identification." While working for the Paris police in a low-level position filing identification cards on criminals, Bertillon noticed that the descriptions on the cards were so vague that any card could describe hundreds of different individ- uals. The descriptions did not even include accurate measurements of height, weight, hair, or eye color. He also disliked the extremely random way in which information was recorded about the indi- vidual offenders. This made it difficult to compare individuals who already had been caught with individuals who committed new offenses. Sometimes, multiple cards existed for one person. If mea- surements were taken by different officers, they tended to vary. There was little consistency.

Bertillon devised what he believed was a much better system based on body measurements, tattoos, scars, and personality traits. All of these characteristics combined created a formula that would lead to the identification of only one person. His system gained popularity due to the fact only three months after it was implemented in 1883, a criminal was caught (Swanson et al. 2000).

FINGERPRINTS   Much to Bertillon's displeasure, his system of identification was supplanted by one of the most important developments in criminalistics—dactylography, otherwise known as "the study of fingerprints." Not only were fingerprints a much better method of identification during the time of their development at the end of the nineteenth century, they are still an important form of identification today—fingerprinting is the oldest forensic technique still in use.

Fingerprints had been used as a form of identification, much like a signature, to enter into contracts, by a variety of ancient and modern societies. But it was the work of two individuals, William Herschel and Henry Faulds, who were primarily responsible for early interest in using fingerprints as a means of classifying and identifying offenders. As early as 1858, Herschel had used palmprints in business dealings in India, where many individuals were not literate, hoping to keep people honest. Prior to 1880, Faulds was able to identify a thief based on a print that had been left at a crime scene. Unfortunately for both of these men, the interest in fingerprints did not catch on at the time (Swanson et al. 2000).

There really wasn't significant interest in fingerprints until 1897 when Edward Henry's classification system was put into place in India and three years later in England. This system made it easy to both catalogue and retrieve fingerprints (DeForest et al. 1983). In the days before computer databases, this advance could save hours of hand-searching through disorganized files.

At first, fingerprints were used as a means of classifying offenders along with their photograph. If the offender came back into the system, because his picture and fingerprints were already in the system, his card could be found and the arresting officer knew that he wasn't just an offender but a repeat offender. Soon fingerprints were also used as a method to link an offender to a crime scene. If officers successfully retrieved fingerprints from a crime scene, those fingerprints could be compared with those fingerprints of known offenders. If the crime scene fingerprint shared enough characteristics with a known-offender's fingerprint, it was considered to be a *match* and the officer knew who had left the fingerprint and presumably committed the crime.

It can't be overstressed how important the development of fingerprints as a means of classifying criminals has been to law enforcement. Prior to the widespread use of offender fingerprint and photographic classification, individuals who were arrested would simply give false names since there was no way to prove who they were. There was no way to link them to either their past offenses that they had been arrested for or their past crimes for which they had not been arrested. Without a means of properly and efficiently classifying criminals, criminals had a much greater ability to operate freely. It was not a panacea. Offenders could leave a particular jurisdiction and quite literally leave past crimes behind. It was quite a while until there were good state and federal databases of fingerprints. By the early 1920s, many police departments in major metropolitan areas had established a fingerprint catalogue of offenders. Photographs, along with identifying information about very dangerous and wanted criminals who were at large, were often posted in post offices and other public places. The FBI issued its first "wanted" poster in 1919 (http://www.fbi.gov/page2/dec06/firstio121506.htm).

Fingerprint Databases   The Bureau of Criminal Identification (BCI) was created within the Department of Justice in 1905. The BCI maintained a federal repository of fingerprint cards. The International Association of Chiefs of Police also created a repository of fingerprint cards. In 1926, these two collections became the responsibility of the Bureau of Investigation—the forerunner of the FBI (http://www.fbi.gov/libref/historic/history/lawless.htm). The creation of a federal fingerprint database allowed even those criminals who might move from state to state to be tracked. However, the system was often quite cumbersome to use and it might take weeks for a search to be completed when a request came in by local law enforcement. In 1999, the FBI instituted The Integrated Automated Fingerprint Identification System (IAFIS). The IAFIS has increased the use of the federal fingerprint database significantly. Currently, frequent travelers to the United States are also having their fingerprints submitted to the FBI database as the federal government has expanded the use of the database to deal with the threat of terrorism.

FORENSIC PHOTOGRAPHY   In 1888, Bertillon introduced photographs to his identification system. These photographs were very much like the *mug shots* that we are familiar with today—frontal and profile photos. The photographs were even better than his measurements at documenting the likeness of the offender.

Bertillon did not confine his work with the camera to taking pictures of criminals; he also was influential in the use of the camera to document the crime scene. Photographic documentation of events became common during the American Civil War—the first war to be widely documented with photographs. The camera had been used in criminal investigations since 1859, and even earlier than that, the French had been making daguerreotypes—an early form of photographs—of criminals since the 1840s (Eckert 1997; Swanson et al. 2000).

In modern crime scene processing, photography is a standard method of documenting even the most simple and routine crime scenes. Since the early days of crime scene photography the purposes of photography have not changed but the technology has changed considerably. Cameras first became smaller and easier to use, and flashes went from being ignitable powders to flash bulbs to the wide variety of light sources that are available today, including both infrared and ultraviolet light. Digital cameras became available in the 1980s. The digital camera has many advantages over the traditional 35mm camera, including ease of use and the ability to allow the photographer to immediately see the photograph. Also, most patrol officers can be equipped with a digital camera so that evidence that might quickly fade can be recorded. Although many jurisdictions currently admit digital photographs into evidence, there has been considerable debate regarding whether or not they should be since they can be altered more easily than photographs from 35 mm film.

AUGUST VOLLMER   In the second half of the nineteenth century, forensic development in the United States lagged behind Europe. This state of affairs did not change until the 1920s, when August Vollmer's work significantly changed policing. He favored college education and increased training for police officers, instituted car patrols, and was instrumental in the inception of the first forensics laboratory in the United States.

BALLISTICS   How people are murdered has frequently served to move forensics forward. Just as the widespread use of poison as a murder weapon helped move toxicology forward; the use of firearms as a murder weapon moved ballistics forward. Henry Goddard, in 1835, obtained the first confession based on bullet evidence. Goddard noticed that all of the bullets at a crime scene had similar markings on them—indicating that they belonged to only one individual and not many. Richard Kockel, an early German researcher in firearms identification focused on recording the details of bullets (Eckert 1997). Calvin Goddard (1858–1946) perfected the bullet-comparison microscope. This made a much more detailed analysis of bullet evidence possible. It was not until after the end of World War I that investigators began looking at a broader range of factors other than bullets, such as cartridge cases. The lack of expertise in ballistics after the 1929 St. Valentine's Day massacre helped bring about the establishment of a crime laboratory in Chicago (DeForest et al. 1983).

DOCUMENT ANALYSIS   Document analysis should not be confused with handwriting analysis. Handwriting analysis involves examining the structure of handwriting for keys to the writer's personality. It dates back at least to ancient Greece and has many practitioners today. However, it is generally not accepted as being scientifically based and is not admissible in our court system. While handwriting may be analyzed as a component of document analysis, it is not analyzed to determine personality traits but rather to determine if the document was written by a particular person.

Document analysis once comprised a significant portion of the work of policing. As was the case with offender identification, document analysis was carried out by law enforcement officers within their own organizations, not by outside scientists. Training was done in-house and on-the-job. Even today most of the training that analysts receive is obtained through the FBI or other law enforcement organizations once the individual is working in the field—universities do not grant degrees in this area.

Modern document analysis encompasses the analysis of all forms of papers and documents. This includes handwriting and signature identification; analysis of inks (to a much lesser extent pencil graphite), writing instruments, and papers; and also all documents produced by copier, fax, and printer (much less is done regarding typewritten documents today). Document analysis also encompasses the area of counterfeit money, false identification, counterfeit tickets, records alteration, checks, wills, suicide notes, and certificates. Questions may be answered regarding document age, time of writing, or whether it has been altered. The examiner may need to assist in the recovery or reconstruction of documents.

Glossary

American Law Institute (ALI) Standard—in order to be found to be insane, an individual must lack a substantial capacity to distinguish between right and wrong.

Anthropometry—a system of criminal identification based on body measurements, eventually abandoned in favor of dactylography.

Canonical Law—(also referred to as canon law) law originating from the church.

Code of Hammurabi—a compilation of laws in Mesopotamia by King Hammurabi around 2100 B.C.

Codified—written down.

Common Law—a legal system created by the English, based upon precedent and in use in many former English colonies.

Competency—the ability to knowingly engage in an action.

Coroner system—a system of death investigation that relies on an elected individual who does not necessarily have a medical degree to hold the office.

Dactylography—the study of fingerprints.

Damages—an award given by a civil court to an individual.

The *Daubert* Decision—*Daubert v. Merrell Dow Pharmaceuticals* (1993) supersedes *Frye* and holds that scientific evidence is admissible if the trial judge feels that it is relevant and will assist the triers of fact.

***Durham* Test**—also called the "product test," states that an individual is not "criminally responsible if his unlawful act is the product of a mental disease or defect."

Federal Rules of Evidence—governs what is admissible in court in many U.S. jurisdictions.

Forensic Pathology—a subdivision of pathology, the study of diagnosis of disease.

Forensic Toxicology—the study of poisons and toxins.

Frye Decision—*Frye v. United States* (1923) set the standard that only scientific evidence that related to science that was "generally accepted" in a particular scientific community could be admitted to court.

Guilty But Mentally Ill—an alternative to the insanity plea.

Insanity—a legal term that refers to a defendant's responsibility for his or her actions.

Islamic Sharia—law derived from the Koran.

Justinian Code—a compilation of laws from A.D. 529 which helped cement the power of the Christian church while decreasing the rights of the Jews.

Law of the Twelve Tables—from 451 B.C. Rome, focuses on procedure and due process of law.

Laws—written rules and regulations that govern behavior that are established by a government or a ruler.

M'Naughten Rule—in order to establish the defense of insanity it must be proved that at the time of the act the accused suffered from a "defect of reason, from disease of mind" that was such that he did not know the act he was doing or that it was wrong.

Medical examiner system—a system of death investigation that is headed by a medical doctor who makes determinations regarding cause of death, especially suspicious deaths.

Mores—those rules that are the customs of the group, generally referred to as *mores*.

Roman Law—pertains first to law as it was practiced in Rome, but later to a collection of legal concepts that helped create the legal system that has been dominant in Europe.

Toxic torts—nickname for product liability cases.

Warren Court—the Supreme Court headed by Earl Warren from 1953–1969, known for many liberal decisions that furthered the civil rights movement (e.g., *Brown v. Board of Education* 1954) and the Rights of the Accused (e.g., *Miranda v. Arizona* 1966).

Webliography

Forensic Science Timeline
    http://www.forensicdna.com/Timeline020702.pdf
History of Forensic Pathology
    http://www.autopsy-md.com/History.html
History of Fingerprints
    http://onin.com/fp/fphistory.html
    http://kyky.essortment.com/fingerprinthist_rmmv.htm
    http://www.deakin.edu.au/forensic/Chemical%20Detective/
        fingerprint_history.htm
    http://www.fingerprintamerica.com/fingerprintHistory.asp

http://www.alumni.ca/~diasj/history.html
http://www.edcampbell.com/PalmD-History.htm
http://www.met.police.uk/so/100years/history.htm
Sanity
    http://law.enotes.com/everyday-law-encyclopedia/
        89917#CURRENTSTATUSOFTHEINSANITYDEFENS
        EAMONGTHESTATES
    http://www.newshour.org/wgbh/pages/frontline/shows/
        crime/trial/history.html

References

Bjur, R. and J. Richardson. "Expert Testimony Involving Chemists and Chemistry." In *Expert Witnessing: Explaining and Understanding Science.* Edited by Carl Meyer, 67–87, Chapter 5. Boca Raton, FL: CRC Press, 1999.

Brickley, P. "Science v. Law." *Scientific American* 289, no. 6 (December 2003): 30.

DeForest, Peter R., R. E. Gaensslen, and Henry C. Lee. *Forensic Science: An Introduction to Criminalistics.* NY: McGraw-Hill, 1983.

Dix, J. and R. Calaluce. 1999. *Guide to Forensic Pathology.*

Eckert, William G. ed. *Introduction to Forensic Sciences*, 2nd ed. Boca Raton, FL: CRC Press, 1997.

Eckert, W. G. and R. K. Wright. "Forensic Pathology." In *Introduction to Forensic Sciences*, 2nd ed. Edited by Eckert, William G., 107–132. Boca Raton, FL: CRC Press, 1997.

Edmunds, Palmer D. *Law and civilization.* Washington: Public Affairs Press, 1959

Hileman, B. 2003. "Daubert Rules Challenge Courts." *Chemical & Engineering News* Jul 7, 81, no. 27 (2003): 14.

Hooker, R. 1996. *Mesopotamia: The Code of Hammurabi.* Accessed on August 26, 2006, from http://www.wsu.edu/~dee/MESO/CODE.HTM.

Kiely, T. 2001. Forensic Evidence: Science and the Criminal Law. Boca Raton, FL: CRC Press.

Meyer, C. "Science, Medicine and the U.S. Common Law Courts." Chapter 1 In *Expert Witnessing: Explaining and Understanding Science,* Edited by C. Meyer, 1–29. Boca Raton, FL: CRC Press, 1999.

Saferstein, R. *Criminalistics*, 8th ed. Upper Saddle River, NJ: Pearson, 2004.

Swanson, C., N. Chamelin, and L. Territo. *Criminal Investigation,* 7th ed. NY: McGraw-Hill, 2000.

Wecht, C. "Legal Medicine and Jurisprudence." In *Introduction to Forensic Sciences,* 2nd ed. Edited by Eckert, William G. Boca Raton, FL: CRC Press, 1997.

Wigmore, J. H. *World's Legal Systems.* Washington, D.C.: Washington Law Book Company, 1936.

Review Questions

1. Why do societies develop laws?
2. What are the four most influential ancient societies in the development of law?
3. Why was the Code of Hammurabi so important?
4. Explain how the *Frye* decision changed the way courts viewed scientific evidence.
5. How has the *Daubert* decision functioned to keep reliable science out of the courtroom?
6. How did the Warren Court protect the "rights of the defendant?"
7. What was the main difference between the death investigation system in England and the system in continental Europe?
8. How did Orfila influence the field of toxicology?
9. Trace the development of the "insanity defense."
10. Legal medicine consists of which three separate but often related fields?

Some Things to Think About

1. The authors of the text argue that criminalistics and forensic science are different, yet others have argued that they are the same. What do you think about this?
2. Why do you think it is important to understand the history of forensic science?
3. It has only been since the *Frye* decision in 1923 that questions have been asked about good science and bad science. Why do we ask these questions now?

Processing the Evidence

Section II is comprised of Chapter 3, *The Importance of the Crime Scene* and Chapter 4, *The Crime Laboratory*. Together these two chapters will acquaint you with the key area of evidence processing. Without proper evidence processing, there can be no forensic science testimony in the courtroom. Chapter 3 focuses on the crime scene. Chapter 3 may be the most important chapter in the book. All investigations begin at the crime scene. The crime scene must be properly identified, secured, documented, and searched. When evidence is located it must be packaged in appropriate containers and the proper chain of custody must be followed while it is transported to the laboratory.

Chapter 4 discusses the history and development of the crime laboratory. In the United States each state has its own system of laboratories, and while the FBI offers laboratory services, it does not function as a federal laboratory. State and local laboratories are often divided into separate units to handle different types of evidence. These laboratory units are discussed, along with the forensic techniques that are used to analyze the evidence.

The Importance of the Crime Scene

WHAT IS THE CRIME SCENE?

It may seem a bit obvious to ask a question like "what is the crime scene?" At first glance, the answer may seem deceptively simple: "the crime scene is the place where the crime occurred." On one level, that is the correct answer. The crime scene *is* the place where the crime occurred. Yet many crime scene boundaries are not that clear-cut. Some crime scenes are in one location, some will extend over several locations. Some crime scenes will be neatly bounded by the walls; others have much more uncertain boundaries. In some instances it is obvious that a crime has occurred, and so, that location will be a crime scene. In other cases, it is not so obvious that a crime has occurred at a particular location. In some instances, it is even difficult to establish a crime scene at all. Many types of computer crimes do not leave obvious crime scenes. Sometimes the only evidence of a computer crime may reside on a distant server, or on someone's hard drive or on a very small flash drive. If the crime scene is where the crime occurred, in the case of computer crime this can be very difficult to determine. In some crimes, there may be a primary crime scene and a secondary crime scene.

Determining where exactly the crime scene is can be further complicated when there is a primary and secondary crime scene. If a body is found in a room, the investigator must determine if the room is the crime scene or if the crime took place somewhere else and the body was brought to the room. The room could function as a "dump site" for the body. If we find a body, we may very well have a crime (or the death may have been the result of natural causes), but at first glance, the investigator cannot know for sure that the crime was committed where the body was found. The crime scene is the primary place where the crime was committed and it is possible to have several crime scenes associated with a single crime: there may be a primary crime scene, where most evidence will be found, and one or more secondary crime scenes where more evidence may be found. The possibility of multiple crime scenes should not be overlooked by the first responder when establishing the perimeters for the crime scene.

Each type of crime (robbery, homicide, arson) creates a unique and different crime scene. A homicide creates a very different scene from a burglary; this is something that all good officers and detectives know and they treat these scenes very differently. A seasoned officer can frequently tell what sort of a crime scene it is just from a quick first examination, and evidence collection will be guided by this. These different types of scenes, and their various considerations, will be discussed in detail in the remaining chapters of this text.

THE MOST IMPORTANT JOB IN FORENSICS

Many students will ask: "What is the most important part of the investigation?" or a corollary question: "Who has the most important job in forensics?" Students often believe that the most important person in forensics must have the title of "Detective," or even "Doctor." The impression has been created, mostly through the media and television shows like *CSI,* that forensics is all about the latest technology, that with the most recent advances in, for example, DNA analysis, we will be better able to catch criminals, or be better able to eliminate the innocent from our investigations. Surely the most important job in forensics, then, will entail working with these latest advances in technology. The reality is much simpler—and far less glamorous.

The single most important aspect of all investigations is the crime scene. All investigations begin with the crime scene. In order for any forensic examination to take place—before any evidence can be sent to the laboratory, before any evidence can be collected—the crime scene must be established and protected. This importance *cannot* be overstated. Furthermore, no amount of technological advances will ever compensate for an improperly handled crime scene.

It is true that technology has been very important in forensics. Through the use of technology we are able to do new and different things, or better and faster things, every day. Technological advances are important to the field—and they often drive changes in the field—but they are not the most important aspect of forensics. The most advanced testing for DNA or fibers can only be performed and submitted to court if the crime scene is handled properly. No amount of the latest technology can restore a poorly protected crime scene to its pristine state. If the crime scene has been contaminated, the integrity of all of the evidence from that crime scene may be called into question. All that technology—all those expensive, intricate tests—will amount to very little if the crime scene has not been properly established and protected.

The beginning of the investigation lays the foundation for everything else that follows. If this foundation is not properly laid, the entire investigation is at risk. The most important job in forensics, it could be argued, is not a job in forensics at all, but the job of first responder, the first person who arrives at the crime scene. Some crime scenes become compromised at this point. The first responder is usually a uniformed patrol officer. The first responder may be a seasoned veteran with 20 years experience, but since almost all police officers begin their careers as patrol officers, he or she may be a brand-new officer. For this reason, proper training in crime scene handling and evidence collection is a must for all police academy attendees. Thorough training in these areas will translate to higher conviction rates.

Handling the Crime Scene

The officer who responds to the scene has many duties that occur simultaneously or in quick succession. The first responder must be concerned with a number of things when responding to a call:

- approaching the crime scene
- securing the crime scene
- giving aid to any victims
- apprehending the perpetrator
- protecting and preserving the crime scene

Depending upon the type of call, some of these will be of greater or lesser concern. When a call comes in concerning a crime in progress, obviously apprehending the perpetrator will be of a much more immediate concern, than if the call concerns a crime that has occurred days or even weeks ago. Some crimes, like explosions, may pose significant physical risks, while a burglary may pose none. An assault may have severely injured victims who will require medical services. A victim of theft, unless very distraught, probably won't require any type of medical intervention. Larger, outdoor, crime scenes are harder to protect than small, indoor crime scenes. The first responder must weigh all of these factors and respond to the scene appropriately.

Approaching the Crime Scene

The officer's job does not begin at the scene; it begins the instant the call comes in. How an officer physically approaches the scene depends upon the type of crime and whether or not it may still be in progress. Necessarily, more caution is taken when a crime may still be in progress than when it is known that the offender is long gone. Also, the officer may receive very little information about the crime during that initial call. He or she must keep in mind that there are many unknowns and what is not known can be very dangerous indeed. The officer should assume danger when responding to the call and be prepared for anything.

While driving to a call, and when approaching on foot, the officer should carefully observe as much as possible. A person on the street may be the perpetrator. A car parked at the corner may be a get-away vehicle. Of special concern would be any individuals behaving in an unusual way, running, showing signs of injury, or carrying objects. Anyone who seems out-of-place or nervous could be of interest. The officer should also be making note of possible entrance and exit routes that were available to the offender. The perpetrator had to get to the scene and leave the scene in some way, and it may very well have been along the same path that the officer is driving.

When approaching the crime scene, being aware of the possibility that the perpetrator is nearby, and the risk this may pose, is not the only concern for the first responder. The first responder should also be aware of the relative risks that may be involved in and around the crime scene. If the perpetrator is long gone, a burglary scene may not be particularly dangerous—although there may be broken glass or weapons at the scene. However, other sorts of scenes pose significant hazards. If there has been an explosion—whether accidental or intentional—there may be secondary explosions yet to detonate. At a suicide scene there may be noxious chemicals present. Terrorist attacks present a whole host of possible hazards; in fact, the element of the unknown in a terrorist attack is often considerable. Perhaps the biggest danger arises simply because the first responder may have little idea what awaits at the crime scene. The initial call may be no more than: "burglary in progress at . . ." or "Shots fired at . . ." Because so much is unknown, the first responder must be prepared for anything and it is advisable to approach the crime scene with extreme caution.

Consider what was initially known by emergency workers in New York City on the morning of September 11, 2001. When the first plane struck the North Tower of the World Trade Center, at 8:46 A.M. EDT, it was not known that it was a terrorist attack, an accident was suspected. Shortly after impact, it was apparent that there was fire and that people were trapped on the top floors. It was not known how many people were trapped and the extent of the fire and damage to the structure were not known. No one knew for sure what was happening. No one knew how dangerous the scene was or would become. At that point, no one could accurately predict the magnitude of the coming disaster. No one knew how large that crime scene would be or that within hours; both the North and South Towers would be in rubble. If it had been known that both towers were going to collapse, rescue workers would have responded to the scene differently. Of course, it is not possible to know this ahead of time. The vast majority of crime scenes will not pose a danger even remotely close to the danger at the World Trade Towers crime scene, but all crime scenes, because they are unknown, have the potential to injure or kill many people.

Securing the Crime Scene

The first responder is responsible for securing the crime scene. This includes determining the perimeter of the scene, keeping unauthorized personnel away from the scene, and dealing with the press if necessary. The officer must also notify the appropriate people—including the lead detective, the forensic unit, and paramedics so that proper crime scene processing can begin before significant evidence deteriorates. Securing the crime scene also means making the crime scene safe for those individuals who are already there, and those who will be entering the crime scene. Because all crime scenes are potentially very dangerous, the first responder must make the scene safe not only for the victims but for everyone else—paramedics, evidence collectors, and bystanders (Figure 3.1). This will take precedence even over assisting victims. Victims cannot be aided and evidence cannot be collected if the scene is hazardous to everyone who enters it.

There are many types of possible hazards at crime scenes. Among the most frequently encountered are human, biological, animal, physical, electrical, combustible/explosive, chemical, although the list of possible hazards is probably limitless.

Human hazards include encountering the perpetrator at or near the scene or the perpetrator returning to the scene. Biological hazards include blood, semen, saliva, tissue, and organs originating from either perpetrator or victim. Biological agents may also be used to launch a terrorist attack, such as ricin or anthrax. Animal hazards consist of being scratched, bitten, chased, or attacked by a domestic or wild animal at the scene. Physical crime scene hazards encompass everything from glass shards and metal fragments, to collapsing ceilings and flying debris. Structures may be unsound from fires, explosions, or simply the age of the structure and

FIGURE 3.1   A potentially very dangerous crime scene.

neglect. Houses used by drug users and dealers present a variety of hazards, including used needles, bodily products (blood, urine, feces, mucous, semen), and unsound structure. Combustible/explosive hazards may be encountered at a crime scene. Perpetrators who bomb abortion and women's health clinics or other targets will frequently set off multiple explosions or have plans beyond a single crime. The primary explosion will target the clinic; the secondary explosion targets rescue workers. Multiple explosions also keep responders off-balance and increase the chaos and danger at the scene. During a suicide or homicide attempt, household gas may be left on, posing a significant threat to rescue workers. At mass disasters, gas lines may be ruptured and pose a risk for fire and explosion, and live electrical wires may also pose a significant threat. Rescue workers may first need to shut off gas and electric lines at the scene. Chemical hazards can arise from chemicals used by drug manufacturers, fumes from household chemicals, or chemical agents used by terrorists.

Most crime scenes require only a moderate and routine level of safety precautions to protect those individuals working at the crime scene and to protect the crime scene and the evidence it contains from destruction. Standard precautions include the wearing of latex gloves. In fact, there is a wide variety of gloves available depending upon the type of hazards that are encountered. Latex is often used and will provide a good level of protection; however, latex will degrade when exposed to certain acids, gasoline, and heat. Nitrile gloves provide more protection from acids and solvents; they also offer superior resistance to cuts and punctures. Protective eyewear should be worn if alternate light sources are used at the crime scene; eyewear also provide protection from the splattering of bodily products or chemicals into the eyes. A facemask is a good idea for anyone working closely with the collection of small evidence, not only to protect themselves from hazards, but also to protect the evidence from contamination. This is especially true for certain types of mtDNA (mitochondrial DNA) evidence that can be easily contaminated by droplets of saliva. The wearing of a respirator is necessary for crime scenes where hazardous and noxious fumes may be present, including methamphetamine laboratories. Sturdy shoes are necessary for all crime scene workers, not only for walking in all types of environments, but to protect the bottoms of the feet from cuts or punctures. Sometimes shoe covers, which look like large booties, will be worn by technicians to prevent evidence contamination. Some crime scenes will also require head protection. This is especially the case for buildings where explosions or fires have

---

Protective Gear

Gloves for protecting the crime scene and the crime-scene worker's hands

    Latex used for standard crime scenes

    Nitrile provide increased protection against certain types of chemical hazards, are less likely to tear

Footwear protects the crime scene from having extraneous materials tracked in, also protects the crime scene worker's feet

    Booties cloth covers for shoes, used to protect the crime scene

    Sturdy shoes or boots protects the crime-scene worker's feet

Eyewear goggles may be incorporated into a facemask, or may be worn alone

Facemask protects worker from possible splattering; also protects evidence from contamination if the worker sneezes

Respirator protects from airborne hazards

Headgear used to protect the head from falling debris.

Jumpsuit may be required in very hazardous chemical and biological crime scenes

Thermal Protective Gear for use mostly by firefighters during fires

Diving gear used for protection during diving

    Wetsuit for warmer water diving

    Drysuit for cold water diving, protects against hypothermia

    Diving gloves and boots protect worker's hands and feet in the underwater environment

---

occurred, or other scenes that require personnel to enter structures that may be unsound. At crime scenes that have known hazardous biological and chemical agents present, crime scene technicians may wear jumpsuits not only to protect themselves, but to protect the crime scene from adulteration.

SPECIALIZED SERVICES   Other crime scenes will require handling by personnel who have specialized training. This includes emergency medical technicians (EMTs)/paramedics, firefighters, hazmat teams, bomb squads, and sniper squads (Figures 3.2 and 3.3). Since the terrorist attacks of September 11, 2001, greater emphasis has been placed on disaster and emergency preparedness. Each jurisdiction should have a plan prepared to deal with any potential hazard that may occur. And while large-scale hazards occur only rarely, smaller incidents occur daily.

At crime scenes where there are injuries, EMT/paramedic services are required. At mass disasters, they will most certainly be required. EMTs and paramedics are trained to provide medical services. They will stabilize injured individuals and transport them to the hospital.

Firefighters will be required to combat active or suspected fires. Usually, however, they do not have to be summoned to the scene, in a significant majority of cases when emergency services are summoned; firefighters are the first responders to the scene. If there is an active fire, and even after the fire has been extinguished, no one should enter the building until the fire fighters have declared that it is safe. Even if it has been determined that the structure is still relatively safe and evidence can be collected, fire and arson scenes present many hazards and require at least head and foot protection.

The hazmat team is called to a crime scene when there are known or suspected chemical and biological hazards. Most frequently, hazmat teams respond to chemical hazards. The team will

FIGURE 3.2   Firefighters may be required at some crime scenes.

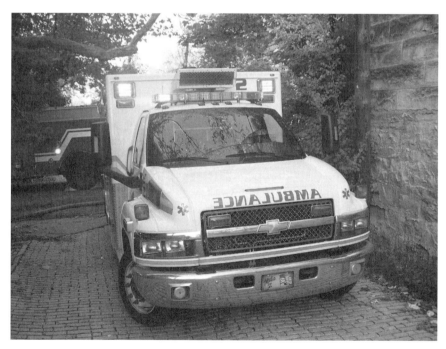

FIGURE 3.3   Paramedic services are required when there are injuries.

contain the hazard and clean it up, which includes decontamination of the area. When the hazard is unknown, the team can determine what the hazard is and how much of a threat it poses and the sort of protective gear that is required for the scene. Hazmat teams must follow the regulations of Occupational Safety and Health Administration (OSHA) and the Environmental Protection Agency

(EPA) in dealing with hazardous materials. Today it is not uncommon for hazmat teams to use computer modeling to help determine what sort of hazard is being faced.

If it is suspected that there are unexploded devices at the scene, the bomb squad must be notified. It may be that a bomb threat has been called in, that a suspicious package has been located, or if a bomb has already been detonated, there may be others that are unexploded in the vicinity. Under no circumstances should untrained personnel ever handle suspected explosive devices.

A sniper squad may be brought to the scene to deal with a perpetrator who has created a barricade or one who is holding hostages or one who simply poses a significant threat to the public. These individuals are trained to shoot and kill with high-powered rifles. While it is the goal of the police to apprehend and not kill the perpetrator, the safety of the public and others involved in the incident is primary to perpetrator safety.

Aiding the Victims

After the crime scene has been secured as much as possible, rendering aid to any victims present is the next most immediate concern for the first responder. This takes precedence over apprehending any perpetrators. This may include administering cardiopulmonary resuscitation (CPR), basic first aid, or calling for an ambulance. The first responder should assess the situation and determine what sort of assistance is needed by the victims. Generally, paramedics will be among the first responders to a major crime scene and officers will not need to summon them. It is always advisable to allow medical personnel to assess the situation and determine what the needs of the victims are. All victims who have been involved in any sort of physical altercation should be assessed by medical personnel. A victim is not the best judge of whether or not medical intervention is necessary. Levels of adrenaline in the bloodstream may be high, and this will mask pain from injuries. The psychological needs of victims should not be forgotten. While these will not be as immediate as medical concerns, psychological assistance should be made available for victims.

Apprehending the Perpetrator

If the officer is responding to a call of a crime in progress, then the offender may be pursued if it can be done in a safe manner, without further endangering victims and others. When approaching the crime scene, the first responder should be looking for suspicious individuals leaving the crime scene because the perpetrator might be among them. It is especially important to pursue the offender when possible because the earlier an arrest is made; the more likely it is that there will be a conviction.

Although it is certainly a goal of officers to apprehend the perpetrator as soon as possible, the real goal is to apprehend the *actual* perpetrator and make an arrest that results in a conviction, not just an arrest of someone who may or may not be connected with the crime. Care should always be taken not to use racial profiling when apprehending individuals. While the perpetrator may have been a black man, this is not a good enough reason to arrest every black man in the area. This type of profiling wastes law enforcement resources.

Protecting and Preserving the Crime Scene

An important part of preserving the crime scene is simply keeping everyone except the authorized few away, which is easier said than done. At this early stage the crime scene is at its most vulnerable to damage from both intentional and unintentional harm. Intentional harm may come from the perpetrator trying to destroy possible evidence, or from someone trying to protect the perpetrator by altering or destroying evidence. Individuals trying to protect the perpetrator are sometimes well-meaning. This can be in the case of a suspected suicide. A family member may try to make the suicide look like an accident. This may be done to save the family from

The Lindbergh Case—Failure to Secure the Crime Scene

The Lindbergh baby case clearly illustrates three important points. First, it is very important to an investigation for law enforcement to protect and have control over the crime scene. Second, it illustrates the difficulties of investigating a case that involves a celebrity. Third, it shows how detrimental media exposure can be to the proper investigation of a crime.

In 1932, the infant son of Charles Lindbergh, Jr, who had made the first solo flight from New York to Paris in 1927, and Anne Morrow Lindbergh, was kidnapped. The child was subsequently murdered. Charles Lindberg III was kidnapped from his nursery on the night of March 1, 1932. Although a ransom note was found, and the kidnapper left a ladder outside the window, and the remains of a child were found in the nearby woods, and Bruno Hauptmann was executed for the crime, there is still considerable doubt regarding who actually killed the child, and, indeed, if the child was ever found.

Within hours of reporting the crime, the Lindbergh estate was inundated with New Jersey State police. President Herbert Hoover offered to assist in any way possible, even though, at the time, kidnapping was a local crime, not a federal crime. Huge rewards were offered. The Bureau of Investigations (which would later become the FBI) became involved.

It is not uncommon when a famous individual is involved in a crime that law enforcement experiences challenges handling the case. The Lindbergh case presented many such challenges. After police arrived, no attempt was made to cordon off the crime scene. Instead officers walked around the grounds freely, obscuring any shoe impressions that may have been near the location of the ladder. No shoe impressions were photographed or cast. Although the house and grounds were searched for miles, it was not done in a systematic fashion. Possible evidence may have inadvertently been trampled. Although the body of a young child was found in the nearby woods months later, there were discrepancies between that body and the description of the Lindbergh baby. Also, no forensic examination of the body took place by a qualified pathologist. The body was cremated, quickly destroying all chances for later examination. Lindberg himself was allowed to exercise considerable control over the case, in large part due to his fame. When a second ransom note was received, instead of giving it to the police, Lindbergh gave it to a man who worked for the *Daily News*, who copied and published the ransom note. This made all of the notable individual characteristics in the writing useless for further identification since the entire contents of the letter were public.

There were numerous theories about what happened to the Lindbergh child. Violet Sharpe, a young maid at the house was accused when she was not consistent with her story. This young woman killed herself by swallowing cyanide, not because of guilt, but because she had been out at a club and feared she would lose her job for such behavior. In the end, Bruno Hauptmann was tried, convicted, and executed for kidnapping and killing of the Lindbergh baby. Even today, doubt regarding his guilt still exists.

the difficulty of having to acknowledge the suicide, or to allow the beneficiary to collect on insurance policies. Crime scenes may even sometimes be altered by law enforcement. This may be done to attempt to cover up an officer's involvement in illegal activity, or to cover up for someone else. In some cases, law enforcement may alter a crime scene to create an impression that a particular suspect is guilty, or it may be done to help back up other officers' statements. Intentionally altering a crime scene, regardless of who attempts to do so or why it is done, is a crime and should be treated as such.

Most of the individuals who alter and do harm to the crime scene do not do so intentionally. They include victims and witnesses, home or property owners, the press, bystanders, and even other police officers who are just curious. Home or property owners may begin to clean up and repair damage that has been done. Even using a broom to sweep a walkway may cause trace evidence to be destroyed. A crime scene is *not* an open invitation for everyone connected with law enforcement to have a look around. This can be especially difficult because the first responder may be a patrol officer with little rank and experience and must give in to superiors who want to enter the crime scene.

The media can pose a particular problem for law enforcement. While the public does have a right to know that a crime has been committed, they are not entitled to all the details of the crime, especially when disseminating those details can—and often do—hamper an investigation. However, the media should not be looked at as the enemy. In fact, savvy law enforcement agencies can form positive relationships with the media and even use the media to help further the investigation.

If a significant crime has occurred, there should be a media liaison to provide the necessary information to the media without compromising the crime scene or the investigation. This balances the public's right to know with proper crime scene protection. It also provides law enforcement with a certain amount of control regarding what information is released to the public and when.

ESTABLISHING PERIMETERS   Establishing physical perimeters around a crime scene is the first step in keeping the crime scene safe from intentional or unintentional destruction. This is the area that will be marked off and searched for evidence, as such, it must encompass the entire area where evidence will be found, or at least as much of this area as possible. To properly protect the crime scene, establishing three perimeters is recommended. The outer perimeter is established to keep the public out, and the scene safe. A media station may be set up just outside this perimeter. The middle perimeter is established outside the actual crime scene. This allows a variety of official personnel to get close to the scene without endangering the evidence. The inner perimeter is established around the actual crime scene; only select personnel are allowed into the inner perimeter: crime scene technicians, the lead investigator, the medical examiner. Possible entry and exit routes for the perpetrator should also be protected. Entrances and exits into the scene must be kept to a minimum and preferably should all follow the same route. This will aid both in controlling access to the scene and in keeping unauthorized people out.

The initial perimeter established by the first responder should be as large as possible to err on the side of caution and to preserve any outlying evidence, such as tire tracks and shoe impressions. An indoor crime committed in a room in a house or other building has the natural boundary of walls. The walls establish the perimeter of the crime scene. When the crime is committed outside, it is much harder to establish an appropriate perimeter. The first responder must make some guesses and err on the side of caution. It is better to create too large of a perimeter rather than one that is too small.

The type of crime will also help the responding officer determine the perimeter of the scene. Crimes like explosions will have a much larger crime scene. In some cases it may well be impossible to set the perimeters of the crime scene large enough to encompass all evidence: consider how to secure the scene created by an explosion, by the destruction of the World Trade Center, or by the explosion of space shuttle *Columbia.* These scenes were so huge and encompassed so much area that it would be impossible to set perimeters outside of the scene. In the instance of *Columbia,* that would have encompassed several states! In these extreme cases, investigators need to do the best they can trying to collect as much evidence as possible without being able to make the entire area a crime scene.

CONDUCTING INTERVIEWS

In a criminal investigation, interviews may be conducted at many points during the investigative process. While this chapter discusses the crime scene, this section will address not only the process of conducting initial interviews at the crime scene but also the process of conducting later interviews and interrogations.

The Crime Scene Interview

While some individuals are interviewed on several occasions, the initial interview may be the most important interview that is conducted, for several reasons. First, for some witnesses, this will be the only time that they get to talk to an officer. Second, memories are most fresh right after an incident has occurred and the officers are most likely to get the most detailed, truthful statements at this time. Third, these initial interviews will very likely have a significant impact on how the investigation develops. If the initial interviews are done by skilled interviewers, they will yield a wealth of leads and may even result in an immediate confession. Because of the importance of these interviews, care must be taken that they are done competently, thoroughly, and as completely as possible.

As soon as possible after the crime scene has been stabilized, the interviewing of witnesses and victims should begin. Witnesses should be isolated from each other to preserve their stories. Having two or more officers conduct interviews will help speed the process along and minimize contamination amongst witnesses. This will help insure consistency of statements. If witnesses are allowed to talk to one another about what has occurred, their statements will change. This is not necessarily intentional, but once an individual hears another perspective regarding what happened—or many perspectives—that individual's statements will begin to conform to the details that others have provided and disregard memories that appear inconsistent with the perceptions of others. It is also a good idea to conduct these interviews as soon as possible because memories will quickly begin to fade, especially fine details of those memories.

If some individuals are not interviewed quickly, they may leave the crime scene and never be found again. Then their story will be lost. The evidence that they know will be lost. If it is not possible to thoroughly interview all witnesses, their names and contact information should be obtained so that they can be contacted later.

THE INTERVIEW PROCESS   At the outset of the interview, the officer wants to try to establish a positive rapport as much as possible. If the witness is the victim, the officer will want to appear empathetic to the victim's feelings. And while the officer is just doing his or her job, it can be detrimental to appear too businesslike. The victim is a person and in crimes like assault and rape, the victim may be significantly traumatized. Even in crimes that do not involve physical injury and danger, the victim may experience trauma. It is always best to begin the interview by letting the victim know that by telling their story, they will aid the investigation and the process of justice. If the story is traumatic, acknowledge that it is traumatic. The officer should never appear judgmental. If the interview is being conducted with a female victim of sexual assault, it is often a good idea to have a female officer conduct the interview to make the victim feel more at ease.

It is often a good idea to have the witness tell his or her story in chronological order, using only minimal prompts like: "tell me what you were doing prior to the crime." If the witness's statement seems to have gaps, the officer may give small prompts: "where were you when you heard the glass breaking."

Gain as much information as possible to prepare for subsequent interviews. Probe for as much detail as possible, but do not ask leading questions: who, what, when, where, why. Ask why they think someone did something, it can provide insight. What is the interviewee's motivation for cooperating or not cooperating with you?

COGNITIVE INTERVIEW TECHNIQUE   The cognitive interview is not just one technique, but rather a number of techniques that can be used both in the field and in a controlled interview setting to enhance the memory of a witness or victim. (There is a similarly named technique that is used during therapy.) Some of the techniques are very lengthy and the field setting might not be conducive to their use; however, others are less involved and can be employed by police officers.

The cognitive interview technique enhances memory by encouraging the witness to focus in a different way. He or she may be encouraged to remember everything about the physical surroundings rather than focus on the event. He or she may be asked to report everything that is remembered, regardless of how unimportant it may seem. He or she may be encouraged to retell what happened from a variety of chronological points (beginning to end, end to beginning, from a point in the middle). He or she may be asked to recall the event from a variety of points of view.

Conducting Follow-Up Interviews

It is often necessary to conduct follow-up interviews with key witnesses to major crimes. The suspect may be interviewed on a number of occasions. Unlike the initial interview which is often conducted at the crime scene, this interview is more likely to be conducted in a controlled setting if it is with the suspect, such as an interview room at the police station. The interviewer should take time to prepare thoroughly for the interview. He or she should review all the facts of the case and also all information known about the suspect. This includes previous contacts with the law, work habits, friends, and associates. Especially when interviewing the suspect, information is the interviewer's key weapon. The more that is known about the suspect the better.

Conducting Interrogations

Most cases are solved by a confession. An interview is *not* an interrogation. There are several key differences between an interview and an interrogation. The main goal of an interview is to gain information. The main goal of an interrogation is to gain a confession via direct or indirect admission to the crime. During an interview, the person being interviewed is free to leave the interview at any time. During an interrogation, the person being interrogated is not free to leave the interrogation at any time. In fact, it is this distinction that triggers the Miranda requirement—when the suspect is *in custody,* in other words, not free to leave.

A witness or suspect is always free to request that an attorney be present during the interview or interrogation process, however, it is only prior to the interrogation that the suspect must be informed of his or her right to have an attorney present. Prior to an interrogation, the suspect must be read the Miranda Warnings. In general, suspects in an investigation are read the Miranda Warnings, witnesses are not.

There is not always a clear distinction between an interview and an interrogation. An interview can become an interrogation, depending upon what is revealed in the interview. If that happens, the Miranda Warnings must be read, or the information gained will not be admissible in court. However, keep in mind, that voluntary statements made to officers during an interview are admissible. If an individual is being asked routine questions and decides to confess to the crime, that confession is still admissible because it was given freely and voluntarily and the individual was not being interrogated at the time the confession was given.

The interrogation process is very different from the interview process. In the interview process, the officer's goal is to gain information to further the investigation. In the interrogation, the officer's goal is to gain a confession to the crime. The interrogation is often very structured, to include the suspects retelling of what happened, after which the officer points out inconsistencies in the story and asks for clarification. The purpose of the clarification is to allow the suspect to make further statements that are clearly not true, or contradict an earlier version of his story. The witness may also be told about evidence that exists against him and asked for explanation. When confronted with the evidence that law enforcement has, he may confess.

LYING TO AND COERCING A SUSPECT   Interestingly, to gain a confession, law enforcement may legally lie about the evidence they have against a suspect. While law enforcement may not fabricate evidence that will be presented in court, it is perfectly okay to make statements like: "our testing reveals that there is a high likelihood that you fired the murder weapon," when, in fact, the ballistics testing did not reveal this. An interrogator may state: "your friend told us that you were the one who actually raped the victim, he wasn't even in the room." When, in fact, no such statements have been made. The interrogator's story may prompt the suspect to counter with: "that's not true, we both raped her."

There are certain forms of coercion that are allowed during interrogations. Officers may keep the suspect in a room that is not terribly comfortable. It may be a bit too hot. The chairs may be hard. The lighting may be very harsh. While the suspect may not be deprived of drink and food indefinitely, even water does not have to be immediately provided.

The Miranda Warnings

In *Miranda v. Arizona* (1963), a confession made by Ernesto Miranda was thrown out because he was not advised of the fact that he could choose not to answer officer's questions and that he could have an attorney present during questioning. The Supreme Court ruled that a defendant in any case in which loss of freedom could result, must be advised about certain rights; the right to remain silent and not make statements to officers because those statements can be used in a court of law, and the right to have an attorney represent him or her. The Miranda warnings are so entrenched in our society that they can be heard on almost any police show on television on any day of the week!

    The basic Miranda warnings are as follows:

    "You have the right to remain silent. Anything you say can and will be used against you in a court of law. You have the right to speak to an attorney, and to have an attorney present during any questioning. If you cannot afford a lawyer, one will be provided for you. Do you understand these rights as read to you?"

The suspect cannot be threatened during interrogation, either physically or psychologically. Even implied threats are not allowed. Also, interrogators cannot threaten the suspect's family or friends. An individual cannot be held indefinitely without being charged.

CRIMES MOST LIKELY TO YIELD FORENSIC EVIDENCE

Forensic evidence is not collected for every crime that is committed. This would be far too time consuming, and also too costly. Some crimes are too petty to warrant forensics, for example, small thefts. Frequently, when citizens have something stolen from their house or car they feel that the responding officer should "dust for fingerprints," just like they have seen done on television, in order to apprehend the thief. Yet, if the item stolen was inexpensive, going through the process of collecting forensic evidence is not a good use of limited law enforcement resources. These resources are best reserved for more serious offenses. Although the theft victim may not like hearing this, the reality is that only serious crimes are processed for forensic evidence, or even followed-up. This selective investigation can negatively impact the public's perception of the police. Yet, the reality of police work is that everything costs money and many jurisdictions have a very limited budget and monies are allocated to the most serious and high-profile crimes first.

Certain offenses, generally speaking, demand processing for forensic evidence. There are three reasons why a crime scene is processed. First, it may be processed for statutory reasons; such as drug offenses and DUI offenses. When an arrest is made, the substance seized must be analyzed and its chemical makeup determined—after all a bag of oregano is strange but not illegal. An arrest for DUI must be backed up with a blood-alcohol analysis. Second, serious felonies, like murder, and many sexual offenses, will always be processed for forensic evidence. Third, there are certain crimes that are most likely to yield forensic evidence: drug crimes, murder, rape, burglary, arson and explosives, accidents, and hit and run.

PROCESSING THE CRIME SCENE

The Fourth Amendment

The Fourth Amendment protects individuals from unreasonable searches and seizures. When law enforcement responds to a call, they are legally allowed to collect any and all evidence related to the crime. Law enforcement should make every effort to collect all evidence at this time, not only because subsequent searches will require a warrant but also because any remaining evidence may be destroyed.

If a subsequent search is required after the initial crime scene search, a warrant must be obtained. That warrant must describe exactly the objects and evidence to be seized. The warrant must also clearly describe the area to be searched and provide a specific time frame. If the warrant states that drug paraphernalia is being searched for in the house, the officers cannot look for and seize child pornography that is stored in the detached garage.

Processing the crime scene includes the crime scene search; thorough written and photographic documentation of the crime scene (possible video documentation); evidence collection, packaging, and transporting; and continued protection of the crime scene.

Documenting the Crime Scene

The crime scene must be documented as fully and completely as possible. It is only through thorough documentation that judges and juries can be presented with the facts of the case. Documentation is the way to preserve the crime scene as it was when it was first discovered after the commission of the crime.

The number of people working and documenting the crime scene is often dependent upon both the size of the department and the type and extent of the crime, but it should always be kept to a minimum. It is important that control of the crime scene be established as quickly as possible and only a few authorized individuals be allowed to be inside of the crime scene. The first responder should begin a crime scene log to document everyone who enters or leaves the crime scene. This begins to establish the chain of custody for all of the evidence that will be taken from the crime scene. Carefully following this procedure also serves to protect individual police officers and the police department by helping to insure that evidence has not been planted or compromised.

NOTES AND REPORTS   The first and most basic way that the crime scene can be recorded is through note taking. Note taking is an essential part of any investigation. Even a minor call will result in some note taking and a report; these together will serve as the narrative of the case. To facilitate note taking, all patrol officers, detectives, and investigators should carry a notebook that is easily portable, generally fitting into a pocket. A notebook is still essential so that the officer can record information whenever it is encountered.

In this era of ever-expanding technology, more than 50 percent of police officers (and this includes even the smallest of departments) have mobile data terminals in their patrol cars. Not only do officers use this technology to enter notes concerning the crime scene, they also can link to major databases to send and receive information. Even during a routine traffic stop, an officer can enter license plate and driver information and immediately receive notification regarding any outstanding warrants. This also allows information from crimes to be shared among local, state, and federal jurisdictions.

This type of sharing and linkage among departments is essential in our post-9/11 world. One of the reasons why the attacks on September 11 occurred was due to linkage blindness—the non-sharing of information among law enforcement agencies. This has also been a problem in tracking and capturing criminals who move across state lines or even from one local jurisdiction to another. The cost of linkage blindness is very high. Now, due to initiatives from the Department of Homeland Security and the advances of computer technology, jurisdictions are more willing and able to share information on criminal activity.

The first responder creates the first record of the crime scene, and will begin taking notes as soon as is reasonably possible and will maintain notes on what crime has been committed and where the scene is, recording what is seen, heard, and smelled. The sense of smell is often overlooked but can yield very important information, especially regarding chemicals, gases, and decomposition. It is especially important to pay attention to odors that are present at the crime scene early on because the human nose becomes accustomed to smells very quickly. After 15–20 minutes odors will no longer be noticeable to someone who has been on the scene, or they may dissipate altogether.

Notes should be clear and concise and comprised of facts, not opinions. They should be written during the officer's interaction or shortly thereafter. It is better to take brief notes during discussions and while walking through the scene and fill in details shortly thereafter. In this way, the officer can pay attention to what is going on at the scene, or with the interviewee. The taking of these short notes can be very important, just as witnesses' perceptions can become altered if they interact with each other, officers perceptions can also become altered as they interact with other officers and witnesses and victims at the scene. It is important that each officer strives to record only facts and not impressions or biases.

All information that will be needed to write a comprehensive report should be included in the notes (who, what, when, where, how, and why). If a case goes to trial—and very few do—those same notes can be used in court to refresh the individual's memory of the case. Because notes will serve as the basis for writing the report and may serve as the basis for courtroom testimony—and are accessible by both the defense and the prosecution—they must be well written.

Reports, unlike notes, are formal documents. In a small department, the report may be written by the first responder. In a large department, it will be written by the detective or lead investigator who is assigned to the case. The report, whether it is written by the first responder or the principal investigator, is the official narrative of the case. Reports are generated for many reasons: tracking criminal offenses, justifying personnel, or for use in court. Even for minor offenses, accurate report-writing is important, but it becomes increasingly important as the severity of the crime increases. However, no officer or detective should ever assume that a case will not go to trial. All reports should be written as if the case will go to court. Because of the importance of the official report, clarity, conciseness, and accuracy are extremely important. The report must be written in a professional manner, using proper grammar and spelling. It is important that the report be accurate because even small inconsistencies can undermine the prosecution of a case.

The first responder will also begin a "crime scene log" to track all individuals who enter or leave the crime scene until the arrival of the detectives. If a case goes to court, this document will be used to establish chain of custody for all physical evidence collected from the crime scene.

CRIME SCENE SKETCHES   The narrative account of the incident, in the form of notes and reports, is important, but it is not the only way in which a crime scene can and should be documented. Crimes that will be receiving more than an initial report may also be documented through the use of sketches, drawings, and diagrams. The first responder will sketch the crime scene prior to any evidence being removed. If the investigation is turned over to a lead investigator or detective, that person will also create sketches of the crime scene.

Sketches do not have to be artistic or exact. It is not uncommon to focus on certain areas in a sketch: the area around the body, the area in the vicinity of the weapon. Several sketches should be done of the entirety of the crime scene. These are generally at several distances (close up, moderate distance, and farther back), and at all four compass points (north, south, east, and west). Other sketches will be done of specific points of interest at the crime scene including the body, any weapons, tool marks on door jambs or window frames, bloodspatter, footprints, and so forth. These sketches will focus on specific salient details.

Sketches will be used by artists to create drawings to be used in the courtroom. When the artist converts the sketches into drawings for the courtroom they will be exact in respect to size and placement of objects. These will be used to illustrate points in the courtroom. Crime scene drawings will show where the body was found in the crime scene and where, in relation to the body, the weapon was located. In this book, for some of the crimes that are discussed, a crime scene photo will be presented along with a crime scene sketch of the same crime scene. This will allow you to compare these two methods of crime scene documentation.

PHOTOGRAPHY   Photography has long been used to document crime scenes. The actual process of photographic documentation has not changed considerably in over 100 years, but the equipment used, of course, has changed considerably. The advent of digital camera technology, for example, has allowed many patrol officers to have a camera in their automobile as standard equipment. This gives them the ability to photographically record evidence that might otherwise be lost—like wet footprints on concrete.

The purpose of crime scene photography is to document what the crime scene looked like and the evidence it contained as it was found by investigators. This is done so that jurors, who, naturally, will not be able to view the pristine crime scene, can see what it looked like. Crime scene photographs help to visually tell what happened at the crime scene.

The first photographs that are taken should orient the viewer to where the crime occurred. If it is an indoor crime scene, these photographs are taken outside, perhaps at the closest street corner or to include a recognizable landmark. Another photograph should be taken of the outside of the building. It is also a good idea to photograph the cars parked on the street in front of the building, behind the building, and nearby—it is not unheard of for a perpetrator who has been surprised to have left a car behind at the scene.

The next set of photographs should document possible entrance and exit routes from the crime scene. These are especially important because evidence may have been left or discarded in these areas. This will include front, back, and side doors; windows; and alleyways.

Once inside, photographs should be taken of all rooms, with most of the photographs being taken in rooms that contain evidence. Rooms that contain evidence should be photographed from the four separate compass points (N, S, E, and W), or from the four walls of the room. Photographs are taken of all evidence at the scene before removing any object to be processed. Each piece of evidence should be photographed from at least two angles, a distance shot which will show the object in relation to other objects in the room, and a close-up of the object with a scale (generally a small ruler) included. Other markers may be used in photographs. If the crime scene contains multiples of one type of evidence, numbers may be used to differentiate them in photographs.

VIDEOGRAPHY   Increasingly, videography is being used to document the crime scene. As video cameras have become smaller and less expensive, more jurisdictions are purchasing and using video equipment. Patrol officer may have a video camera in or on the patrol car to document traffic stops and the actions inside the patrol car. In general, official video documentation of a crime scene is done by a trained videographer. Just like photography, this is a way to show the jurors what the crime scene looked like when it was found.

EVIDENCE COLLECTION

Searching the Crime Scene

Once the crime scene has been thoroughly documented through the use of notes, sketches, and photographs, the crime scene must be processed. Some evidence at the crime scene will be readily apparent. At a homicide, the body is obvious and the majority of evidence will be found in the vicinity of the body. However, to locate all evidence, a comprehensive crime scene search must be conducted. The crime scene must be searched systematically and carefully, preferably by only a few individuals. This care is taken so that as little evidence as possible is missed or inadvertently destroyed. Common crime scene search patterns include spiral, strip, grid, wheel, and zone. The spiral search pattern begins at two opposite edges and has the officers proceed inward in a spiral pattern. In the strip search pattern the search proceeds from one side to the other, back and forth, until the entirety of the scene has been searched. The grid search pattern is really like conducting a strip pattern both back and forth and up and down. The wheel search pattern begins at the outer edges of the spokes of the wheel and progresses inward, toward the center. Finally, the zone search pattern divides the crime scene up into sections that are searched individually (Figure 3.4). As the crime scene search is conducted, each piece of evidence is thoroughly documented regarding where it was found and what it is.

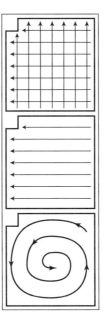

FIGURE 3.4 Common crime scene search patterns.

Who Collects

Depending upon the size of the department, the first responder may be one of the individuals who collects evidence at the crime scene, or a forensic team may collect the evidence. In the case of evidence that will rapidly deteriorate, such as possibly wash-away from an approaching storm or snow melting, the first responder may be in a position to need to either document the evidence with photographs and/or collect that evidence before it is lost forever. Again, this stresses the utmost importance both of the role that the first responder plays in the investigation and that all first responders are thoroughly and properly trained.

Generally, the size and budget of a jurisdiction will determine who is collecting the evidence. As a general rule, the larger and better funded a jurisdiction is, the more specialized forensic personnel they will employ. In a large, well-funded department, the forensic team will handle most evidence collection. In smaller, not-so-well-funded departments, a lead detective or other officer may collect the evidence. One exception to this rule is when a particularly serious crime occurs in a jurisdiction that has little funding. Some rural areas may have very small police department that have no forensic capabilities at all. In that case, the local jurisdiction can ask the county, state, or even the FBI for assistance. Help is most likely to come from the county and state, as far as evidence collection. The FBI would be most likely to assist in an investigation through use of their databases (DNA, fingerprint).

How to Collect

At any crime scene, safety is always the main concern. As discussed earlier, crime scenes may contain a variety of dangers including blood, tissues, body parts, shattered glass, metal shards, needles, noxious fumes, hazardous byproducts, and unexploded devices. The most potentially dangerous aspect of any crime scene, however, is the unknown—and at the beginning of any investigation, much is unknown. It must always be assumed that a variety of dangers will be encountered at any crime scene, and all crime scene personnel should observe appropriate safety precautions.

Evidence collection should not begin until the crime scene is secure and the more deadly hazards have been dealt with. Some scenes that contain hazardous waste or fumes may need to be visited by a hazmat team. At the scene of an explosion, it may be necessary to ascertain whether additional explosives are present. At an arson scene, it may be necessary to ascertain how sound the structure is before evidence can be gathered. Even after the more obvious dangers have been accounted for, things can still go wrong. There is some risk inherent in working many crime scenes; because of this, crime scene workers should always be on guard for potential hazards.

Often it is not possible to make the crime scene "perfectly safe," because doing so would obliterate evidence; therefore, crime scene workers need to protect themselves from potential hazards. Sturdy shoes or boots are a necessity. Gloves are also necessary and should be worn while collecting evidence to prevent contamination and to protect the crime scene worker from contact with bodily products. Crime scene workers should wear other protective garments to prevent contamination, illness, and injury. For example, masks should be worn while working an arson or explosion investigation to help prevent breathing in hazardous fumes. Mass disasters such as the destruction of the World Trade Center in New York City can create a serious air hazard.

Taking proper precautions not only protects crime scene workers but also protects evidence from damage before it can be collected. Once the evidence has been collected, it must also be packaged and transported correctly to ensure that it will be intact and available for analysis.

PACKAGING AND TRANSPORTING EVIDENCE   There are a variety of options available for proper packaging of evidence, from large and small envelopes to large and small plastic containers, to boxes and vials. One consideration when choosing a container is the size of the evidence. Very small evidence, powders, trace evidence, and dust, can be packaged in small envelopes. Sometimes it is advisable to place the smaller envelope containing the evidence in a larger envelope for transport. This helps guard against the possibility of the smaller envelope being misplaced. In an emergency, when an envelope is not available, very small evidence may be placed on a clean sheet of paper which is then folded into a druggist fold.

Evidence envelopes come in a variety of sizes. They can hold everything from very small amounts of powder cocaine to articles of clothing. Envelopes are also good for evidence that requires air circulation. This would include cloth evidence (sheets, clothing) that contains bodily products (blood, semen). In an airtight container, the growth of bacteria and mold become much more likely. If this happens, the evidence cannot be processed at the laboratory.

Evidence may also be packaged in plastic containers. This is especially good for evidence from a suspected arson because the airtight container will preserve chemical residues. In a breathable envelope, these residues would evaporate and could not be analyzed later. On the other hand, plastic containers are not appropriate for other wet evidence because it will encourage the growth of bacteria—again rendering the evidence useless for analysis.

Vials can be used for the collection of liquid blood or other fluids when there is a sufficient amount present. When there are only small amounts of blood, or it has already dried, swabs are used for collection. Once the blood has been transferred to the swab, it is allowed to air-dry and placed into an envelope. If the swab is not allowed to air-dry, bacterial growth will be encouraged and the evidence will not be useful.

Boxes are especially useful for packaging evidence that is large, awkward, or sharp. Large pieces of glass collected from a broken window cannot be placed in an envelope; a box should be used to protect not only the evidence, but everyone who will come in contact with the evidence. Specially sized boxes can also be used for seized computers or drug paraphernalia.

CHAIN OF CUSTODY   All packing containers should be labeled with the case number, what the evidence is, and the names of everyone who has had contact with the evidence. This begins the *chain of custody*. The chain of custody is very important to the prosecution of a case. In order to prosecute a suspect based on the evidence, the prosecutor must be able to demonstrate that the evidence collected at the scene has not been tampered with, and that it is in the same condition as when it was collected: that is has not been altered. In order to do this, a chain of custody is established for each item of evidence. This is a document that lists every person that had any contact with the item, from the individual who collected it at the scene, to the individual that processed it in the lab, to anyone who examined the evidence at any time.

What to Collect

Knowing what to collect is as important as knowing how to collect it properly. Through experience and training, the investigator develops a skill for knowing what to collect and where evidence is most likely to be found. This comes down to knowing that certain types of crimes generally produce certain types of evidence. Subsequent chapters in this text will focus on the types of evidence found at different types of crime scenes.

CHALLENGING CRIME SCENES

Although the processing of most crime scenes is very routine, some present unique challenges for the investigator. Outside forces, like the media and the public can make even a routine crime scene challenging at times. In an effort to get a good story and increase ratings, the media may broadcast information that compromises the investigation, or interview witnesses before statements can be taken. Law enforcement should always be firmly in charge of the crime scene and relate information to the media as needed. Although the public does have a right to know and we do have a free press, this does not extend to interfering with an investigation. Some departments will have a media liaison to handle media issues. Regardless, the media should never be allowed to intrude upon an ongoing investigation. Law enforcement, however, may use the media as a tool during an investigation to disseminate information to the public. For example, a description of the perpetrator may be released to the media immediately and the public encouraged to respond with any information that they might have. This is also done when there is an Amber Alert. If a child is reported missing, immediately, with the Amber Alert system, a description of the individual or the vehicle involved in the abduction is broadcast. In this way, law enforcement can use the many eyes and ears of the general public.

Crimes that occur in public spaces present unique difficulties. Onlookers pose a threat. It can be difficult to cordon off public areas such as a beach or a park. Trace evidence may be trampled underfoot. Evidence may be accidentally or purposefully removed or altered. It can be difficult to isolate witnesses from each other so that statements remain untainted. Extraneous people should be moved back to the outer-most perimeter of the crime scene as quickly as possible. Other challenging types of crime scenes include outdoor crime scenes and underwater crime scenes.

Outdoor Crime Scenes

Any crime scene that is located outside presents a challenge because it is much more exposed than crime scenes that are indoors. Outdoor crime scenes are exposed to the elements, to animals, and to human beings. Indoor crime scenes are, by their very nature, more protected. (This does not mean that they are perfectly protected, when a homicide occurs in room where the temperature is 100 degrees, the body will decompose faster than if the homicide occurred in a room where the temperature is 40 degrees.) An indoor crime scene can remain relatively unchanged for days. Outdoor crime scenes must be processed quickly and efficiently because evidence is likely to deteriorate at a much greater rate than the same evidence would deteriorate inside. More so than many other crime scenes, the investigators will not get a second chance to go back for more evidence at outdoor crime scenes because the evidence may no longer exist.

As soon as is reasonably possible, the outdoor crime scene should be protected from the elements and a reasonable decision must be made regarding the outer perimeter of the crime scene.

One method of protecting the crime scene from the elements is tenting, which can be essential if it is raining or snowing—two factors that increase the speed of deterioration.

In an indoor crime scene, walls generally create a perimeter. An outdoor crime scene has no such natural boundaries. The first responder must make an educated guess as to how far to extend the crime scene. Only so much space can be reasonably secured. Outdoor crime scenes also make it more difficult to determine the perpetrator's point of entry and exit.

Underwater Crime Scenes

Crime scenes that are partially or completely underwater can be very challenging and hazardous. Water washes away trace evidence. If the water is a moving body of water, such as a river, lake, or ocean, evidence may be carried far away. A body in water is also subjected to being partially eaten by a variety of underwater animals. Some bodies may be found because they float to the surface. However, if a body is believed to be in water after a suspected drowning, divers will be sent out to search for the body; recovery can be hampered by the depth of the water, the strength of the current, the clarity of the water, and the water temperature. Whenever evidence must be recovered from within a body of water, specially trained search and rescue divers must be part of the investigative team.

In May of 1996, ValuJet Flight 592 crashed into the Florida Everglades shortly after taking off from Miami International Airport. The search and recovery effort was made difficult not only because the airplane crashed into water, but because of extreme heat, the muddy nature of the area, and the alligators that inhabit the Everglades. At this crime scene, we have a number of factors that are working against investigators. First, the crime scene was remote and not easily accessible by recovery workers. Second, the water served to wash away evidence and the muddy nature of the Everglades served to engulf evidence. The water and mud also create a difficult environment for evidence collection. Third, the alligators could have posed an ongoing hazard to the crime scene workers, but probably because of the chemicals from the jet fuel that were released at the crash site, they pretty much remained at a safe distance from the crime scene. Fifth, the media also were an ever-present issue that had to be dealt with by investigators.

Crime-Scene Technician

Job Description:

The crime scene technician is responsible for the identification, collection, preservation, and processing of physical evidence. This individual will be called to the scene of higher-priority or difficult crime scenes and may be required to work on-call hours. This individual will also prepare reports and testify in court. In this position, frequent interaction with law enforcement, prosecutors, medical examiners, and pathologists is required.

Knowledge, Skills, and Abilities:

Crime scene technicians must be familiar with all areas of recognition and crime scene reconstruction. Certification and training is required in multiple areas of recognition, especially proper evidence-collection techniques. A two-year or four-year college degree is desirable. Crime scene experience is required. Excellent written and oral skills are a must.

Salary Range

Varies considerably from jurisdiction to jurisdiction across the country, but starting salary is generally between $35,000–45,000.

Glossary

Amber alert—a system to alert the public as quickly as possible when there has been a known or possible child abduction.

Chain of custody—the official tracking of the movement of a piece of evidence from the crime scene to the courtroom.

Cognitive interview technique—an interview technique that uses a variety of nonstandard techniques to help the witness tell his or her story.

Crime scene perimeter—area around the crime scene that is protected for the purposes of evidence collection.

Druggist fold—a way to fold a piece of paper to hold small evidence. Druggists used this fold for medicines in the days prior to the widespread use of bottles.

DUI—driving under the influence: a crime in all jurisdictions in the United States. In some cases it may be referred to as DWI (driving while intoxicated).

EMT/paramedic—emergency medical personnel.

EPA—Environmental Protection Agency.

Grid search pattern—like conducting a strip pattern both back and forth and up and down.

Hazmat team—team of individuals trained to deal with possible or known chemical or biological hazards.

Mobile data terminal—a laptop used by a patrol officer in a squad car.

OSHA—Occupational Safety and Health Administration.

Spiral search pattern—begins at two opposite edges and the individuals proceed toward the center in a spiral pattern.

Strip search pattern—the search proceeds from one side to the other, back and forth.

Wheel search pattern—begins at the outer edges of the spokes of the wheel and progresses toward the center.

Zone search pattern—divides the crime scene up into sections that are searched individually.

Webliography

www.crime-scene-investigator.net This is a good site for students interested in learning more about forensic science and the crime scene. There are specific links to schools that offer degrees in areas related to forensic science and there is advice on how to begin a career in forensic science or crime scene investigation. faculty.ncwc.edu.toconner/315/315lect04.htm http://www.planecrashinfo.com/pictures.htm Aviation accident photos.

Review Questions

1. Why can it be so complicated to answer the question: "what is the crime scene?"
2. What's the difference between the primary and secondary crime scenes?
3. Why does the first responder have "the most important job in forensics?"
4. Why can't technology make up for an improperly handled crime scene?
5. Explain why all crime scenes are potentially dangerous.
6. Why is it better to make the crime scene perimeter larger than necessary rather than smaller?
7. What methods are used to document the crime scene?
8. Explain the importance of maintaining a "chain of custody."
9. List and discuss four serious mistakes made at the Lindbergh crime scene.
10. How does the cognitive interview technique differ from standard interview techniques?

Some Things to Think About

1. Certain types of crimes receive more attention and processing of forensic evidence. Explain whether or not you think this is fair.
2. In the text we discussed some challenging crime scenes, for example, those that are outside or under water. What other crime scenes would be particularly challenging? Why?
3. How would you address some of the challenges posed by crime scenes that involve famous individuals?

CHAPTER 4

The Crime Laboratory

CHAPTER OUTLINE

HISTORY OF THE CRIME LABORATORY

There are two distinct threads to the history of the crime laboratory, the development of European crime laboratories and the development of U.S. crime laboratories. Laboratories were founded earlier in Europe, around 1910, and developed at a faster rate, in part due to centralization of laboratory control. Once individual European governments felt they had a need for crime laboratories, they devoted the money and resources necessary to found or run them. United States laboratory development lagged behind Europe by almost two decades at least partly because it was left to local (not even state) jurisdictions, who frequently had little money and no trained laboratory personnel, to develop their own laboratory services. In many jurisdictions the laboratory services that were offered went little beyond the very rudimentary services of fingerprinting or document evaluation.

European Developments

Prior to jurisdictions having their own laboratories and their own personnel, they depended upon working relationships that had been established with university scientists. For areas such as chemistry and biology, this was a more than adequate arrangement. Law enforcement asked questions regarding how a particular chemical behaved or where a certain plant could grow, and the scientist answered the questions. In these cases, science could serve the law very well.

Sometimes, however, the problem arose that the interests of law enforcement and the interests of science did not overlap, a problem which continues to this day. This disjunction in the interests of law enforcement and science occurs because law enforcement and scientists use scientific information in vastly different ways. The law enforcement professional wants to know a particular fact in order to understand what happened, to solve a case, or to obtain a conviction. The scientist wants to know a particular fact in order to understand how some facet of the world works. Sometimes these two uses overlap. For example, in the area of toxicology, the toxicologist wants to know how a poison behaves in the body in order to treat patients. The police want to know how a poison behaves in the body so that a determination can be made as to whether or not an individual's death was intentional. While the information that the scientist and the police officer seek is the same, how each one will use that information differs considerably. Because toxicology has been of interest to medicine and the scientific community in general, considerable research has been conducted in this area and the knowledge base continues to grow. We'll discuss toxicology more in Chapter 5.

Problems soon arose with relying upon university scientists for all of the scientific information needed in the courtroom because law enforcement often wants to answer questions that are not of particular interest to traditional science—for example, in the areas of document, tool mark, and fingerprint analysis. Document examination has long been of interest to law enforcement and the courts. A document examiner can help determine if a signature on a will is genuine, or if a 50-dollar bill is counterfeit, or if a page has been added to a contract, or if a suicide note was written by the deceased. And while these questions are very interesting to the court, they are not necessarily interesting to scientists.

Tool mark analysis may be very important to law enforcement at the scenes of burglaries and some homicides, rapes, or other crimes, yet, the marks that tools make on doorjambs and windowsills hold little interest for scientists (Figure 4.1). Some archeologists may study tools and their markings at archeological sites to determine how humankind has previously used tools, but overall, tool mark analysis is of very little interest to the scientific community in general.

Fingerprint examination has long been a key area of law enforcement, being one of the oldest methods of identification still in use today. Yet the scientific community in general has taken little notice of fingerprints—except possibly to note that while identical twins have the same DNA, they will not have the same fingerprints—this is due to the fact that an individual's DNA is created at conception, while fingerprints develop long after the zygote has split into two (Figure 4.2).

Hitler's Diaries

Historians sometimes need to answer questions regarding who wrote a document or the age of a particular document. In 1983, for example, a set of 62 notebooks reported to be war diaries of Adolph Hitler were purchased for almost 10 million German Marks (about $4.5 million). Both historians and war memorabilia collectors were initially very excited about the discovery. Previously it had not been believed that Hitler had maintained any sort of a personal written record of what occurred before and during the war. However, a cursory examination of the diaries by experts revealed them to be a forgery. Although the handwriting was well imitated, the paper the diaries were written on was of postwar manufacture, as was the ink. (As we will see in Chapter 6, both inks and papers changed during the 1940s and 1950s.) Details were often historically inaccurate. While historical finds do not usually generate interest from law enforcement, in the case of the Hitler diaries, the veracity of the documents was of great interest not only to historians, but also to law enforcement because a large sum of money was paid by a publisher for the rights to the fakes. The forgers, Konrad Kujau and Gerd Heidemann, were eventually sent to prison.

Crime laboratories were created not only because law enforcement wanted to be able to have control over and perform their own analyses of crime scene evidence without having to rely upon outside experts, but because there were numerous areas in which law enforcement had an interest but the scientific community clearly did not. This became very influential. If the scientific community in general was not interested in areas such as fingerprints and tool marks, they would not be studied in any significant detail and advances would not be made. It was up to law enforcement to study the world on its own, to research and advance areas that were important for crime scene processing and court prosecution. This was the impetus for the birth of all crime laboratories.

It was not the case that law enforcement would no longer call upon scientists who had specialized knowledge that was of interest to the courts, but rather that law enforcement would now be able to set its own research agenda within its own laboratories. Crime laboratories were established throughout Europe during the early part of the twentieth century. Italy had its first laboratory in 1908, France in 1910, and Austria in 1918 (Eckert 1997).

FIGURE 4.1 Tool marks left at a burglary scene.

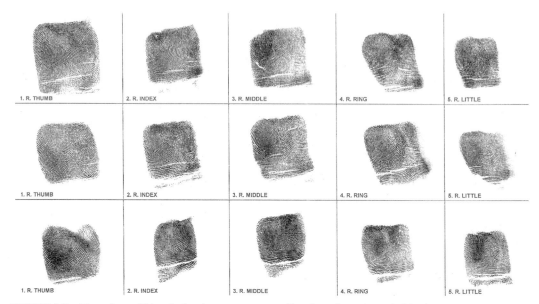

FIGURE 4.2   The prints of identical twins are no more alike than the prints of siblings.

LOCARD'S INFLUENCE   Although there were many individuals who were important in the development of forensic science in Europe, few had the broad impact of Edmund Locard, who was born in France in 1877. He was trained in medicine and law and later became professor of forensic medicine at the University of Lyons. He was a student of Bertillon and did significant work in the area of fingerprint examination; he suggested using 12 matching points in order to establish positive fingerprint identification—16 points are employed in the current system.

In 1910 Locard began the first police laboratory in Lyons. The laboratory provided examinations in ballistics, toxicology, and document examination. He began slowly, with little more than a microscope (Saferstein 2004), but because of his work and dedication, he became a leader in his field and the driving force in establishing crime laboratories in many European nations. Locard published several important criminological works, including *L'Enquête Criminelle et les Méthodes Scientifiques* (1920), *Manuel de Technique Policière* (1923), and the well-known *Traité de Criminalistique* (1931–1940). In *Traité de Criminalistiqe,* Locard articulated his infamous "exchange principle." This principle states that whenever a criminal comes into contact with a crime scene, the criminal cannot help leaving something behind. His focus was on trace evidence, microscopic evidence that the criminal would leave behind at the crime scene or carry away from the crime scene. Locard's exchange principle has been the guiding principle in forensics. Forensics is always looking for that which the criminal has left behind, that remnant of the criminal at the crime scene. Locard remained an active researcher until his death in 1966.

U.S. Developments

By the 1930s, European laboratories had advanced considerably. This may be due, in large part, to the fact that crime laboratories are centralized in Europe and controlled by their respective federal governments. This centralization allowed for uniform services to develop across each country. Laboratory services in the big city of Paris would be the same as laboratory services in the countryside.

In the United States, however, laboratory services lagged behind. Local jurisdictions relied upon local funding, which often was not adequate, for crime laboratories. Training and personnel were also inadequate. This was not a problem that was limited to the laboratory. Many police forces were also poorly trained and inadequate.

By the Saint Valentine's Day Massacre in 1929, it became apparent that even large cities, like Chicago, lacked personnel with the experience necessary to analyze basic forensic evidence. Chicago, like many other large cities, also faced the additional problem of corruption and politicization within its police department. Too often law enforcement was more involved with reinforcing the political power of certain individuals than with protecting the general public. The resolution of criminal cases often resulted from a coerced confession—coerced by police officers who applied physical and psychological pressure upon individuals.

AUGUST VOLLMER AND CALIFORNIA'S CRIME LABORATORIES   Just as Edmund Locard was a driving force in the development of forensics in Europe, August Vollmer was a significant individual in the early development of forensics (and policing) in the United States. Vollmer was born in New Orleans, Louisiana, in 1876. He received no formal education beyond grade school—truly a self-made man. He held a variety of positions, including feed–store worker, letter carrier, and fire fighter. He also served for a year in the Spanish-American War (www.prospector-utah.com, www.ci.berkeley.ca.us).

At the young age of 29, he was elected Berkeley town Marshall in 1905 and became the first Chief of Police in 1909. He was responsible for the development of major police reforms, including the quasi-military organization of police departments and professionalism in policing. Although he did not receive any formal schooling beyond the sixth grade, he understood the value of education and advocated for the college education of police officers—though even today many jurisdictions do not have officers with college degrees. He established the first "police school" in 1908. He pioneered bicycle, motorcycle, and automobile patrol. He supported the early work in police psychology and was a proponent of the intelligence and psychiatric screening of police officers. Vollmer sat on President Hoover's Commission on Law Enforcement and on the Wickersham Commission (www.prospector-utah.com, www.ci.berkeley.ca.us).

Vollmer's impact on forensics includes the first use of forensics in the investigation of a case in 1907, which included analysis of blood, fibers, and soil. Vollmer instituted procedures for the proper

---

Policing and the Powerful

The history of policing within the United States is not necessarily the history of an organization that has as its goal serving the public or even solving crimes. The history of policing within the United States tends to be the history of an organization that has as its goal helping the powerful to retain their power.

One of the early duties of the U.S. Marshals was to maintain order in the western territories of the young United States. This frequently meant quashing uprisings of Native Americans. In the South, many police organizations were begun as slave patrols, charged with the duty of returning slaves who had run away, to their masters. In the North, many police organizations were founded to serve as strike-breakers for large industrialists, like Andrew Carnegie. Carnegie employed Pinkerton Guards during the Homestead, Pennsylvania, steel strike of 1892. He and the Pinkertons were responsible not only for breaking early steel unions, but for the deaths of seven striking workers.

Throughout history, law enforcement agencies have been used to maintain the status quo and the existing power structure. Law enforcement has focused on solving the crimes and problems that were mostly of importance to the wealthy, not in seeing that justice was done. Much of the focus of the criminal justice system has been on the crimes committed by the lower classes—burglary, theft, street crimes. It wasn't even until the early part of the twentieth century that the phrase *white-collar crime* was coined by Edwin Sutherland to refer to the crimes committed by the middle class and wealthy. Even today, the crimes that affect the wealthy receive more attention that the crimes that affect the poor. Why did the brutal rape of a wealthy, white jogger in Central Park receive so much attention and the rape of a poor, black woman (who was thrown from a window) blocks away garner no press coverage? And why was it so easy to convict five young, minority men for the rape of the white jogger even when there was no DNA evidence linking them to the victim?

handling of evidence. He taught at the University of California from 1916 to 1932 and established contacts there to assist with evidence analysis. He was also partially responsible for establishing a special unit to handle forensic evidence in the LAPD, in 1927, where he served as Chief of Police from 1921 to 1922. In the early 1950s he contracted throat cancer, and he ended his own life in 1955 (www.prospector-utah.com; www.ci.berkeley.ca.us).

THE SAINT VALENTINE'S DAY MASSACRE   As is often the case in forensics and criminal justice, the field is moved forward by the need to solve new and different sorts of crimes. The Saint Valentine's Day Massacre in Chicago, Illinois, was one such new and different crime. On February 14, 1929, seven men were gunned down in a warehouse in Chicago's North Side. The gangland killings that became famously known as *The Saint Valentine's Day Massacre* were a driving force in the advancement of ballistics and forensics in the United States.

Six of the victims died at the scene. One survived the trip to the hospital but died a few hours later. All of the men had been shot multiple times in the back at close range. The killers used machine guns, a sawed-off shotgun, and a .45 caliber gun from which spent cartridges littered the floor of the warehouse where they killed. The killers dressed as police officers and used a stolen police car to escape. To exonerate the police, the machine gun cartridges left behind were examined by Calvin Goddard using the comparison microscope. Goddard had to be brought in from New York because there was no local ballistics expert. The fact that Illinois had no expert who could assist in the case led to the establishment of the first independent crime laboratory, *The Scientific Crime Detection Laboratory* at Northwestern University. Unlike other laboratories in existence in the United States at that time, the Northwestern laboratory operated within the university and not within a state or local system of law enforcement. This gave the laboratory more autonomy than many other laboratories and made it more like the forensic laboratories in Europe. However, throughout the entire history of forensic laboratories in the United States, the Northwestern laboratory is the exception—not the rule. Most forensics laboratories have been under direct state or local control (http://www.isp.state.il.us/Forensics/ISPHTML/History.htm).

ORGANIZATION OF LABORATORIES

To this day, laboratory services remain centralized in Europe. A centralized system allows for consistency of services across a country and relieves local jurisdictions from the cost of supporting a laboratory. In the United States, the establishment of crime laboratories has largely been left up to the local and state jurisdictions, much the way the organization of state and local courts are left to those jurisdictions without interference from the federal government. The federal government has also been reluctant to try to institute a federal police force, and the states have been reluctant to grant the power to the federal government. Individual states want to have autonomy; they want minimal interference from the federal government. The majority of criminal prosecutions are conducted at the state, not the federal level. Prior to the mid-1980s, almost all criminal prosecutions were carried out by the states, even after the expansion of federal drug laws in the mid-1980s, most prosecutions are still a state matter. As a result, there is considerable unevenness in the availability of services. Coordination of laboratory systems and the services that those laboratories offer is variable and their funding has largely been left to individual state and local jurisdictions. Smaller, less well-funded laboratories offer fewer, more limited services, while larger, well-funded laboratories offer a wider range of services. In some instances, a larger neighboring jurisdiction can be called upon to offer assistance in the processing of a complex crime scene, but this also does not assure competent handling of a case. In one instance, a coroner from a nearby county who was assisting in a murder case retrieved and refrigerated a body before the time of death had been established—thus eliminating the possibility of determining time of death from core body temperature. Unevenness of services, lack of funding, and variations in levels of competence have led to cases being lost or not even pursued.

Federal, State, and Local Laboratories

The FBI, then the United States Bureau of Investigation, began operating a forensic laboratory in 1932. In the early years, the laboratory conducted firearms and handwriting analysis, paralleling the types of investigations that were common in law enforcement at the time. In 1981, the Forensic Science Research and Training Center (FSRTC) was established. FSRTC specializes in cutting-edge analysis and training (www.fbi.gov/hq/lab/labhome.htm).

Although the FBI operates a forensic laboratory, the United States does not have a federally coordinated system. The FBI assists state and local law enforcement with investigations in the following areas: chemistry; computer analysis and response; DNA analysis; evidence response; explosives, firearms, and toolmarks; forensic audio, video, and image analysis; forensic science research; forensic science training; hazardous materials response; graphics used in investigations and in courtrooms; latent prints; materials analysis; questioned documents; racketeering records; special photographic analysis; structural design; and trace evidence. However, assistance from the FBI is by request only, the FBI do not step in on their own.

The FBI maintains the Integrated Automated Fingerprint Identification System (IAFIS) and Combined DNA Index System (CODIS) databases. IAFIS is a national fingerprint and criminal history system that was developed in 1999. This database contains the fingerprints of more than 36 million people. Law enforcement can use IAFIS for automated fingerprint search capabilities, searches for latent prints, electronic image storage, and electronic exchange of fingerprints. Because this is an electronic service, it is available at all times. This service allows even small departments with very limited budgets to benefit from access to a large database of fingerprints (http://www.fbi.gov/hq/cjisd/iafis.htm).

The IAFIS can be utilized by law enforcement in a number of ways. It can be used to search for a prior arrest record when an arrest is made and it can assist in maintaining arrest records for individuals. Law enforcement can use the database to compare new arrest records against prints taken from unsolved crimes. The FBI also maintains the largest repository of fingerprint records in the world in the Criminal Justice Information Services Division (http://www.fbi.gov/hq/lab/org/lpu.htm).

The FBI Laboratory's CODIS allows crime laboratories at the national (NDIS), state (SDIS), and local (LDIS) levels to exchange and compare DNA profiles electronically. All DNA input is at the local level, which allows each jurisdiction to input data according to state statutes. CODIS maintains both a *Forensic Index* of DNA profiles that have been taken from crime scenes and an *Offender Index* of DNA profiles taken from convicted sex offenders and other violent criminals. (What types of offenders are included in the database depends upon state statutes. Each state has determined which crimes will result in the DNA of the offender being included in the database.)

Through the use of the CODIS database, crime scenes can be linked together even though the crimes occurred in separate jurisdictions. This represents a significant advance for law enforcement. It used to be very difficult to link together or solve crime that occurred in disparate jurisdictions because there was little to no communication among jurisdictions—even jurisdictions that lie within the same state. CODIS allows for communication among jurisdictions regarding DNA crimes. Another advantage of the CODIS system is that it is not labor intensive. DNA information can be easily entered into the system and the database identifies other crimes that contained the same DNA (http://www.fbi.gov/hq/lab/codis/index1.htm).

Each state determines how its laboratory system will be set up and run. This is one factor that has led to the wide variance of how things are done from state to state. Virginia, for example, has created what is referred to as a *regional system*. Virginia has a central laboratory in Richmond, the capital, a northern laboratory in Fairfax, a western laboratory in Roanoke, and an eastern laboratory in Norfolk (Figure 4.3). Kentucky also employs a regional system; there is a central laboratory in Frankfort and five regional laboratories in Louisville, Madisonville, London, Ashland, and Cold Springs (Figure 4.4). A regional system is designed to provide adequate laboratory coverage for the entire state, regardless of where a crime occurs. Local law enforcement can call upon

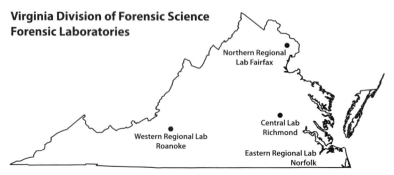

FIGURE 4.3   Location of Virginia's forensic labs.

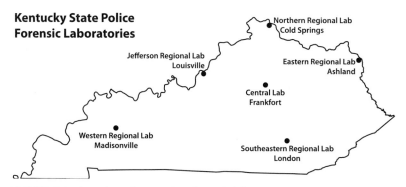

FIGURE 4.4   Location of Kentucky's forensic labs.

state facilities when necessary and not have to submit their evidence to a laboratory on the opposite side of the state. This is an efficient and effective way of running a state's laboratory system. Some states will have several full-service laboratories and several satellite laboratories that offer more limited services. It is not uncommon for smaller laboratories to concentrate on drug-related submissions.

Some jurisdictions have responded to the problem of providing equitable services to far-flung regions by establishing mobile crime scene units. These have also been used to remedy the problem of transporting samples to a laboratory. With a mobile laboratory, the lab services are housed within a vehicle, usually a large van or truck or bus. Within the vehicle, many standard laboratory tests can be performed without having to transport evidence to a laboratory hours away. On a smaller scale, mobile crime scene units can be used to coordinate all of the personnel needed to completely process a crime scene, rather than relying on law enforcement personnel.

Training and Licensing of Forensic Personnel

Training and licensing are both methods of ensuring high-quality forensic services. Continuing education is also a means for professionals to remain abreast of the latest techniques in the field. Almost all fields require continuing education. The individual in that area—even medical doctors—must continue to take courses on a regular basis (every one, two, or three years). Broadly, training consists of instruction or education in a particular area. Training comes in many forms. It may be formal schooling at the college or postgraduate level, or it may be specific courses/workshops offered by the

---

The Pros and Cons of a Centralized Federal System

This chapter highlights the fact that in Europe, as well as in many other nations of the world, each country has a centralized laboratory system run by their respective federal governments. These systems have worked very well around the world, yet there has not been much consideration given to a federal laboratory system in the United States.

There are obvious pros to a federalized system. A federalized system would eliminate the inequity of funding among jurisdictions. The federal government would allocate a certain portion of the federal budget for laboratory work. All laboratories would be subject to the same sort of oversight by the federal government. All laboratories would offer the same services, or at least the services that the federal government determined were necessary for that jurisdiction. Laboratory personnel could also be hired and promoted according to one standard.

There are also obvious cons to a federalized system. The United States is a collection of semi-independent states. It is up to each state to create its own legislation and govern itself. Criminal justice matters have historically been left up to individual states. To shift a significant portion of this responsibility to the federal government would require a considerable adjustment in how criminal justice matters are handled across the United States—it would be a major change. If the federal government controlled a federal laboratory system, the federal government would decide which cases to pursue and which ones not to pursue. States would lose a considerable amount of autonomy in determining which cases are important and deserving of funding. A federal system would most likely be very cumbersome. Presumably, there would be federal laboratories in each state, in much the same way as there are federal courts, and coordination among these laboratories would present many problems. The federal budget would need to be increased; individuals paying federal taxes in Wisconsin might not be anxious for their money to be spent in California—where the population is much greater and the need for laboratory services is far more pressing. Also, even though all of the same services could be offered in each laboratory under a federal system, this would not take into account the different needs of each state. Interior states, like Colorado, have different needs than border states, like California, or port states, like Florida. States that are densely populated have more of a need than sparsely populated states.

FBI, a college or university, or an organization. One of the first changes Vollmer called for when he sought to modernize and professionalize policing in Berkeley was that police officers be college educated. Training first teaches forensic personnel what their duties are, and then keeps them abreast of changes in techniques. A standardized curriculum helps to ensure that all forensic personnel in a particular job have received similar training.

Forensic scientists and crime scene personnel are only as skilled and competent as their training. Without proper and thorough training, evidence will be overlooked or mishandled, cases will be lost, and although a lot can be learned by reading on your own, forensics is not a self-taught field. There is considerable value to working under another professional who can oversee and guide your early work. Some forensic disciplines, like forensic pathology, require not only a four-year college degree and a medical degree, but continuing medical education as well. Other disciplines, like fingerprint technician, require only a high school diploma or GED in some jurisdictions. Anyone who is interested in pursuing a particular career in forensics should investigate what the educational requirements are to enter that field. A student who wants to be a medical examiner but does not want to go to college is likely to be very disappointed. Many fields require only a general two or four-year college degree, in addition to specific training in that area.

Conferences and training are also offered by many of the state and regional forensic science associations. At a conference, members may attend presentations on cutting-edge topics that last for a few hours. Conferences provide members with the opportunity to brainstorm with others regarding key issues in the field. Individual professionals are given the opportunity to present their work and research at conferences to audiences who can provide them with informed feedback.

Some of the following associations may offer longer training programs: The Northwest Association of Forensic Scientists (www.nwafs.org), The Northeast Regional Forensic Institute (http://www .albany.edu/nerfi/), Southern Association of Forensic Scientists (www.southernforensic.org), Mid-Atlantic Association of Forensic Scientists (www.maafs.org), Midwest Association of Forensic Scientists (www.mafs.net), the Northeast Association of Forensic Scientists (www.neafs.org), The Southwestern Association of Forensic Scientists (www.swafs.us).

The FBI laboratory in Quantico, Virginia, offers in-service training in a variety of forensic specialties for law enforcement. This includes arson, explosives, computer crimes, death investigation, narcotics, evidence collection, weapons, hostage negotiations, and photography (a complete list of training programs is available in the Bureau of Justice Assistance database located at: http://bjatraining .ncjrs.gov/).

A few state forensic laboratories also offer training. The web site for the Washington State Patrol Crime Laboratory Division states that they offer the following training to criminal justice agencies: crime scene investigation, death investigation, crime laboratory services, leaf marijuana identification, controlled substances, sexual assault evidence, physical evidence recognition and handling, latent fingerprint processing, arson investigation, rape evidence collection (to hospital emergency room personnel), documents, traffic investigation, and crime scene photography (http:// www.wsp.wa.gov/crime/crimlabs.htm). The New York State Division of State Police offers a variety of forensic training seminars not only to New York State Police personnel but to outside law enforcement organizations as well (http://www.troopers.state.ny.us/Forensic%5FScience/Training/).

Not all forensic positions are licensed. Licensure is regulated by the individual states. All medical doctors must hold a license to practice medicine in the state in which they work. Licensing is a way of having the government, generally the state government, regulate a particular field. While its goal is to ensure higher quality professionals within a specific field, sometimes licensure and training can function as a way of keeping certain individuals out of a profession. This was evidenced in the early portion of the twentieth century in medicine. Licensure and training were structured to exclude women and African-Americans from working as medical doctors.

Certification/Accreditation of Laboratories

Generally the words *certification* and *accreditation* are used interchangeably. Accreditation is a certification, usually given by a regulatory body that oversees a particular field. The accreditation of laboratories is a means of ensuring higher quality laboratory services. The American Society of Crime Laboratory Directors/Laboratory Accreditation Board (www.ascld-lab.org) certifies forensic laboratories both across the United States and internationally. Currently, only Delaware, North Dakota, South Dakota, Rhode Island, and Wyoming do not have laboratories accredited by the ASCLD/LAB.

The accreditation process consists of application, evaluation, and inspection. Any lab that is seeking accreditation must first apply. The laboratory must be self-evaluated and it must be evaluated by a team of inspectors from ASCLD/LAB. Once a lab is accredited, that accreditation is reviewed on a yearly basis and there is a full re-inspection every five years. This process is purposefully rigorous to help ensure the highest quality laboratory services from any laboratory that holds the distinction of ASCLD/LAB accreditation (http://www.ascld-lab.org/legacy/aslablegacyprocess.html).

WHY DO WE EXAMINE PHYSICAL EVIDENCE?

In a textbook on forensics, it may seem a bit odd to ask the question: "why do we examine physical evidence?" It may seem as though it should be taken for granted that this is something that we do in forensics. We examine physical evidence because we believe that it can help us to understand the facts of the case. It can help us to know what happened. It can help us sort through conflicting stories. When no one has witnessed the crime, the physical evidence stands as witness.

We examine the physical evidence in order to understand what happened during the crime. This has not always been the case. Historically, as was discussed in Chapter 2, it has not been the physical evidence that has been so important, but eyewitness testimony, what was directly seen by an individual. Eyewitness testimony is known as *direct evidence.* Physical evidence, in fact, does not speak for itself. Physical evidence *denotes* something else; this is why it is considered to be *circumstantial evidence.* It is an indicator of what happened. Often, it may not clearly point to what happened and there may be more than one explanation for the physical evidence. Fingerprints on a drinking glass do not necessarily indicate that someone was at the crime scene. It may not even indicate that someone held the glass, but it does indicate that his or her fingers touched the glass—it may have been placed in his or her hand while he or she was unconscious and then placed at the crime scene. Physical evidence, because it cannot *speak* for itself, must be interpreted by the forensic scientist. The forensic scientist tells us what might have happened; he or she offers an interpretation. Often there are other interpretations that are equally plausible. Each side in a court case may present their own experts who testify about the same piece of evidence, yet present opposite conclusions. This is what concerns many about allowing expert witnesses to testify. It sometimes seems to jurors and the public that expert witnesses twist the evidence to suit their own needs. The job of the expert witness, however, is *not* to reinterpret the evidence to suit the needs of either side in a criminal or civil case. It is the job of the expert to base his or her conclusions on what the evidence shows. An expert who tailors opinions to suit the attorney who is paying the bill becomes a *hired gun* and that individual's opinion is not trusted. After all, if the other side were paying the bill, that expert would be saying exactly the opposite! In Chapters 13 and 14 we will discuss the ethical issues involved in testifying in court.

Saferstein (2004) notes that, in general, physical evidence is examined for identification or comparison purposes. Undertaking an examination of the physical evidence for identification purposes will tell us what the substance is, for example, the evidence seized is heroin and not cocaine. Undertaking an examination of the physical evidence for comparison purposes will tell us if the evidence in question comes from the same source as another substance, for example, if the fingerprints on the murder weapon belong to the suspect.

CLASSIFICATION OF PHYSICAL EVIDENCE

In large part, the physical evidence that investigators search for is determined by the type of crime that has been committed. Semen and DNA evidence are frequently found at sexual assault crime scenes, but rarely at computer crime scenes. It seems obvious to look for these types of evidence when investigating a sexual assault. Good investigators do not eliminate the possibility that unusual forms of evidence will be found at a crime scene, but they concentrate on what their experience and training tells them is most likely to be there. As we discuss each type of crime in subsequent chapters, we will focus on the varieties of evidence most likely to be found at those specific crime scenes.

One of the reasons seasoned investigators and crime scene technicians know what to look for and where to look for it is because they have learned specific classification schemes for evidence. A classification scheme allows the investigator to quickly deal with the crime scene. All human beings are quite naturally predisposed to organizing, grouping, or classifying all information they receive. This helps us deal with the world in a number of ways. First, it allows us to acquire new information by comparing it to what we already know and placing it in existing schemes that we have created. We get to know the evidence by finding things that are alike. Second, once we determine what this new thing is like, we know how to deal with it. Classification schemes in forensics are designed for exactly these reasons; to place a piece of evidence into existing schemas and then to know how to handle that piece of evidence. When we discuss how to classify objects in the world, we are faced with an infinite number of classification schemes. In biology, we might choose to group living things according to kingdom, phylum, class, order, family, genus, or species. In chemistry, we might group substances by chemical composition. In psychology and psychiatry, we use the *The Diagnostic and Statistical Manual of Mental Disorders*-Fourth Edition-Text Revision (*DSM-IV-TR*) to classify mental disorders. How we classify depends significantly upon what exactly we want to do with the information we have.

Within forensic science, there are a variety of ways in which physical evidence can be classified, and, in fact, we could create an infinite number of different ways to classify evidence and objects. Not all classification schemes are equally useful. In some instances, the classification scheme depends upon what you want to do with the evidence. DeForest et al. (1983) suggests four very useful ways that physical evidence can be classified; according to type of crime, by the type of question to be resolved, according to the way the evidence was produced, by the appropriate laboratory approach.

CLASSIFICATION ACCORDING TO TYPE OF CRIME

Evidence that is classified according to type of crime illuminates the fact that certain crimes are more likely to produce forensic evidence and also that particular crimes (e.g., rape) are more likely to produce certain types of evidence (semen stains). However, this approach is also limited by the fact that almost any type of evidence can be found at any type of crime (e.g., toolmarks may be found at the scene of a burglary—which is where they are most often found—but they may also be found at a rape or homicide). This classification system may be most useful to the novice investigator, patrol officer, or crime scene technician to use as a reminder of the most common types of evidence to look for—as a memory jogger.

The knowledge of what sorts of evidence are found at which types of crime scenes helps *guide* the evidence collection. However, this type of classification scheme should never be used to limit the search for evidence to just what is expected or what is most common. If this happens, key evidence can be overlooked. An investigator must always be on the lookout for *unusual* or uncharacteristic physical evidence—for example, semen at a crime scene may denote a sexual motivation, even if that sort of crime is not usually thought of as sexual. A crime scene that first appears to be a routine burglary can become a sexually related offense when semen is located at the scene.

CLASSIFICATION BY THE TYPE OF QUESTION TO BE RESOLVED

Physical evidence is examined for a variety of reasons and in many cases a single piece of evidence may be examined for multiple reasons. Evidence can be classified by the type of question to be resolved. Evidence can be used in one or more of the following ways: to reconstruct the crime, to prove an element of the crime, to link the suspect to the victim or to the crime scene, to exclude a suspect, to corroborate or disprove an alibi, to provide investigative leads, to secure a search warrant, and it can be used in court to secure a conviction.

Crime Reconstruction

Evidence can be used to reconstruct the crime scene or an accident scene. Photographs are taken of skid marks at a vehicle crash site that will be used to determine the speed of the vehicle prior to the crash. Bloodspatter is examined to determine the angle from which a fatal blow was delivered. Footprints under a window or near a door can indicate how the perpetrator entered or exited a crime scene.

Prove Element of the Crime

There are seven elements that must be present in order for a crime to have occurred; *actus reus* (it must be an act that is against the law), *mens rea* (the person must know that it is against the law), harm (the act must cause harm), causation (the individual must have caused the act), concurrence (you must have both *actus reus* and *mens rea*), legality (there must be a law that prohibits the act), and punishment (there must be a punishment already set forth for the act). Evidence can be used to prove one of these elements. Most often the element that physical evidence is used to prove is *actus reus*—that the action was a crime. Statutory analysis of drugs is performed to prove *actus reus*.

The physical evidence may be used to establish that a crime has taken place, the *corpus delecti*. Examination of the body may prove that a homicide, rather than suicide, has occurred; and core body temperature can be used to establish a timeframe for death and consequently further clarify if, in fact, a crime has been committed. Laboratory examination of suspected illegal drugs will establish that the substance seized was, for example, heroin. Because the bulk of all forensic evidence examined is drug- and alcohol-related evidence collected for statutory purposes, the bulk of all forensic evidence is examined to establish that a crime has taken place.

Currently the majority of forensic laboratory work that occurs across the country is what is known as *statute work*—work that must be done in order to obtain a conviction—the identification and quantification of drugs and alcohol falls under this category. Before a conviction can be obtained in a court of law, it must be established that the substance collected was, in fact, cocaine (and not, say, powdered sugar!). Possession of large quantities of powdered sugar, under current statutes, is not a crime—unusual perhaps and indicative of a bakery, but not a crime! This is forensic examination for the purpose of identification.

Evidence can be introduced to prove *mens rea* is not present. For example, the testimony of a forensic psychologist might be used to show that the suspect was suffering from a severe mental illness at the time of the commission of the crime that interfered with his ability to know what was going on.

Linking the Suspect to Victim or Crime Scene

The physical evidence can link a suspect with a victim. Bite marks on the victim will match the bite pattern of the suspect. Semen or other bodily fluids on the victim will contain the DNA of the perpetrator. When forensic scientists answer questions regarding whether or not the blood on the suspect's car matches the victim's blood type, or whether or not plant spores stuck in the tread of the suspect's shoes match plant spores found at the crime scene, they are asking questions concerning comparison. In a comparison, an examination of a known substance is compared to an unknown. A decision is made regarding whether both substances share the same point of origin. A considerable amount of evidence is used to link the suspect either to the victim or to the crime scene (in some cases the investigator may also want to link the victim to the crime scene). Fingerprints found at the crime scene can link the perpetrator to that scene. Fibers found on the victim may be the same type of fiber as in the suspect's shirt. Carpet fibers found on a victim who has been kidnapped may be the same type of fiber that is found in the trunk of the suspect's car.

The physical evidence can link a person (victim or perpetrator) to a crime scene. A suspect may carry dirt or unusual plant material away from the scene on shoes or clothing. A murder victim who was transported from the "kill site" to a "dump site" may pick up carpet fibers from the trunk of the perpetrator's car or from the floor of the perpetrator's living room.

Excluding a Suspect

Physical evidence can also very clearly exclude a suspect. If a rapist deposited semen on the victim's clothing and the DNA contained in that semen does not match the DNA of the perpetrator, then he did not commit the rape (Figure 4.5). While the victim may testify that the defendant is the individual who raped her, if the semen collected does not contain his DNA, he is excluded.

Corroborate or Disprove an Alibi

The physical evidence can support or disprove witnesses' or suspects' statements. Analysis by a ballistics expert will confirm that an individual was shot in the back while running away from the crime scene, rather than in the chest while approaching the shooter. Establishment of time of death may conflict with a suspect's statement that the victim was alive the last time they interacted.

DNA Matching

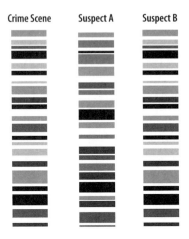

The DNA pattern of "Suspect B" matches the pattern of the evidence found at the crime scene.

FIGURE 4.5   Suspect DNA and DNA taken from the crime scene that do not match.

If a suspect states that he or she has never been in the apartment where the crime took place, yet their fingerprints are found in multiple places around the apartment, this evidence clearly contradicts her statement. If the suspect claims that when he or she saw the victim eight hours ago, the deceased was alive, but time of death is established as approximately ten hours earlier, then his or her statement is false.

Provide Investigative Leads

Physical evidence almost always provides investigative leads. Muddy tire tracks in the driveway can tell investigators that a large truck was at the crime scene. Tool marks on a door frame can indicate a possible point of entry. If we examine the tool marks closely, they may also tell us that the crowbar that was responsible for opening the door had a jagged end. Investigators can search for a crow bar with a jagged end when they search the suspects home, car, and garage.

The physical evidence can help identify a "person of interest." Footprints in soggy ground may point to a heavier individual as the burglar. The angle of cuts on a victim can point investigators in the direction of a left- or right-handed person.

Secure a Search Warrant

In some cases, physical evidence can be used in court to secure a search warrant to search for particular items in the car, home, or business of the suspect. If crowbar marks are found at a burglary scene, but the actual crowbar is not found at or near the crime scene, investigators can present this evidence to a judge in order to get a warrant allowing them to search the suspects home, car, and garage.

Used in Court to Secure a Conviction

Of course, the goal for any prosecutor who uses physical evidence in court, or during a plea bargain, is to secure a conviction. During interrogation, a suspect may be presented with the evidence against him, which may encourage him to sign a confession. During a trial, the totality of the physical evidence will hopefully lead the jury to bring back a guilty verdict from their deliberations.

CLASSIFICATION ACCORDING TO THE WAY THE EVIDENCE WAS PRODUCED

Evidence at the crime scene can be classified according to the way in which it was produced. This process involves looking at the evidence as a record of how individuals and objects in the environment have interacted. This sort of evidence can be subclassified in numerous ways: position (how something was moved); imprints and indentations (toolmarks, tire tracks, bite marks); striations (marks made when two objects in motion come into sliding contact with each other); tears, breaks, and cuts; mutual transfer of matter (two cars that scrape each other); deposits, dispersals, and residues (spattered blood, gunshot residue); nature of evidential material (identification is the objective); and identification of the evidence (DeForest 1983).

Investigators often use evidence in this way to show who was at a crime scene and what happened at the crime scene. This is especially important when reconstructing a crime scene. The physical evidence can establish the way in which a criminal commits a crime, or the *modus operendi*. A particular burglar may always enter through a basement window—leaving tool marks on the window frame—rather than entering through a door. This signature action of the criminal can allow investigators to link a series of burglaries together. A rapist who always uses a condom, forces the victim to shower afterward, and takes her clothing and the sheets with him has probably raped before because his behavior exhibits considerable knowledge of where evidence is likely to be found. Both the prosecuting and defense attorneys will also use the evidence to construct their theories. They will present these theories to the jury to explain why the suspect did or did not commit the crime in question.

CLASSIFICATION BY THE APPROPRIATE LABORATORY APPROACH

Evidence can be classified by the appropriate laboratory approach, whether it will be used for identification, individualization, or reconstruction. Identification will tell what the substance is—is it cocaine or heroin? Individualization will tell the exact origin of the substance—is it the suspect's semen? Reconstruction will allow investigators to recreate exactly what happened—was the motorcycle speeding when it crashed into the automobile making the left-hand turn onto the bridge?

FORENSIC TECHNIQUES

There are a multitude of techniques employed to assess and examine evidence in forensic science; these include physical methods, chemical methods, and biological methods. The purpose of any of these methods is to tell the forensic scientist, and in turn the investigator, something about the object in question—whatever that object may be—and its role, if any, in the commission of the crime.

Physical Methods

There are a variety of nondestructive physical methods of analysis that are used in forensics. These are the most rudimentary and basic types of analyses that can be done. Because they are nondestructive they are frequently performed first, as they will not alter or destroy the evidence so it can still be analyzed further using other techniques. Techniques that will destroy the evidence are performed later. Common nondestructive techniques include measurement, physical matching, comparison of markings, determination of physical properties, and photography.

Measurement is probably the most basic method of assessing the crime scene. The crime scene as a whole will be measured. Objects within that crime scene will be measured. Measurement is an important part of diagramming the crime scene. The diagram is a drawing of the crime scene with measurements included: objects at the crime scene are measured in relation to each other and in relation to the totality of the crime scene. When crime scene photographs are taken, a scale (usually a small ruler) is included. This scale is included to let the viewer know the size of the object.

Laboratory Services

Biology, Toxicology, DNA, Serology Unit

In some laboratories, all biological services are provided by one unit, the Biological Unit; this includes toxicology, DNA, and serology. Toxicology analyzes bodily specimens for the presence of chemicals (alcohol, tranquilizers, sedatives, stimulants, narcotics) and poisons. Thin-layer chromatography and ultraviolet spectrophotometry are frequently used by the biological unit.

DNA and serology analyze and compare blood and bodily fluids connected with crimes. The DNA unit will handle all analysis of materials and samples that may contain DNA evidence; this includes all bodily fluids like blood, semen, and saliva.

Physical Science (Trace Evidence) Unit

The members of the physical science unit utilize chemistry, geology, and physics to analyze evidence. Often this unit will also focus on the analysis of trace evidence, including soil, paint, and glass. At the scene, the trace evidence unit frequently uses specialized vacuums to gather evidence. In the laboratory, a variety of microscopic techniques will be used to identify and compare small particles.

Firearms and Toolmarks Unit

The Firearms and Toolmark Unit examines firearms, bullets, projectiles, shell casings, and indentations and serrations made from toolmarks. Many of these comparisons rely upon microscopic analysis. Firearms analysis also includes examination of gunshot residue and performs both weapons and projectile comparisons. The scanning electron microscope and transmission electron microscope can be used to analyze gunshot residue.

Document Examination, Computer Crime Unit

Documents may be examined for forgery and alteration. Signatures and handwriting can also be examined. The document examiner compares questioned handwriting, typewriting, printing, computer documents, papers, and inks; examines checks, fraudulent tickets and wills; and both suicide and threat letters. To conduct analysis of documents, examiners may digitally enhance information, use alternate light sources, or chromatography techniques.

The computer crime unit deals with the seizure of computer evidence. They work with databases, hard drives, peripherals, and the retrieval of digitally stored (and even erased) evidence. These individuals are trained computer scientists.

Photography Unit

Since the advent of digital photography, many patrol cars (budget permitting) have a digital camera as standard equipment. This enables the first responder to begin to document the scene photographically—which is especially important when there is fragile evidence which may be lost prior to the forensic unit arriving on the scene. The photography unit specializes in crime scene photography and special photographic techniques, like luminol blood visualization.

Photography is one of the three major ways in which the crime scene will be documented, along with field notes and diagrams. Photographs will be taken of both the interior and exterior of the crime scene. All evidence must be photographed using both close-up photographs to show details and mid-range photographs that show the evidence in relation to other evidence in the crime scene. Also, injuries to victims must be photographed—they are part of the crime scene.

Latent Print Unit

A latent print unit will process prints obtained from crime scenes. They will also compare latent prints to known prints and make use of databases such as IAFIS. Prints are produced by the ridges that are found not only on the tips of the fingers, but also on the palms of the hands and the soles of the feet.

Latent prints can be made visible through the use of chemicals, powders, lasers, and alternate light sources. Latent prints can be lifted from both smooth and rough surfaces, and even off of the human body through the use of super glue fuming.

Polygraph and Voiceprint Analysis Unit

A polygraph and voiceprint analysis unit is responsible for using these lie-detection techniques during an investigation and recording various responses to stimuli to determine the veracity of statements. There is considerable variation among states on whether or not polygraph testimony is admissible in court.

Evidence-Collection Unit

The evidence-collection unit consists of specially trained evidence-collection technicians. These individuals may specialize in fingerprint development and collection, trace-evidence collection. This unit may assume total responsibility for evidence collection, or may provide investigative direction or support.

Accident and Crime Scene Reconstruction

The accident and crime scene reconstruction unit is responsible for examining the physical evidence and determining how an accident or crime took place. At an accident scene these individuals will attempt to determine factors such as position and speed of the vehicles involved. At a crime scene they will attempt to determine the sequence of events during a crime. Upon arrival at an accident or crime scene they will take photographs and measurements from a variety of angles; the calculation of measurements and angles being done by computer software.

In determining how a fatal blow was stuck, the distance from where the victim stood to droplets of blood on the wall and ceiling will be measured. The angle will also be measured. Through the use of measurement, various conditions can be determined; if the victim was standing up or on his knees when the fatal blow was struck, if the victim was struck multiple times, if the blood on the wall was cast-off from a weapon that was already covered in blood, or if it resulted from a major artery being opened.

Forensic personnel may also attempt to physically match certain types of crime scene evidence. This frequently happens at accident and hit-and-run crime scenes when there are large pieces of broken glass or plastic, the forensic scientist will try to match the broken pieces to create a whole. This could link broken glass at the crime scene to the broken headlight of the suspect's car. At a burglary crime scene it could be matching a broken piece of wood with the broken handle of a hammer in the suspect's car. This type of physical matching is done simply by fitting one piece together with another piece to determine if the pieces fit together and were once part of the same object.

Another nondestructive analysis technique that can be employed is the comparison of markings left at the crime scene and test markings made by investigators. This might occur in a burglary crime scene. If a crowbar has been seized from the truck of the suspected perpetrator's car, the lab technician may use it to create test markings; these test markings can be compared to the markings that were discovered at the crime scene. This can also be done by test firing a weapon seized from the suspect and comparing the striations left on the bullet during this test fire to striations on any bullets found at the scene. A forensic odontologist can compare bite marks left on the body of the victim to the bite pattern of the suspect.

For some types of evidence it is worthwhile to determine its physical properties, including density, freezing point, melting point, and boiling point. These are most commonly used in the analysis of drug and toxicological evidence. If a drug has been mixed with another substance, this can be determined by heating the mixture. The drug will melt at a known temperature and any substance that it has been cut with (e.g., protein powder) will melt at another temperature.

Photography, which was discussed in Chapter 3, is a key way in which the crime scene is documented. Not only is photography nondestructive, but it can also be employed without anyone having to actually touch anything at the crime scene—in fact, it is recommended that photographs are taken of the crime scene and all evidence prior to anything being touched or moved. Photography is not only used to document what the investigator can see, but also to expose what cannot be seen with the use of the naked eye. Photographers may use contrast agents, different filters and films, and a variety of lighting techniques including ultraviolet and infrared; all in an effort to make visible the difficult or impossible to see.

Evidence can also be examined without being destroyed through the use of a microscope. Forensics deals with a considerable amount of evidence that is either difficult or impossible to examine closely with the naked eye. This would include all sorts of trace evidence; such as fibers, hairs, glass fractures, and paint chips. All of these require a microscope for better examination. Forensic science utilizes a variety of microscopes, including simple, compound, stereoscopic, polarized-light, comparison, and electron microscopes.

The simple microscope was created by Leeuwenhoek in 1674. It is little more than a magnifying glass, having one double convex lens that will enlarge objects to 266×. There are many occasions in forensics when this low level of magnification is useful. Document examiners may examine a document with a magnifying glass. At the crime scene, tool marks may be examined with a magnifying glass.

The compound microscope magnifies in two stages and is made up of two or more double convex lenses. It has an eyepiece that magnifies objects and an objective lens that also magnifies; this gives it considerable magnifying power. The compound microscope is commonly used in biology, medicine, and forensics.

Unlike the simple and compound microscopes, the stereoscopic microscope provides a three-dimensional image of the object in question. It is able to do this because both of its eyepieces magnify objects and provide a different viewing angle, making the stereoscopic microscope a useful tool for dissection or for other work that requires being able to manipulate a three-dimensional environment.

The polarized-light microscope is especially useful with drug evidence and trace and transfer evidence. It is useful in determining size, color, and refractive index. Roughly 10 percent of materials, referred to as isotropic materials, have identical optical properties in all directions. However, about 90 percent of all solid substances are anisotropic and have optical properties that vary. When the substance is rotated its color and brightness will change.

The comparison microscope is really two microscopes connected by a bridge that allows for a comparison to be made between two different objects. This is an exceptionally useful tool in forensics, especially for matching. The microscope allows the images of the objects to be superimposed, one on top of the other, which allows for a comparison to be made efficiently.

Finally, there are two types of electron microscopes that can be used: the transmission electron microscope, and the scanning electron microscope. Electron microscopes use an electron beam to examine objects. They render a three-dimensional image at high magnification. The transmission electron microscope, which was invented in the 1930s, passes electrons through a very thin sample. The scanning electron microscope examines thick samples and does not pass electrons through the sample but around the sample. The scanning electron microscope is very good for fine details.

Chemical Methods

A wide range of chemical methods can be employed to determine the nature of a substance. These include chemical identification methods, chemical separation methods, chromatographic methods, spectroscopic methods, X-ray diffraction, and mass spectrometry.

CHEMICAL IDENTIFICATION Chemical identification seeks to discover the chemical makeup of a substance. Tests may be performed to determine how the substance reacts with other chemicals or how it reacts under a variety of circumstances such as changes in pressure, application of heat, and so forth.

The use of reagents is a simple method of chemical identification. Reagents can be used at the crime scene to quickly test for the presence or absence of a suspected substance. Confirmation tests still need to be performed at the laboratory in order to obtain a conviction. Reagents are specially created chemical preparations that react only with a specific substance or substances. The reagent is applied to the unknown or suspected substance; if it reacts in the predicted way, identification has been made. Reagents can be especially useful in the field for identifying dried blood or drugs. For example, the Kastle-Meyer test, which uses phenolphthalein as its chemical indicator, turns pink in the presence of blood. A reagent of para-benzoquine in dimethyl sulfoxide becomes fluorescent if cyanide is present. Marquis reagent, a mixture of formaldehyde and sulfuric acid, is used to identify a variety of alkaloids, each of which turns the reagent a customary color. The Marquis reagent can test for Ecstasy (turns the reagent deep blue or black), heroin (turns the reagent purple), amphetamines (turns the reagent orange, red, or brown), methamphetamine (turns the reagent deep blue). Cobalt thiocyanate reagent is used to test for cocaine. The Mandelin reagent can also be used to test for Ecstasy and amphetamines.

CHEMICAL SEPARATION   Chemical separation techniques allow a compound to be separated into its component parts; these techniques are commonly referred to as separation tests. In forensics it is common to need to separate two or more substances, especially when conducting a chemical analysis of illegal drugs. After separation has occurred, confirmatory tests can be conducted.

Separation can be achieved through distillation, sublimation, crystallization, solvent extraction, and the various chromatographic methods. Distillation heats a liquid substance until it becomes a vapor. This vapor is then cooled, which results in a substance with fewer impurities. Sublimation is similar to distillation, except it is performed on substances that can pass from the solid state to the gaseous state without becoming a liquid. When sublimation occurs, the substance starts as a solid, becomes a gas, and then is converted back to a solid to remove impurities. Crystallization functions in a similar fashion, turning a compound into crystals in order to remove impurities. Finally, solvent extraction uses two liquids that will not mix (are not miscible), like oil and water. When solvent extraction occurs, the substance will remain in one of the liquids and the impurities will remain in the other.

There are a variety of chromatographic methods that have been developed to separate substances, including paper chromatography, thin-layer chromatography, column chromatography, high-performance liquid chromatography (HPLC), and gas chromatography. All of the chromatographic methods use motion to separate chemicals. Chemicals are identified based on how they move during a two-phase process that has both a mobile phase and a stationary phase. Some substances are more likely to become mobile and some are more likely to remain stationary. This tendency for a substance to become mobile or to remain stationary is used to separate the substances.

Paper chromatography uses special types of paper in its process and measures how quickly the substance migrates across the paper. Thin-layer chromatography uses a thin layer of absorbent material like silica gel rather than paper in its process. Column chromatography uses an open-topped vertical glass tube up which various components of the sample mixture climb at differing rates. HPLC is very similar to column chromatography except it uses a closed system. Gas chromatography utilizes a boiling liquid like oil to separate substances.

SPECTROSCOPIC METHODS   Spectroscopic methods measure how a chemical reacts with a portion of the electromagnetic spectrum (of which visible light is only a very, very small proportion); these tests include emission spectrography, ultraviolet spectrometry, infrared spectrometry, spectrophotofluorometry, and surface enhanced Raman spectroscopy (SERS). These techniques are also commonly referred to as confirmatory tests because they are generally utilized after separation testing to reveal the specific identity of a substance that has been separated from one or more other substances.

Emission spectrography is a highly useful technique because it can analyze a number of chemicals concurrently. It works because when chemicals are exposed to a flame, they change the color of that flame. In some cases, the flame needs to be broken down into a spectrum so that the difference can be seen. Atomic absorption spectrophotometry is the reverse of measuring emissions. It measures the absorption of light by atoms of interest. Ultraviolet-visible spectrometry relies on the ultraviolet and visible ranges of wavelengths, whereas infrared spectrometry relies on the infrared wavelength range. Infrared spectrometry is the technique of choice with organic substances, for example, drugs, fibers, plastics, paint. Unlike emission spectrography, which can be used to analyze a number of chemicals, infrared spectrometry is used to analyze only pure substances. Spectrophotofluorometry utilizes the fluorescence spectra. It is commonly shown on television crime scene dramas when investigators use a UV lamp at the crime scene to visualize substances, especially bodily products. Fluorescent fingerprint powders are also commonly used with UV lamps. Neutron activation analysis measures the production and analysis of gamma rays. X-ray fluorescence analyzes the radiation that is emitted when the radiation interacts with a specimen.

SERS creates a *chemical fingerprint* of a sample. This technique can be used for both identification and comparison purposes. A light, usually a laser, is shone on a sample. The sample then reacts with the light. It will absorb it, scatter it, and re-emit it. This light is then analyzed, for light intensity, wavelength, direction, and polarization. All of this will create a unique chemical fingerprint. There are three significant advantages to this technique: ability to use small samples, portability, and speed. This technique can be performed using samples on the micrometer scale. SERS can detect very small amounts of drugs, explosive residue, inks, bodily fluids, and other substances. In recent years, this technology has become very portable so analyses can be conducted at the crime scene, not at the laboratory. Analyses can also be done very quickly, within seconds, not minutes or hours, thus giving this confirmatory test the speed of older spot tests (http://www.eequalsmcsquared.auckland.ac.nz/sites/emc2/videos/nz-stories/surface-enhanced-raman-spectroscopy.cfm).

OTHER COMMON METHODS   X-ray diffraction is used to analyze crystalline substances. It measures how crystals diffract X-rays. It compares how an unknown substance diffracts to how known substances diffract X-rays. Because many materials contain crystals (e.g., drugs, soil, minerals, paint pigments) this procedure has wide application in forensics.

Mass spectrometry is not a spectroscopic method because it does not rely on the electromagnetic spectra. This technique is generally used in conjunction with gas chromatography. Gas chromatography first separates the substance in question into its constituent parts, and then mass spectrometry analyzes the substance.

Biological Methods

The most basic biological method is comparison through observation using the naked eye or microscope. There are a wide range of biochemical methods, which tests for the presence of a specific enzyme, like the ones that are present in DNA. There are also immunological methods; this includes blood typing and many of the tests used in serology.

PROBLEMS THAT HAVE OCCURRED IN LABORATORIES

The mishandling and misidentification of evidence are the two major problems that have occurred in laboratories in the United States. It is difficult to determine how serious or widespread these problems are, since much of the evidence that is submitted to laboratories for analysis is never used in court and its veracity is never questioned.

Laboratory mistakes are not usually the result of a lack of proper equipment. Although there is a wide variance in the funding that laboratories receive from jurisdiction to jurisdiction, generally, U.S. laboratories are better funded than laboratories in many other parts of the world and are also more likely to contain the most state-of-the-art equipment. Most laboratory problems in the United States do not have to occur and there are several things that can be done to help solve these problems.

First, there must be a quality check on the substances that come into the laboratory. If evidence has been mishandled prior to arriving at the laboratory, all the laboratory tests in the world will not help. Proper chain of custody must be observed at all times. The tests that a laboratory runs are only as valid as the substances it receives. Whoever receives the substances to be analyzed into the laboratory should double-check to be sure that proper documentation accompanies the samples.

Second, only qualified, well-trained individuals should be hired into laboratory positions, and individuals who are already employed should constantly update their skills. Incompetence is not an option. It is also advisable that laboratories are accredited.

Third, proper handling procedures should be put into place and followed. Some mistakes happen because there is no one set way of doing something. All procedures, no matter how simple, should be written down and followed. Shortcuts are never appropriate. Along with this, the laboratory should not be an open environment. Only a few authorized individuals should have access to the forensic laboratory. All comings and goings in the laboratory, just like at any crime scene, should be documented.

Fourth, all procedures, tests, and results must be fully documented. Appropriate chain of custody is not only important in the field, but in the laboratory as well. Every individual who handles the evidence and every test that is performed must be documented. This documentation can be very important in the courtroom. Improper documentation, while it may not ruin a case, can seriously limit the usefulness of a piece of evidence in the courtroom.

While it is true that all successful prosecutions do begin at the crime scene, there is no point to collecting evidence at all if it will not be handled and processed properly in the forensic laboratory. Proper handling and proper identification of evidence can be the difference between highly useful evidence and evidence that never makes it to a courtroom.

Glossary

Chemical separation techniques—laboratory techniques that are used to separate two or more chemicals.

Chromatography—(paper, thin-layer, column, high-performance liquid, gas) a technique that uses motion to separate chemicals.

CODIS—Combined DNA Index System, a DNA database maintained by the FBI.

Circumstantial evidence—evidence that denotes something else.

Comparison microscope—allows viewing of two objects at once for comparison.

Crystallization—turning a compound into crystals in order to remove impurities.

DSM-IV-TR—*The Diagnostic and Statistical Manual of Mental Disorders, Fourth Edition, Text Revision*. Used by psychiatrists and psychologists to diagnose mental disorders.

Direct evidence—evidence that was directly seen by an individual, eyewitness testimony.

Distillation—purifying a liquid by heating it until it becomes a vapor and then cooling it.

Eyewitness testimony—what was directly seen, heard (although not what someone else said), smelt, touched, by the witness.

IAFIS—The Integrated Automated Fingerprint Identification System, a fingerprint database operated by the FBI.

Latent prints—prints that are not visible to the naked eye.

Locard, Edmund—Very influential individual in the development of forensic science in Europe, including opening the first police laboratory in Lyons, France. His exchange principle, that the criminal always leaves something behind at the crime scene, is a guiding principle of forensics.

Luminal blood visualization—a special photographic technique to photograph blood that cannot be seen with the naked eye.

Mens rea—literally means "guilty mind," that the perpetrator knew the action was wrong.

Modus operendi—the way a criminal commits a crime.

Polarized—light microscope utilizes polarizing light to identify substances.

Saint Valentine's Day Massacre—Gangland slaying that took place in a garage in Chicago in 1929.

Scanning electron microscope—examines thick specimens by passing electrons around them.

Serology—the study of bodily fluids.

Solvent extraction—using two non-miscible liquids to separate substances.

Statute work—laboratory work that must be done in order to obtain a conviction.

Stereoscopic binocular microscope—provides a three-dimensional image of the object being viewed.

Stereoscopic methods—(emission, ultra-violet, infra-red, spectrophotofluorometry) measure how a chemical reacts with a portion of the electromagnetic spectrum.

Sublimation—purifying a substance that passes directly from a solid to a gas.

Trace evidence—soil, paint, glass, and other types of small evidence.

Vollmer, August—influential in the development of both policing and forensic science in the United States.

Wickersham Commission—Formed by President Hoover in 1929 to evaluate Prohibition.

Zygote—the fertilized egg in its initial stage of development. Later it will become an embryo and then a fetus.

Webliography

Many states have very informative web sites for their crime laboratories. Just a few are listed below.

Washington: http://www.wsp.wa.gov/crime/crimlabs.htm

Wisconsin: http://www.doj.state.wi.us/dles/crimelabs/

Montana: http://www.doj.mt.gov/department/forensicsciencedivision.asp

Texas: http://www.txdps.state.tx.us/criminal_law_enforcement/crime_laboratory/index.htm

Mississippi: http://www.dps.state.ms.us/dps/dps.nsf/Divisions/cl?OpenDocument

Georgia: http://www.state.ga.us/gbi/fordiv.html

California: http://ag.ca.gov/bfs/index.htm

South Dakota: http://dci.sd.gov/lab/labexam.htm

Louisiana: http://www.lsp.org/crimelab.html

New York: http://www.troopers.state.ny.us/Forensic_Science/

References

ASCLD/LAB. *Legacy Accreditation Process.* Accessed on February 25, 2007, from http://www.ascld-lab.org/legacy/aslablegacyprocess.html.

Bureau of Justice Assistance. *Training and Technical Assistance, Law Enforcement Training Database.* Accessed on May 29, 2006, from http://bjatraining.ncjrs.gov/.

DeForest, P., R. Gaensslen, and H. Lee. *Forensic Science: An Introduction to Criminalistics.* NY: McGraw-Hill, 1983.

Eckert, W. ed., *Introduction to Forensic Sciences*, 2nd ed. Boca Raton, FL: CRC Press, 1997.

E = MC Squared. *Surface Enhanced Raman Spectroscopy.* Accessed on February 25, 2007, from http://www.eequalsmcsquared.auckland.ac.nz/sites/emc2/videos/nz-stories/surface-enhanced-raman-spectroscopy.cfm.

Federal Bureau of Investigation. *Combined DNA Index System.* Accessed on May 13, 2006, from http://www.fbi.gov/hq/lab/codis/index1.htm.

Federal Bureau of Investigation. *Integrated Automated Fingerprint Identification System.* Accessed on May 13, 2006, from http://www.fbi.gov/hq/cjisd/iafis.htm.

Federal Bureau of Investigation. *FBI Laboratory, Latent Print Unit.* Accessed on May 13, 2006, from http://www.fbi.gov/hq/lab/org/lpu.htm.

Illinois State Police Division of Forensic Services Forensic Sciences Command. *Our History.* Accessed on May 15, 2006, from http://www.isp.state.il.us/Forensics/ISPHTML/History.htm.

Saferstein, R. *Criminalistics*, 8th ed. Upper Saddle River, NJ: Pearson, 2004.

New York State Division of State Police. *Forensic Training Seminars.* Accessed on May 16, 2006, from http://www.troopers.state.ny.us/Forensic%5FScience/Training/.

Washington State Patrol-Crime Laboratory Division. *Forensic Laboratory Services.* Accessed on May 16, 2006, from http://www.wsp.wa.gov/crime/crimlabs.htm.

Review Questions

1. Why did forensic laboratories tend to develop faster in Europe than in the United States?
2. How was Locard influential in the development of forensic science in Europe?
3. How did the Saint Valentine's Day Massacre in 1929 influence the development of forensic laboratories in the United States?
4. When did the FBI first begin operating a forensic laboratory? What services did they provide at that time?
5. What is the difference between the IAFIS and CODIS databases?
6. Why is continuing education important for forensic science professionals?

7. What sorts of microscopes are commonly used in a forensic science laboratory?

8. What is the difference between examining physical evidence for identification purposes as opposed to comparison purposes?

9. How are separation and confirmation tests used in conjunction with one another?

10. List and discuss at least three ways that laboratory mistakes can be prevented.

Some Things to Think About

1. Why is Locard's exchange principle the guiding principle in forensics?

2. Would it be a good idea to have a federally coordinated laboratory system in the United States? Explain your answer fully.

3. If the U.S. justice system became less focused on the illegal use of substances what would be some of the positive and negative repercussions for the field of forensics?

Drugs, Documents, and Doorjambs

Section III begins to look at specific crimes and the types of evidence most commonly associated with those crimes—and some types of evidence that are not so commonly associated with those crimes. This section includes Chapter 5, Chapter 6, and Chapter 7. Chapter 5, *Toxicology, Drugs, and Chemical Analysis,* covers the most commonly collected forensic evidence—drug and alcohol evidence. These are statutory analyses. In order for a successful prosecution of a drug or DUI case, the evidence must be correctly identified and quantified. Chapter 5 also examines the forensic analysis of poisons and the use of biological and chemical weapons by terrorists.

Chapter 6, *Document Analysis, Computer Forensics, and Fraud Investigation,* weds one of the oldest areas of criminalistics, document analysis, to one of the newest, computer forensics. These two areas have some similarities—many documents are now computer generated. Since the advent of widespread interconnectivity, computer forensics has been a rapidly growing area of study. Fraud is also discussed in this chapter because so much fraud occurs in relation to documents or computers.

Chapter 7, *Burglary, Theft, and Accident Investigation,* examines the types of forensic evidence found at burglary scenes and accident scenes, for example, fingerprints, trace and transfer evidence, and tool marks. It also covers accident and crime scene reconstruction. In some jurisdictions, accident calls are one of the most frequent types of calls that an officer responds to, this is especially the case in rural areas.

Toxicology, Drugs, and Chemical Analysis

TOXICOLOGY

History of Toxicology

Three factors have made poison a weapon of choice for thousands of years. First, many poisons could be derived from common plants. This made them readily available to anyone who had only minimal knowledge of plants. Second, many poisons, once made, had little taste or odor and could be disguised in foods or liquids. This made them easy to use without the victim becoming suspicious. Third, until the nineteenth century, there were no reliable tests to determine if poison had been ingested and, in many cases, the symptoms of poisoning were difficult to distinguish from the symptoms of common diseases. This made it easy for deaths by poisoning to occur without being questioned or detected by either law enforcement or the medical community. (Figure 5.1)

It was not until Mathieu Orfila, the "father of toxicology," published the *Traité des Poisons* in 1814 that toxicology was born as a separate discipline and we began to be able to classify and detect various poisons. In *Traité des Poisons* he presented a classification system of poisons based upon experimental observation, and while this classification is no longer in use, it served as a valuable tool for early toxicologists. Orfila also published several other major works, including an important work

FIGURE 5.1 Common poisonous plants (l–r, t–b): Oleander (*Nerium oleander*), Foxglove (*Digitalis purpurea*), Clematis (*Ranunculacae clematis*), Poinsettia (*Euphorbia pulcherrima*), Datura (*Datura metel*), Mountain Laurel (*Kamia latifolia*), a close relative of the also-poisonous Rhododendron.

on the effects of arsenic (*Recherches sur l'empoisonnement par l'acide arsénieux*). At the time, arsenic was the poison of choice—highly toxic and undetectable. The first U.S. work on the subject of poisons was not published until 1869. This was Theodore Wormley's *The Microchemistry of Poisons.*

Around 1838, James Marsh developed what would become known as the *Marsh test* to detect arsenic. Although there were earlier methods that had been used to isolate arsenic poisoning, the Marsh test was far more sensitive. For the first time in history, this very common poison could reliably be detected. In 1840, Orfila testified in the highly publicized LaFarge poisoning case in France. Not only did the evidence he presented from the Marsh test help to convict the defendant, but the trial publicity spread the word about the effectiveness of the Marsh Test and very quickly the rate of arsenic poisoning in France dropped.

Early in his career, Louis Lewin worked with the hallucinogen, Peyote cactus. He later created a broad drug classification system. His system focused on how the drugs affected the body and placed substances in one of the following categories: inebriantia (intoxicants like alcohol), exitania (stimulants like amphetamines), euphorica (narcotics like heroin), hypnotica (tranquilizers like Kava), and phantastica (hallucinogens like peyote). Although we no longer employ this system, it is easy to see how similar it is to how we now classify drugs. The exitania are our modern day stimulants. The phantastica are our hallucinogens. The hypnotica are our antianxiety agents and sleep medications—which, even today, are sometimes referred to as hypnotics.

Chelsea Physic Garden

The Chelsea Physic Garden, founded in 1673, is located in London, England. It was originally called the *Apothecaries' Garden.* Since the inception of the garden, its goal has been to study the medicinal effects of plants, and to facilitate the growing and studying of new and different species of plants. Early in the garden's history, it worked mostly with native species of plants, but it soon began importing and exporting species of plants. In modern time the garden has established itself as Britain's first garden of ethnobotany; it is devoted to studying the botany of different ethnic groups around the world. Because there is a renewed interest in herbal remedies today, the garden continues to explore how plants can treat illnesses and enhance health (http://www.chelseaphysicgarden .co.uk/index.html).

What Is Toxicology?

There is a famous saying in toxicology that all substances are poisonous—it all depends upon the dosage. Toxicology is not black-and-white. Most often it is *not* the case that something either is a poison or is not a poison—it is all a matter of degree. A substance which in a high dose will kill a person, in a low dose may do nothing. Even drugs that are used to heal can kill if too high of a dosage is taken or do nothing if too low of a dosage is taken. A substance that can be tolerated by adults (like lead) is highly toxic to infants and children. Even water ingested in large amounts will lead to death!

Toxicologists are involved in the study of the effects of substances, toxins, and poisons on the body. The toxicologist will determine if a particular substance is toxic and how harmful it may be. They are also concerned with the detection of and remedies for poisoning. Within the discipline of toxicology there are also many smaller subdisciplines. Reproductive and developmental toxicologists study how toxins affect the developing fetus. Environmental toxicologists study the effect of chemicals in the environment. Ecotoxicologists look at the effect of toxins on ecosystems and stress that the effects of a toxin cannot be limited to one organism but rather impacts the whole ecosystem. Occupational toxicologists focus on harmful substances in the work environment. Forensic toxicologists apply the principles of toxicology to the legal arena and focus specifically on those chemicals that cause harm and death.

Most of the work in toxicology is not forensic toxicology, as the majority of toxicologists are employed in industry developing products, evaluating product safety, and assisting with regulatory compliance issues. Many toxicologists with doctorate degrees are employed in academia, and make their living conducting research and educating the next generation of toxicologists.

Toxicology brings together many disciplines to determine the toxicity of substances. The toxicologist must be well versed in the fields of analytical chemistry, bio-chemistry, biology, anatomy, pharmacology, epidemiology, pathobiology, and molecular biology, among others.

Research in Toxicology

Toxicological research frequently centers on the questions, "what substance caused this to happen?" and "how will this substance affect the human body?" Research is conducted to determine how substances hurt or heal the body, along with the causes of death, disease, and poisoning. This can be an important part of the development of new drug treatments to counteract diseases and the effects of harmful substances. In the legal arena, in the area of toxic torts, research is often conducted to determine how substances have affected individuals. The investigation may be concerned with whether or not a substance is a carcinogen, that is, whether it causes cancer. A researcher might investigate the higher instance of a disease that occurs near a chemical plant to determine if pollution or byproducts from the plant in the air or water could have caused the disease. Toxicologists can investigate how a substance affects "at risk" groups such as fetuses, infants, children, and pregnant women. Toxicological research is also conducted prior to the approval of new drugs being released to market and to determine the safety of new cosmetics and perfumes. Food toxicologists study the safety of food additives and preservatives (http://www.toxicology.org/AI/APT/careerguide.asp#Where%20 Do%20Toxicologists%20Work?).

Toxicological research can be conducted on the micro and macro levels and at many levels in between. Toxicological research may be focused on the molecular level (molecular toxicology) and examine microscopic occurrences like cell death. The researcher may examine how dust can kill cells in the lungs (inhalation toxicology), or how injecting rats with a certain drug affects them. Immunotoxicologists study how the immune system is impacted by exposure to a chemical. Others examine how drugs affect the body as a whole. Still others examine how toxic substances may impact a population as a whole (epidemiology is a related area that studies how diseases spread and develop within a population).

Toxins may be of synthetic (man-made) or natural origin. There are many naturally occurring toxins that exist all around us in the world. Ancient societies knew this and much of their

---

Toxicology Journals

There are numerous toxicology journals, both in print and online. Below is a sampling of just a selection of these journals. Also listed is the year in which the journal was first published. The earliest listed was first published in 1911. There was a proliferation of journals that began publication in the 1970s and 1980s.

Toxicological Sciences, 1911

The Archives of Toxicology (a European toxicology journal), 1930

The Annual Review of Pharmacology and Toxicology, 1961

Bulletin of Environmental Contamination and Toxicology, 1966

Critical Reviews in Toxicology, 1970

Archives of Environmental Contamination and Toxicology, 1973

Drug and Chemical Toxicology, 1977

Immunopharmacology and Immunotoxicology, 1978

Journal of Applied Toxicology, 1980

Journal of Biochemical and Molecular Toxicology, 1986

---

medicine was based on the administration of these substances. Many powerful naturally occurring toxins—such as arsenic—can be transformed into even more potent semisynthetic toxins, or turned into a more toxic compound. For example, the compound dioxin is hundreds of times more toxic than arsenic.

CHEMICAL AND BIOLOGICAL TERRORISM

There is a growing concern that naturally occurring toxins or naturally occurring toxins that have been altered may be used in a terrorist attack. *Most* terrorist attacks have employed conventional weapons (explosives, firearms) and not biological or chemical weapons. This is due to the fact that conventional weapons have had great success in the hands of terrorists and terrorists know these weapons very well. Terrorists stick to the methods that they know well and have been successful. This is not to say that both chemical and biological weapons have *not* been used by terrorists and in state-sponsored terrorism. It is also certainly not to imply that there is no danger of terrorists employing either chemical or biological weapons in the future. This is a very real danger, however, it is more likely that terrorists will continue to attempt attacks with predominantly conventional weaponry until they can become more comfortable using chemical and biological methods.

The following sections will examine common chemical and biological agents. Some of these agents have been used during wartime. Some have the potential for use by terrorists during an attack. Others have been used in homicides and suicides.

Chemical Agents

The Centers for Disease Control and Prevention (CDC) categorizes chemical agents as follows: biotoxins, vesicants, blood agents, caustics, pulmonary agents, incapacitating agents, long-acting anticoagulants, metals, nerve agents, organic solvents, tear gas, toxic alcohols, and vomiting agents. Certain categories are of greater interest because agents within those categories are more likely to be used during a terrorist attack and will be discussed further. These include biotoxins, vesicants, blood agents, metals, and nerve agents.

BIOTOXIN   A biotoxin is a poison derived from plant or animal sources. Possible biotoxins include digitalis, nicotine, and ricin. Digitalis, derived from the foxglove plant, is used to treat congestive heart failure and arrhythmia. It works by slowing the heart rate and has been used in modern medicine for more than 200 years.

Individuals can also suffer from nicotine poisoning. Nicotine is commonly found in cigarettes. Poisoning can occur in very young children who are exposed to smoke. Adults can be poisoned through excessive smoking, by continuing to smoke while wearing a nicotine patch (or patches), or through exposure to pesticides that contain nicotine. Often there are no symptoms of nicotine poisoning. Treatment can include giving the victim activated charcoal. There are also specific drug treatments.

Ricin, derived from castor beans, could be employed by terrorists. It can be inhaled, ingested, or injected. Because ricin comes from a bean, it is most often ingested. Symptoms of ricin poisoning include abdominal pain, vomiting, and diarrhea. After several days, a victim may experience dehydration, decreased urine output, and lowered blood pressure. Generally, if the victim survives five days post exposure, he or she will survive, although organ damage is likely. Ricin interferes with the ability of the cells in the body to produce proteins, which leads to cell death. Because ricin kills cells, there are medical applications using ricin to kill specific cells, like cancer cells, or neurons. During World War I, attempts were made to weaponize ricin, but they were never employed. In fact, ricin has at least two serious disadvantages as a terrorist weapon. First, although ricin is easy to produce, it is not very toxic. Second, when it is released into the air, it has a normal tendency to oxidize and become harmless.

VESICANTS   Vesicants cause blistering to the skin, eyes, and possibly the lungs, but most often vesicants affect the skin. Mustard gas is the most common vesicant. It can be released as a vapor into the air or into the water. Exposure to mustard gas does not generally result in death; it most often leads to burns, respiratory disease, and blindness. There is no antidote to mustard gas exposure, all that can be done is to remove clothing that has been contaminated and wash contaminated parts of the body. It was used during World War I against troops and proved to be very effective. Once a person is exposed; it is very difficult to decontaminate him or her because mustard gas is not very water soluble—it will not dissolve easily in water. Effective decontaminants for mustard gas have become available only recently.

BLOOD AGENTS   Blood agents are absorbed into the blood. They prevent the normal utilization of oxygen. Blood agents include cyanide in its various compounds and carbon monoxide.

Cyanide   Cyanide is another very powerful naturally occurring toxin. It can cause death within minutes when taken orally. During World War I, several nations experimented with the use of cyanide gas to kill opposing troops. This posed some difficulties because some compounds are very light and dissipate quickly. During World War II, the Nazis used hydrocyanic acid in combination with Zyklon B (a rodenticide) to kill millions of people. The Zyklon B made the hydrocyanic gas heavier; it did not dissipate as quickly as cyanide alone and was a very effective killing agent.

Luckily, outside of military uses, the use of cyanide is fairly rare. Most individuals who are exposed to cyanide come into contact with the chemical in their work. It is used in chemical synthesis, in the processing of plastics, and as a fumigant. Cyanide also naturally occurs in a variety of foods, including lima beans, cassava beans, and roots. Cyanide may be released during a house fire when rubber or plastic burns. Cigarette smoke also contains cyanide.

Cyanide kills by blocking the body's ability to use oxygen. Many of the symptoms of cyanide poisoning are similar to the symptoms of any other type of oxygen deprivation; weakness, confusion, sleepiness, coma, and finally, death. Like a victim of carbon-monoxide poisoning, a victim of cyanide poisoning will also have a cherry-red appearance. Because it is so rare, cyanide poisoning can be difficult to recognize and treat in an emergency room. Many physicians will never see a case of cyanide poisoning in their practice. Contact with cyanide most frequently occurs via skin contact or ingestion. If it is suspected that the victim had skin contact with cyanide, all clothing should be removed and the victim should be washed to eliminate continued exposure. Medical staff must be very careful not to expose themselves or others when removing or disposing of contaminated clothing. If recent cyanide ingestion is suspected, the victim's stomach can be pumped. Also, some victims may improve through the use of oxygen, although this has not been medically proven. While cyanide is toxic, the compound hydrogen cyanide is even more toxic.

Dietz (http://www.facsnet.org/tools/ref_tutor/tampering/prolif.php3) notes that there have been five incidents of product tampering that have resulted in death. All involved cyanide. In 1982, acetaminophen capsules were tainted with cyanide. In 1986 two people in Seattle died because of tainted analgesic capsules. That same year, Lipton Cup-a-Soup was found to be tainted. In 1991, three people in Washington State ingested tainted Sudafed capsules. In 1992 Goody's Headache Powder was tainted.

Carbon Monoxide   Carbon monoxide was first created by de Lassone in 1776. One common cause of carbon monoxide poisoning occurs when an individual commits suicide using the exhaust from an automobile—usually in an enclosed garage. Suicides by carbon monoxide poisoning are easy to spot because the body takes on a characteristic cherry-red appearance due to the excessive amount of carbon monoxide in the blood stream and lack of oxygen. Accidental poisoning can occur in enclosed spaces when gas-fueled appliances such as furnaces, hot-water heaters, and gas dryers leak. Poisoning can also occur when propane heaters, grills, and barbeques that burn charcoal are used indoors without ventilation, in automobiles where the exhaust leaks into the passenger compartment, and in underground mines.

Symptoms include headache, nausea, dizziness, and confusion. In severe cases the individual may be unconscious or even comatose. Even mild, chronic exposure can lead to permanent neurological damage. The effects of carbon monoxide poisoning are especially devastating in fetuses. A pregnant woman who has only mild symptoms of carbon monoxide poisoning may spontaneously abort her fetus or the child may be born with physical disabilities.

Treatment is very simple and consists of the administration of oxygen. What is not so simple is recognizing that carbon monoxide poisoning has occurred, because the symptoms of mild poisoning look so much like flu symptoms and are most likely to present during cold weather months—when gas furnaces are most likely to leak.

METALS   Metals contain metallic poisons, such as arsenic, mercury, and lead. The vast majority of exposures to metals is accidental and occurs at the workplace. Heavy metal poisoning is generally treated with chelating drugs that remove the metal from the body by binding to it.

Arsenic   Arsenic is a very powerful metallic poison that can lead to multi-organ failure. Throughout history, arsenic has been a poison of choice because of its great potency. Arsenic also does not break down like many other substances, so it will remain wherever it was used. Surprisingly, arsenic was used medicinally prior to the advent of modern antibiotic treatment, and prior to the invention of sulfa drugs it was used to treat syphilis. Arsenic was in a variety of other medical preparations and during the Victorian era it was used by women to whiten their skin. It was used in a variety of different types of cosmetics; many individuals who used these products became unwitting victims of arsenic poisoning. Arsenic was also used in the pigment emerald green and may have contributed to some of the illnesses that many of the Impressionist painters experienced. Arsenic has been used in pesticides and insecticides. It also occurs naturally in certain geological regions.

Starting in the 1930s, arsenic was used to treat wood to prevent rot. This *pressure-treated wood* is very durable and can last upwards of 20 years. It was commonly used for residential decks and other outdoor applications until 2004 when it was banned. Unfortunately, significant problems can occur when pressure-treated wood is burned and the gases are inhaled. Arsenic was used as an insecticide in apple orchards, because it does not break down over time, when these orchards were sold to developers for housing, arsenic was found in the soil of many of the yards. Arsenic has also been used in herbicides; even many years later, high levels remain in the soil in these areas.

In large portions of South America and Asia, high levels of naturally occurring arsenic have been found in drinking wells. In response to this serious public health threat, the National Academy of Engineering has awarded $1 million to Abul Hussam, a professor at George Mason University, for his design of an inexpensive filtering system to remove arsenic from drinking water (Ritter 2007).

Although not nearly as common today because it is easier to detect, in the past, arsenic was frequently a weapon of choice to commit murder. The first sign of arsenic poisoning is generally a mild headache that progresses to lightheadedness. Other symptoms of arsenic poisoning are thirst, stomach pains, and vomiting. These symptoms are not specific to arsenic poisoning; they can occur with many other types of poisoning. In fact, the symptoms of arsenic poisoning are common symptoms of a variety of disorders. This is unfortunate for the victim of arsenic poisoning because if treatment is not received, death will result. Treatment of arsenic poisoning often consists of the use of a chelating drug which will chemically bind to the arsenic, render it harmless, and carry it out of the body. There are other concerns regarding exposure to arsenic because it is a carcinogen. Exposure in smaller amounts, amounts that are too low to cause death, can result in cancer.

Mercury Mercury is a common toxin. The vast majority of mercury poisonings have occurred accidentally. It most likely would have no terrorist applications. Mercury continues to be used in dental fillings, which are actually several metals combined to form an amalgam. It is still being debated whether the mercury in older dental fillings may be released over time and cause harm. Modern dentistry offers a variety of other options for fillings, including ceramics, composites (made up of glass or quartz and resin), and glass and resin ionomers, but amalgam remains the most durable of all filling materials and is still preferred for large fillings in areas of the teeth that are especially subjected to the stresses of a lot of chewing.

Mercury used to be employed in the hat-making process. A mercury nitrate solution was used by hatters (hat-makers) to make animal fur into felt for felt hats. Hat makers were exposed to high levels of mercury and often began to behave oddly. The character of the Mad Hatter in *Alice in Wonderland* was based on the erratic behavior of hat makers. Mercury is no longer used in this manner.

It has been suggested that mercury poisoning may be a cause of autism in young children, but this has yet to be thoroughly researched and substantiated. Individuals may come in contact with mercury if the contents of broken mercury thermometers are not properly cleaned up. One of the authors remembers quite vividly a friend bringing a very small tube of mercury to school and playing with the oddly beading silvery liquid on the desks. The teacher even allowed the vial to be passed around and the mercury to be touched! Luckily, in many cases, even this sort of direct exposure will not make someone sick.

Mercury poisoning may be acute, resulting from exposure to a high level of mercury over a short period of time or chronic, resulting from exposure to a low level of mercury over a long period of time. Symptoms of acute mercury exposure include cough, tightness in the chest, trouble breathing, and stomach discomfort. Symptoms of chronic mercury poisoning include changes in the mouth and gums, mental and mood disturbance, and nerve damage. A doctor can test for mercury poisoning through either a blood or urine level. Treatment of mercury poisoning consists of the use of chelating drugs—special drugs that, when taken by a poisoned individual, will bind to the poisonous substance in that person's system and as the drug passes out of the body, so does the poison. Chelating drugs may also bind to the poison and through an interaction render the poison harmless to the body.

Lead Among all the toxins that workers are exposed to, lead is perhaps the most common. Individuals in a wide range of industries are frequently exposed, including those who work in manufacturing, the chemical industry, construction, the plastics industry, radiator repair, the rubber industry, gas-station attendants, and of course those who work with lead in any way—mining, smelting, soldering, or refining.

FIGURE 5.2 Old cans of lead-based paint pose a hazard if not disposed of properly.

While lead poisoning is not commonly seen in adults, it is frequently seen in children, especially those who live in older houses that have not had lead-based paints properly removed. Houses built prior to 1978—when lead-based household paint was banned completely—are at risk for having remnants of lead paint inside, especially if these houses have not been maintained well, if they are in disrepair, or if paint has been allowed to peel and chip (Figure 5.2). This is a hazard that disproportionately strikes poorer children who are more likely to live in older homes that have not been properly maintained. Lead exposure can come from ingesting paint chips, from sucking on window sills, or from ingesting lead dust. Old vinyl blinds imported from foreign countries also pose a risk. Frequently, lead was used in the blinds as a binder (to get the paint to properly coat the blinds) and after years of use and exposure to sunlight, lead dust may form on the surface of the blinds. Children may also be exposed to lead through contaminated soil. Younger children have a greater risk of poisoning from lead not only because they are more likely to put everything they can into their mouths, but also because their systems are still developing. High levels of lead in children can lead to behavioral problems, brain damage, and cognitive impairment. Studies have shown that a significant proportion of violent inmates, especially serial murderers, have high levels of lead in their bloodstreams. The detrimental effects of lead exposure to young children is so well known, that pediatricians regularly screen for it in their young patients. Checking blood-lead-levels is generally recommended at two years of age for all children who live or have lived in housing that was built before the mid-1970s.

Symptoms of lead poisoning in adults include headaches, weakness, vomiting, abdominal pain, and anemia—although a poisoned individual may experience no symptoms at all. Symptoms in children include crankiness, vomiting, confusion, seizures, and coma. Kidney damage, brain damage, and death may result. Treatment consists first of stopping exposure to lead and then using chelation drugs to remove lead from the body. Even after treatment, children who have suffered from lead poisoning may experience permanent kidney or brain damage.

NERVE AGENTS Nerve agents, for example, sarin, soman, Tabun, and VX interfere with the nervous system's ability to function properly. Nerve agents have frequently been used during wartime.

It is possible to be exposed to sarin gas through air, water, food, or even from the clothes of others who have been exposed. Sarin affects the muscles of the body and the body's ability to regulate musculature. Signs of minor exposure include runny nose, eye pain, blurred vision, rapid breathing, diarrhea, headache, vomiting, changes in heart rate and blood pressure. If the exposure is extensive enough, the person may no longer be able to control breathing, and may experience respiratory failure and convulsions. People generally recover from mild and moderate exposure.

Tabun gas is a nerve agent. Exposure may occur via air, water, eye, or skin contact. The possible effects are very much like those of sarin gas. A severe exposure is likely to result in death.

VX gas is a nerve agent. Possible effects of exposure include breathing problems, asphyxiation, blindness, vomiting, diarrhea, burns on the body, convulsions, and coma. If death does not result, victims may become blind, may have a variety of respiratory, digestive, and neurological disorders, a variety of cancers, and birth defects (http://www.state.gov/r/pa/ei/rls/18714.htm).

ADDITIVE EFFECTS OF CHEMICAL AGENTS   During the Iran–Iraq War that raged 1980–1988, it is known that Saddam Hussein attacked Iran using chemical weapons. (Some sources claim that Iran also responded with chemical weapons.) The U.S. State Department claims that Hussein used a mixture of the chemical weapons mustard, sarin, tabun, and VX gases against the Kurds in northern Iraq. When gasses are combined, the immediate and long-term effects are greater than the effects would be from using any one gas.

Biological Agents

Just like chemical agents, the threat of biological agents being used in terrorist attacks is a growing concern. Some biological agents can be turned into an airborne or water soluble form where they can be delivered easily to a large segment of the population. Of particular concern are anthrax and smallpox.

ANTHRAX   In an October, 2001 terrorist attack, anthrax was mailed to people in the media and to two U.S. senators. Five people died and seventeen others became ill. Overall, anthrax has not proved very useful in attacks because it is difficult to use it to kill high numbers of individuals. There are three types of anthrax: skin, lung, and digestive. Most anthrax is contracted by farm workers who have contact with infected animals. The digestive form can be contracted from eating infected, undercooked meat. As a potential weapon, a powder form of anthrax, which contains anthrax spores, is used. This form of anthrax must be inhaled into the lungs. Inhaled anthrax is the most lethal of the three types of anthrax; however, it is very difficult to grow enough anthrax and to convert it into a form that could be used to affect large numbers of individuals (say released into the ventilation system at a mall, or dispersed by plane over a large city). Also individuals who would try to create this form of anthrax put themselves at significant risk of infection.

SMALLPOX   After September 11, 2001, there was concern that smallpox may be used as a terrorist weapon. The disease smallpox has been eradicated from the face of the earth, but still exists in laboratories and there is worry that these laboratory samples could be used to create very powerful biological weapons, especially samples that may have been located in the former Soviet Union. Historically, only the United States has successfully used smallpox as a biological weapon; in the early part of U.S. history, 1763, the government distributed blankets that once belonged to smallpox victims at Fort Pitt in Pittsburgh, Pennsylvania, to Native Americans. The natives had no resistance to the disease and others that were common in Europe at that time; the effects, as the government expected, were devastating. In fact, overall, more Native Americans died as the result of disease than in confrontations with white, European settlers—although not all contagion of the disease was deliberate, Europeans infected the natives repeatedly with a variety of illnesses.

Until the early 1970s, children in the United States were routinely immunized to protect against smallpox. When smallpox ceased to be a threat, the last case occurred in Somalia in 1977, vaccination was stopped, leaving the population open to infection if an outbreak should occur.

The Biological and Chemical Weapons Conventions

The 1972 Biological Weapons Convention

The Biological Weapons Convention is a multilateral disarmament treaty banning the production of biological and toxic weapons. Governments that have signed the treaty have agreed not to produce or stockpile biological weapons or toxins except for protective purposes. They have also agreed not to retain biological weapons, to destroy existing stockpiles of weapons, and not to assist other nations in acquiring biological weapons. By 1975, 22 governments had signed the convention and currently, 155 governments have ratified the convention.

The 1997 Chemical Weapons Convention

The 1997 Chemical Weapons Convention is a multilateral disarmament agreement. It prohibits the development, production, acquisition, stockpiling, transfer, and use of chemical weapons. It categorizes chemicals into one of three schedules, depending upon the possible uses of a chemical. Schedule I chemicals have no uses other than as chemical weapons. The amount of these types of chemicals that a nation may possess is strictly limited. Schedule II chemicals have uses other than as chemical weapons but only in small amounts. Manufacturing that uses these chemicals is tracked. Schedule III chemicals are commonly used for purposes other than chemical weapons manufacturing in large amounts. There are restrictions imposed on the export of these chemicals. As of August 2000, 140 nations had signed the convention.

In order to use the smallpox virus that exists in laboratories as a weapon it would first need to be released into the air so that it could be inhaled. Once inhaled, approximately one-third of those individuals who were infected with the disease would die.

OSHA and the CDC

Two key government agencies that assist in the regulation and investigation of substances are The Occupational Safety and Health Administration (OSHA) and the Centers for Disease Control and Prevention (CDC).

OCCUPATIONAL SAFETY AND HEALTH ADMINISTRATION   OSHA, a division of the U.S. Department of Labor, was founded in 1971 and is responsible for setting standards for creating safe working environments. OSHA also works to provide both technical and regulatory information on a variety of biological agents that could be employed by terrorists (www.osha.gov).

THE CENTERS FOR DISEASE CONTROL AND PREVENTION   CDC is a part of the U.S. Department of Health and Human Services. It was founded to fight the disease malaria in 1946. The modern CDC has greatly expanded its mission and currently conducts research in a wide range of areas; to combat diseases, injuries, workplace hazards, and environmental health threats. You will notice in many places in this text statistics regarding illness, injury, and death are quoted from the CDC. The CDC tracks all of these and disseminates information to the public and professionals.

The CDC tracks information on bioterrorism, mass casualties, chemical emergencies, and radiation emergencies. Concerning bioterrorism, the CDC provides up-to-date information for first responders, how to submit samples to the laboratory, and what to watch for regarding different agents. The CDC maintains a list of biological agents that have the potential to be used by terrorists. The list is separated into three categories based upon the type of threat that the individual agents pose to the general public. Those in Category A pose the highest risk. They tend to be easily spread and would likely result in high death rates, panic, and disruption. Agents in this category include anthrax, botulism, plague, and smallpox. Agents in Category B pose less of a threat. They aren't as easy to spread and would not result in as high a death rate as those agents in Category A. Agents in this category include salmonella, *E. coli*, ricin, and typhus. Category C includes agents that are just emerging as new threats. These emerging agents may be readily available, easily disseminated, and may have potentially high mortality rates. Agents in this category include Nipah virus and hantavirus (http://www.bt.cdc.gov/agent/agentlist-category.asp#catdef).

The CDC disseminates information concerning mass casualties which can occur after a variety of natural and man-made events, including hurricanes, earthquakes, explosions, and plane crashes. They provide information and training for first responders and other individuals who deal with a variety of traumas, including blast injuries, wound management, and posttraumatic stress (http://www.bt.cdc.gov/masscasualties/).

A chemical emergency occurs when a chemical agent has been released and harm may result. Chemical emergencies may be either unintentional or intentional. The CDC provides information for the general public and professionals. The general public can find information on creating a safe shelter in their own homes, evacuation during a chemical emergency, and how to deal with contaminated clothing. The CDC provides training for first responders, medical management guidelines, and laboratory information.

Radiation emergencies include the deliberate release of radioactive materials and the detonation of nuclear weapons. Besides providing information for the general public, the CDC also provides information for first responders, clinicians, hospitals, and the public health community.

The CDC founded the Laboratory Response Network (LRN) in 1999 to respond as quickly as possible to biological and chemical attacks. The biological portion of the LRN is a Network of 140 state, local, and international laboratories. There are a variety of types of laboratories, including public health, military, food-testing, environmental, and veterinary. In the case of a biological threat, local, hospital-based labs serve as sentinel labs that recognize possible emerging threats. Once a suspicious case occurs, a local reference laboratory is notified. These laboratories either confirm or deny the suspicions of the sentinel laboratory. Finally, national laboratories can handle the most highly infectious and dangerous threats (http://www.bt.cdc.gov/lrn/factsheet.asp).

The LRN structure for responses to possible chemical threats is similar and consists of 62 laboratories (Figure 5.3). All laboratories perform level 3 functions. At this lowest level, the laboratories

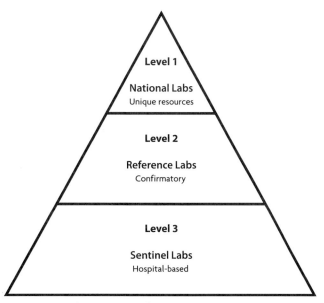

FIGURE 5.3 The structure of the Laboratory Response Network.

are referred to as "sentinel labs," and like sentinels these laboratories watch out for potentially suspicious samples. If a potentially suspicious sample is identified, the sentinel laboratory does not examine the sample or confirm the identity of the sample. The sentinel laboratory will pass the sample along to a level 2 laboratory.

Thirty-seven of the 62 laboratories also perform level 2 functions. These laboratories are referred to as "reference labs." When a suspicious sample is received, the reference lab will perform tests to confirm the identity of the sample. Rather than rely on the laboratories at the CDC, these labs are local and facilitate a quick response to chemical threats. If a laboratory identifies a highly infectious agent, a national lab will be notified. Ten laboratories participate in level 1 activity. At this highest level, the laboratories deal with most dangerous and infections agents (http://www.bt.cdc.gov/lrn/factsheet.asp).

Toxicology and Torts

Since 2001, there has been an increase in interest in toxic substances because of their potential to be used as part of a terrorist attack. Previously, much of the interest in toxic substances focused on the potential of a chemical, pharmaceutical, or product to cause harm to people. This is an area known as *toxic torts*. A toxic tort is a civil case in which an individual claims that a chemical caused harm (or sometimes death). The toxic substance may be a chemical, pharmaceutical, or products that the individual was exposed to in the environment, at home, or at work. In a toxic tort, the injured party, the plaintiff, asks for damages to be awarded from the corporation that was responsible for the harm. Damages are generally awarded in the form of a large sum of money. A successful toxic tort can result in both the plaintiff and the attorney receiving millions of dollars.

While there are toxic substances all around us, most people are not exposed to them in a great enough quantity in their daily lives to incur harm. Many people who are exposed to hazardous chemicals are exposed at work. This exposure tends to be much worse than casual exposure in the environment because the chemicals are often more concentrated, in greater quantities, and the workers may not be aware of the need for protective gear.

A number of chemicals have been the subject of toxic tort cases, including benzene, asbestos, and silica. Benzene has a wide range of applications. Previously it has been used as a gasoline additive and even to decaffeinate coffee. Currently, it is a solvent and is used to manufacture drugs and plastics among other products. Contact with benzene can cause a wide range of problems depending upon the form of contact. Breathing in benzene can cause confusion, dizziness, or even death. Ingesting benzene in tainted food or water can cause vomiting and convulsions. Benzene is a carcinogen. Long-term exposure damages bone marrow, weakens the immune system, and causes leukemia.

Asbestos has long been used in a wide range of applications because of its insulating properties, its strength, and its resistance to both fire and chemicals. It's use was documented in ancient Egypt and it is naturally occurring. Currently it is used in brake shoes on cars, as insulation, in plasters, and in stuccos. Unfortunately, breathing in asbestos fibers causes cancer. Asbestos causes the following diseases: asbestosis, mesothelioma, and cancer.

Silica is found in nature. It is used in glasses, plaster, and as a food additive. Breathing crystalline silica dust can be harmful. It has been linked to silicosis and cancer. The safety of silicone breast implants has been the subject of considerable debate.

TOXIC TORT CASES Although the focus of this text is on the criminal applications of forensics, most of the work in forensics actually occurs in civil court. In fact, the impetus for opening the courtroom to a wider variety of expert witnesses came from toxic tort cases. These cases not only opened the doors for many different types of expert witnesses, but it could be argued that some of the more famous cases have changed how we view scientific evidence, how we view responsibility, how we view harm, and how we protect ourselves.

In this section we will discuss six cases in chronological order: the Thalidomide case, the silicone breast implant cases, the Halcion cases, the Kerr-McGee case, the Pacific Gas & Electric Company (PG&E) case, and the Bendectin (*Daubert*) case. Thalidomide, Halcion and Bendectin (*Daubert*) all dealt with possible negative side effects of medications. Kerr-McGee and PG&E both dealt with toxic chemical exposures resulting from a company's improper handling of hazardous substances. The cases are presented in chronological order because the outcomes of earlier cases, even when an earlier case is not specifically cited in the later case, necessarily affect those cases that come after.

Thalidomide The case involving Thalidomide is not interesting because it resulted in significant litigation or massive amounts of damages being awarded to victims. Thalidomide is interesting because it never received approval in the United States—an action which prevented scores of birth defects. Mothers who took Thalidomide during the first trimester of pregnancy produced babies with severe limb defects. Thalidomide was originally produced in Germany. It came to market in 1957 as a treatment for insomnia and morning sickness. It was aggressively marketed as a safe alternative to barbiturate sedatives (e.g., Seconal) that could easily result in overdose and death. By 1960 it was the most common sedative in Germany, taken by adults and children alike.

Thalidomide was licensed in the United States in 1958 and samples of the drug were sent to physicians as part of a continuing aggressive marketing plan. Approximately 16,000 patients were given the drug, some of whom were pregnant; luckily only 17 children were born with birth defects. Thalidomide was never approved in the United States; this was due almost wholly to the actions of Frances Oldham Kelsey at the FDA who repeatedly asked for more documentation of the drug's safety.

Outside of the United States, over 10,000 children were born with birth defects, almost half of them in Germany. The Thalidomide case resulted in stricter controls being put into place at the FDA for approval of new drugs. There have been U.S. lawsuits involving the drug and damages were paid to victims. Thalidomide was withdrawn from the U.S. market for many years. It is currently used under very controlled circumstances to treat leprosy and certain types of cancer. Any potential user, male or female, must take precautions to prevent conception.

Silicon Breast Implants There have been numerous lawsuits involving silicon breast implants. Most of the lawsuits involve early versions of the implants that ruptured and leaked silicone. Silicone breast implants were invented in the early 1960s. The first lawsuit against Dow Corning was filed in the 1970s. In 1984, an attorney successfully argued that silicone that had leaked out of an implant had caused a woman's autoimmune disease. In 1991, there were two large awards for plaintiffs in breast implant lawsuits ($5.4 million and $7.3 million) and by the end of that year, over 100 individual lawsuits had been filed against Dow Corning. Although the scientific evidence that established any link between the illnesses the women were suffering and their implants was shaky, more and more lawsuits were filed and more damages were awarded. By the end of 1992 over 3,500 lawsuits had been filed. A year later, the number was over 12,000, and by the end of 1994, the number was 19,092.

In 1994 a class action lawsuit settlement was approved and women could apply for money without having to go to court or prove that their implants caused their illnesses. That same year, studies began to appear in medical journals indicating that there was no link between silicone breast implants and illness. Since then the body of research that supports the safety of implants has grown considerably.

Halcion Halcion is a benzodiazepine derivative, an antianxiety agent. Like other benzodiazepines this medication is designed to help people relax and has been used to treat insomnia. The drug was removed from the market in Great Britain and was removed from the United States market for a while due to the significant psychiatric side effects that have been associated with the drug at high dosage. These side effects have given rise to lawsuits against the manufacturer. Some individuals who have taken the medication have become violent. There have been documented suicides and homicides.

Silkwood Case Karen Silkwood worked as a chemical technician at a Kerr-McGee nuclear plant. She was also an activist for worker safety and had testified before the Atomic Energy Commission regarding the lack of safety at the plant. In early November 1974, she was found to be contaminated with dangerous levels of plutonium while working at the plant. There was some debate regarding how she had become contaminated. The company stated that she had contaminated herself, hoping to blame the company. Silkwood maintained that she was purposefully contaminated by the company because of her actions with the Union and the Atomic Energy Commission revolving around the safety of the plant. She died under suspicious circumstances in mid-November. Her father and children successfully sued Kerr-McGee for being responsible for her contamination with plutonium. Regardless of whether she had been purposefully exposed to plutonium or the contamination had occurred during routine work exposure, the company was held liable for that exposure. Foul play was never proved regarding the circumstances of her death. Interestingly, it has not been proven that the facility Silkwood worked in actually posed a hazard either to worker safety or to the community's safety.

Pacific Gas and Electric Erin Brockovich was responsible for helping to successfully prosecute the Pacific Gas & Electric Company. PG&E contaminated the ground water of the town of Hinkley, where their compressor station was located, with hexavalent chromium. Hexavalent chromium is a known carcinogen. PG&E knew that they had contaminated nearby groundwater and wells by 1965, yet they continued to pour water containing hexavalent chromium into unlined holding tanks. To make matters worse, in 1988, the company told residents that they knew of the contamination but that it was not bad, that it was safe to bathe in it or fill their swimming pools with it. Many residents were injured, including unborn children, during the 1960s, 1970s, and 1980s. The company was forced to pay a settlement of $333 million.

Daubert v. Merrell Dow The *Daubert v. Merrell Dow* (1993) case, discussed in depth in Chapter 2, is well known in criminal justice and forensics. The *Daubert* ruling significantly changed the way scientific evidence was viewed in the courtroom, establishing the judge as the gatekeeper for expert testimony at trial. In *Daubert* the plaintiffs argued that the drug Bendectin had caused birth defects in their children. Merrell Dow was named in over a thousand lawsuits.

Drugs and Chemical Analysis

The majority of the work in forensic laboratories consists of analyzing drugs and alcohol for statutory submissions. This mirrors the cases and arrests in the criminal justice system in general.

SUBSTANCE USE, ABUSE, AND DEPENDENCE In nonscientific conversation, substance use, abuse, and dependence can be defined in a variety of ways. Almost everyone has had some interaction with an individual who abused or was dependent upon a substance, however, for the purposes of this text, we will use the definitions provided by *The Diagnostic and Statistical Manual of Mental Disorders-Fourth Edition-Text Revision* (*DSM-IV-TR*) (2000). The *DSM-IV-TR* divides the substance-related disorders into substance-use disorders and substance-induced disorders. Substance-use disorders consist of substance dependence and substance abuse. The substance-induced disorders mimic other mental disorders (anxiety disorder, sleep disorder, for example), except they are brought on by ingesting substances.

Substance use is defined as the use of a substance, generally for its perception altering properties. Substance use is not confined to the use of illegal substances. Alcohol is considered to be a substance. The *DSM-IV-TR* does not define substance use because it is not considered to be a mental disorder. Almost all people will use a substance at one time or another, even if it is just a "glass of wine to relax."

Substance abuse is defined in the *DSM-IV-TR* as "a maladaptive pattern of substance use manifested by recurrent and significant adverse consequences related to the repeated use of substances" (p. 198). In order for a mental health professional or a physician to apply the diagnosis of substance abuse, the individual must meet specific criteria set forth in the *DSM-IV-TR*.

Substance abuse can lead to dependence. According to the *DSM-IV-TR*, "Substance Dependence is a cluster of cognitive, behavioral, and physiological symptoms indicating that the individual continues use of the substance despite significant substance related problems" (p. 192). In substance dependence, which may or may not exhibit physiological dependence, the individual using the substance has experienced significant difficulties because of the substance but continues to use it. Keep in mind, drug and alcohol addiction has a medical component, which, for an addicted individual will make it very difficult to stop using.

WHY DO INDIVIDUALS USE SUBSTANCES?   Criminals and noncriminals use substances for a variety of reasons. Substances may initially be used because they make the users feel good—or not feel as badly as they did before. Young people may use substances to fit in with others in their peer group. Some people abuse drugs to avoid reality and their problems. Some people who abuse drugs do so out of a constant need to alter reality, out of a need for stimulation, and to alleviate boredom.

There is anthropological evidence to indicate that human beings have always used substances to take away pain, to feel better, and to alter perception. A variety of roots and plants have been used medicinally throughout time. Some anthropologists have speculated that it may very well be the case that using substances is highly adaptive and has helped human beings to survive under very adverse conditions.

The Drug–Crime Relationship   The relationship between drugs and crime is a convoluted one at best. The use and abuse of drugs and alcohol contributes to crime in a variety of ways. In the majority of street-crimes, 75 to 80 percent, drugs or alcohol are involved in the commission of the crime. The offender was either under the influence at the time of the crime, or the crime committed was a drug-related crime (e.g., possession of a controlled substance).

Drugs as Motivation for Crime   Drugs may be a prime motivator for crime. This is especially the case for property offenses. Abusers frequently need cash to support their addictions and lifestyles. They steal to get the money they need in order to buy drugs or to buy other items necessary for a drug-abusers lifestyle—for example, they may use the money to buy things for a girlfriend or a child that they are supporting.

Drugs as Catalyst   The use of drugs or alcohol may also make crime more likely to happen. Drugs and alcohol serve as a disinhibitor to many crimes which are sexual in nature and violent as well. Individuals who are under the influence are less likely to employ good judgment. A drug like alcohol slows reaction time, making it less likely that an individual will be able to respond quickly if the situation calls for it. Drugs also impair impulse control. Although some drugs depress the system, other substances (like crack or crystal meth) make the user very aggressive and more likely to react violently to perceived threats.

Many individuals who use substances do so in an attempt to alleviate problems—unfortunately, this often serves to compound their problems. A significant portion of heavy users use substances as a means of self-medication for depression. The use of substances further impairs their ability to constructively address problems.

Drugs and a Criminal Lifestyle   Heavy users of illegal substances are far more likely to engage in a lifestyle that brings them into contact with more criminals and more opportunities to break the law. Individuals who use illegal substances must maintain contacts with individuals who can supply those substances. Individuals who have been arrested for drug-related crimes face enormous barriers to finding legitimate jobs. It is often much easier for them to return to a life of drugs and crime.

COMMONLY USED AND ABUSED DRUGS   Alcohol is the most commonly abused substance in the United States. While alcohol is legal for adults who are 21 years of age or older, it still causes significant problems for many users. There are many illegal substances that are abused and the list of illegal substances continues to grow. As new chemical compounds are tried and abused, the government responds by adding these chemical compounds to the list of illegal drugs.

While the list of possible illegal substances that an officer can encounter at a crime scene is very long indeed, most officers, in the course of their daily work, encounter the same substances repeatedly. Which substances the officer will encounter depends upon where the officer works (certain areas are more likely to have so-called club drugs; crack cocaine is more often encountered in poorer areas) and even what year the officer works on the street. Illicit drugs tend to go through phases of popularity and high use and then periods of low or no use, like any other fad. Also, as substances become illegal, new combinations are made by drug manufacturers. During the 1980s, the inexpensive form of cocaine referred to as *crack* became popular, and some argue it is more addicting than cocaine. It does produce a more intense high than cocaine, but the high tends to be very brief, driving the user to want more very quickly.

Designer Drugs   Designer or *club drugs* first became popular in the 1990s. These drugs are referred to as club drugs because users often take them at clubs. They are called designer drugs because they take advantage of the fact that all substances that are controlled are listed by chemical make-up. Until the exact chemical make-up of a substance is placed on a schedule, it is not illegal. Individuals who run drug labs will chemically alter an illegal substance; the *new* form of the drug, while producing similar effects, is not illegal. States and the federal government respond by continuously updating the list of chemical substances that are illegal.

Methamphetamine Laboratories   In some cases, a substance that is being abused may be controlled in a different manner. Efforts have been made to curtail the meth-lab problem by creating laws criminalizing the possession of precursors and equipment used to manufacture methamphetamine. For many years, pseudoephedrine (found in Sudafed, a Pfizer brand name) has been the main ingredient used to manufacture methamphetamine. As a decongestant, its legitimate use is for relief from a runny nose. While legislators did not want to put pseudoephedrine on the illegal substance list, they did want to control it and wrote legislation to require pharmacies to keep it behind the counter and require customers to show identification in order to purchase the product. This is a step beneath requiring a prescription to obtain a product. Canada has reacted in a similar fashion. The Department of Justice (2006), notes that these *precursor laws* have been so successful that much of the methamphetamine manufacturing in California has moved to Mexico.

While drug abuse is typically seen as an *inner-city* problem, illicit methamphetamine laboratories tend to be a significant problem in rural areas. Individuals who work in these laboratories often steal commonly used farm chemicals (anhydrous ammonia, which is used in nitrogen fertilizer—incidentally, this type of fertilizer was also used to create the bomb that blew up the Oklahoma City Federal Building) to manufacture methamphetamine. Interestingly, other than common farm chemicals, there is a whole host of common substances that can be used to manufacture methamphetamine, including acetone, rubbing alcohol, engine starter, and drain cleaner, to name a few.

Abuse of Inhalants   Inhalants are commonly abused by young people because they are readily available in homes and they do provide a high. Young people will inhale a variety of household chemicals to get high, including hair spray, gasoline, lighter fluid, helium from balloons, canned air, correction fluid, nail polish remover, insecticide, to name just a few.

Generally, the chemical is sprayed into a bag and inhaled from the bag. The high that the user obtains comes from being deprived of oxygen. In most cases, if inhalant use is not chronic, there is little danger to the user. Extended use of inhalants can result in brain and other organ damage. Perhaps the greatest danger arises because the user often has little control over how much substance is taken into the body, unlike pills or alcohol, which give the user some measure of control, inhalation abuse most frequently results in accidental overdose.

Abusing Legally Prescribed Medications   Often overlooked by law enforcement, by far the most frequently abused drugs are those that are obtained by legal prescription. Many individuals become addicted to medications that were prescribed by their doctors. Sometimes it is pain medication (Demoral, Percodan), in other cases it may be an antianxiety agent (e.g., Xanax or Valium). An addicted individual may take more than the prescribed amount, may take the medication for much longer than it is necessary, or may obtain prescriptions from several doctors for the same or similar medications. They may also use alcohol or other medications to achieve a more intense effect than the prescribed medication alone.

Not only can prescribed medication be abused by the individual for whom it was prescribed, but prescription medications can be abused by other individuals who have access to them. Teenagers may take or sell their parents' antianxiety or pain medications. They might also sell the attention deficit hyperactivity disorder (ADHD) medication taken by their younger brothers or sisters. This form of *drug dealing* often goes unnoticed among high school or college students.

VOLUME DRIVING THE FIELD   The sheer volume of drug cases has driven developments in the field. The need to analyze increasing quantities of drug samples has spurred the growth of not only more laboratories but larger ones. This increase in drug submissions to laboratories does not mean that there has been an increase in individuals who are addicted to substances; rather, this increase was driven by changes to the drug laws during the mid-1980s. President Reagan's sweeping changes to the drug laws and the creation of new federal drug laws allowed for more drug prosecutions and those prosecutions required the submission of drug evidence to laboratories.

While the growth of laboratories has been a positive for drug analysis, it does not necessarily mean that more evidence is being analyzed from homicides, rape cases, and other felonies (also, there has not been an increase in homicides or rapes, in fact, these types of crime have been decreasing, so there is actually less evidence from these felonies to be analyzed). Sometimes forensic evidence from these other felonies is not sent to the laboratory for analysis because there is no statutory requirement that it must be analyzed. Sometimes it is merely the fact that end users of forensics (investigators) are not fully aware of the benefits of having forensic evidence sent to the laboratory. As more and more criminal justice professionals understand the benefits of forensic analysis this volume will also go up.

There has also been an increase in the forensic evidence, especially DNA evidence that is being reexamined. Small amounts of blood evidence that were too minimal to be analyzed for DNA 10 years ago can now be analyzed due to technological advances.

CLASSIFICATIONS OF DRUGS   While there are many ways in which drugs can be classified, this text is concerned with only the medical and legal classifications of drugs. In medicine, a wide range of drugs is commonly used to address many, many different types of medical problems. Medications are prescribed to lower blood pressure and to lower cholesterol. Medications are prescribed to facilitate kidney function, to fight infection, to help regulate heart function, and so forth. We are not directly interested in all of these medications, although certainly, too much of almost any drug can cause death or dysfunction, not all medications are equally harmful.

The medical classification of psychoactive drugs categorizes substances according to the effects they have on the body, and divides psychoactive drugs into four groups: opiates, stimulants, hallucinogens, and depressants. For the medical practitioner, drugs are categorized in this way to facilitate their use in a medical setting. Certain medications are commonly used prior to surgery to anesthetize a patient, others paralyze the patient. Some drugs are given for their calming properties

Opiates, such as opium and all of its derivatives [heroin, morphine, codeine, hydromorphone, oxycodone (Percodan), meperidine (Demerol), and methadone], bind to the opiate receptors in the brain. These drugs relieve pain, suppress cough, alleviate diarrhea, dull the senses, and induce anes-thesia, and have a variety of medical uses—as well as the potential for illegal use and abuse. Under a doctor's care, these drugs can be administered orally, transdermally (on the skin through the use of a skin patch), or injected. When used illegally, they are commonly taken orally, smoked, sniffed, or injected. The opiates reduce stress, tension, anxiety, and aggression and have been used for centuries. Even the fictional character Sherlock Holmes used opium. During the nineteenth century, opium was widely used and legally available throughout the United States, where its use greatly increased. This was due in part to Civil War veterans to whom it had been administered for its pain-relieving properties, and also to the influx of Chinese immigrants who brought with them the custom of smoking opium to the western United States. There are both natural and synthetic forms of opiates. Morphine was first isolated in 1806, and codeine was isolated in 1832. Laudanum—an opiate—was commonly given to women during menopause to cure mania. In the 1800s, opiates were also in preparations that could be purchased over the counter for cough, crying babies, and "women's com-plaints" to mention a few of the many, many uses of opium.

Drugs classified as stimulants work on the nervous system; as their name indicates, they stim-ulate the individual and increase alertness. These drugs increase heart rate, respiration rate, and blood pressure, and they suppress appetite. This class of drugs includes amphetamines, cocaine, crack, and ecstasy. Prescription stimulants include Adderall, Dexedrine, and Ritalin—all three of these are used to treat ADHD. Caffeine falls into this category and is a mild stimulant. When pre-scribed, these drugs are taken orally. When abused, these drugs may be taken orally, smoked, or injected. Amphetamines have also been used for weight loss because of their appetite-suppressing properties. Cocaine has a long history as a medicine. It was used to treat depression, and has widely been used as an anesthetic. It was given to women during pregnancy to cure morning sickness as well as other "female complaints." Of course, cocaine was in the original recipe for Coca-Cola, whose name is a derivative of the word cocaine. When cocaine could no longer be included as an ingredi-ent, the manufacturer substituted caffeine.

Hallucinogens distort an individual's perception of reality, which may include changes in what the individual sees, feels, and hears. Common hallucinogens include lysergic acid diethylamide (LSD), Phencyclidine (PCP), and "magic mushrooms" (these are actually mushrooms that contain psilocybin). These substances can be ingested or smoked; mushrooms can be consumed in hot water. These drugs produce increased heart rate and blood pressure, loss of appetite, and sleepless-ness, although the most notable changes are changes that occur in the user's sensory perceptions.

Depressants produce the opposite effect of the stimulant drugs; they depress the central ner-vous system. Perhaps the most used and abused of the depressant drugs is alcohol. The illegal use and overuse of the substance alcohol contributes considerably to the volume of forensic laboratory work in the United States. Blood-alcohol results are statutorily required for every DUI/DWI arrest. Other common depressants include tranquilizers, antianxiety agents (hypnotics), and barbiturates. Many drugs in this class have street value because they produce a noticeable and desirable effect on the body. Some individuals will use stimulants to start their day and end their day using a depressant to go to sleep. All of these drugs are potentially addictive. It is not a bad thing to need help falling asleep or waking up on occasion; it is a bad thing to need help all the time. Individuals who have a chronic sleeping problem and who do not have other medical problems need to make lifestyle changes and address the cause of the sleeping problem. These changes may include eating better, exercising, and reducing levels of stress. Taking medication to go to sleep every night does not address the problem and is only a short-term solution. If an individual becomes dependent upon the medication, that only adds to the other problems.

Commonly prescribed antianxiety drugs include Valium, which was heavily abused in the 1960s and 1970s, and its more recent cousin, Xanax. Depending upon the mental state of the person when the drug is ingested, the effects will vary. If a calm person takes an antianxiety agent, he or she may fall asleep, whereas an agitated individual may only feel much less agitated. These drugs are intended to calm down the user; they produce feelings of overall well-being. Valium, tends to remain in the bloodstream for quite a while, users sometimes complain that they feel fuzzy the next morning. Xanax, on the other hand, clears the bloodstream much quicker and does not tend to produce the ongoing effect of fuzziness.

PSYCHOTROPIC MEDICATIONS Psychotropic medications include any medication that is capable of altering mood, perception, sensation, emotions, or behavior. There are three classes of psychotropic medication: antipsychotics, antianxiety agents, and mood stabilizers. Antipsychotics were first widely used in the 1950s. Medications like Thorazine allowed many formerly hospitalized schizophrenics to leave the hospital and become more participatory members of society. The difficulty with first-generation antipsychotic medication lies in a very significant side-effect profile. With long-term use, all of these early medications produced Parkinson's-like side effects; these individuals often began to have severe motor disturbances. More recent antipsychotics have less severe side-effects.

Although individuals have used all sorts of substances throughout history to alleviate anxiety—most notably alcohol—antianxiety medications were first widely prescribed in the 1960s. Women's use of these medications was especially notable and so common that The Rolling Stones produced the song *Mother's Little Helper* about the "little yellow pill," Valium. This highlights the fact that the majority of drug users who are addicted to substances obtain them legally through a doctor's prescription.

The third class of psychotropic medications consists of the antidepressants and mood stabilizers. Antidepressants, as their name states, work to relieve depression, while mood stabilizers are used with individuals who feel episodes of both depression and mania. The first medication prescribed as a mood stabilizer was lithium. Lithium is a naturally occurring substance and is the third element on the period table. In general, this class of medications doesn't have a high potential for abuse because they do not produce a noticeable "high." It takes a considerable period of time—generally a week or two—of daily use for these drugs to build up in a person's bloodstream and produce their effect. Most individuals seeking a high want to feel the effects immediately.

THE CONTROLLED SUBSTANCES ACT There have been a variety of attempts over the past century to regulate the use of substances. In 1906, the first food and drugs act (the Wiley act) was passed. This regulated foods, drugs, and alcohol. It subjected all of these items to government inspection.

The Harrison Narcotics Tax Act of 1914 regulated the sale and distribution of opium, coca leaves, and their derivatives. It required individuals who dispensed the drug (doctors, veterinarians, and dentists) to keep records. It also imposed a tax on these substances.

During Prohibition (1920–1933), alcohol was outlawed. Far from this prohibition curbing alcohol use during this time, it increased; it also created a very large illegal market for the substance and contributed to the growth of organized crime. Prohibition was a resounding failure and was repealed in 1933 by the ratification of the Twenty-First Amendment to the Constitution.

The Controlled Substances Act became law in 1970 (21 USC, Chapter 13, Subchapter I, Part B, SS 812), making it the legal classification of substances. This federal classification created five "schedules" of drugs. Determination of which schedule a substance will be classified under is dependent upon three criteria. The first is its potential for abuse; the second is its medical use in the United States; the third is its potential for physical and psychological dependence. Schedule I consists of those substances that are deemed to have the highest potential for abuse and dependence, while having no recognized medical use. Schedule V consists of those substances that are deemed to have the lowest potential for abuse and dependence, which also have accepted medical uses. Each state may also create its own schedule of drugs. Some have created a schedule VI for over-the-counter medications.

In order for a drug to be listed on schedule I, it must meet three criteria: it must have a high potential for abuse; it must have no currently accepted medical use in the United States, and there must be a lack of accepted safety for the use of the substance. Heroin, LSD, and cannabis are on this schedule. It is somewhat controversial that cannabis is listed as a schedule I substance—whereas cocaine is a schedule II substance—as a number of states permit cannabis (marijuana) to be used for medical purposes. Since the enactment of the Controlled Substances Act, critics have argued that cannabis has much less potential for abuse and dependency than the other substances on schedule I and does have known medical uses, including as a treatment for pain in cancer patients.

In order for a drug to be listed on schedule II, it must meet three criteria. It must have a high potential for abuse; it must have a currently accepted medical use (sometimes with severe restrictions), and abuse of the substance may lead to severe psychological or physical dependence. Cocaine and Ritalin are on this schedule.

Drugs listed on schedule III meet these three criteria: the substance has less of a potential for abuse and misuse as the substances in schedules I and II; the substance must have a currently accepted medical use in the United States, and it may lead to moderate or low physical dependence or high psychological dependence. Steroids are listed on this schedule. While perhaps not highly addictive; steroids do have the potential for abuse, especially by athletes who abuse them to enhance performance.

When a drug is listed on schedule IV, it meets these three criteria: it must have a low potential for abuse (lower than those drugs in schedule III); it must have a currently accepted medical use in the United States; and abuse of the substance may lead to limited physical dependence or psychological dependence. Drugs such as Xanax, Valium, and the sleep agent Ambien are listed on this schedule. The so-called date rape drug Rohypnol is also on this schedule.

In order for a drug to be listed on schedule V, the substance must meet these criteria: the substance must have a lower potential for abuse than the schedule IV substances; have a currently accepted medical use in the United States; and have little potential for physical or psychological dependence. These drugs may be available over-the-counter, such as some cough medicines that contain only a small amount of codeine.

COLLECTION AND PRESERVATION OF DRUG EVIDENCE   How drug evidence is collected and preserved depends upon at least the following three factors: the nature of the call, the state and type of the drug, and the quantity of the substance found. Because drugs and drug paraphernalia come in many forms, drug evidence is packaged in a variety of ways. Pills and powders can be packaged in appropriately sized evidence envelopes. Liquids should be packaged in glass bottles with lids to prevent leakage. Paraphernalia can be packaged in appropriately-sized boxes. Paraphernalia includes pipes, spoons, and needles used to take various drugs; scales, cooking instruments, and precursor substances used in the manufacturing of drugs.

Drug evidence is not only found at drug crime scenes, it can also be found at any crime scene. How important the evidence turns out to be depends upon the quantity found, whether or not the officer decides to write a citation, and the prosecutor's decision to prosecute or not.

During a drug raid, when there is a search warrant, officers will search for all drug evidence, drug paraphernalia, and related items at the scene. This might include guns and ammunition along with large amounts of cash. Because there is a search warrant, they will conduct a search for these items in all of the areas listed on the warrant—for example, in all rooms of the house and in, on, and under all surfaces in those rooms. However, if the officers are called to the residence because of a domestic dispute, they cannot conduct a search for drugs. However, if the officers see drugs or drug paraphernalia lying out on a table or another place that is in *plain sight*, they will seize it. This is an example of a legitimate seizure and is covered under the plain sight doctrine. The plain sight doctrine states that the officer can seize those objects that are within plain sight or plain view without having a warrant. However, the officer must still have probable cause to believe that the item they are seizing is illegal. At this point, the drugs may simply be seized and destroyed or the individual may be cited. Interestingly, the plain sight doctrine has been expanded to include plain feel, plain smell, and plain hearing.

DRUG IDENTIFICATION   Drugs can be identified through either qualitative or quantitative analysis. Often, a full analysis combines both. A qualitative analysis will answer the question: "what is this?" It is designed to tell us if a substance is a drug and not something else (e.g., blood). Qualitative analysis will also reveal the identity of the substance (heroin as opposed to cocaine). Many of the tests conducted in the field are qualitative in nature, designed to tell forensic professionals what the substance in question is. Once it is ascertained that the substance is an illegal drug, it can be sent to the laboratory for confirmatory testing.

Quantitative analysis tells us how much of a substance is present. This can pertain to a mixture of substances. If several substances have been mixed together, it is important to know the percentage and quantity of each. In many jurisdictions, the question of amount is very important, since the statute requires that the perpetrator possess a *useable quantity* in order for it to be deemed illegal.

There are three types of tests that make up forensic drug identification: screening tests, separation tests, and confirmation tests. Screening tests are used to narrow down the possibilities the drug sample might be and are usually one of three types: spot or color tests, microscopic tests, and spectroscopic tests. Separation tests are usually a form of chromatography and are used to separate a drug from other substances with which it may be mixed. Confirmatory tests, which are used to positively identify a substance as one particular substance, are usually spectroscopic.

Screening Tests   Spot tests are a very quick way to tell if a particular drug is present within a sample. These tests are qualitative in nature and can be done by technicians in the field. These tests work because specific drugs produce certain colors when a chemical reagent is applied to them. For example, the Marquis reagent can be used to test for a variety of substances. The reagent will turn purple when it comes into contact with heroin. It will turn orange, red, or, brown when it comes into contact with amphetamines. The Scott test, which is actually a series of reagents, produces a blue color when cocaine is present.

Microcrystalline tests can also be performed. These tests are more specific than spot tests and also very quick; however, the results are not as specific as chromatography. In a microcrystalline test, a small amount of the substance is placed on a microscope slide along with a liquid reagent. The two substances react and form a crystal. The crystal that is formed is examined under a microscope and can then be easily identified. There are literally hundreds of different microcrystalline tests that have been developed to test for the many illegal drugs and substances.

Separation Tests   Separation tests separate illegal drugs from each other and from other substances. Once they are separated, the sample can be analyzed more fully. These tests are performed in the laboratory and are very useful because it is rare to find a pure chemical substance when drugs are seized in the field. Generally, illicit drugs are not pure and contain a variety of other substances, including sugars, which sometimes can even increase the effectiveness of certain drugs. Sugars, however, are not illegal, and the court is interested in the type and amount of illegal substance that has been seized. Thin-layer chromatography, gas chromatography, and high performance liquid chromatography can all be used at the laboratory to identify drugs submitted for analysis. These tests take more time than spot test or microcrystalline tests, but they are more exact. In order for prosecution to be successful, often these tests are required.

Confirmation Tests   Confirmation tests are used to identify which specific drug has been seized. Gas chromatography and mass spectrometry are used together. Gas chromatography will be used to separate the substances, and then mass spectrometry will be used to ionize the sample, allowing a mass spectrum to be created for each component of the separated substance. Mass spectrometry also has the advantage that only a small sample is needed to obtain identification. Prior to a successful criminal prosecution, confirmatory tests must be performed and the exact chemical makeup of the substance must be determined.

MANDATORY DRUG TESTING Laboratories may receive drug submissions not only from law enforcement departments that are investigating crimes, but offices of probation or parole may submit samples for testing, as do workplaces that screen applicants. Offices of probation and parole require both routine and unannounced drug testing of their clients who have been convicted of drug-related offenses, as well as for many other offenses. The stipulation of nonuse of drugs and alcohol during probation or parole is very common. Some workplaces require drug-testing prior to employment. In the military, soldiers are screened regularly for drugs. Many athletes are also screened for drugs. Three ways in which a laboratory can test for the presence of drugs in an individual are through the use of hair, urine, or blood samples. These types of tests will be discussed in Chapter 9.

Alcohol

Alcohol is legal for individuals over the age of 21. The number of young people below the legal drinking age who use and abuse alcohol is a significant problem. Of legal alcohol users, only about one-quarter have a significant problem with it; those individuals spend a significant amount of healthcare dollars and cause considerable emotional distress to family and loved ones who may be treated poorly, abused, and left behind when the alcoholic dies in a car accident or from end-stage liver disease. The use and abuse of alcohol is a significant social problem in the United States. The numbers of individuals who are addicted to alcohol far surpass the number of individuals who are addicted to illegal substances. Alcohol use and abuse is a contributing factor in many deaths. In 2003, chronic liver disease and cirrhosis was the twelfth leading cause of death (27,503). That same year the leading cause of death was heart disease (685,089) and homicide was fifteenth (17,732) (http://www.cdc.gov/nchs/data/nvsr/nvsr54/nvsr54_13.pdf).

It is illegal in all 50 states to operate a motor vehicle with a tested blood-alcohol content level (BAC) at or above 0.08. In most European countries, the BAC limit is lower than in the United

---

Working in Toxicology

According to a survey conducted in 1997 by the Society of Toxicology more than half of the trained toxicologists entering the workforce take industrial positions, as opposed to positions in academia or government (http://www.toxicology.org/AI/APT/jobmarketsurvey.asp). Many of these individuals will work in the area of product testing, safety, and regulatory compliance.

The Society for Forensic Toxicologists Inc. maintains an employment exchange on their web site. A variety of positions are available at any time (http://www.soft-tox.org/Default.aspx?pn= employment_exchange). Jobs are available for toxicologists with associate's, bachelor's, master's, and doctoral degrees, and also for individuals with postdoctoral training.

An entry-level forensic toxicologist would be employed in a laboratory and would be expected to perform qualitative/quantitative analysis of alcohol and drugs in human biological materials submitted by law enforcement agencies and others. The position would require knowledge of chemical and instrumental screening methods, extraction and purification procedures, and sophisticated instrumental analysis methods. The forensic toxicologist would also be required to prepare technical reports that support analytical findings and testify in a court of law as an expert witness.

Minimum educational requirements for an entry level forensic toxicology position is a bachelor's degree in a physical or natural science, toxicology, pharmacology, criminalistics, forensic science, or a related discipline with at least 24 credit hours in chemistry. Depending upon region of the country, starting salary ranges from the mid-30s to lower-40s. Most individuals begin their career in forensic toxicology at the entry-level, and through experience and education will prepare themselves for more advanced and supervisory positions. Laboratory director positions generally require a master's degree (or more) with at least five years of experience.

States, around 0.05, several countries have a limit of 0.02. In some Middle Eastern countries, consumption of alcohol is entirely prohibited, as is driving under the influence.

A quick test of alcohol that is exhaled in the breath can be done in the field. There are a variety of devices that measure blood-alcohol levels in exhaled breath that are used by law enforcement. Generally, measurement of blood-alcohol will be done with a handheld device at the scene; these are fuel cell-based instruments or semiconductor oxide-based testers. Some manufacturers are even marketing handheld alcohol testers to the public. "Breathalyzer" is the brand name of a device made by Smith and Wesson that measures blood-alcohol content by measuring the alcohol in exhaled breath. The Alcohawk ABI Digital Breathalyzer is one such device; it retails for about $119. (http://www.breathalyzer.net/alcohawkabi.html).

Field devices give a general indication of the blood-alcohol level, but cannot be submitted as evidence in court. In order for the results to be admissible in court, a measurement must be taken with a much more accurate machine at the station. These machines are spectrophotometers. One problem with measuring the blood-alcohol later on, at the station, is that the blood-alcohol level continues to rise after the individual has stopped drinking. In many cases, the blood-alcohol level taken an hour after the individual has ceased drinking will be higher than the blood-alcohol level taken immediately after the individual ceases drinking. There is software available for forensics professionals to use to calculate blood-alcohol levels.

Glossary

Biotoxin—a poison derived from plant or animal sources.

Blood agent—a substance absorbed into the blood.

CDC—Centers for Disease Control and Prevention, a governmental agency that investigates disease prevention and control.

Carcinogen—a substance that causes cancer.

Chelating drug—a drug used to remove a toxin from the body.

Club drugs—drugs like ecstasy that are commonly used in clubs by young people.

Conventional weapons—explosives and firearms.

Crack—freebase form of the drug cocaine.

DSM-IV-TR—*Diagnostic and Statistical Manual of Mental Disorders, Fourth Edition, Text Revision.* Published by the American Psychiatric Association.

Ecotoxicology—effects of toxins are not limited to one organism but impact the entire ecosystem.

Epidemiology—the study of how diseases develop and spread within a population.

Exitania—stimulants.

Euphorica—narcotics.

Hypnotica—tranquilizers.

Immunotoxicologists—toxicologists who study how the immune system is impacted by being exposed to a chemical.

Inebriantia—intoxicants.

Laboratory Response Network—a network of laboratories founded by the CDC to respond to possible biological and chemical attacks.

Marsh Test—designed by James Marsh to detect arsenic.

Mathieu Orfila—considered to be the "father of toxicology."

OSHA—the Occupational Safety and Health Administration, oversees safety and health regulations for businesses.

Phantastica—hallucinogens.

Pharmacology—the study of drugs.

Synthetic—created by humans.

Sulfa drugs—a group of drugs derived from sulfanilamide which inhibit the growth of bacteria. Rarely used today due to the advent of antibiotics.

Toxic tort—a civil case in which an individual claims that a chemical caused harm.

Toxicology—the study of poisonous substance.

Toxin—a poisonous substance.

Vesicant—a substance that causes blistering to the skin, eyes, and other parts of the body.

Webliography

http://www.toxicology.org/index.asp
This is the web site for the Society of Toxicology.

http://www.geradts.com/anil/ij/vol_003_no_002/others/bc/bc001.html
An interesting site discussing Orfila and his classification of poisons.

References

American Psychiatric Association. 2000. *Diagnostic and Statistical Manual of Mental Disorders, Fourth Edition, Text Revision.* Washington D.C.: American Psychiatric Association.

CDC. *Emergency Preparedness and Response: Bioterrorism Agents/Diseases.* Accessed on November 27, 2006, from http://www.bt.cdc.gov/agent/agentlist-category.asp.

CDC. *Facts About the Laboratory Response Network.* Accessed on August 24, 2006, from http://www.bt.cdc.gov/lrn/factsheet.asp.

CDC. *Mass Casualty Event Preparedness and Response.* Accessed on November 27, 2006, from http://www.bt.cdc.gov/masscasualties/.

CDC. 2003. *National Vital Statistics Reports.* 54 (13). Accessed on February 25, 2007, from http://www.cdc.gov/nchs/data/nvsr/nvsr54/nvsr54_13.pdf.

Chelsea Physic Garden. Accessed on April 15, 2007 from http://www.chelseaphysicgarden.co.uk/index.html.

Dietz, P. February 14, 2000. *Product Tampering.* Accessed on November 27, 2006, from http://www.facsnet.org/tools/ref_tutor/tampering/prolif.php3.

Job Market Survey: Past, Present, and the Future SOT Placement Committee Report. Accessed on May 24, 2006 from http://www.toxicology.org/AI/APT/jobmarketsurvey.asp.

Ritter, S. K. February 5, 2007. Chemist Wins Gold in Million-Dollar Arsenic Challenge. *Chemical and Engineering News.* Accessed on February 25, 2007, from http://pubs.acs.org/cen/news/85/i07/8507prize.html.

Society of Forensic Toxicologists Inc. Accessed on May 24, 2006 from http://www.soft tox.org/Default.aspx?pn=employment_exchange

U.S. Department of Justice: National Drug Intelligence Center. November 2006. *National Methamphetamine Threat Assessment 2007.*

U.S. Department of State. March 14, 2003. Saddam's Chemical Weapons Campaign: Halabja, March 16, 1988. Accessed on November 27, 2006 from http://www.state.gov/r/pa/ei/rls/18714.htm.

Review Questions

1. How does the CDC function in relation to toxicology?
2. Explain the difference between quantitative and qualitative drug analysis.
3. Describe the differences among the five schedules of drugs.
4. What are the differences between separation tests and confirmation tests?
5. What does the broad field of toxicology study?
6. What type of analysis is done most often in forensic laboratories?
7. List and describe the three classes of psychotropic medications. Which of these has the greatest potential for abuse?
8. Why might a drug manufacturer try to develop new "designer drugs?"
9. What are some of the limitations of using hair for drug analysis?
10. We all know that illegal substances are abused, but what are some of the common legal substances that are misused and abused?

Some Things To Think About

1. Construct an argument for moving cannabis off of Schedule I.
2. The text states that while the number and size of forensic laboratories has increased, there has not necessarily been an increase in the forensic evidence from nondrug felonies. Develop some ways in which submission of forensic evidence from nondrug felonies might be increased.
3. When might the use of substances be an adaptive rather than a maladaptive behavior?

CHAPTER 6

Document Analysis, Computer Forensics, and Fraud Investigation

Health Care Fraud

Insurance Fraud

Securities Fraud

Bank Fraud

Telemarketing and Computer Fraud

Tax Fraud

Identity Theft

The areas of document analysis, computer forensics, and fraud investigation are often intertwined. Document analysis has traditionally been investigated by law enforcement. In the modern era, document analysis has expanded to include examination of all sorts of computer-generated documents and their corresponding inks and papers. The advent of the laser color printer has been a boon to would-be counterfeiters. Computer forensics includes not only papers, documents, and even currency generated by computers but also data stored on computers. A vast majority of fraud investigation will involve either the analysis of documents or computer forensics as investigators follow the paper trail and the money trail to the perpetrator.

DOCUMENT ANALYSIS

Criminalistics focuses on areas that have been useful to law enforcement and advanced by law enforcement, but were not of interest to the scientific community in general. This is why document analysis is a subarea of criminalistics. It has been of interest mostly to the law, whether it is civil law that is concerned with the authenticity of a will or criminal law that is concerned with the source of counterfeit money. Throughout history, the origin of signatures, documents, and currency have been questioned. Like the area offender identification (e.g., fingerprints), document analysis historically was carried out by law enforcement officers within their own organizations. Law enforcement did not seek the assistance of scientists at universities to analyze documents. Training was done in-house and on-the-job.

Document analysis comprises the analysis of just about everything that has to do with any type of document. This includes handwriting and signature identification; typewriter, computer printer, fax machine and copier machine identification (and documents produced by copier, fax, and printer); and analysis of inks, pencil lead, writing instruments, and papers. Document analysis also consists of the examination of money, forms of identification, wills, tickets, checks, certificates, and suicide notes. Document analysis may also answer questions concerning document age, time of writing, alteration, forgery, recovery, and reconstruction.

There is a wide array of professional organizations to which a forensic document examiner can belong, including the International Association of Questioned Document Examiners, World Association of Document Examiners, American Association of Handwriting Analysts, and the National Association of Document Examiners. There are also regional document examiner associations, and state document examiner associations. It is not necessary for an examiner to belong to many different organizations, but it is a good idea to belong to one or more that will provide opportunities for professional growth, including access to training, journals, and colleagues in the specific subareas of document examination. Like all of the subareas of forensic science, document analysis changes rapidly because of advancing technology. It is only through continuous training and education that the document examiner can stay abreast of what is happening in the field.

Working and Training in Document Analysis

While many subareas of forensic science require specialists to have master's or doctoral degrees, document specialists are usually police officers who have worked and trained in this specialization. They may have obtained a college degree, but the most common educational background is completion of high school and the police academy. Also, there is no set training program through which a document analyst must progress, and no specific degree or certification that qualifies an examiner. It is recommended that the individual who is interested in document analysis earns a bachelor's degree. Although this degree could be in a physical or biological science, it could also be in criminal justice or any other area, as long as some coursework in microscopy has been completed. Of all the tools that can be used in document examination, the microscope is probably the single most important tool—other than the examiner's own eyes. The document examiner in training should also complete a supervised apprenticeship. During the apprenticeship, the examiner will work under a more senior professional. This allows the apprentice to be exposed to the field, to conduct analyses, and even to make mistakes under the guidance of someone who can turn those mistakes into opportunities to grow and gain confidence.

Tools Used in Document Analysis

The most important tool in a document analyst's arsenal is the microscope and the magnifying glass. Unlike those areas of forensics that conduct analyses on the molecular level, document analysts mostly employ low-powered magnification. Other commonly used tools include cameras, a variety of light sources, and thin-layer chromatography.

Both microscopes and magnifying glasses are used to examine the surface of papers and documents. A document that looks legitimate to the naked eye may reveal, through very low magnification, erasures, additions, broken lines, and differences in ink. Using a camera gives the document examiner the advantage of being able to photograph the document using different filters. An infrared filter can be used to make erased signatures and alterations on a document visible. Ultraviolet light can be used to differentiate between different inks or visualize other substances on the paper. Oblique lighting can help the examiner to visualize indentations. Thin-layer chromatography on occasion can be used to determine the chemical makeup of an ink, although this is often avoided because it is a destructive technique.

Handwriting and Signature Identification

Handwriting and signature identification are based on the following two principles: first, if there are enough known examples of an individual's writing, it is possible to determine if the writing sample in question is authentic or a fraud; second, every person's writing exhibits numerous individual characteristics and through these individual characteristics, identification can be made. It is generally possible to identify most handwriting and signatures when there are enough known samples of the individual's writing and if the existing samples exhibit enough individual characteristics (Brunelle in Saferstein 1982).

The basis of all handwriting and signature identification lies in the examiner having known samples of the individual's writing. These are samples in which there is no doubt regarding their authorship. They may be documents that were signed in the presence of others, handwritten letters that are not questioned, or even a journal kept by the individual. The journal can be of considerable value because it will contain a considerable amount of writing and will exhibit many individual characteristics. Prior to beginning any analysis, the document examiner should ask for as many samples—produced under as many different conditions as possible—to be supplied. It is better to collect "naturally occurring" samples, in other words, specimens that were spontaneously written, rather than those generated by asking a suspect to provide a writing sample. It is very common for an individual who is asked to provide a sample to attempt to alter or disguise his or her writing. While these attempts are not generally successful, they make it much more difficult to discern the author's true individual characteristics and will add a layer of difficulty to the analysis. A naturally occurring sample will provide the examiner with a look at the author's normal writing and individual characteristics should be apparent.

The document analyst relies upon individual characteristics being apparent in writing. If handwriting exhibited no individual characteristics, everyone's would be identical. When young children learn to write, they are taught a specific method of making all of the letters. New writers tend to exhibit few individual characteristics in their writing because they are copying an example. Children spend several years in school copying examples, first letters, then words, then entire sentences. In the beginning, all children concentrate on their writing. They concentrate on following the example that the teacher has written on the board, or that is in their workbook, or on a handout. As the child gains more confidence in making letters and words, he or she no longer has to concentrate as much on the physical action of writing. In time every one of us can write without giving it much thought at all. Think about it, how much thought did you give it the last time you signed your name? Was it on a credit card receipt, or on a birthday card? Perhaps you don't even remember. That would not be unusual because your writing, at least the physical action of your writing, is now automatic. It no longer takes a conscious effort to write. As we age, and are no longer copying an example or thinking about our writing, our writing becomes more and more unique and individual characteristics emerge. The greater the number of individual characteristics, the easier it is for the document examiner to make confident statements about the author of the document.

If samples that were written under different conditions are available, they should be provided. One fact that any document examiner knows is that a person's writing varies under differing conditions, as does a signature. Variation is normal and does not necessarily indicate forgery. The document examiner may need to make a determination as to how much variation is normal and how much indicates forgery. When examining any particular document or signature, the document examiner must be aware of these two diametrically opposed facts. First, almost everyone's writing will exhibit individual characteristics, and second, variation is normal. Take a look at your own signature; actually, take several looks at your signature on a variety of documents over time. For most individuals, the signature will look basically the same over time. In some cases, your writing may be neater. The signature on your driver's license will tend to be neater than your signature on a credit card receipt. In some cases an individual's signature will change. Perhaps you stopped using a middle initial. Perhaps, because you have to sign your name frequently, you only clearly write the first letters of your first and last name and the remainder of the signature has become more of a scrawl. Regardless of these changes, all of these examples are still your authentic signature. Unfortunately, there are not specific guidelines as to how much variation is *normal*. The document examiner does not have a specific formula to use that differentiates between legitimate variation and a forgery.

A variety of factors can affect an individual's writing. These include health, age, tiredness, stress level, hurriedness, intoxication, writing instrument, writing surface, movement, and duress. Any one of these factors may cause writing or a signature to take on a very different appearance from the individual's usual writing. Also, the reason why the signature was originally produced will affect its appearance. A signature on a formal document, like a will, tends to be different from a signature on a credit card receipt. The individual signing the will or other legal document produces a more careful signature because of the importance of the document. The individual signing the credit card receipt is more likely to scrawl a form of signature. The seasoned examiner knows that it is not the best idea to expect exemplars from credit card receipts or hotel registers to exactly match the signature on a will. Generally, individuals who suffer from ill health, have poor eyesight, or who are intoxicated, overly tired, or of advanced age tend to exhibit writing that is sloppier, more poorly connected, varied considerably, of inconsistent pressure, and deviating from the lines on the paper. Such differences should not be taken as definite proof that the writing or signature is not valid. A will signed 20 years ago by a 57-year-old may have a considerably different signature than a codicil signed a month ago by a 77-year-old. Yet both signatures may very well belong to the testator.

When examining a written document, not only does the examiner look at the writing, but also takes into account line and letter spacing, pressure, margins, size of letters, pen lifts, and connecting strokes. All of these characteristics may become individualized. So the document examiner does not take a signature by itself, unless that is all there is to examine—which is rarely the case—but instead looks at the overall document that was produced. It is much more difficult for a forger to fabricate an entirely written document, like a letter or holographic will. The lengthier the writing is, the more likely that the forger's own individual characteristics will become apparent. This is one of the reasons why many forgers confine themselves exclusively to signatures.

Most forged signatures are forged in one of three ways. The signature can be traced, simulated, or simply written in the forger's own handwriting—this latter method isn't really a forgery at all. A traced signature is produced by copying over an authentic signature. This can be done using a sheet of carbon paper or the forger can place the document to be signed directly under the signature which is traced by copying the indentation on the paper in ink. The forger can also place the document to be forged on top of the authentic signature and, if the document is sheer enough, trace the signature through the forged document. All of these methods produce signatures with unnatural pressure indentations and flow. If the forger uses carbon paper to create the signature, there is the added problem of the chemical transferred from the carbon paper which is easily identified upon analysis.

A simulated forgery is a freehand drawing of a signature. The forger will copy and practice the signature to be forged repeatedly and then sign the document to be forged. These types of forgeries produce more natural pressure variations; however, the forger's own individual writing characteristics tend to come through. Shapes of letters tend to vary, as do finishing strokes. Just as in the traced forgery, there tends to be pressure and flow variations in a simulated forgery. It is difficult to write a forged signature with the same natural flow that you would your own signature.

A third type of forgery isn't really an attempt at forgery at all. The forger simply signs the document in his or her own handwriting, making no attempt at all to reproduce a signature that is not distinguishable from the legitimate signature. This type of forgery, of course, takes little or no planning and, if questioned, is easy to identify. Since the forger uses his or her own writing, with all of its individual characteristics, it is also easier to uncover the identity of the forger. This type of forgery can be found when an individual steals credit cards or applies for credit cards under the names of other people. Often the forger will commit this crime repeatedly and eventually law enforcement will become aware of a pattern. Most petty thieves commit their crimes in the localities in which they live and work, so law enforcement can concentrate their efforts. The forger can also sign stolen checks. This crime can occur in a variety of ways, someone might find a lost checkbook, or an individual who works for an elderly woman may steal several checks from her checkbook and then fill them out (to herself, a friend, or to CASH) and cash them. If the checkbook is balanced, the discrepancy is bound to become apparent on a subsequent statement.

Document examiners may also deal with disguised writing. In some instances a writer may not make an attempt to copy someone else's style of writing, but may simply try to disguise his or her own writing. This individual may change their handwriting's slant; write with their nondominant hand, use block lettering or printing, or irregular spacing. Disguised writing often appears forced and unnatural. Such writing is commonly found in ransom notes, written threats, hold-up notes, and similar documents—or when an individual is asked to present a writing sample.

Machine Identification

The document examiner may be asked to identify the machine that produced a certain document. Historically, much of this work was typewriter identification. Typewriters could develop a variety of individual characteristics; there might be defects in the letters, defects of spacing, and defects in the ribbon. However, as typewriters have become largely obsolete, this type of analysis is now very rare. It is far more likely an examiner is asked to identify a fax machine, copier, or printer that produced a document—and far more difficult because these devices are less likely to develop individual characteristics. When a fax is received, the receiving machine will print out an identifying line of characters. However, this identifies the fax number more than the actual machine. Copiers and printers, unlike their earlier counterpart the typewriter, generally do not develop individual characteristics unless something is wrong with the machine. An older printer may not distribute toner evenly or may collect debris that can affect the quality of printing or produce irregular lines on documents that emerge from the machine. It would be very difficult to locate one particular machine in the absence of a suspect. However, if there is a suspect and he or she had access to certain machines, a particular defect would make it easier to determine which machine was responsible for the copy in question. Also, it can clearly be stated on a search warrant that copiers and printers are to be seized from the home or place of business of a suspect and then law enforcement can examine these machines for the defect.

Analysis of Inks, Pencil Lead, Writing Instruments

A document examiner may also examine inks, pencil lead, and other writing instruments, although, by far, the most common analysis of these would be ink analysis. Documents written in pencil just are not all that common and neither is the analysis of other writing instruments, but inks are very common in our everyday world.

Different sorts of chromatography can be used to analyze inks, along with eletrophoresis techniques. These techniques separate out the various component parts of ink. These are all destructive techniques and would be used after nondestructive techniques such as lighting techniques. Ballpoint inks prior to 1950 were solvent based and post 1950 were water based. Different inks are used for printers and fax machines. Ink-jet inks can be either water based or solvent based as well.

Sometimes the document examiner will be asked to identify a particular ink. The question can also be whether all of the ink on a document comes from the same source. Although all of the writing on a check may look like the same black ink, analysis can reveal that some of the numbers were added or written over.

Counterfeiting

Document analysts also examine counterfeit monetary instruments. After the inception of a national monetary system in the United States, counterfeiting became a significant problem. It has been estimated that in 1860, between one-third and one-half of all U.S. currency was counterfeit. So severe was the problem of counterfeiting that the United States Secret Service was formed on July 5, 1865, to deal with the problem. Within 10 years, the Secret Service had considerably curtailed the counterfeit problem (http://www.frbsf.org/federalreserve/money/funfacts.html).

During the past decade or so, there has been a resurgence of counterfeiting activity. With the advent of computer and laser printing technology and desktop publishing it is possible to create good counterfeit money with few counterfeiting or computer skills. This has been one of the driving forces behind the security enhancing changes in United States paper currency instituted by the U.S. Bureau of Engraving since 1996 when the $50 note was redesigned.

COMMON METHODS OF COUNTERFEITING One simple way to counterfeit is to cut the corners off of a higher-denomination bill (like a $50) and glue them onto a smaller-denomination bill (like a $1). The bill is generally presented folded, with the face of the bill covered, in the hopes that the cashier or other unsuspecting person will not look closely at the bill. Of course, this is a very crude method of counterfeiting and is easily detected (Figure 6.1).

Another crude method is to photocopy legitimate 20s or 50s using a black-and-white copier and then to *colorize* the counterfeited bills to resemble the familiar dark green of United States currency. These types of counterfeit bills do not feel like U.S. currency because they are made of lightweight copy paper. U.S. currency is made of rags. It is very heavy and very durable—ever notice that a dollar bill will survive a normal wash cycle none the worse for wear? This type of counterfeit is also easy to spot because the ink on the counterfeit bill will have a tendency to smear when rubbed.

FIGURE 6.1   Notice the error in this poorly counterfeited bill.

This is a very basic way to tell if a bill is legitimate—rub it on a piece of paper. U.S. currency will not smear; however, ink will come off onto the paper.

The vast majority of technologically advanced counterfeiting used to be accomplished through the lengthy process of offset printing. Using this process, photographic negatives are created of actual bills, and then these negatives are used to create plates that contain different details of the bill. When the counterfeit bills are produced, these different plates layer the details of the bill. Although a time-consuming process, the counterfeit bills that are created are of high quality.

Modern desktop publishing and color laser printers have made the colors of U.S. currency much easier to duplicate. While serious counterfeiting used to be left to professionals who used offset printing presses, technology has made it possible for many small-time criminals to dabble in counterfeiting. Although these desktop-counterfeiters do not create counterfeit bills in the high volume that professional counterfeiters would, desktop counterfeiting continues to account for a greater and greater proportion of the counterfeiting that occurs within the United States.

COMBATING COUNTERFEITING   Measures can be taken both as new currency is printed to decrease the ease of counterfeiting and measures can be taken by businesses that take in currency to lessen the likelihood that counterfeit bills can be successfully passed. To combat the increase in desktop counterfeiting, the Bureau of Engraving and Printing began making changes to currency to enhance security. Changes have been made to all notes except the $2 and $1 notes. A watermark has been added. This is done during the printing process by impressing a metal stamp onto the currency. The watermark can be seen by holding the bill up to the light. *Color-shifting ink* is used on portions of the bill, so that when you tip the bill, the colors change. Microprinting is utilized on the bill. Microprinting is very tiny printing that is used in several places on the bill and is difficult to duplicate. The new bills use several colors, rather than the dark green that was used in the past (http://www.moneyfactory.gov/section.cfm/7/35).

One of the easiest ways to combat all but the best counterfeiters is to look for these security features on all bills that are received. Counterfeit detection pens are a common tool that can be used at cash registers to detect counterfeit bills. These pens use an iodine solution that reacts with the wood-base of most copier papers and will *mark* counterfeit bills in one color and legitimate bills in another color.

When counterfeit bills surface, they are collected and compared to others. Generally, when numerous counterfeit bills come to light they are from a single source. Often they are all of a single, higher denomination, like 20s or 50s. Investigators will examine all seized bills looking for common items or common errors on each bill. The same sort of smear or an incorrectly made letter or line usually indicates a common source. Eventually all of the bills can be submitted as evidence to gain a conviction.

Check Alteration

A check can be altered in three ways: erasures, additions, and writing over. Erasures on a check may be made mechanically or chemically. Mechanical erasures are done using an eraser and result in some of the paper the check is made of being lost. This is often clearly visible upon close inspection with the naked eye or through the use of a low-powered microscope. Chemicals may also be used to dissolve the ink on the check, referred to as *check washing*. Check washing is very easy to do. Criminals will frequently use acetone (nail polish remover) and place the check or a portion of the check in the acetone. Acetone dissolves the dye-based ink on the check and the criminal can simply rewrite the check. Frequently, all but the signature will be submerged in the acetone, leaving the legitimate signature on the check; the criminal will simply write the check out to a different person for a different amount. Checks can be pretreated with chemicals that make check washing more difficult. These chemicals can cause the word *void* to appear on the check when chemicals are applied to it.

Checks may also be altered by making additions to the writing that exists on the check. Most often the criminal will alter the amount of the check. This type of alteration can be very easy to detect, especially if the inks used are visibly different. If the difference is not visible to the naked eye, it may be visible upon closer inspection (Figure 6.2). There will probably also be pressure differences and other differences in the legitimate and added writing. Checks can be altered simply by writing over the original writing. This is a very unsophisticated technique and can generally be detected with the naked eye.

Document Age

Sometimes document examiners are asked to establish the age of a document, or to certify whether or not all portions of the document are of the same age. In this case, the examiner will focus the examination on the paper and the ink. A document purportedly produced in the 1920s would not be on copier paper, nor would it be printed by a computer. A legal document generally is printed on a heavier paper than a memo. Historically, writing papers have varied considerably and the older the document, the easier it is to establish a timeframe for when it was written. The same can be said for inks. Inks produced from the 1950s onward are very different from most inks produced prior to 1950. The

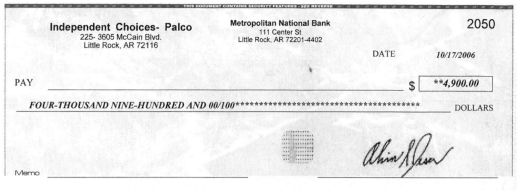

FIGURE 6.2   The errors in this counterfeit check are not obvious to the untrained observer.

document examiner establishes the likely age of the paper and the age of the ink. If these are inconsistent with the supposed age of the document, something is likely amiss. The document examiner also needs to examine many portions of the document in question. In longer documents, while much of the entire document may be legitimate, one or two pages may be added. If it is a written document, especially a letter or a handwritten will, it is possible that words or phrases have been added at a much later date than the original was produced. Of course, the signature must also be examined.

Time of Writing

Occasionally, a question will arise as to when a document was written or signed, or if the document was written and signed at the same time. A blank piece of paper might have been signed and then the body of the document written. In some cases, it can be very difficult to determine the time of writing accurately. If a document was written in the 1940s, but the ink used for the signature was not manufactured until the 1950s, obviously the document was signed much later. When there is a considerable time span between the two writing times, this can be a very difficult question to answer. A difference in pen inks can also indicate a difference in writing time.

Document Alteration

Documents can be altered in many different ways. Three common methods are through erasures, obliterations, and additions. Each can be easily detected by the trained document examiner. When an erasure is done, the forger simply uses a method to erase ink from the paper; this may be done either physically or chemically. Physical erasure causes disturbance of the paper fibers which—if not visible to the naked eye—is certainly visible under a low-powered microscope. Chemical erasures are not as easy to detect but can become apparent through the use of nonstandard lighting, colored filters, and high-contrast photography.

Obliterations are an attempt to conceal what was originally written by writing or even scribbling over it. Obliterations are obvious and, through the use of infrared lighting and colored filters, the document examiner can filter out the ink that was used to obliterate the writing underneath.

Additions are another common method of forgery. The forger may simply add more writing to a document—changing the amount on a check, for example. In this case, the examiner will focus on whether or not different inks are used, as well as identify any unexplained variation in the writing.

Document examiners must be familiar with pencil lead and a wide variety of inks. The vast majority of all writing that is analyzed is produced by some type of ink—whether it is ink from a ball-point pen or ink from a computer printer.

Document Recovery and Reconstruction

Forensic document examiners may be asked to recover or reconstruct documents that have suffered considerable damage—intentional or unintentional—from water or fire. Documents that have been submerged in water can be dried by the examiner. If the ink on the document has faded or disappeared entirely, the examiner can use infrared or ultraviolet light, side-lighting, and photographic techniques to successfully visualize the writing.

Charred documents can be very difficult to work with. They are usually very brittle and may break or disintegrate when touched. Some success can be achieved if the document is moistened. Depending upon the extent of the burning much of the contents may be unrecoverable.

Suicide Notes, Ransom Notes, Threat Letters

All documents give clues to their authorship. Counterfeit money is examined for similar mistakes, leading to the creator. Likewise, anonymous ransom notes and threat letters are examined for individual properties that point to their authorship. In some cases, suicide notes, ransom notes, or threat letters may be examined for handwriting to determine their authorship. A forged suicide note can be an attempt to disguise a homicide.

FORENSIC LINGUISTICS Forensic linguistics looks beyond the mechanics of writing. Forensic linguistics examines the words that are used, their patterns, grammar, syntax, and misspellings. It looks at how language is used to identify the author. It can be used in written document analysis to determine if a portion of a handwritten document was added by someone other than the primary author of the document.

Forensic psychiatrist James Brussel used forensic linguistics to examine notes left by the Mad Bomber (see Chapter 11). Through analysis of the vocabulary (the author of the notes used archaic phrases like *dastardly deeds*) and sentence construction (the author used the construction *the ConEd* instead of *ConEd* when referring to the electric company that he held a grudge against) he determined that the individual responsible for the explosive devices was of Eastern European descent.

The unabomber, David Kaczynski, was caught, in part, due to the use of forensic linguistics. An analysis was conducted to compare the "Manifesto" that the unabomber had written, which was published by the *New York Times* and the *Washington Post* in 1995, to copies of handwritten letters David Kaczynski had written to his brother. They were remarkably alike in both vocabulary and spelling mistakes.

On a more mundane level, forensic linguistics can also help determine if a paper written by a college student was plagiarized. Forensic linguistics will examine the language used throughout the paper. If significant portions of the paper were stolen from a source, this will be revealed. If the entire paper was stolen, forensic linguistics can still help spot this crime. The paper in question can be compared to other known sources of the students writing, for example, essays written in class. While polished papers are written differently than essays that are written without research or editing, the student's basic linguistic style will not vary considerably. Many professors use a rudimentary form of forensic linguistics when they determine that a suspicious paper *doesn't sound like the student wrote it*.

COMPUTER FORENSICS

If any area of forensics is new, it is computer forensics. Computer forensics is not a forensic science in the way that forensic anthropology is a forensic science. Computer forensics brings together the disciplines of computer science and forensics. It is the use of computer science applications for the investigation of possible crimes.

The Impact of the Computer and the Electronic Age on Crime

Twenty years ago, there were few activities that would fit the current definition of computer crime. Although the Internet existed, its connectivity was limited to the government and major research institutions and universities. Twenty years ago, computer crime consisted of entering and altering databases. This was generally done by someone within the company that had access to computer mainframes used to store data. Computer crime also, in a limited way, may have consisted of criminal enterprises that kept their records on computers—although this certainly would have been limited in nature. Twenty years ago, very few people had the knowledge or ability to commit computer crimes.

As technology advanced and as the Internet became more accessible during the mid-1990s and more people and data went online, the opportunities for computer crime increased, including identity theft. Computer knowledge went from being the purveyance of relatively few to being something that the vast majority of the population possessed. In 1995, fewer than one out of seven individuals was online. By 2005, that number was closer to two out of three (Almasy 2005).

In 1985, there were relatively few individuals with the requisite skill to commit computer crimes. It required a lot of specialized knowledge. More than 20 years later, it requires very little skill to commit computer crimes. Some crimes do require considerable skill or access to protected databases, so an individual with basic knowledge of how to use e-mail can commit fraud. Teenage hackers routinely hack into government web sites—among others. They do this for fun and the challenge of getting into a web site. Hacking into government sites can be especially attractive to teenage hackers simply because it is seen as an extra defiant act. Some teen hackers go on to become legitimate computer specialists who advise companies and governments concerning computer security. But hacking any site is a crime and perpetrators, whether teens or older are subjected to fines.

Technology in and of itself is neither good nor bad, it just *is*. Technological advances create opportunities for new sorts of crimes. In the Old West, criminals stole horses. When the railroad linked the eastern and western United States, criminals robbed trains. With the advent of the automobile, the getaway car was born. The advent of the computer age has allowed criminals to use this tool in their criminal enterprises as well.

Terrorist Use of Computer and the Internet

Terrorists, like everyone, have adjusted to the expanded use of the computer. Technology has always been a great asset to terrorists. Better explosives have made it possible to bring down larger buildings. The modern telephone system in Paris enabled Ayatollah Khomeini to consolidate his power and organize the overthrow of the Shah of Iran in 1979—something that could not have been done with the poor telecommunications in Iran. Cyberterrorism also presents opportunities to terrorists. Cyberterrorism can be used both as a terrorist tactic and as a *force multiplier*.

Cyberterrorism can be used as a terrorist tactic, just like other tactics of kidnapping, hijacking, and suicide bombings. Because cyberterrorism tends not to involve as much of a direct threat of violence as more traditional terrorist tactics, it is more likely to be used in conjunction with more traditional techniques, as a force multiplier.

A force multiplier increases the potential harm that can be caused by terrorists. The Internet can be used by terrorist groups to create the image that they are much larger and more powerful than they actually are. Terrorists can also communicate with each other via the Internet. They can encrypt messages on web pages. Terrorists can spread their message via the Internet in the same way that hate groups spread their message. By spreading their message, terrorists can also use the Internet to create a larger support network.

Why Computer Crimes Are Increasing

While trends indicate that the crime rates for most types of crimes are falling, the rate of computer crimes is increasing. This is due to four factors: first, there are many more computers and users; second, much more information is in electronic form on computers and in databases, and a significant proportion of this data is sensitive and wanted by criminals; third, more people have the necessary skills required to use computers and get online; and fourth, the level of interconnectivity has greatly increased. All of these factors help create more opportunities for computer crime.

The increase in the number of computers has provided opportunities for more users to get online. Many homes have computers, and also many schools, universities, and libraries are connected. There has also been an increase in handheld computer devices and an increase in cellular technology.

More information than ever before is stored in electronic form in databases that are vulnerable to attack. Data that is transmitted from computer to computer can be intercepted as it travels from server to server. A lot of sensitive data is available online that can be useful to criminals, for example, credit card companies have databases of customers' credit card numbers.

While it may have been unusual 20 years ago for someone to have the requisite computer skills to hack, now many people have the skills required to use computers, get online, and hack. The population in general is acquiring computer skills earlier. Children in kindergarten frequently use computers.

If computers were isolated, there wouldn't be much of a problem with computer crime. But with many, many computers being connected by the Internet, this connectivity provides access for both good and evil purposes.

Computer crime provides advantages over more traditional forms of crime. The computer is fast. The computer also provides access to many more victims. Whether it is a scam artist or a pedophile, the computer allows the would-be offender to set up and commit a crime easily, with great speed, and in many cases, almost unlimited access to possible victims.

Recognizing and Recovering Computer Evidence

Every law enforcement officer is trained at the academy to recognize and collect evidence at crime scenes. Yet this training does not extend to the recognition and collection of computer crime evidence. The hard-drive of a desktop computer may contain evidence of a computer crime. A laptop may contain computer crime evidence. Evidence may also be found on disks and a variety of "mass storage devices." Computers also have a variety of peripherals that may contain evidence, such as zip drives. Information can also be stored on a variety of handheld devices, like PDAs. With the exception of the hard-drive in a desktop, all of these items have a considerable amount of portability. Unless the data on a device is examined in detail, it is impossible to know if it may or may not contain evidence.

Recovering evidence from computer crimes can be very tricky. A key problem is that most officers and first responders are not properly trained in the recovery of computer evidence. Mistakes can often be made at this initial stage that will cause more damage to the evidence.

If a computer is networked or accessible to the Internet the owner may still have access to it from a remote site and may be able to remove digital evidence. Also, the owner may have written commands into the computer to destroy files and folders when an unauthorized user attempts to access the computer.

Perhaps the most important thing a first responder can do is make sure that trained individuals are called to the scene to handle all evidence. Anyone who has not had special training in recovering computer evidence should not touch computer evidence or try to unplug or seize devices.

It is often recommended that a copy of the hard drive is created prior to any attempt to access information on the drive. Law enforcement can work with the copy while retaining the hard drive in exactly the condition that it was found.

If a computer-savvy criminal wants to hide evidence on a hard drive, it is possible to make it almost impossible to access information. This can be done by creating virtual hard drives, or it can be done through encryption. Some individuals, rather than store illegal images on their own computer, will hack into other computers to store their data. However, most individuals do not make a concerted attempt to hide evidence on their hard drives. Most information is either readily available or the only attempt to hide evidence is through simple passwords.

Types of Computer Crimes

There is not one computer crime. There are many different types of actions that may be classified as computer crimes. It is useful to break-down computer crimes into three subareas: computers used to assist in other crimes, computer-specific crimes, and use of the computer as a force multiplier.

COMPUTERS USED TO ASSIST IN OTHER CRIMES   The ways in which computers can be used to assist in the commission of crimes is almost limitless. Illegal gambling operations can track winnings and losses on computers. Illegal prostitution operations can track patrons on computers.

Legitimate businesses that engage in money laundering activities can keep duplicate sets of books using computers. E-mail may be used as a means of communication during the planning, commission, and cover-up stages of a crime. Computers allow for the quick transfer of data across the world. Criminals can easily carry computer chips, flash drives, and other mass storage devices across borders. Cell phone technology allows for better voice-to-voice communication. Any technological advance that has been beneficial to business, education, or law enforcement has also been beneficial to criminals.

Cyberstalking Cyberstalking is harassing and threatening behavior in the online environment. It can range anywhere from annoying e-mails to unwanted digital pictures to verbal threats. In extreme cases, the behavior will carry over into the real world. These cases are generally those in which offender and victim are known to each other and have a previous relationship. It is difficult to estimate how many individuals have been stalked online because, like the traditional form of stalking, it is underreported to law enforcement. Most Internet service providers have specific policies governing how to handle unwanted online behavior.

A handful of states have specific statutes regarding online stalking. Other states deal with the crime through more general harassment statutes. Depending upon the exact nature of the stalking, other statutes may be brought into force as well, for example, if the perpetrator makes specific threats, that individual may be prosecuted under statutes that govern making terroristic threats.

Computer Use and Sexual Predators As a tool for the pedophile, the computer serves a multitude of purposes. It reinforces the compulsivity of sexual offending; the anonymity lessens the chance of being caught while disinhibiting the offender; it provides opportunities to interact with other offenders; it provides almost limitless access to victims; and finally, it provides a convenient storage place for child pornography.

The immediacy of the computer environment reinforces the compulsivity of sexual offending. For sexual offenders who already have a problem with pornography or online sexual activity, the online environment provides almost limitless access only a click away. This 24/7 access reinforces the addiction. The anonymity of the Internet lessens the chance of being caught. The computer can also serve as a disinhibiter. An individual who would never approach a child in real life can experiment with and practice this behavior online and gain confidence.

The online environment provides the offender with opportunities for interaction with other offenders. This networking helps the offender to feel normal in his deviant thought-patterns (which are shared by other offenders). And, like any other networking, it helps him to learn better ways to approach victims, and better ways to avoid detection by law enforcement or by family and friends. Pornography can be exchanged. It can even present opportunities to exchange victims.

The computer provides the opportunity to look for victims with some level of anonymity. The offender can assume a fictitious identity and change his identity depending upon what the victim wants. Rather than relying on real-life interactions with young people, he can go into chat rooms and web sites frequented by children. He can post on newsgroups and bulletin boards (BBS) and identify vulnerable targets.

The offender has almost unlimited access to victims across state lines or across the world. For sexual offenders, much of their time is spent grooming potential victims. In grooming, the offender determines if the child would be a good victim; he also draws the child into his behavior as a participant, even going so far as to make the child the primary actor. In an online environment, it is possible for the offender to spend a significant portion of the day searching for potential victims. He is limited only by the amount of time he can spend on the computer. The offender may spend months grooming a target; and can groom many, many targets at once.

The computer provides a convenient storage place for child pornography, including images and stories. Offenders may save pornography that other offenders have sent them, or they may save pornography that they have created themselves. During an investigation, everything that has been downloaded and stored onto a computer hard drive will become evidence. Even images that the offender believes have been erased will be reconstructed.

COMPUTER-SPECIFIC CRIMES Computer-specific crime is a category of crimes that exists solely because of the advent of the computer. These crimes did not exist prior to the widespread use of computers and significant interconnectivity. These are crimes such as stealing, altering, and destroying computer data; spamming; denial-of-service attacks; hacking; and cracking.

Theft, Alteration, and Destruction of Computer Data The most obvious computer-specific crime would be the theft, alteration, or destruction of data stored on disks, drives, mainframes, or other computer devices. Data theft occurs far more often than companies and individuals are aware. Data may be stolen with little or no trace that anyone entered the system. A common instance of this is the theft of credit card information.

Criminals may also access databases and alter or destroy data. In some cases, this data may be unrecoverable. This represents a considerable and expensive loss for the company that experiences this sort of crime. Data recovery and reconstruction is an expensive process and is sometimes impossible. Contrary to popular belief, most of the individuals who steal, alter, or destroy data are not outsiders; usually they are current or former employees of the company that experiences the crime.

Spamming Another common computer-specific crime is spamming. Spamming is the sending of unwanted and unsolicited e-mails to individuals or businesses. Spammers (those who send spam) may be trying to sell legitimate products or services, or they may be attempting to defraud, or to distribute pornography.

Internet service providers typically try to filter as much spam as possible. This can be done by looking for certain words or images that frequently appear in spam messages and blocking them. Users can also mark messages as spam and all other e-mails from that address will also be blocked. Of course, as anyone with an e-mail account knows, spammers find clever ways around spam filters.

DoS Attacks A denial-of-service attack (DoS attack) is carried out by sending a high volume of e-mails to a specific server, which causes the server to shut down. This type of attack is generally aimed at a specific company or institution with the purpose of disrupting business. Harm results from a loss of business, or loss of communication while the server is down, and the cost of restoring services; these attacks generally do not result in any permanent losses but instead interfere with the business function of the company.

Hacking and Cracking Hacking and cracking are two final computer-specific crimes. Hacking is gaining unauthorized access to computer data, whereas cracking is gaining unauthorized access to computer data with *malicious* intent.

The profile of the "average" hacker is a young, white, male between the ages of 14 and 24. Over the past 20 years, an entire culture has grown up around hacking. Hackers have formed online communities and even have conventions (DefCon is held in Las Vegas each year). While the image of these hackers is benign, gaining unauthorized access to data on web sites is illegal and causes considerable damage each year. Hackers attempt to enter sites simply for the challenge of entering unauthorized sites. Crackers attempt to enter sites for revenge, to steal or alter data. Although any site can be vulnerable, many hackers especially enjoy the challenge of entering government web sites. Crackers, choose sites that are meaningful to them, for example, former employers.

USE OF THE COMPUTER AS A FORCE MULTIPLIER The computer can be used as a "force multiplier." A force multiplier is something that increases the damage that can be done by a criminal. The computer is not used as a weapon but to increase the force of an attack or a crime. It allows criminals to reach more people. During a traditional terrorist attack, such as a bombing, the terrorists could use the computer to hack into the 911 system and disable it so that help cannot be notified or so that it is delayed in arriving. While the computer attack in this example doesn't actually harm anyone, it allows more harm to occur because of the delay of appropriate emergency response personnel. The scam artist can talk only to a limited number of people during a single day, but e-mail can allow him or her to reach thousands of people in a single day.

COMPUTER USE IN FRAUD AND SCAMS Criminals who used to carry out scams had to do so in person. This limited the number of contacts that could be made in a single day. Criminals who used the mail could reach more individuals. The advent of e-mail has logarithmically increased the contacts that can be made. Now a scam artist can contact thousands of individuals in a matter of seconds, which increases the likelihood that someone will respond.

Carrying out a computer scam also requires less effort than carrying out a traditional scam. The scam artist can sit at a computer and with an e-mail program send out tens of thousands of e-mails—all before breakfast.

RECOVERING EVIDENCE OF COMPUTER CRIMES Computer evidence is not always easy to recover. A savvy computer user can employ encryption techniques that are readily available on the Internet (www.truecrypt.org) to encrypt a partition or file in excess of 128-bit encryption, making it almost impossible to decrypt. A criminal who has some computer skills and takes the time to use them can successfully encrypt anything so that it will remain hidden from law enforcement.

It can be easier, in some cases, to recover evidence from computers than it is to recover traditional "forms of evidence." Once physical evidence is destroyed, it is usually gone for good. While disks and computer storage devices can be destroyed, short of destroying the hard drive, it is difficult to actually get rid of all of the information stored on a computer hard drive. Although files may be "deleted," they are rarely gone—except when the drive reaches capacity and begins to overwrite the "deleted" information; most modern hard drives are so large this rarely happens. This means that all of the information that has been on that drive can possibly be reconstructed from the "ghosts" that exist on the hard drive. These ghosts can be beneficial to law enforcement, but the average computer user should be aware that when a computer is discarded, all of the information that had been written to the hard drive is still there, unless the system is physically destroyed, or erased using special disks—the same sort of an erasure that the military would perform.

Why Businesses Are Reluctant to Cooperate with Law Enforcement It is very difficult to accurately estimate the prevalence of computer crime. Many computer crimes frequently occur without being detected, where data is copied without anyone realizing that someone has gotten into the system. Hackers obtain access to web sites and leave without a trace. Businesses that are victimized are reluctant to report break-ins to law enforcement because the investigation and possible seizure of computers as evidence would cause more monetary losses and greater disruption of business than the initial break-in. It may also be the case that businesses do not welcome the opportunity to have law enforcement in their private computer systems.

Computer evidence should be seized only by experts specially trained in dealing with computers. One of the reasons why businesses have been reluctant to cooperate with law enforcement is because of the fear of untrained or poorly trained law enforcement personnel causing more damage than the initial attack.

Computer Emergency Response Team Computer Emergency Response Team (CERT) is housed at the Software Engineering Institute at Carnegie Mellon University in Pittsburgh, Pennsylvania. CERT is a center for analyzing and protecting against Internet security problems. In fact, CERT was founded after the "Morris worm" of 1998 that paralyzed much of the Internet.

CERT maintains statistics on computer attacks that have been reported to them. When vulnerabilities are discovered, they make fixes or patches available to the public. CERT offers a selection of workshops and training and also works with the Department of Homeland Security to protect against serious Internet attacks.

What Is Needed to Successfully Investigate a Computer Crime? The investigation of computer crimes is very different from the investigation of traditional crimes. Perhaps the most important factor in the successful investigation of computer crime is "awareness." Law enforcement must be aware of at least five things for the successful investigation of a computer crime:

1. that the possibility of a computer crime exists
2. how to recognize computer evidence
3. protection of computer evidence before it is collected
4. proper techniques for collection of computer evidence
5. and preservation of computer evidence.

How Do Computer Crimes Come to Light? The truth is that many computer crimes are never detected, especially crimes that involve merely copying data as opposed to altering or destroying it. A semiskilled hacker can access a site, copy data, and exit again without leaving much of a detectable trail. And the trace that does exist may be very difficult to find unless you know exactly what to look for. Computer crimes are more likely to come to light when the attack has significantly altered or destroyed data, or in instances where the data reappears and is used elsewhere.

Does Law Enforcement Lag Behind in Computer Technology? Unfortunately, while computer crimes have been increasing, law enforcement's methods for dealing with such crimes have lagged behind. Many law enforcement agencies still lack the skilled personnel necessary to investigate and combat this form of crime. This is largely due to the fact that until just recently, most police officers had few, if any, computer skills. Until recently, even officers with college educations had little or no computer training. Also, those individuals with degrees in computer science generally do not enter police work because the pay is much higher for positions in other fields. Slowly, this is changing. Many large police departments and federal agencies actively recruit individuals with computer skills and degrees.

Slowly, police departments are becoming more and more computer-savvy. Computers in police cars and in precincts are now far more common. At least half of all police vehicles have a mobile data terminal. All but the smallest and most rural police departments employ some sort of desktop computing. The days of being able to ignore a speeding ticket received in another state are over!

CYBER INVESTIGATIONS—FBI In response to the growing threat of the possibility of computer attack at the personal, corporate, and national level, the FBI responded with a Cyber Investigations division which includes Cyber Action Teams and Computer Crimes Task Forces and an Internet Crime Complaint Center (http://www.fbi.gov/cyberinvest/cyberhome.htm). Cyber Action Teams respond to emerging cyber threats all over the world. The Computer Crime Task Forces respond to calls from victims of cyber crime, look for Internet sexual predators, and examine computer evidence that has been seized from criminals. The Internet Crime Complaint Center (IC3) is a joint venture between the FBI and the National White Collar Crime Center. The IC3 handles criminal cyber complaints, and acts as a bridge between victims of cyber crime and the appropriate investigating agencies (federal, state, and local) (http://www.ic3.gov/).

FRAUD

Fraud is a deliberate misrepresentation of the truth that leads to loss. A company can misrepresent its liabilities and assets to drive up its stock price, as key management personnel at Enron did, or an individual can misrepresent herself as the owner of a stolen credit card while purchasing online goods. Fraud can be classified in many different ways, depending upon the targets of fraud or the motivation for fraud. This section will discuss health care fraud, insurance fraud, securities fraud, bank fraud, telemarketing and computer fraud, tax fraud, and identity theft. Fraud investigation may encompass both computer forensics and forensic accounting.

Investigation of Fraud

Most fraud comes to light when the victim realizes that there has been a loss. In some instances considerable time can lapse from when the loss occurred. This makes successful identification of the perpetrator more difficult. Fraud investigation involves following both the paper trail and/or the money trail involved in the crime. The investigator gathers as much information as possible about the victimization.

The United States Secret Service operates a Financial Crimes Division that investigates bank fraud, credit and debit card fraud, telecommunications (dealing with cloned cell phones) and computer crimes, fraudulent identification, fraudulent securities, and electronic funds transfer fraud (http://www.secretservice.gov/financial_crimes.shtml). The secret service also investigates foreign individuals and groups engaged in defrauding individuals within the United States. The FBI's Financial Crimes Section (FCS) investigates corporate fraud, health care fraud, mortgage fraud, identity theft, insurance fraud, and money laundering (http://www.fbi.gov/publications/financial/fcs_report052005/fcs_report052005.htm).

In sheer numbers, fraud is a very significant crime in the United States. Statistics would indicate that the monetary loss from the various types of fraud is far greater than all of the monetary losses from all forms of street crime combined. These frauds are addressed in this chapter because their investigation often involves the use of computers.

Forensic Accounting

Forensic accounting is a relatively new discipline that has emerged as a significant subdiscipline since the Enron scandal. Forensic accounting is accounting that can be presented in a court. Forensic accounting is following the money trail. Forensic accountants engage in the verification of financial records. The forensic accountant will verify both income and expenditures. Most forensic accountants are Certified Public Accountants (CPAs), accountants who have passed a series of tests. Not only can forensic accountants review the financial records of an institution, but also during a divorce, one party may hire a forensic accountant to look for hidden assets.

While technically not a forensic science, forensic accounting deserves a brief mention here. Forensic accounting is the application of accounting principles to the legal arena. Since the Enron and WorldCom scandals, in which large-scale fraud occurred, considerable attention has been drawn to the ways in which corporations may commit crimes. Forensic accountants investigate and analyze financial information, not only for companies and corporations, but they may also be involved in marital assets investigation and personal injury claims, and professional negligence.

In their work involving corporations, forensic accountants may review financial records to help resolve disputes involving partners or shareholders; they may be involved in insurance investigations, employee fraud investigations, and business economic loss investigation. Due to the increased use of computers to commit fraud or to store data used in fraudulent operations, the forensic examination of computers is an important part of many fraud investigations.

Health Care Fraud

The FBI estimates that between 3 and 10 percent of all health care spending is fraudulent (http://www.fbi.gov/publications/financial/fcs_report052005/fcs_report052005.htm). Health care fraud takes a variety of forms. It can be committed by a healthcare provider who submits false or elevated claims for procedures or falsifies dates of service or services provided. In some cases, a doctor may tell the insurance company that he or she charges a higher price for services but bill a patient at a lower rate. A psychotherapist may tell an insurance company (or the government in the case of individuals who are covered under Medicaid or Medicare) that he is treating a patient for one mental disorder because it is covered but actually be conducting therapy for symptoms that aren't covered. Health care fraud can be committed by a health care institution that bills for services never provided or double bills for services. Individuals who are insured may assist providers and institutions in committing health care fraud by allowing the doctor or hospital to make false claims or by substantiating those claims.

Health care fraud is punishable by both criminal and civil penalties. In the first half of 2005, there were $803 million in restitutions, $4.9 million in recoveries, $28.4 million in fines, and $22.2 million in seizures (http://www.fbi.gov/publications/financial/fcs_report052005/fcs_report052005 .htm).

Health care fraud investigation can begin with information sharing among the various investigating agencies. These types of fraud investigation may involve the FBI, the Secret Service, or the Internal Revenue Service (IRS). The IRS can be a good place to begin because fraud often involves considerable amounts of cash, especially because a lot of health care fraud involves over-billing or billing for services that were never received. When large amounts of money are deposited into an individual's or company's bank account, the IRS may investigate to ascertain that the money derived from a legitimate source. Fraud may also come to light during an audit. An audit will evaluate the financial records of the health care system in question. Through careful analysis, irregularities will come to light.

Insurance Fraud

The FBI estimates that insurance fraud costs more than $40 billion each year (http://www.fbi.gov/ publications/financial/fcs_report052005/fcs_report052005.htm). The majority of insurance fraud is committed by corporations who divert policyholder premiums; also unauthorized companies may sell insurance products. Insurance fraud also occurs when an individual files a false claim with an insurance company. This can be with an auto insurance company or a home insurance company or a business insurance company. This also includes false workers' compensation fraud. Arson can be a form of insurance fraud. Arson becomes insurance fraud when the purposeful burning happens so that the owner of the property can profit from the burning.

In the first half of 2005, FBI investigations into insurance fraud resulted in $100.1 million in restitutions being paid, $0.874 thousand in recoveries, $45.4 thousand in fines, and $1.5 million in seizures (http://www.fbi.gov/publications/financial/fcs_report052005/fcs_report052005.htm).

Securities Fraud

Securities are regulated by the Securities Exchange Commission (SEC). Securities fraud occurs when investors are deceived and because of this deception theft results. The Internet has significantly increased opportunities for this type of crime.

INSIDER TRADING   Insider trading is a form of securities fraud. Insider trading happens when a corporate insider trades stock or securities based on inside information, such as when news of an impending merger or sale or negative company report has not yet been released to the public. In the Enron scandal, numerous company executives and their accounting firm conspired to artificially raise the company's stock price by incorrectly reporting the company's liabilities and debts. Then, as the company collapsed, company executives and others who received insider information dumped their stock. In a dramatic collapse the company's stock shares dropped from $90 to $0.30 a share.

Enron had far-reaching effects on the accounting world. The scandal resulted in massive fines and prison sentences for executives. Many executives also accepted plea agreements and testified against top executives in exchange for lesser sentences. Investors and employees of Enron lost all

---

Financial Software

Financial software has been designed to track monetary transactions by spotting trends in the movement of money. This can be used in a variety of applications from organized crime to white-collar criminals to terrorists. The financial marketplace realized a long time ago that people who trade in the stock market follow certain trends in buying and selling securities and the SEC developed software to track common trends in order to identify unusual buying or selling activity indicative of insider trading and other various securities violations. This same software has been used by lending corporations to monitor credit card accounts. The software examines buying activity that deviates from the normal purchasing activity of the buyer and then alerts the cardholder about possible credit card or identity theft. This software has also been extremely useful to law enforcement to identify white-collar criminals and the crimes they commit, the laundering of drug transactions and the laundering of money for organized crime. There are now corporations that specialize in this type of security analysis on every individual who has established credit. These databases have been expanded to include the financial history compiled on individuals as well as their personal spending habits, likes, dislikes, and credit history. This can be very useful when developing an interrogation format for a suspect. It can also be used to locate suspects who are on the run, by tracking their purchases.

---

savings and pensions. Not only did the scandal take down Enron, but also its accounting firm, Arthur Andersen. Arthur Andersen was convicted of obstruction of justice and forced to surrender its licenses to practice accounting. From the wreckage of both companies, the Sarbanes–Oxley Act of 2002 was created. The purpose of this act was to create oversight into public-company boards, management, and public accounting firms. It includes enhanced penalties for securities violations and misrepresentations of financial statements, accelerated reporting of insider trading, independent auditing of companies, and additional disclosure.

In the Martha Stewart case, Stewart sold shares in a pharmaceutical company, ImClone, based on information that her friend, and founder of ImClone, Samuel Waksal gave her. She was eventually sentenced to five months in prison, five months of home confinement, two years of probation, and fined $30,000.

In the first half of 2005, through FBI investigations into corporate fraud alone, there were $2.2 billion is restitutions, $34.6 million in recoveries, $79.1 million in fines, and $27.9 million in seizures (http://www.fbi.gov/publications/financial/fcs_report052005/fcs_report052005.htm).

Bank Fraud

One form of bank fraud is mortgage fraud. Mortgage fraud consists of misrepresenting information on a mortgage application; it can be misrepresenting income by borrowers, identity theft, and property flipping (a process in which an owner buys a property and then quickly resells it for a profit) using false appraisals. Because there is no standardized reporting of mortgage fraud, it is difficult to know the true extent of this crime. Bank fraud may be committed by insiders, those employed by banks, or by outsiders. Insider bank fraud includes fraudulent loans, wire fraud, forged documents, uninsured deposits, and demand draft fraud. Bank fraud committed by outsiders includes altered checks, stolen checks, accounting fraud, check kiting, booster checks, stolen credit cards, duplication of credit card information, identity theft, fraudulent loan applications, and prime bank fraud. FBI investigations into mortgage fraud led to $91.9 million in restitutions, $31 thousand in recoveries, $208 thousand in fines, $8.9 million in seizures during the first half of 2005 (http://www.fbi.gov/publications/financial/fcs_report052005/fcs_report052005.htm).

Telemarketing and Computer Fraud

Computers are frequently used as a tool in many fraudulent schemes. Telemarketing fraud frequently involves promises of large cash prizes or lottery winnings in exchange for a fee paid to access the winnings. Of course, once the victims pay the fee, they never see their winnings. Similar scams are also seen on the Internet. FBI investigations in the first half of 2005 resulted in $483.6 million in restitutions, $500 thousand in fines, and $161 thousand in seizures (http://www.fbi.gov/publications/financial/fcs_report052005/fcs_report052005.htm).

Nigerian Scam

One common scam that occurs either by mail, or now via e-mail, is known as the *Nigerian Scam*. In this scam, unwitting individuals are asked to assist an official in getting funds released. In order to do this the victim is eventually asked to pay a certain amount of money. Sometimes this money is to bribe officials. Below is an example of the Nigerian Scam received as an e-mail by one of the authors.

CENTRAL BANK OF NIGERIA
TINUBU SQUARE, VICTORIA ISLAND, LAGOS-NIGERIA
(OFFICE OF THE DEPUTY GOVERNOR)
TINUBU SQUARE, LAGOS-NIGERIA.
Our Ref: CBN/IRD/CBX/021/07
ATTN: Sir/ Madam,
IMMEDIATE FUND RELEASE NOTIFICATION

Compliments! I am Dr Ola Ahmed, The Deputy Governor, Central Bank of Nigeria (CBN). I have been instructed by the Federal Government of Nigeria, Revenue Office to legally transfer your contract payment valued at Twenty One Million, Five Hundred Thousand United States Dollars ($21.5M). We apologize for any inconvenience as a result of delay in transaction.

However, during the auditing and closing of all financial records of the Central Bank of Nigeria (CBN), it was discovered from the records of outstanding contractors and inheritance funds due for payment with the Federal Government of Nigeria that your name, email and company was next on the list of the outstanding contractors who have not yet received their payment.

I wish to officially notify you that your payment is being processed and will be released to you as soon as you respond to this letter. Be assured that this transaction is 100% hitch free and my promise is that you will receive your fund without any delay.

To facilitate the process of this transaction, please kindly re-confirm the following information as stated below:

1. Your full name and address.
2. Phone, Fax and Mobile #.
3. Company name, position and address.
4. Profession, age and marital status.
5. Complete bank account information.

Upon the reconfirmation of the above information, your payment will be released to your doorstep in a certified bank draft, Diplomatic courier delivery service or wired to your nominated bank account directly from Central Bank of Nigeria. You are therefore advised to reply urgently as soon as you receive this letter for further discussion and more clarification.

Best Regards,
Dr Ola Ahmed
Deputy Governor,
Central Bank of Nigeria (CBN)

Tax Fraud

Tax fraud or tax evasion can range from a few dollars to millions of dollars. It is any form of cheating on income taxes. It can take the form of receiving payment for services *under the table* rather than through income that is reported to the Internal Revenue Service. Individual tax payers who make an average income frequently commit tax evasion by over-reporting deductions. Tax payers who are in higher income brackets commit tax evasion on a larger scale. Illegal businesses also commit tax fraud. Drug dealers do not report their illegal income so it is not taxed.

Organized criminal operations engage in *money laundering* to hide income. Through money laundering, illegal assets are converted into legal assets. During the first half of 2005, FBI investigations led to $98.7 million in restitutions, $6.7 million in recoveries, $270 thousand in fines, and $324 thousand in seizures (http://www.fbi.gov/publications/financial/fcs_report052005/fcs_report052005.htm).

Identity Theft

Identity theft is a federal offense under Chapter 47, Title 18 of the United States Code. All states recognize identity theft as an offense and consider it as a felony or misdemeanor, often increasing the punishment depending upon the monetary amount involved. The FBI sees identity theft as one of the most pressing white-collar crimes of the twenty-first century, with opportunities for committing this type of crime on the rise (http://www.fbi.gov/publications/financial/fcs_report052005/fcs_report052005.htm). FBI investigations in the first part of 2005 resulted in $10.2 million in recoveries, $152 thousand in fines, and $2.1 million in seizures (http://www.fbi.gov/publications/financial/fcs_report052005/fcs_report052005.htm).

Glossary

Booster check—a non-sufficient funds (NSF) check used to make a payment on a credit card account. This works because credit companies must post payments prior to checks clearing. This is used to boost the individual's credit limit.

Check kiting—also referred to as "paper hanging," an individual takes advantage of the "float" (when the check is written and used and when it clears the bank) to draw on funds before a check clears.

Check washing—using chemicals to remove the ink on checks.

Color-shifting ink—ink used on money that appears to change color when the bill is moved.

Counterfeit detection pens—pens that utilize an iodine solution that marks counterfeit bills.

Cracking—hacking with malicious intent.

DOS attacks—sending a high volume of e-mails with the intent of shutting down a server.

Desktop publishing—using software programs and a printer to produce high-quality publications.

Electrophoresis techniques—a chemical separation technique used to analyze substances.

Force multiplier—increases the potential harm caused by a criminal.

Fraud—a deliberate misrepresentation of the truth that leads to loss.

High-contrast photography—a photographic technique that emphasizes the differences between light and shadow in a photograph.

Infrared filter—allows only infrared light to pass through.

Microprinting—very small printing utilized on money as a security feature.

Oblique lighting—lighting from the side.

Prime bank fraud—an organization claims that they offer an exclusive banking opportunity of guaranteed deposits in "prime banks," or "constitutional banks." While these sound official, they serve merely to defraud investors.

Spamming—sending of unwanted e-mails.

Webliography

CERT Coordination Center
(www.cert.org)

The International Association of Computer Investigative Specialists
(http://www.iacis.info/iacisv2/pages/home.php)

References

Almasy, S. October 10, 2005. "The internet transforms modern life," CNN.com. Accessed on November 27, 2006, from http://www.cnn.com/2005/TECH/internet/06/23/evolution.main/index.html.

Brunelle, R. L. "Questioned Document Examination." In *Forensic Science Handbook*. Edited by R. Saferstein, 672–725. Englewood Cliffs, NJ: Prentice Hall, 1982.

Cyber Investigations. Federal Bureau of Investigation. Accessed on June 28, 2006, from http://www.fbi.gov/cyberinvest/cyberhome.htm.

Federal Bureau of Investigation. May 2005. *Financial crimes reported to the public.* Accessed on November 27, 2006, from http://www.fbi.gov/publications/financial/fcs_report052005/fcs_report052005.htm.

Federal Reserve Bank of San Francisco. *Fun facts about money.* Accessed on November 27, 2006, from http://www.frbsf.org/federalreserve/money/funfacts.html.

Internet Crime Complaint Center. Federal Bureau of Investigation. Accessed on June 28, 2006, from http://www.ic3.gov/.

United States Bureau of Engraving. 2006. *Anti-Counterfeiting.* Accessed on November 27, 2006, from http://www.moneyfactory.gov/section.cfm/7/35.

United States Secret Service. *Financial Crimes Division.* Accessed on November 27, 2006, from http://www.secretservice.gov/financial_crimes.shtml.

Review Questions

1. How have copiers and fax machines impacted forensic document analysis?
2. Why are exemplars (known samples of writing) so important in document analysis?
3. What are some ways in which the age of a document can be established?
4. What type of a signature forgery isn't a forgery at all?
5. What are the three types of computer crimes?
6. Why are so many businesses reluctant to report computer attacks to traditional law enforcement?
7. What does CERT do?
8. What does a forensic accountant do?
9. Discuss two common types of fraud.
10. Which government agencies may be involved in fraud investigation?

Some Things to Think About

1. The chapter discussed sexual predators and the Internet. Can you think of ways in which children can be protected from this sort of behavior on the Internet?
2. Law enforcement tends to lag behind in computer technology, how can this problem be addressed?
3. Explain the interrelatedness of document analysis, computer forensics, and fraud investigation.

CHAPTER 7

Burglary, Theft, and Accident Investigation

CHAPTER OUTLINE

This chapter is divided into two sections. The first section will cover the crimes of burglary and theft. These crimes are related because they both involve the loss of goods. Theft as a criminal category is exceedingly broad. This section discusses such diverse topics as art theft and horse and tack theft! Some forms of theft you will immediately recognize, for example, car theft, others may be completely new, for example, freezer crimes.

The second section addresses accident and hit-and-run investigations. Hit-and-run investigations are always criminal matters, but an accident may also be a criminal matter—depending upon the cause of the accident (e.g., driver impairment and driver carelessness). Both accidents and hit-and-run crimes involve at least one vehicle; in some cases they may involve a vehicle and a pedestrian or a vehicle and a stationary object.

BURGLARY

Like most crimes, the burglary rate has been falling steadily over the past 20 years. In 1986 the rate was 1,349.8 per 100,000 inhabitants. In 2005 the rate was 726.7 per 100,000 inhabitants (http://www.fbi.gov/ucr/05cius/data/table_01.html). Over one-quarter of burglaries are committed by blacks and almost two-thirds are committed by whites (http://www.fbi.gov/ucr/05cius/data/table_43.html).

The definition of *burglary* has gone through considerable change over time. This crime once required the following three components: the structure to be a dwelling, the entry to be forced, and the crime to be theft (Figure 7.1). Current statutes do not require these elements any longer. The structure does not have to be a dwelling. A burglary *may* be committed by an individual who has entered a warehouse through an opened window or door. The warehouse, clearly, is not a dwelling. Entry does not have to be forced. In this example, the burglar entered through an open window. The intended crime need not be theft; it can be assault, rape, homicide, or any other criminal act. The crime of burglary now involves unlawfully entering a structure to commit a crime. Criminal offenses are generally addressed by state statutes. It is up to each individual state to define those actions that are crimes, as such; the exact wording of the statute covering burglary varies from state to state.

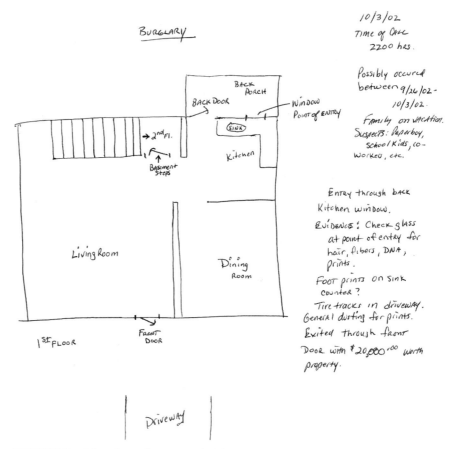

FIGURE 7.1 A burglary crime scene sketch.

Burglary Statutes

The Pennsylvania and Minnesota statutes are included here as examples of how burglary may be defined in statutes:

Pennsylvania statute (Title 18, Part II, Article C, Chapter 35, Subsection 3502) states, in part, "A person is guilty of burglary if he enters a building or occupied structure, or separately secured or occupied portion thereof, with intent to commit a crime therein, unless the premises are at the time open to the public or the actor is licensed or privileged to enter."

Note the inclusion of the phrase "or separately secured or occupied portion thereof . . ." This phrase would include within the statute actions like stealing items from an attached garage, even if the perpetrator did not enter any other portions of the house. If the garage is detached and cannot be occupied, stealing items from it would be considered *theft* and not burglary. If, however, the detached garage also has an apartment above it, it would be considered a dwelling and, therefore, stealing items from inside would be burglary. The difference between occupied and unoccupied, although seemingly small, is a really significant difference. It is assumed that if the structure is a dwelling, then human lives could possibly be at risk if someone enters it with the intent to commit a crime—therefore the crime is different and the penalties are different.

Minnesota statute (609.582, Subdivision 1) states, in part, that an individual has committed burglary in the first degree under the following circumstances: "Whoever enters a building without consent and with intent to commit a crime, or enters a building without consent and commits a crime while in the building, either directly or as an accomplice, commits a burglary in the first degree . . ."

Burglary Evidence

Although in this text, evidence is frequently discussed in terms of the crimes in which it is most commonly found, remember that almost any type of evidence *can* be found at any type of crime scene. That being said, there are certain types of evidence that are commonly found at many burglary sites, including tool marks, tire and shoe impressions, fingerprints, soil, and—sometimes—DNA. Not only are certain types of evidence likely to be present, but also evidence is generally found in certain areas.

The seasoned investigator will know what types of evidence are most likely to be present at the burglary scene and where that evidence is likely to be found—although nothing is ever ruled out prior to a thorough search of the crime scene. In fact, the seasoned investigator, because he or she knows what types of evidence will usually be found at a burglary scene, will be more likely to collect evidence that is not ordinarily found at a burglary scene.

Investigators always search the entirety of any crime scene. At a burglary crime scene, the search will focus on areas in which evidence is most likely to be found; the entry and exit points, the pathways to that entry and from the exit; areas from which items were taken; and the areas where other crimes were committed during the burglary.

Pathway to Entry and Pathway from Exit

Even before arriving at the crime scene, the investigator is trying to determine how the perpetrator entered the crime scene and how the perpetrator exited the crime scene. Both of these pathways—and they may be the same pathway—are likely places for evidence. There may be shoe prints or impressions, depending upon the condition of the ground. If the area is wooded, hair or fibers may have gotten caught on branches. Blood may be found on jagged edges of metal fencing.

If the point of entry is a likely place for evidence to be found, it is even more likely that evidence will be found along the exit path (Figure 7.2). If the burglar was surprised by the residents (returning home or waking up), or left hurriedly, stolen items that were too heavy or awkward to carry may be discarded along this path. The path may lead investigators to where an automobile was

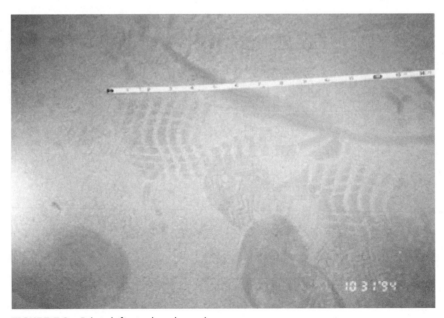

FIGURE 7.2 Prints left at a burglary crime scene.

parked that was used to escape—or even where an automobile remains because the perpetrator could not get back to it.

Point of Entry and Exit

Just as there must be a pathway that the perpetrator took to and from the burglary scene, there must also be a point of entry and a point of exit. The criminal must enter the crime scene in some manner. This may be through a door, window, or other opening. The point of entry can be determined in a variety of ways. First, investigators will note all doors and windows, as these are all likely points of entry (Figure 7.3). Ground-floor doors and windows can be especially vulnerable. Doors and windows that cannot be viewed from the street because of trees, shrubs, or other obstructions provide a convenient place for would-be burglars to work unseen.

Once the point of entry is determined, investigators will carefully examine the surrounding area for evidence. The burglar may have spent a significant amount of time lingering here waiting for the opportunity to enter and may have left cigarettes, partially eaten food, and shoe impressions in the vicinity. Footprints and impressions may be near the point of entry. Investigators will also look for tool marks on door jambs and window casings. A careless burglar who did not wear gloves may leave fingerprints at the point of entry. Tools used to gain entry, such as a screwdriver or a crowbar may also remain at the point of entry.

Unless the criminal remains at the scene, there must be a point of exit. Generally, it is not as likely that investigators will find tool marks at the point of exit from the crime scene. Since the burglar is already inside, there is little need to pry open a door or window—however, either one may be left open as the burglar flees, giving clear indication of where exactly the point of exit was. In some instances, the point of exit is not carefully thought out before hand. A burglar may break a window if it will not open. If the burglar is interrupted during the commission of the crime he or she may choose a point of exit that is closest and easiest. A burglar who is interrupted merely wants to get away from the scene. All other thoughts are secondary. A burglar who is interrupted may also be careless, knocking objects over, dropping objects, or tripping an alarm. If this is the case, more evidence will be created and the chance of the burglar being identified increases. If objects are knocked over, glass may break and cut the burglar, or a plant may tip and the burglar may pick up dirt or plant material on shoes or pants. All of this creates more evidence.

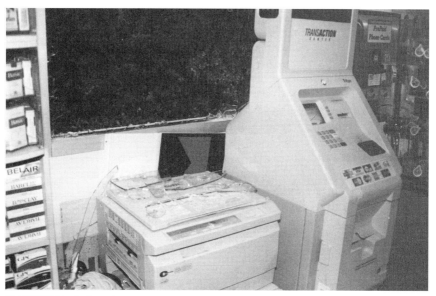

FIGURE 7.3   Point of entry.

Areas from Which Items Were Taken

The owner can provide investigators with a list of what is missing and where these items were kept. Any area within the crime scene from which items were taken will be focused on during evidence collection. These are places where the perpetrator had to stop—if only momentarily. He or she may have touched other items in the vicinity of the missing items. Other items may have been moved. In some cases, a careless burglar may even remove his or her gloves to touch something that is particularly attractive to him or her.

Noting the specific areas from where items were taken can also help determine the path the burglar followed through the crime scene. It may be apparent that the burglar spent very little time in most of the house and concentrated on taking objects in certain rooms. It should be noted if the perpetrator seemed to miss certain valuable objects. This could indicate any of the following:

1. The burglar was surprised and fled.
2. The burglar was not thinking clearly.
3. Burglary was not the primary crime, but was intended to cover up another crime.
4. The crime was committed by the owner who removed only insured pieces.
5. The burglar was familiar with the residence and came to take specific items.

The investigator will consider all of these possibilities and look at the overall pattern that the evidence creates.

Areas Where Other Crimes Were Committed

A considerable amount of evidence will be found in areas where other crimes were committed during the course of a burglary. A homicide will be investigated as a homicide; a rape will be investigated as a rape. Generally, these crimes leave considerable amounts of evidence—more than the average burglary. It will also be important for investigators to determine if burglary was the primary intention of the perpetrator and he committed the other crime because an opportunity presented itself, or if the homicide or rape was the original intent of the perpetrator and he also removed items from the scene. He may have removed these items to hide his identity or he may have taken them as souvenirs of his crime.

Photographing the Burglary Scene

Crime scenes are photographed to preserve evidence and to tell a story. The photographs will make a permanent record of the crime scene as it was found because the scene itself cannot be indefinitely preserved. These photographs will also be used to communicate the story of what happened during the commission of the crime to the jury.

Crime scenes in general are photographed from the outside toward the inside. This is done to insure minimal destruction of evidence while the photographs are being taken. The crime scene photographer will take a series of photographs. The first photograph will be taken at the closest intersection or other landmark to establish the general location of the burglary. It's a good idea to also take photographs of the cars parked on nearby streets—in case the burglar fled and left a vehicle behind. The next photographs will show the front, back, and sides of the exterior of the building. The entry and exit pathways are photographed along with the points of entry and exit.

Each room of the crime scene should be photographed separately, focusing on rooms in which items were taken, damage was done, or other crimes were committed, as these rooms are most likely to contain evidence. Each piece of evidence should be photographed at least twice. The first photograph shows the evidence in relation to other objects in the room. The second photograph is a close-up of the evidence. A scale (tape measure or ruler) is included in the second photograph to show how large the object is. Most crime scene kits contain many small rulers or tape measures for just this purpose.

THEFT

Theft is unlawful taking, also referred to as larceny. Many thefts are never reported because they involve such small amounts—often under $200—otherwise known as petty theft. Most jurisdictions will not investigate thefts of less than $5,000 in loss. Smaller thefts are simply not worth the investigative effort. Larger thefts, especially those that occur repeatedly in a limited geographical area and those that target specialized items, are investigated.

Theft also is not a mutually exclusive category; a theft may also be a fraud or a burglary. Remember the definition of fraud from Chapter 6: "a deliberate misrepresentation of the truth that leads to loss." Some thefts overlap with the category of burglary. Remember, the definition of burglary is "entering a structure with the intent to commit a crime." If a particular crime meets the statutory definition for a number of crimes, it may be charged under separate counts—that is, the offender will be charged with all possible offenses (this can become an issue during plea bargaining, and the offender may be allowed to plea down to the lesser offense, or to only one offense).

The entirety of the Minnesota theft statute has been included here. From reading the statute, it is clear to see the breadth of the crime of theft. This statute covers such diverse areas as theft of trade secrets, theft of cable and telecommunications, theft of items from a workplace, theft of services, and theft of motor vehicles. It also has provisions covering theft by deception, by fraud, and by concealment. As broad and inclusive as this statute seems to be, mail theft, identity theft, and receiving stolen property are covered under separate statutes.

Minnesota Theft Statutes 609.52, Subdivision 2

Subdivision 2. Acts constituting theft. Whoever does any of the following commits theft and may be sentenced as provided in subdivision 3:

1. intentionally and without claim of right takes, uses, transfers, conceals or retains possession of movable property of another without the other's consent and with intent to deprive the owner permanently of possession of the property; or
2. with or without having a legal interest in movable property, intentionally and without consent, takes the property out of the possession of a pledgee or other person having a superior right of possession, with intent thereby to deprive the pledgee or other person permanently of the possession of the property; or
3. obtains for the actor or another the possession, custody, or title to property of or performance of services by a third person by intentionally deceiving the third person with a false representation which is known to be false, made with intent to defraud, and which does defraud the person to whom it is made. "False representation" includes without limitation:

    i. the issuance of a check, draft, or order for the payment of money, except a forged check as defined in section 609.631, or the delivery of property knowing that the actor is not entitled to draw upon the drawee therefor or to order the payment or delivery thereof; or
    ii. a promise made with intent not to perform. Failure to perform is not evidence of intent not to perform unless corroborated by other substantial evidence; or
    iii. the preparation or filing of a claim for reimbursement, a rate application, or a cost report used to establish a rate or claim for payment for medical care provided to a recipient of medical assistance under chapter 256B, which intentionally and falsely states the costs of or actual services provided by a vendor of medical care; or
    iv. the preparation or filing of a claim for reimbursement for providing treatment or supplies required to be furnished to an employee under section 176.135 which intentionally and falsely states the costs of or actual treatment or supplies provided; or

(continued)

v. the preparation or filing of a claim for reimbursement for providing treatment or supplies required to be furnished to an employee under section 176.135 for treatment or supplies that the provider knew were medically unnecessary, inappropriate, or excessive; or

4. by swindling, whether by artifice, trick, device, or any other means, obtains property or services from another person; or

5. intentionally commits any of the acts listed in this subdivision but with intent to exercise temporary control only and:

   i. the control exercised manifests an indifference to the rights of the owner or the restoration of the property to the owner; or
   ii. the actor pledges or otherwise attempts to subject the property to an adverse claim; or
   iii. the actor intends to restore the property only on condition that the owner pay a reward or buy back or make other compensation; or

6. finds lost property and, knowing or having reasonable means of ascertaining the true owner, appropriates it to the finder's own use or to that of another not entitled thereto without first having made reasonable effort to find the owner and offer and surrender the property to the owner; or

7. intentionally obtains property or services, offered upon the deposit of a sum of money or tokens in a coin or token operated machine or other receptacle, without making the required deposit or otherwise obtaining the consent of the owner; or

8. intentionally and without claim of right converts any article representing a trade secret, knowing it to be such, to the actor's own use or that of another person or makes a copy of an article representing a trade secret, knowing it to be such, and intentionally and without claim of right converts the same to the actor's own use or that of another person. It shall be a complete defense to any prosecution under this clause for the defendant to show that information comprising the trade secret was rightfully known or available to the defendant from a source other than the owner of the trade secret; or

9. leases or rents personal property under a written instrument and who:

   i. with intent to place the property beyond the control of the lessor conceals or aids or abets the concealment of the property or any part thereof; or
   ii. sells, conveys, or encumbers the property or any part thereof without the written consent of the lessor, without informing the person to whom the lessee sells, conveys, or encumbers that the same is subject to such lease or rental contract with intent to deprive the lessor of possession thereof; or
   iii. does not return the property to the lessor at the end of the lease or rental term, plus agreed upon extensions, with intent to wrongfully deprive the lessor of possession of the property; or
   iv. returns the property to the lessor at the end of the lease or rental term, plus agreed upon extensions, but does not pay the lease or rental charges agreed upon in the written instrument, with intent to wrongfully deprive the lessor of the agreed upon charges.

For the purposes of items (iii) and (iv), the value of the property must be at least $100. Evidence that a lessee used a false, fictitious, or not current name, address, or place of employment in obtaining the property or fails or refuses to return the property or pay the rental contract charges to lessor within five days after written demand for the return has been served personally in the manner provided for service of process of a civil action or sent by certified mail to the last known address of the lessee, whichever shall occur later, shall be evidence of intent to violate this clause. Service by certified mail shall be deemed to be complete upon deposit in the United States mail of such demand, postpaid and addressed to the person at the address for the person set forth in the lease or rental agreement, or, in the absence of the address, to the person's last known place of residence; or

10. alters, removes, or obliterates numbers or symbols placed on movable property for purpose of identification by the owner or person who has legal custody or right to possession thereof

with the intent to prevent identification, if the person who alters, removes, or obliterates the numbers or symbols is not the owner and does not have the permission of the owner to make the alteration, removal, or obliteration; or

11. with the intent to prevent the identification of property involved, so as to deprive the rightful owner of possession thereof, alters or removes any permanent serial number, permanent distinguishing number or manufacturer's identification number on personal property or possesses, sells or buys any personal property knowing or having reason to know that the permanent serial number, permanent distinguishing number or manufacturer's identification number has been removed or altered; or

12. intentionally deprives another of a lawful charge for cable television service by:

    i. making or using or attempting to make or use an unauthorized external connection outside the individual dwelling unit whether physical, electrical, acoustical, inductive, or other connection; or by
    ii. attaching any unauthorized device to any cable, wire, microwave, or other component of a licensed cable communications system as defined in chapter 238. Nothing herein shall be construed to prohibit the electronic video rerecording of program material transmitted on the cable communications system by a subscriber for fair use as defined by Public Law 94-553, section 107; or

13. except as provided in paragraphs (12) and (14), obtains the services of another with the intention of receiving those services without making the agreed or reasonably expected payment of money or other consideration; or

14. intentionally deprives another of a lawful charge for telecommunications service by:

    i. making, using, or attempting to make or use an unauthorized connection whether physical, electrical, by wire, microwave, radio, or other means to a component of a local telecommunication system as provided in chapter 237; or
    ii. attaching an unauthorized device to a cable, wire, microwave, radio, or other component of a local telecommunication system as provided in chapter 237.
    The existence of an unauthorized connection is prima facie evidence that the occupier of the premises:
    a. made or was aware of the connection; and
    b. was aware that the connection was unauthorized; or

15. with intent to defraud, diverts corporate property other than in accordance with general business purposes or for purposes other than those specified in the corporation's articles of incorporation; or

16. with intent to defraud, authorizes or causes a corporation to make a distribution in violation of section 302A.551, or any other state law in conformity with it; or

17. takes or drives a motor vehicle without the consent of the owner or an authorized agent of the owner, knowing or having reason to know that the owner or an authorized agent of the owner did not give consent.

Blue-Collar Theft

Blue-collar theft is not a statutory definition. These thefts would be classified as *unlawful taking,* in some cases *burglary* or *robbery.* They are referred to as *blue-collar thefts* because of the offenders who commit the thefts and the motivation behind the thefts. A motivational typology can be useful for apprehending perpetrators. Blue-collar thefts are carried out either by an unskilled individual or a small group. They aim for petty targets. They are motivated by thrills, drugs, and alcohol, and the need to support their lifestyle. They focus upon houses, small business, and individuals. The gain from this type of theft is usually very small and consists of either products or cash. Because the crimes are usually impulse driven, they are not well thought out, and are poorly executed. Offenders are often caught because of their carelessness and not through particular investigative effort.

White-Collar Theft

White-collar thefts, when compared to blue-collar thefts, are executed by a more intelligent individual or group. These crimes are well thought out, very organized, and focused upon larger targets. The gain from this type of theft is usually larger amounts of cash or product. These offenders are more likely to rely on loopholes in the system and utilize businesses that appear legitimate to launder stolen products or cash in exchange for a share of the profit. These thefts are conducted more like business transactions than thrill-seeking and are not executed out of necessity but out of want. White-collar offenders commit crimes because they want significant amounts of money to support their middle-class lifestyle.

Organized Theft

Organized theft accounts for considerable monetary losses each year to businesses and individuals. The losses are considerable because organized thieves can take significantly more merchandise much more quickly than individuals can on their own. There are numerous types of organized theft—referred to as "major thefts" by the FBI—including retail theft, cargo theft, vehicle theft, art theft, and jewelry and gems. Organized thefts require special skills on the part of the thief and specialized investigative techniques on the part of the investigator. They also frequently require an organized network of individuals to dispose of the product (fences), and established legitimate businesses to launder the profits from the theft. Interestingly there is no Minnesota statute covering organized theft, although Section 609.521 covers possession of shoplifting gear. The threat of organized theft to businesses is very high and the potential for loss is significant. Because law enforcement has been slow to adequately deal with the problem of organized groups that commit theft, many professional organizations have formed their own response to theft in the form of security bulletins and training, web sites, and benchmarks for security.

RETAIL THEFT   Retail theft is any theft from a retail store, commonly referred to as "shoplifting." Shoplifting has been seen as a petty crime, most often perpetrated by young teenagers who steal goods that they can immediately use or sell. In the eyes of the law, shoplifting is a petty offense. It is usually a summary offense or a misdemeanor (unless the offender has multiple previous retail theft offenses or the amount stolen is over a certain dollar amount).

Although shoplifting may seem like an inconsequential crime, the majority of loss that retail stores experience is through retail theft, and while shoplifting is frequently committed by teenagers, it is also committed by professional shoplifting rings. These rings pose a much greater risk for loss for the average retail store than shoplifting teenagers. The FBI estimates that the retail industry loses between $30 billion and $37 billion a year to organized retail theft (http://www.fbi.gov/page2/april07/retail040607.htm). An organized group of shoplifters can steal hundreds of thousands of dollars of merchandise during a single outing. Because the penalties for retail theft are so light, these offenders see it as a low-risk crime. Once merchandise is stolen, it is almost impossible to track. The stolen merchandise is sold at flea markets, out of homes, and on the Internet. The Internet, especially sites like e-Bay, has been a particular boon to thieves looking to dispose of product.

Law enforcement has been slow to respond to organized retail theft, so retail business have developed loss-prevention techniques to protect themselves—in store cameras, antitheft devices on clothing, and employment of loss-prevention personnel. The National Retail Federation recently created the Retail Loss Prevention Intelligence Network Database. This database allows retailers and law enforcement to work together to curb organized retail theft. Through the database information can be shared among businesses and law enforcement agencies—since some organized theft groups operate across multiple jurisdictions (http://www.lpinformation.com/Default.aspx?tabid=259).

In January 2006, the U.S. government finally responded to the growing losses experienced through retail theft. President George W. Bush signed The Organized Retail Theft Bill into law.

This law established the Organized Retail Theft Task Force at the FBI (http://www.nrf.com/modules .php?name=News&op=viewlive&sp_id=36). In April 2007, the FBI launched the Law Enforcement Retail Partnership Network (LERPnet). This database will help track information on organized retail theft across jurisdictions (http://www.fbi.gov/pressrel/pressrel07/database040507.htm). The best way to combat these offenses is to lessen the ability of offenders to move from store to store and town to town carrying out the same offenses over and over. The database will track offenders and their methods of operation. When offenders are caught, it will be possible to link them to past offenses in other jurisdictions.

CARGO THEFT Cargo theft is the theft of goods that are being moved from point to point. Thieves can steal goods from trucks, planes, trains, and ships (generally in large containers)—any means of transportation that carries large amounts of goods can be targeted. The FBI estimates that cargo-theft losses cost $15–$30 billion a year; a single truck trailer alone can be worth between $12,000 and $3 million (http://www.fbi.gov/page2/july06/cargo_theft072106.htm).

Thieves who target cargo almost always work within an organized network that knows what goods are being shipped, where those goods can be disposed of, and where to launder profits (Figure 7.4). Law enforcement apprehends thieves by tracking patterns of theft. They recognize that there are certain hot spots for this type of theft. This is the main reason the FBI has established task forces in the following cities: Memphis, Houston, Newark, New York, San Juan, and Miami (http://www.fbi.gov/page2/july06/cargo_theft072106.htm).

VEHICLE THEFT During the past 20 years, the rate of motor vehicle theft per 100,000 inhabitants has been declining overall—although not steadily. The rate was highest in 1991 at 591.3 and it currently stands at 416.7, although in 2000 it was at its lowest at 412.2 (http://www.fbi.gov/ucr/05cius/ data/table_01.html). The American Association of Motor Vehicle Administrators maintains a web site and encourages partnership with law enforcement to combat theft (http://www.aamva.org/).

The typical auto theft involves a young male or group of males stealing a car to use and then abandon. Most of these cars are found within a few days of being stolen. They are not usually damaged, except by the method used to break into the car. Another type of vehicle theft is organized auto theft. Organized auto thieves target certain types of cars for theft. In some cases, they will steal high-priced

FIGURE 7.4 Cargo theft can occur at busy seaports.

sports cars and luxury vehicles for specific buyers. In other cases they will steal very common cars (Honda Accord, Toyota Camry) because they can sell them easily and cheaply.

The FBI is tracking and combating a new twist on car theft—"car cloning," where a vehicle identification number is copied from a car (same make, model, and color) with a clean (not stolen) title and put onto a stolen vehicle. This stolen vehicle, because it has a clean title, can be sold for a considerable amount more than a normal stolen vehicle could be sold for (http://www.fbi.gov/page2/march07/carcloning032907.htm).

ART THEFT The FBI estimates that as much as $6 billion dollars of art is stolen each year. (http://www.fbi.gov/hq/cid/arttheft/arttheft.htm). Art theft, or art and cultural theft, is a highly specialized form of theft. An art thief must have knowledge about breaking into secure museums (although not all expensive art pieces are kept in secure conditions); they must also have contact with clients or fences who will buy the pieces they steal. They must have a working knowledge of which art pieces are valuable and which do not have a market.

Famous art objects are stolen for a very specific audience. When a Picasso is stolen, it does not appear the next day on eBay. Often pieces are stolen for specific collectors who have requested them, or requested pieces from a certain artist. Art thieves are unlikely to be local and will quickly leave the area with the pieces they have stolen to get them to a buyer. This is the prime reason investigators should move quickly. Many pieces do not remain in the country from which they were stolen. Once the thieves leave the location where the theft has occurred, they are more difficult to track. Because they often do successfully leave the area, art theft investigation requires an international effort. The FBI has 12 special agents dedicated to art theft investigation (http://www.fbi.gov/hq/cid/arttheft/arttheft.htm).

Nazi Stolen Art

From 1933 to 1945, when the Nazi's were in power in Germany, they looted art from collections. A considerable amount of art that was stolen by the Nazi's during World War II is still missing. In some cases, pieces have shown up in legitimate art galleries, having been purchased unknowingly. The Nazis looted both public and private art collections. In many cases, art collections were required "donations" in exchange for exit visas. Art was confiscated from the collections of many rich and famous Jews and others who were enemies of the state. It is astounding that although some of these works were stolen more than 70 years ago, in many instances it has been only over the past decade or so that attempts have been made to identify possibly stolen objects.

Looted art works exist not only in many museums in Germany, but all over the world, including the United States. In 1998, the Association of Art Museum Directors (AAMD) published a report on art objects that were possibly looted during World War II and now reside in U.S. art museums. The AAMD encouraged all museums to review and research their collections and identify questionable pieces and find a way to return them to their rightful owners (http://www.aamd.org/papers/guideln.php).

Identifying possibly looted works of art and returning them to their rightful owners has proven very difficult. Owners were often killed during the war or have since died and their heirs may not even be aware of the pieces. Memories of particular pieces have faded over time. Many American museums, including the Museum of Modern Art, the Metropolitan Museum of Art, the Art Institute of Chicago, and the Museum of Fine Arts in Boston have reviewed the history of ownership of all of their paintings. These reviews have revealed numerous paintings of questionable origin. At one point in time, the Getty Museum estimated that almost half of its collection had questionable wartime ownership.

The Lost Art Internet Database was set up to assist in locating artworks and cultural pieces that were stolen by the Nazis in the 1930s and 1940s. Through the database, individuals can report missing or found cultural objects, research cultural objects, and consult a variety of publications (http://www.lostart.de/index.php3?lang=english).

Art recovery takes a considerable coordinated effort; this effort has been assisted through the use of databases. The FBI maintains the National Stolen Art File (NSAF), a computerized database of historically and artistically significant pieces that have been stolen (http://www.fbi.gov/hq/cid/arttheft/nationalstolen.htm). Interpol also maintains a "Stolen Works of Art" file. These databases can be accessed by investigators, museum curators, and the public. Information can be uploaded and shared (http://www.interpol.int/Public/WorkOfArt/Default.asp).

JEWELRY AND GEMS   The FBI estimates that jewelry and gem thefts cost over $100 million in losses every year. There are two typical types of thefts, thieves target traveling gem salespersons who carry samples of gems, and smash-and-grab operations carried out in jewelry stores. Unlike other forms of organized theft that are carried out without victims realizing what is happening (and often at night), these thefts often involve face-to-face contact between perpetrators and victims and the use of weapons. Like art theft, these crimes cross state and international boundaries (http://www.fbi.gov/hq/cid/jag/jagpage.htm).

Except for very individualized pieces, most gems are not easy to trace. Gems, like other stolen goods, are often stolen in one area and fenced in another. The FBI notes that fencing activities are highest in Los Angeles, Houston, Miami, and New York City. The FBI partners closely with industry to investigate thefts. The FBI also maintains the "Jewelry and Gem Database" that tracks suspect descriptions, methods of operation, and descriptions of stolen goods (http://www.fbi.gov/hq/cid/jag/jagpage.htm). The Jewelers' Security Alliance has been helping fight jewelry crime since 1883 (http://www.jewelerssecurity.org/index.php4).

Rural Thefts

The generic heading of *rural thefts* encompasses those forms of theft that occur in predominantly rural areas. These include freezer crimes, horse and tack theft, and theft of farm chemicals. The motivation behind each of these three types of theft is vastly different.

FREEZER CRIMES   Freezer crimes occur on large cattle ranches—not only in the United States but also internationally. Australia has a particular problem with livestock theft. Thieves will often kill a few head of cattle in the middle of the night, cut off the parts that are not needed, and cart away the remaining meat. These crimes are very hard to stop and solve. Generally these ranches have thousands of cattle and are comprised of hundreds of acres of land. It is not possible to patrol the entire ranch 24 hours a day. Thieves will operate during the night. Because of the large size of the ranches, it may be days or weeks before the crime is discovered. By that time, the thieves are long gone. It is difficult to steal cattle and sell them on the legitimate market because cattle are branded. In some cases, thieves may try to devise a brand that can be stamped over the original brand to look like a legitimate brand.

Mississippi formed an agricultural theft bureau in its Department of Agriculture and Commerce in 1993 to handle the following rural crimes: livestock theft, the shooting of livestock, timber theft, farm equipment theft, saddle and tack theft, and agricultural chemical theft. They also maintain the registration of livestock brands (http://www.mdac.state.ms.us/n_library/departments/ag_theft/index_agtheft.html).

HORSE AND TACK THEFT   Surprising to many city folk, both horses and tack (all of the equipment that is used in riding them) can be very expensive. Horse and tack theft is actually burglary. It occurs on a farm in the dead of night when the owners are asleep. The primary motives are money and revenge over competitive events that have been lost. Upstate New York has a significant problem with organized horse theft. Many show horses are extremely valuable on the open market. Tack is also very valuable. Custom made saddlery can cost more than $100,000 and there is always an open market for the quick resale of these items. Because there is no title to a horse or equipment, anyone can sell a horse or tack without any record of the transaction and at any price. Many times the fencing price is driven by the eye of the beholder. Stolen horses are often trafficked by a select group operating as *school horse distributors*. Such distributors pick up a horse from a horse thief and place it on the open market to particular barns with whom they have a relationship for such quick sales. There are no papers, no trail, and no taxes, only profit. Florida has many horse auctions where thousands of horses are processed. The problem is not limited to theft within the United States. Horses are an international market with Japan buying large numbers of them. This is an excellent place to sell a stolen horse because no one can track it and no one can prove it. There is very little tracking of horses. Racehorses and elite breeds are all tattooed inside the upper lip. Exotic breeds such as Dutch warm bloods are tattooed on the hind quarters.

THEFT OF FARM CHEMICALS   Farm chemicals are stolen for use in clandestine methamphetamine laboratories. These thieves are local. They live in the vicinity of their crime targets and operate their methamphetamine laboratory nearby. When significant amounts of farm chemicals are reported stolen, law enforcement should concentrate their investigation in the local area, and look for other signs of methamphetamine laboratory activity or drug sales. The motivation for this crime is profit through the sale of drugs. Although these crimes appear to be thefts, they should be investigated as drug crimes. They are also prosecuted as drug crimes which result in tougher penalties for the perpetrators. These crimes are more common in states that have large farming operations where significant quantities of the chemicals are used in the farming process.

Theft Against Organizations

When the crime is a theft against an organization, the target is a very large corporation—generally one that is publicly traded. These crimes can involve insider trading and accounting theft, such as the crimes that were seen in the Enron case that was discussed in considerable depth in Chapter 6. These offenders often abuse generally accepted accounting principles to manipulate the nondefinitive nature of certain accounting practices to reconcile the books. These offenders are extremely intelligent and operate either alone or with a few select others.

The risk in these crimes is considerable, especially due to the heightened awareness of both the public and SEC of the possibilities and dangers of these crimes. When these criminals are caught, the penalties are significant. However, the rewards are magnificently large and often transmitted to offshore accounts to minimize tracking and possible seizure by the authorities.

Theft Against Governments

One common way for theft against the government to occur is in the wake of a disaster. This offense involves so-called plastic contracts with phony vendors who are needed quickly by the government due to political/social pressures to respond quickly after a natural or man-made disaster has occurred. Wall (2005) identifies five types of disaster fraud: solicitations by illegitimate charities, forgery, home repair fraud, insurance fraud, and price gouging. These frauds may target the government or individuals.

It is very difficult for law enforcement agencies to appropriately track fraud and other crimes immediately following a disaster due to the urgency of the situation and the ensuing chaos (Quarantelli 2001). The perpetrator can overcharge for products and services that are difficult to trace because of poor tracking systems (or no tracking systems) implemented by the government and by the vendor delivering the service or product. The fraud occurs in the form of price gauging and under delivery of service or product to the targeted area, with surplus being re-routed to others who then pay full price. In this way, the offender is paid twice—once by the government, once by the individual who pays full price. Very little systematic research on disaster fraud has been conducted. Davila (2005) found that the average victim is over 60 years old, about half are Caucasian, and 65 percent are female.

Offenders are often quick start-up businesses, feeding upon social chaos and public grief surrounding the disaster. Some will target individuals with fraudulent home repair schemes. The rerouting of charity donations obtained by government endorsement are prime targets because the government wants the positive publicity but often does not follow through with good internal accounting procedures for the donations of cash or goods.

CLASS EVIDENCE AND INDIVIDUAL EVIDENCE

All forensic evidence can be broken down into the two broad categories of class evidence and individual evidence. Class evidence cannot be linked to a particular individual or object but only to a class of objects. The vast majority of evidence that is dealt with in the criminal justice system is class evidence. Glass evidence, paint evidence, shoe print evidence, ballistic evidence, fiber evidence, and tool marks are all class evidence. Class evidence can only link an object to a certain class of evidence; for example, a particular type of glass, such as window glass or auto glass, may be linked to a crime scene. Conversely, individual evidence can be linked to one individual or to a specific object. Fingerprints are perhaps the best example of individual evidence. Not even DNA is as individual as fingerprints. No two people have identical fingerprints, but identical twins have identical DNA!

Class evidence, however, may acquire individual characteristics over time. Through wear and tear, or other changes, certain class evidence can take on distinct characteristics and become individual evidence. The longer a tire has been on a vehicle, the more likely that it will develop individual wear patterns that can link a tread mark to the particular tire that made it. New shoes have only class characteristics, but because every person wears out shoes differently, over time they develop individual characteristics. The wear pattern on the bottom of a shoe becomes unique. All new shoes of any type are exactly the same, but when a burglar has worn a pair of shoes for many months the wear pattern becomes distinct: heels may be worn more on one side of the shoe, or tread may be nonexistent in some spots. Similarly, with glass evidence, the color, refractive index, and other physical and chemical properties can lead to a successful identification of a class of glass. A fragment of glass, however, can take on individual characteristics when it is apparent that the particular piece of glass under examination could only be a fragment of a particular window because it fits perfectly with the broken pieces recovered from the crime scene.

In an investigation, it is hoped that individual evidence will be found. Individual evidence can be linked directly to a particular individual. Your fingerprints are unique to you, just as the fingerprints of the person sitting next to you in class are unique to that person. If your fingerprints are found on a glass, it is safe to assume that your hand was on that glass (it is important to point out that it cannot be proven that you *held* the glass; the fingerprints do not prove that, as someone may have placed your hand around the glass while you were unconscious). In the many years that fingerprints have been used as a means of criminal identification, no two individuals have ever been found to have the same exact fingerprints.

Other individual identifiers include palm prints, sole prints, voice prints, bite marks, and perhaps both ear prints and lip prints. Hospitals often use sole prints taken in the delivery room as a method of identifying infants; while everyone has unique sole prints, because most criminals wear socks and shoes, it is not likely that sole prints will be left at the crime scene. Voiceprint analysis is a developing area that has received some acceptance in the courts; and bite marks are frequently used to link a suspect to a victim in sexual assault. While all of these forms of evidence may be individual, they have not been used to classify criminals. No one has developed a classification system based on lip prints or even sole prints. Many of these individual identifiers are not common enough to be used for criminal identification—how often does the offender leave lip prints at the crime scene? Fingerprints have been used so successfully for such a long period of time because fingerprints are adaptable to a system. It is also quite easy to leave a latent fingerprint on many types of surfaces—so fingerprints, whether we can see them or not, are fairly common in our environment.

TRACE AND TRANSFER EVIDENCE

Trace and transfer evidence is a broad class of evidence that includes an almost limitless range of substances. Trace evidence is any evidence that is very small. This type of evidence requires special collection techniques. Some forensic laboratories will have dedicated trace evidence units. Transfer evidence is anything that can be exchanged from one place to another as the result of contact. Trace evidence can refer to oils, tars, paints, cosmetics, hair, feathers, fur, dust, and pollens, among other things.

FIBER ANALYSIS

The world around us is full of fibers. In the room in which you are sitting and reading this text, chances are there are dozens of different fibers—carpeting, clothing, pillows, blankets, and upholstery, to name a few. Fibers may be of natural or synthetic origin. Natural fibers include vegetable fibers (cotton and hemp), animal fibers (wool and cashmere), and mineral fibers (asbestos). Synthetic fibers include a wide range of fibers (e.g., acetate, nylon, polyester, rayon, saran).

Because fibers are so prevalent in our everyday lives, they will also be prevalent at the crime scene. Fibers from clothing, bedding, house carpeting, and vehicle carpeting are common at crime scenes. These fibers are found most commonly in crimes that require close contact, such as sexual assault and murder. However, hit and run and robbery can also yield fiber evidence. During a hit and run, fiber from the victims' clothing may be found on the bumper of the car or in the tire tread. At a robbery crime scene, fibers from the perpetrator's clothing may be found on broken glass and other sharp objects.

Fiber Collection and Analysis

At the crime scene, fibers are collected in the same manner as hair evidence. Since most fibers are not readily apparent, areas that are most likely to contain such evidence should be vacuumed separately and the contents of each collection packaged separately to avoid contamination.

In the laboratory, most fiber analysis is conducted microscopically. The laboratory determines whether the fiber in question is natural or synthetic and what type of fiber it is. The color and shade of the fiber are noted, as are the shape and texture. The analyst can also examine the optical properties of the fiber. Through the use of a polarized light microscope or infrared spectroscopy, the molecular composition of the fiber can be determined.

SOIL EXAMINATION

When a crime occurs outside, either in whole or in part, the forensic examination of soil may be involved. Soil is not one material, but rather many types of material together. Soil is defined as rocks, minerals, vegetation, and animal products. It is comprised of many particles, and may be characterized in many ways, such as sandy, rocky, loamy, or claylike. Soil examination may reveal a whole host of organic products. Soil examination also encompasses analysis of manufactured products that may be contained within the soil, like paint, glass, and plastics. It is not an exaggeration to state that an almost limitless list of materials may be contained within a soil sample.

Forensic examination of soil occurs in many different types of investigations. Most commonly it is used in kidnapping, burglary, rape, and homicide investigations. Soil analysis may be useful in any crime, in which the perpetrator transports soil from another location and deposits it at the crime scene, or in which the victim carries soil with him/her. Soil may be carried on the suspect or victim, or deposited on the tires or underside of a vehicle. It may be found not only at the primary crime scene but also at secondary crime scenes. Soil examination can be extremely important when a body is found in a shallow grave. It is not uncommon for evidence that originated on the perpetrator to be found within the grave—even cigarette butts, gum, or partially eaten food discarded by the perpetrator may be uncovered. It is important for investigators to take into account weather conditions around the time of the commission of the crime. Rainy conditions will make footprints more likely. If there is snow on the ground, investigators may be required to act very quickly to preserve evidence.

Soil Collection and Analysis

When collecting soil at the crime scene, like any other type of evidence, it is important to first take photographs of the area before anything is disturbed. These photographs record the crime scene as it was found. After the initial photographs are taken, soil samples should be taken both from the area in question and from nearby areas. Many crime scene photographers will also document the area after samples have been removed. The soil samples from nearby areas will serve as a reference for determining the baseline qualities of the soil in that location. Experienced technicians will pay particular attention to areas where soil or plants have been disturbed, as these are most likely to yield useful results. The trained eye will look for differences in the soil. These may be color differences or texture differences. Plants may be broken or moved aside. Anything that is a disturbance in the normal growth pattern of the plants at the scene will be examined further.

In the laboratory, the composition of the questioned samples and the reference samples will be analyzed for differences. The soil should be dried first and examined under a microscope using low power. First the examiner will note the gross features of the soil, such as color and particle size. This alone can tell a great deal about a sample, and the examiner can compare the color to a collection of reference samples. If, for example, the sample taken from the suspect's shoes and the sample taken from the crime scene are unlike in color they are not likely to have come from the same source. In general, in this type of examination, it is much easier to exclude samples. In other words, if the two samples are different, it is usually the case that they did not originate from the same source. On the other hand, if two samples are similar, more caution should be exercised before concluding that they are from the same source.

FORENSIC BOTANY

Forensic botany is the study of plants and plant material in connection with criminal proceedings. Forensic botany is used to examine plant matter found in or around the crime scene or on victims or suspects. The basic purpose of this evidence is to link the suspect to the victim, or the suspect or victim to the crime scene. Recall Locard's "exchange principle" which states that the criminal always leaves traces of himself at the scene.

The forensic botanist might be called in to examine plant material at the site of a shallow grave. If foreign plant material is found, the forensic botanist may be able to give an indication as to where that material may have originated, as certain plants, seeds, and spores are endemic to particular climate zones, areas, or elevations. Likewise, if a victim was abducted and transported, plant material can be helpful in telling investigators where the body may have been prior to being found. This can be very important in tracking the perpetrator or setting up a chronology of events, and in locating what may be the primary crime scene or secondary crime scenes.

Forensic botany is interested in all plant materials, including; plants, leaves, seeds, pods, spores, and pollens. A forensic botanist should have a Ph.D. in biology, specializing in botany. Because the services of a forensic botanist are not frequently used, these individuals generally work in other areas of botany—often as university-level professors—and are called upon when their services are needed. They provide valuable input in a wide variety of cases, including burglaries, homicides, rapes, and kidnappings. While a homicide can occur in one location and the body may be deposited in another location, it may harbor plant materials from where the killing took place. Even bodies that have been buried for a long time—including those showing considerable decomposition—may be found with plant material that is foreign to the burial site. During a rape, because of the close contact between victim and offender, there is often an exchange of many types of forensic evidence—plant material may be among these. During a kidnapping, the victim may also retain plant materials from the perpetrator or from remote locations.

Collection and Analysis of Forensic Botany Evidence

Forensic botany evidence would generally fall under the category of trace evidence. Although large plant debris may be found, especially in gravesites, the investigator deals with very small, sometimes microscopic particles. The analysis will take place in the laboratory. First, the item will be visually inspected. Larger botanical evidence can be identified without the assistance of a magnifying glass or microscope. Smaller botanical evidence will be examined in a way similar to soil evidence.

TOOL MARKS

Tool marks can provide a seasoned investigator with much information. First, they are likely to indicate point of entry. Second, they will be found on objects that had to be pried open, like doors or lock boxes. Third, if a tool is found in the possession of the suspect that makes a mark identical to a mark made at the crime scene, it can reveal who committed the crime.

Tool-mark evidence can be left in many ways during the commission of a variety of crimes. A slim jim used to open a car door may scratch the paint; however, tool marks are generally caused when a forced entry occurs during a burglary or other crime. Tool marks are often found near the locking mechanism of a door or window. A tool mark occurs when a tool is used to force open a door or window and leaves impressions on the window, door, or casing. Tools commonly used include crow bars, screw drivers, the nail-pulling prongs of hammers, jimmying devices designed for the purpose of opening locks, metal bars, and axes. New tools have class characteristics, over time and with repeated use, the tools may develop individual characteristics. Metal may become bent, scratched, or broken. A screw driver that once had a flat edge may develop an edge with four small notches in it. It is the investigator's hope that such a thing has happened and that tool marks found at the scene can be successfully matched to a tool found in the possession of the suspect (in the suspect's car, truck, garage, basement, workplace, etc.). During an investigation, law enforcement will look at known offenders who have employed the same or similar breaking and entering methods of operation to identify possible suspects.

Tool Mark Collection and Analysis

In some cases, if the entire surface that contains the tool mark can be collected, it will be. In many cases, because tool marks are found on door jambs and window casings, they must be documented photographically. The photographs will be compared to test marks made by tools seized from the suspect.

TIRE AND SHOE IMPRESSIONS AND TRACKS

An impression is an indentation made by a harder substance into a softer substance. Depending upon the conditions at the scene of a crime, a perpetrator may leave behind tire and shoe impressions. Usually, these impressions will be left in moist ground, but they can be left in any soft substance, including sand or even a body. This would include things like wet footprints or footprints in snow. Footprints in snow—while subject to deterioration or obliteration as a result of temperature change or because of foot-traffic—can often be protected until crime scene technicians arrive. These footprints, like all evidence that is outdoors, require protection from the elements (rain can be especially harmful) or deterioration will be rapid, and the evidence irretrievable. Footprints and tire tracks in snow must be cast quickly using specialty casting materials formulated to not generate heat. It is difficult to preserve wet footprints at a crime scene because of their ephemeral nature; this evidence can easily be lost to evaporation or rain. It is essential for first responders to be equipped

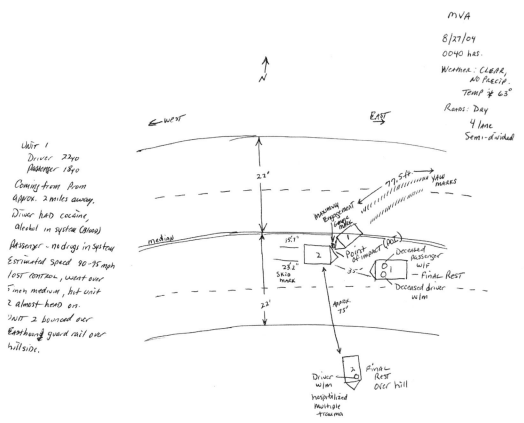

FIGURE 7.5 A motor vehicle accident crime scene sketch.

with cameras as this may be the only opportunity for such evidence to be recorded. As with all evidence, a scale should be included in the photo, and shots should be taken both at close range and at a greater distance to show where the impression is located in relation to other important objects at the crime scene (Figure 7.5).

Impression and Track Collection and Analysis

To cast the impression, all debris that has fallen on the impression should be removed; however, debris that is imbedded in the impression should remain because it will generally cause considerable destruction to remove embedded debris. By the time embedded debris is removed, the impression may be significantly destroyed. An impression in very loose soil or sand can be stabilized with hairspray. In some cases, a contrasting powder can be used to make the impression more visible prior to photographing. Impressions are cast using special plaster media.

Databases of Impressions

Unlike the DNA database kept by the FBI, there is not a similar single database for identifying tire and shoe impressions. The best sources of information on these prints are professional industries. Both the tire and shoe industries have generally been cooperative with law enforcement. A seasoned impression specialist can usually narrow down the type of shoe or tire and then contact manufacturers, who then, after viewing a photo of the impression, can identify the make and model of the tire or shoe. This, however, will not lead to a specific shoe or tire, but it can be enough to obtain a warrant from a judge to search a suspect's home for a particular type of shoe, or the suspect's car for a particular brand of tires. These shoes or tires can help link the suspect to the crime scene.

FINGERPRINTS

The history of fingerprints stretches back into antiquity. Fingerprints have been used as a form of signature since ancient times. It was not until the last quarter of the nineteenth century that they were used as a means of identifying criminals. At that time, several individuals in different parts of the world were working with fingerprints. Until the advent of DNA, fingerprints were the key forensic method of positively identifying individuals. Even now, fingerprints are still the only truly individual type of evidence; not even DNA is completely individual, since identical twins have the same DNA. Identical twins, however, do not have identical fingerprints because fingerprint ridges are formed in utero during the second trimester, and identical twinning occurs before the twelfth day postconception.

On the surface of everyone's feet, toes, hands, and fingers are ridges of skin. These are known as friction ridges. These ridges aid in gripping. These ridges consist of lines that form a variety of patterns. On the tips of the fingers there are larger patterns, which consist of arches, loops, and whorls, and there are smaller details, known as minutiae. Once fingerprints develop while the fetus is in utero, they do not change during a person's lifetime, except to become larger. Also, each fingerprint is unique—not only will no two people have the same fingerprints but also one person will not have two fingerprints that are the same.

Fingerprint Patterns and Subtypes

There are three basic fingerprint patterns: arches, loops, and whorls; and eight subtypes. All fingerprints are classified based on the characteristics seen in all 10 fingers.

Fingerprint matches are not made solely on the larger details of each fingerprint, that is, on the loops, whorls, and arches, but also there are often many, many smaller details, referred to as minutiae, in any print that help make identification possible. The lines that comprise the fingerprint may begin and end and split, there may be scarring, there may be creases, all of which are permanent. Also, there may be temporary changes in the fingerprint caused by warts or cuts, among other causes. It is the unique pattern of these small details that creates the individuality of fingerprints. In many cases, these little details serve to highlight the individuality of the fingerprints, and while many individuals have similar fingerprint patterns, these little details are individual.

Print Collection and Analysis

While this discussion focuses on fingerprints, prints can also be left by the palm of the hand and the soles of the feet. The same search, development, and collection techniques would apply to these prints also. Like any search for evidence, the search for fingerprints must be systematic. The search will focus on areas that are most likely to contain fingerprints, starting with the area surrounding the crime scene. Fingerprints are also likely to be found at the points of entry and exit to the crime scene and especially on any items that have been moved.

There are three types of prints that may be found at the crime scene: visible, plastic, and latent. A visible print may be found in colored material like paint or blood. It will require no further development or enhancement before it can be photographed and collected. Plastic prints are found in soft surfaces like wax or clay. They can be photographed or even cast.

Latent prints are not readily visible and require development before they can be photographed and collected. In some cases, when the surface is smooth and nonreflective, oblique lighting may enhance the print enough to be photographed. The most commonly used method for fingerprint development is dusting with a variety of powders. Black powder is the oldest and still very common, now, however, powders are available to contrast with any background. On adhesive surfaces, several powders may be used to create the contrast necessary to develop prints. There are also a variety of chemical methods that can be used to develop prints, including iodine fuming, ninhydrin, silver nitrate, nitric acid, and cyanoacrylate fuming—otherwise known as *super glue fuming*.

Once the prints are developed, they may be photographed and/or collected. During the collection process, gloves must always be worn. The print should first be photographed, and then it should be lifted with lifting tape. The tape will then be placed on paper or a card and labeled, sealed and properly marked.

SUPER GLUE FUMING   The fact that super glue fumes could develop fingerprints was discovered in Japan quite by accident in a super glue factory. Some of the workers noticed that in certain portions of the plant, fingerprints on Coca-Cola cans were visible. Super glue fuming is a deceptively simple technique. The object that contains suspected fingerprints should be placed in an almost enclosed area. At the scene, this can be done by creating a small tent with plastic. In the laboratory, specialized hooded work areas can be utilized. The super glue is spread on a large surface, like a pie plate, and hot air is blown over the surface area of the super glue—creating as many fumes as possible. A common household hairdryer can be used for this process. When there is a sufficient amount of super glue fumes around the object, the latent prints will become visible because the fumes react to the natural oils contained in all fingerprints.

LIFTING FINGERPRINTS OFF OF THE HUMAN BODY   Fingerprints can be visualized on the human body through either the use of a lead powder, which will then be X-rayed, or iodine fumed. It is also possible to use special lighting techniques and lasers to make fingerprints visible. If it is suspected that the body will contain fingerprints, efforts should be made to develop these prints as soon as possible. The natural decaying of the body will erode fingerprints, as will fluctuating temperatures and, of course, any environmental factors that the body is exposed to—like water.

FINGERPRINT COMPARISONS AND MATCHES   Fingerprint matches are based on how portions of the fingerprint relate to each other overall. Because the skin is elastic and because fingerprints will appear differently on different surfaces, it is not generally beneficial to measure distance between points on a fingerprint, however, it is beneficial to measure relative location. The patterns and minutiae of a person's fingerprint should be relatively stable in relation to each other. The examiner will look to see if the same minutiae exist in both prints, in the same locations. Although this was once done through the time-consuming method of fingerprint card searches, it can now be done through computerized technology, such as databases and laser fingerprint analysis.

LASER FINGER PRINT ANALYSIS AND EYE RECOGNITION SYSTEMS   Laser fingerprint analysis and eye-pupil recognition technology utilizes laser scan technology to review a fingerprint and eye composition for identification purposes. This technology is not only used to identify suspected criminals but also for security clearance and access to secure areas and installations. The laser fingerprint scan can be used to cross compare fingerprints across large databases of logged fingerprints of convicted felons. The advantage is that these identification systems are extremely fast and accurate and cannot be exploited by identity thieves unless they have their eyes and fingerprints changed to match a specific target for identity theft.

ACCIDENTS AND HIT-AND-RUN CRIMES

Not all accidents are hit-and-run crimes, of course, not all hit-and-run crimes are accidents. However, the reconstruction of both of these situations is similar. Insurance companies will often do some sort of accident reconstruction when determining fault in even minor accidents. Reconstruction is a method of determining what happened during the event in question. This includes but is not limited to the order of events. Determinations are often made regarding the speed of the vehicles, point of impact, placement of vehicles just prior to the crash, trajectory of vehicles after impact, and final resting spots of vehicles.

Accident Reconstruction

There are many similarities between accident reconstruction and crime scene reconstruction. Both seek to establish what happened and the exact order of events. An accident may quickly become a criminal investigation, depending upon the circumstances and especially if drugs or alcohol were involved; an accident will also require reconstruction for insurance purposes, even if no criminal charges are to be filed.

Accident reconstruction begins at the end and works its way backward to the events that led up to the accident and is primarily concerned with two events: the point of impact, and the final resting spot. In the case of a two-car accident, the reconstruction will begin with photographing of both vehicles at the point where they finally came to rest after impact.

The place at which the vehicles collided and the point of impact, will also be focused upon. The point of impact may be known, because one car was stopped at a light, or because witnesses can state with a great deal of certainty where the point of impact was. There may be debris surrounding the point of impact, because of broken headlights, turning lights, bumpers, and so forth.

Photographing the Accident Scene

The accident scene is photographed in a systematic fashion. The first photographs are taken of evidence that will need to be quickly moved (possibly because it is blocking traffic), or that will deteriorate quickly. When an accident occurs on a busy road, it will need to be cleared as quickly as possible to allow for normal traffic flow to resume; this will necessitate taking photographs quickly.

The point of impact is photographed, more importantly, it figures significantly into measurements that are taken. The measurement of the distance from point of impact to where the cars came to rest after impact can be used to determine the speeds of the vehicles.

Photographs will also be taken of skid marks and yaw marks (the marks tires create on the road surface when moving sideways). Skid and yaw marks are used to determine the direction of travel prior to the crash (Figures 7.6–7.8). Skid and yaw marks are important in determining if one of the drivers tried to stop prior to impact. In some one-car crashes, the absence of skid marks may indicate that the car crash was really a suicide attempt. It can also indicate that the driver was asleep

FIGURE 7.6   Close-range skid.

FIGURE 7.7 Mid-range skid.

FIGURE 7.8 Long-range skid.

at impact or was unaware of the impending impact due to intoxication or for another reason. An absence of skid marks may indicate that a driver died prior to the accident, for example, from a heart attack or embolism. If the driver was already deceased or dying during the accident, he or she cannot be held responsible for the accident.

Individuals who were involved in the crash and other witnesses will be interviewed. Although eyewitness statements, like eyewitness testimony, can be unreliable, they are recorded for reconstruction purposes. In order for statements to be as untainted as possible, witnesses should be isolated from each other as soon as possible so that they cannot discuss what happened. Even unintentionally, discussion among witnesses can lead to changed statements. Not any one eyewitness will have seen everything that occurred, nor will any one eyewitness remember everything. For this reason, the statements of all of the witnesses are considered during reconstruction.

Through the use of all three methods: measurements, photographs, and interviews, accident reconstruction specialists will determine what happened before, during, and after the impact. Engineers who specialize in the stress testing of metals can assist in determining the degree of force and the speed at which a car was traveling during the accident.

Accident Evidence Collection

Because many accidents occur on roadways that cannot remain closed indefinitely for evidence collection, all evidence must be collected quickly and systematically. Once the road is reopened for public traffic, any remaining evidence may be lost. Photographs will be an important method of evidence collection, especially if vehicles are not impounded. They will also be the only permanent record of the end result of the accident.

Vehicles that sustain significant amounts of damage or were driven during the possible commission of a crime will be impounded. There will be ample opportunity for the interiors of these vehicles to be searched during impounding. If drugs or alcohol are suspected as a cause of the accident, these may be found in the vehicle.

Glass fragments are collected from the road. Paint markings are noted and photographed, especially in the case of a hit and run. Metal shards and fragments are also collected. Of course, witness identification and statements are recorded. In some areas where video recordings are used, these may also be available for analysis.

PAINT ANALYSIS

In our daily environment, paint is a very common chemical substance. Paint is found both inside our houses and on the exterior; cups and dishes that we use are often painted; signs may be painted, along with benches, furniture, and many other products. The most common interaction with paint in forensics is with automotive paints and in crimes involving either accidents or hit-and-run crimes. Paint evidence may also be encountered in burglary investigations if paint transfers onto tools. Automotive paint may be found on a victim or on other cars or objects at the crime scene. Paint may be found in the form of smears or chips—with chips being the more useful because they contain information not only about the surface paint, but also about the chemicals contained in the layers beneath the surface. The painting of an automobile is a multilayered process, and insight into the layers can help identify evidence.

Automotive Paint Collection and Analysis

Paint has five components: pigment, oils, driers, paint solvents, and plasticizers (Saferstein 1982). Because various manufacturers use different formulas and processes for each of these components, a paint chip can provide considerable information and lead to identification of the specific manufacturer. For example; Suzuki and McDermot (2006) state that nickle titanate was used in almost three dozen yellow nonmetallic monocoats between 1974 and 1989, while chrome titanate was only used in a few yellow and orange nonmetallic monocoats. Information like this can enable the forensic chemist to quickly narrow down the particular makes, models, and vehicle years in which the paint in question was used. This information can then be collated with information from the department of motor vehicles and a list of possible suspects and their vehicles can be created.

Paint Databases

While the FBI does not maintain a paint database, most manufacturers do keep a record of the variety of paints and paint components that they have manufactured. Just as with shoe marks and tire treads, it is important for the forensic scientist to have a good working relationship with individuals in the industry. The Royal Canadian Mounted Police maintain the International Forensic Automotive Paint Database. Investigators can utilize this source for assistance in matching a paint to a possible source.

GLASS EVIDENCE

Just like soil and paint, glass is very common in our daily environment. Glass is found in automobiles, windows, doors, dishes, bottles, eyewear, televisions, computers, and so forth. Take a look around where you are sitting right now; chances are there are several types of glass that you can see.

Glass is generally considered to be a supercooled liquid, although there is disagreement, sometimes it is considered to be an amorphous solid. It is really neither a solid nor a liquid. It also does not crystallize. Glass can be either naturally occurring, for example obsidian, or synthetic. The earliest forms of glass and most glass that is manufactured today are made from soda-lime. A variety of chemicals can be added to glass to add or change its properties, for example, glass that contains a significant amount of lead oxide is lead crystal. Glass can be treated with heat to temper it, which makes it stronger. Tempered glass is found in automobile windshields; this prevents shattering. Automotive glass, upon impact, will crumble, rather than shatter. This prevents vehicle occupants from being cut with glass shards. It also prevents tempered glass from being cut in any way. Once glass is tempered, it cannot be cut. It must first be formed into the particular windshield shape, and then tempered.

Glass Collection and Analysis

When glass evidence is encountered at the crime scene, the first question that must be asked is "Is a physical match possible?" If the pieces of broken glass can be fit together, every effort should be made to do so. A physical match gives glass evidence, which is class evidence, individual characteristics. When a physical match may be possible, each piece of glass should be packaged separately and all glass must be collected. It is better to collect debris that is not glass and allow the examiner to make the determination of what material is important and what is not. Large glass pieces should be wrapped and packaged in a box. This will not only protect the glass but also those who will work with the evidence. Smaller pieces of glass may be collected in vials.

In the laboratory, glass can be examined for its nonoptical as well as its optical properties. Nonoptical properties of interest to the forensic scientist are hardness and density. Generally, if the nonoptical properties of the piece of glass in question differ significantly from that of the known glass, then the questioned glass did not originate from the same source as the known glass. If the nonoptical properties of the questioned glass are the same as that of the known glass, it is possible that both pieces of glass came from the same source, but it is not definite. The nonoptical properties of glass are class characteristics and not individual characteristics.

The optical properties of glass refer to how the glass interacts with light. Optical properties include the absorption of light, fluorescence, and refractive index. Absorption of light can be measured. Glass that absorbs all wavelengths of visible light equally is clear or grey. Clear glass has a low absorption of light and grey has a high absorption of light. Colored glass will absorb particular wavelengths better than others; this is what creates the appearance of the color to the human eye. Fluorescence occurs when light of a shorter wavelength interacts with the glass to produce light of a longer wavelength. This can be examined visually under a UV lamp. The refractive index refers to how the glass bends light. As with the nonoptical properties of glass, if the optical properties of the questioned glass are the same as that of the known glass, it is possible that both pieces of glass came from the same source, but it is not definite. The optical properties of glass are class characteristics— not individual characteristics.

Glossary

Elements—when referring to a crime, these are the conditions that must be met.

Hot spots—areas where certain crimes occur more frequently.

Larceny—theft.

Scale—used when photographing evidence to record relative size. Usually a small ruler or paper tape measure.

Statute—a written law.

Theft—unlawful taking.

Webliography

American Association of Motor Vehicle Administrators http://www.aamva.org/

U.S. Department of Labor: Occupational Safety & Health Administration http://www.osha.gov/

References

Association of Art Museum Directors. June 4, 1998. *Report of the AAMD Task Force on the Spoliation of Art During the Nazi/World War II Era (1933–1945)*. Accessed on February 25, 2007, from http://www.aamd.org/papers/guideln.php.

Davila, M. *After the flood: Fraud among the elderly after natural disasters*. Unpublished doctoral dissertation. Sam Houston State University, Texas, 2005.

FBI. Art Theft Program. Accessed on February 25, 2007, from http://www.fbi.gov/hq/cid/arttheft/arttheft.htm.

FBI. 2006. Crime in the United States 2005: Table 1. Accessed on November 27, 2006, from http://www.fbi.gov/ucr/05cius/data/table_01.html.

FBI. 2006. Crime in the United States 2005: Table 43. Accessed on November 27, 2006, from http://www.fbi.gov/ucr/05cius/data/table_43.html.

FBI. March 29, 2007. Headline Archives: Car Cloning. Accessed on April 15, 2007, from http://www.fbi.gov/page2/march07/carcloning032907.htm.

FBI. April 6, 2007. Headline Archives: Organized Retail Theft. Accessed on April 15, 2007, from http://www.fbi.gov/page2/april07/retail040607.htm.

FBI. July 21, 2006. Headline Archives: Cargo Theft's High Cost. Accessed on February 25, 2007, from http://www.fbi.gov/page2/july06/cargo_theft072106.htm.

FBI. Jewelry and Gem Program. Accessed on February 25, 2007, from http://www.fbi.gov/hq/cid/jag/jagpage.htm.

FBI. *National Stolen Art File*. Accessed on November 27, 2006, from http://www.fbi.gov/hq/cid/arttheft/nationalstolen.htm.

FBI. April 5, 2007. Press Release: FBI partners with retailers to fight organized retail theft. Accessed on April 15, 2007, from http://www.fbi.gov/pressrel/pressrel07/database040507.htm.

Jewelers' Security Alliance. 2006. Accessed on February 25, 2007, from http://www.jewelerssecurity.org/index.php4.

Minnesota burglary statute (609.582, Subdivision 2). Minnesota Office of the Revisor of Statutes. Accessed on April 15, 2007, from https://www.revisor.leg.state.mn.us/bin/getpub.php?type=s&num=609.582&year=2006.

Mississippi Department of Agriculture and Commerce. Agricultural theft bureau. Accessed on April 15, 2007, from http://www.mdac.state.ms.us/n_library/departments/ag_theft/index_agtheft.html.

National Retail Federation. January 9, 2006. Merchants welcome signing of organized retail theft bill. Accessed on January 21, 2006, from http://www.nrf.com/modules.php?name=News&op=viewlive&sp_id=36.

National Retail Federation. About organized retail crime. Accessed on April 15, 2007, from http://www.lpinformation.com/Default.aspx?tabid=259.

Pennsylvania burglary statute (Title 18, Part II, Article C, Chapter 35, subsection 3502).

Quarantelli, E. L. "Statistical and Conceptual Problems in the Study of Disasters." *Disaster Prevention and Management* 10 (2001): 325–40.

Saferstein, R. ed. *Forensic Science Handbook*. Englewood Cliffs, NJ: Prentice Hall, 1982.

Suzuki, E. M., and M. X. McDermot. "Infrared Spectra of U.S. Automobile Original Finishes. VII Extended Range FT-IR and XRF Analysis of Inorganic Pigments in situ—Nickel Titanate and Chrome Titanate." *Journal of Forensic Sciences* 51, no. 3 (May 2006): 532–547.

Wall, A. D. *Disaster Fraud*. Glen Allen, VA: National White Collar Crime Center, 2005.

Review Questions

1. How does burglary investigation differ from theft investigation?
2. What is the difference between class evidence and individual evidence?
3. What is trace and transfer evidence?
4. What is a toolmark?
5. Compare the challenges that are faced by the first responder in preserving wet footprints and tireprints left in snow.
6. What is the process for identifying a shoe print?
7. For personal identification, what is the best form of individual evidence?
8. How can we lift a latent fingerprint from the body of a deceased individual?
9. What are the components of soil analysis?
10. What types of materials are tracked by a forensic botanist?

Some Things to Think About

1. Why do you think no one has ever classified criminals based on palm prints or the prints from the soles of their feet?
2. How can the investigator work with industry to identify a certain paint?
3. How can forensic botany be useful in an investigation?

Violent Felonies

Section IV consists of Chapter 8 *The Process of Dying and Death Investigation,* Chapter 9 *DNA,* and Chapter 10 *Assault, Abuse and Sexual Crimes.* The crimes covered in Chapters 8 and 10 are some of the most violent and serious crimes investigated by the criminal justice system. Chapter 8 explores the natural process of death, from time of death to decomposition to skeletonization. Through understanding this process, the body reveals significant information to the investigator. This chapter discusses the crime of homicide. Of all crimes, homicide creates the most forensic evidence, and the most significant piece of evidence is the body. To understand what the body is telling us, we will cover a variety of subareas of forensics that may be involved in conducting a death investigation; forensic pathology, forensic entomology, forensic anthropology, forensic odontology, bloodspatter analysis, and ballistics. This chapter also looks at the unique challenges of dealing with the "long" dead.

Chapter 9 is devoted to the most significant advance in modern forensics—DNA. It is difficult to believe that as recently as 20 years ago very little was done in forensics with DNA. Although not quite as individual as fingerprints, the advent of forensic DNA analysis has led to unsolved cases being resolved and the wrongfully prosecuted being released from prison. With the more recent advent of mitochondrial DNA, it is now possible to get DNA from saliva and hair and very small or very old samples.

Chapter 10 discusses the violent crimes of assault, domestic violence, rape, and child abuse. In some cases, the forensic evidence left behind is significant. Investigation of these crimes may involve serology, DNA analysis, hair and fiber analysis, and fragment analysis. In other cases, especially when the crime is not reported to law enforcement immediately, the forensic evidence has been lost—making prosecution much more difficult. This chapter also discusses victimology, the *study of the victim.* Too often, the victim is discounted in the criminal justice system, in forensics, the victim is significant to the development of the case.

The Process of Dying and Death Investigation

Forensic Entomology
  Immediately After Death
  Collection and Preservation of Entomology Evidence

Everybody dies. We are all born and we will all die. The body inevitably breaks down. Sometimes it breaks down even prior to birth and sometimes it breaks down when we are in our nineties. While most of us will die of natural causes—the most common cause being some form of heart disease—in forensics we frequently deal with deaths that are not from natural causes. This chapter begins by covering the natural process of the body's breaking down that occurs during any death. This breaking down is first evidenced by *livor mortis* and *rigor mortis* and later in decomposition. Then we will turn our attention to death and homicide investigation. We will discuss death certification, determining cause and manner of death, death and homicide investigation, and the importance of the autopsy. This chapter also covers several related forensic fields that may be called upon in the identification of bodies: forensic anthropology (the study of bones), forensic odontology (the study of teeth), and forensic entomology (the study of the growth and development of insects that colonize the decomposing body)—especially important when a body is located long after death.

THE PROCESS OF DYING

Death can be defined in a variety of ways. Brain death is the absence of higher-level brain activity, even though the individual may still be breathing and their heart is circulating blood. Noteworthy cases such as those of Terri Schiavo, Nancy Cruzan (from the 1980s), and Karen Ann Quinlan (from the 1970s) illustrate some of the complexities of determining what exactly is meant by *death*. In each of these cases, the young women were *brain dead*, yet were kept alive in persistent vegetative states through the use of artificial respiration and feeding tubes. As our society has become increasingly medicalized, we have come to rely upon a medical definition of death. Certainly, in the absence of brain activity and heart activity the individual is dead. In a society where considerable medical intervention is available, an individual can be placed on a ventilator so that breathing can be assisted mechanically; an individual who cannot maintain his or her own heart rate can be assisted with medication or a pace maker; an individual who is unconscious and cannot eat may be tube-fed. Most of the questions raised by such artificial life extension fall outside of the scope of criminal justice and are better dealt with in the field of medical ethics. In the United States, death is defined as brain death; whereas in European nations, death is defined either as the loss of all independent lung and heart function or the permanent and irreversible loss of all brain function.

According to the Centers for Disease Control and Prevention (CDC), the leading cause of death in the United States in 2002 was heart disease—with 696,947 deaths—followed closely by all cancers with 557,271 deaths, and stroke, a distant third with 162,672 deaths (http://www.cdc.gov/nchs/fastats/lcod.htm). Not only was heart disease the leading cause of death in 2002, but it has been the leading cause of death in the United States every year since 1921. Heart disease, pneumonia, and tuberculosis were ranked as the top three leading causes of death since 1901 (http://www.cdc.gov/nchs/data/dvs/lead1900_98.pdf). In the United States, during the 1930s and 1940s antibiotics were developed to treat bacterial pneumonia and successful treatments for tuberculosis were also developed. Because of these medical advances, pneumonia and tuberculosis became less deadly.

As a cause of death, in 2002, homicide ranked twentieth for Caucasian individuals, seventh for Hispanic individuals, and sixth for African-American individuals in the United States. Assault is the second leading cause of death for individuals 15–24 years of age (http://www.cdc.gov/nchs/data/nvsr/nvsr53/nvsr53_17.pdf). This disparity in chance of experiencing violent death can be partially attributed to economic disparities. Minorities are more likely to occupy inner-city areas and these areas more likely to be economically depressed. The inner city has higher rates of unemployment, gang activity, and more visible drug activity. Minorities are also more likely to be involved in the criminal justice system than Caucasians—even when they commit similar offenses. All of these factors increase the likelihood that minority individuals will be involved in drugs and violence.

In developing countries the leading cause of death is AIDS, followed closely by lower respiratory tract infections—much as respiratory diseases figured so prominently in death statistics in the United States in the early part of the twentieth century. AIDS infection rates are high in developing countries due to the low frequency of condom use among the general population. Once infected, many forms of treatment, especially newer drug treatments, are unavailable in developing countries. Respiratory infections are common because of overcrowded conditions, poor sanitation, and lack of routine medical care in many areas.

Death Certification

When a person dies, a death certificate is issued by the county in which the death occurred. The issuance of a death certificate provides a means for tracking individuals and diseases—this is how we know the leading causes of death during the early part of the twentieth century. The death certificate must be signed by several individuals, including a physician, a funeral director, and the local registrar. Having each of these individuals sign the death certificate serves as a safeguard against the issuance of false death certificates which could be used to obtain death benefits, file false insurance claims, or for other fraudulent purposes.

Many states began tracking deaths and issuing death certificates around 1900—also around the same time that births began to be tracked. Not all deaths and births were recorded in the early years of the system, since many occurred in the home even as late as the 1930s and 1940s (Figure 8.1). When

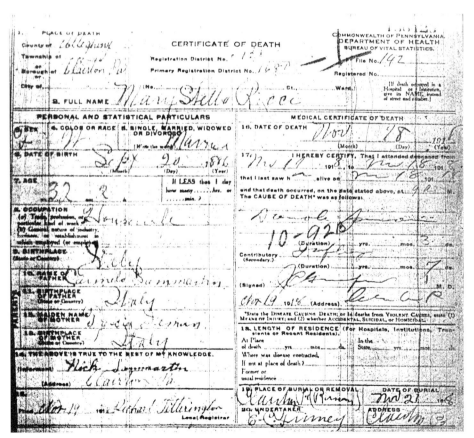

FIGURE 8.1   Death certificate from 1918.

hospital births, attended by physicians, as opposed to home births, attended by midwives, became commonplace in the 1940s, it became easier to track births. Once the use of morticians and funeral directors came into general acceptance—as the mortuary business became increasingly professionalized, and their services were regulated—it became easier to track deaths.

Deaths are tracked for several reasons. First, death may end or trigger payments to individuals and the government. When alive and earning income, a person pays taxes; after death, the estate will pay taxes one final time and then the tax obligation to the government is finished. The death of an individual who has minor children will trigger the payment of survivor benefits. A death may also cause property and money to transfer from one individual to another or from joint ownership to sole ownership, as is the case when a spouse dies, jointly owned assets, such as a house and bank accounts, may transfer automatically to the surviving spouse.

Several causes of death may be listed on the death certificate including the *immediate cause* and the conditions which may have given rise to that cause. For example, heart failure may be the immediate cause of death, but kidney failure and liver failure may be the conditions which precipitated the heart failure (Figure 8.2). When the manner of death is homicide, then the cause of death is of great interest to law enforcement. If the cause of death is attributed to an illness or disease, this will be tracked by epidemiologists and the CDC.

The death certificate lists the decedent's parents' names—if known—and the name of any surviving spouse. While this information isn't particularly useful to law enforcement, it can be useful to genealogists who are tracing family histories. The death certificate also indicates whether or not an autopsy was performed. A physician will sign the death certificate. In most cases, when the individual dies in a hospital, the attending physician will sign the death certificate. When the individual dies under a doctor's care—but not in a hospital—their own physician will sign.

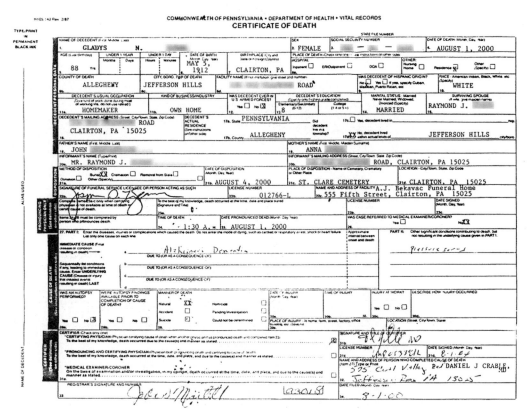

FIGURE 8.2 Death certificate from 2000.

The Unattended Death

A death that is not witnessed will trigger an investigation. This is especially the case if the individual was not under a doctor's care, if the person was young, if the death may have been the result of a homicide or suicide. When a person dies and it is not witnessed, a number of professionals become involved. These may include paramedics, police, and the medical examiner. The following case illustrates how each set of professionals is involved in determining the cause and manner of death.

A 33-year-old male found unresponsive in his bedroom by his housemate. Emergency responders are called to a private residence at 8:45 P.M. Paramedics arrive at the scene at 8:56 P.M., police respond at 9:03 P.M. Paramedics pronounce the young man dead at 8:56 P.M., although it is apparent from the condition of the body that the young man has been dead for at least eight hours. Paramedics depart, leaving the investigation in the hands of the police. The medical examiner's office is contacted.

Three people live at the house, Richard, the young man who called the police, Richard's young son, and the decedent, Frederick. Officers question Richard, who is the nephew of the owner of the house. He states that he and the decedent had watched movies last night until around 1:30 A.M. The decedent then retired to his room. Richard went to work the following morning and had not seen the decedent. When the young man had not seen the decedent by late that evening, even though the decedent's car was parked outside, he went into the bedroom and found him sitting at the edge of his bed slumped over. The young man stated that he tried to rouse the decedent and when he was not successful, he called the police immediately. Richard was visibly very upset while talking to police.

The decedent was found sitting near the bottom left corner of his bed. His right ankle is crossed over his left thigh. The left side of his face rests on a Sudoku puzzle book that is clutched in his left hand. A pen is clutched in his right hand, at his side. He is wearing blue jeans and a grey long-sleeve shirt.

There is one entry into the room and two small windows. There are no signs of a struggle. There is no evidence of trauma to the body. Homicide is tentatively ruled out. No drugs or alcohol were found in the vicinity of the body. Officers did note an ashtray filled with cigarette butts on a table beside the bed. Suicide is tentatively ruled out pending toxicology.

Because there is no apparent evidence of homicide or suicide, police turn the matter over to the medical examiner's office and file a routine report. An investigator from the medical examiner's office arrives at the scene at 10:05 P.M. and takes the body into custody. Investigators note that the body is in full rigor mortis, indicating the decedent had been dead between eight and twelve hours.

A full autopsy is performed the next morning, following standard autopsy procedures. The pathologist notes no exceptional findings to indicate stroke, heart attack, or other indication of a blood clot. Upon gross dissection of the major internal organs, no tumors are noted. It was noted that the lungs weighed close to twice the expected lung weight and were almost filled with fluid, suggestive of left-side congestive heart failure. All major organs were removed and sections were submitted for histology. Toxicology was also submitted. The body is released to the funeral home that afternoon. The death certificate is issued listing the cause of death as *pending*. Histology is completed two weeks later. The toxicology report, due to the volume at the laboratory, is completed three months later. The manner of death is ruled as natural. The cause of death is congestive heart failure. The final report is filed at the medical examiner's office 128 days after death.

Immediately After Death

Immediately following death, the body begins to break down and many processes occur simultaneously. The body cools from 98.6 degrees F to room temperature or whatever the outside temperature is. This cooling process is referred to as *algor mortis*. Once the heart stops beating, the blood will settle to the lowest point in the body. This settling process is referred to as livor mortis. The area where the blood settles will discolor and take on a purplish, bruised appearance as a result of the pooling of blood in the tissues. If a body is moved after livor mortis has occurred, there may be multiple bruising patterns. Also, a stiffening of the joints occurs; this is referred to as rigor mortis, which begins first in the smaller joints and proceeds throughout the body.

As rigor mortis passes, decomposition occurs. The skin will begin to turn green starting at the abdomen, and the body will begin to swell because of the formation of bacterial methane gas. Epidermal sloughing occurs while hemoglobin degradation begins. This is the destruction of the red blood cells in the body. Decomposing blood and bodily fluids are forced out of the body through all of its openings in a process called purging. Under normal circumstances this occurs about four days postmortem. When decomposition is finished, all that remains of the body is the skeleton. Under the right conditions, skeletonization can occur in a matter of weeks—for example in heat and moisture (Dix and Calaluce 1999).

Decomposition is an important indicator when trying to determine the time of death. Unfortunately, the longer a body has been dead, the more difficult it becomes to pinpoint the exact time of death. Bodily indicators become less and less specific. For the long dead, the time of death may be narrowed down to a few weeks or months. There are a variety of factors that significantly alter the rate of decomposition—and even on a single body; different areas may decompose at varying rates. For example, those areas of the body that are exposed to the elements will decompose faster, those areas of the body that are clothed, especially in leather (shoes, jacket) decompose at a slower rate.

Decomposition is not the only process at work that will eventually lead to the destruction of the body. Animals of all sorts may feed off the body. Bodies indoors that are exposed to air will naturally be colonized by insects; these are most likely to be found in the moist regions of the body including the eyes, nose, mouth, genital area, and any areas that have been injured, especially when bleeding has occurred.

In addition to insects, bodies exposed to the elements outdoors may be eaten by animals ranging from rats in the city to predators such as wolves in the wild. While being in water slows down decomposition, it may expose the body to animals that dwell in the water that are especially likely to feed on the facial areas of the body because they are the areas most likely to be exposed.

The Process of Decomposition

Depending upon the conditions that a body is exposed to, it may evidence skeletonization in some areas, while other areas will show little evidence of decomposition. Although the sequence of decomposition remains the same under all circumstances, the rate of decomposition varies considerably depending upon environmental circumstances. The rate of decomposition can even vary in the same body. Decomposition is affected by both factors that are specific to the deceased individual and environmental factors. All of the following factors can significantly impact decomposition: body weight, injury and illness, chemicals, clothing, temperature, water and humidity, burial (also depth of burial), and insect and carnivore activity.

Larger bodies will decompose more slowly than smaller bodies. This can be extended to animals. Larger animals decompose more slowly than smaller animals. Injury and illness impact rate of decomposition. If injury has occurred—especially an injury with bleeding—this area of the body will decompose more quickly than noninjured areas of the body. Insects are attracted to the injured areas of the body and will feed off of the exposed blood there. Illnesses, especially those with fever, hasten the decay process as well. Chemicals, like insecticides, arsenic, and lead, in the body can halt decomposition almost entirely. Clothing, especially leather, generally slows decomposition and can protect the body from being eaten, although fly larvae and ants will still have access to the body. A body that was only partially clothed may show evidence of less decomposition in the areas that are covered, while exposed areas may skeletonize quite quickly.

Temperature can significantly alter the rate at which a body decomposes. A body that has lain outside in the snow will evidence little decomposition. In fact, hospitals and funeral homes often place bodies in refrigerated units while waiting for the family's instructions because refrigeration will halt decomposition. Conversely, bodies exposed to high temperatures will decompose very rapidly; at 100 degrees F, the body may skeletonize within weeks.

Moisture and water can have varied effects on a body. Humidity can serve to preserve a body. In general, the moist areas of the body will attract more insects, which, in turn, will speed decomposition. Bodies submerged in water or exposed to excess water may also become waxy (adipocere). A body submerged in water will remain white and the outer layers of skin can be lost. Decomposition under water progresses at about half the speed of normal decomposition.

Dryness serves to speed up the process of decomposition and skeletonization. Dryness in combination with heat may cause mummification. During the process of mummification the body dehydrates and the internal organs dry up; the skin becomes dark and dry as the body shrinks. The heat and dryness retard bacterial growth. The process of mummification can preserve a body for hundreds—and in the case of the Egyptians who mummified their dead—or even thousands of years.

A buried body will decompose more slowly than one that is exposed to air. Burial will generally prevent the body from being eaten by larger animals—unless the grave is shallow, or the body is unearthed. Burial may also preserve trace evidence, so a burial site should be excavated very carefully so that trace evidence is not accidentally discarded.

Insect and carnivore activity also impact decomposition. Bodies that are outside may be exposed to significant destruction from carnivores. Bodies that are in water will often evidence destruction from sea animals in the facial region. There will always be insect destruction of the body, regardless of where the death occurs.

Investigators face mounting difficulties in determining time and manner of death as the process of decomposition progresses. Trace evidence may be lost to the elements. Internal organs dry up and can no longer be analyzed for toxins. Even clothing may deteriorate, making identification increasingly difficult. At this point, a forensic anthropologist may be needed to assist in making an identification from skeletal remains alone.

Death Investigation

A death investigation is not a homicide investigation. Death investigations are conducted in instances where it is not immediately apparent that a person has died from natural causes. While most deaths in the United States fall under the category of natural causes, some do not, and can be categorized as suicide, homicide, accident, or undetermined (Figures 8.3–8.5).

FIGURE 8.3   Mid-range photograph of a gunshot suicide.

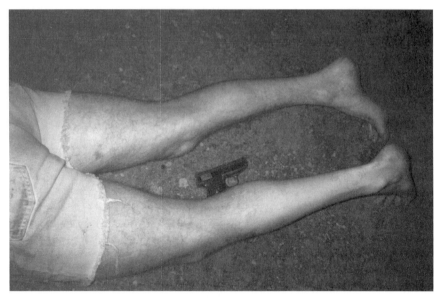

FIGURE 8.4 Photograph of gunshot suicide with gun.

FIGURE 8.5 Photograph of blood pool from gunshot suicide.

Deaths that are ruled suicide or accident require no further investigation. However, it can be difficult to make a clear distinction between some accidental deaths and some suicides. Car accidents that involve only one driver may actually be a suicide. It is also possible to have difficulties distinguishing between some homicides and suicide. A murderer may attempt to set up a death scene to make a homicide look like a suicide.

The category of *undetermined* is infrequently used, and is most often reserved for rare cases when a long period of time has elapsed between death and the discovery of physical remains and there simply is not enough evidence to indicate cause of death.

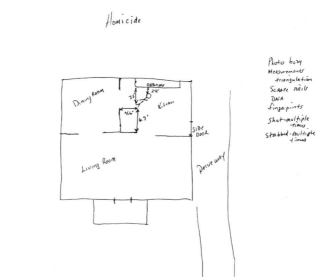

FIGURE 8.6   A homicide crime scene sketch.

Homicide Investigation

A homicide investigation, unlike a death investigation, is a criminal matter. The medical examiner will investigate the cause of death of any individual who did not die of natural causes. The medical examiner also investigates cases in which foul play is suspected, or where civil liability is an issue. In the case of homicide, the medical examiner becomes a part of a law enforcement investigative team (Figure 8.6).

Many police departments, especially larger departments, have specialized units or divisions to investigate all homicides. Homicide investigation may also be the responsibility of violent crimes units. In smaller jurisdictions, a homicide may be investigated by the most senior officers, or it may be investigated by the same officers who investigate all crimes in that area. A smaller jurisdiction lacking the experience or skill to competently investigate a homicide should ask for the assistance of another agency either a nearby jurisdiction that is larger, or an agency that also holds jurisdiction—such as the State Police. This is not always as easy as it sounds. In some cases, serious complications result when a smaller agency seeks the help of a larger agency. Local law enforcement generally dislike the idea of giving up control of investigations within their jurisdiction and they dislike giving up credit for a successful arrest as well. Sadly, sometimes egos get in the way of successful case resolution.

Under most circumstances, the FBI does not assist with the investigation of individual homicides, although all of its databases (fingerprints, DNA, etc.) are accessible to local law enforcement. Because of widespread interconnectivity, these databases are now available electronically 24 hours a day. When the FBI does assist with an investigation, they tend to focus their efforts on serial crimes and other crimes that cross lines of jurisdiction. Sometimes, even in these types of crimes, there is reluctance to ask for assistance from the FBI—again, egos can get in the way of successful resolution of crimes. Unfortunately, the FBI does not have a very good track record for sharing the credit for a successful arrest or sharing the blame when a crime goes unsolved.

HIGH CLEARANCE RATE FOR VIOLENT CRIMES   Violent crimes have a higher clearance rate than property crimes. Homicides generally are not difficult to solve and homicide had the highest clearance rate of all index offenses in the Uniform Crime Reports. In 2005, 62.1 percent of all homicides were cleared (http://www.fbi.gov/ucr/05cius/offenses/clearances/index.html#figure). Although many homicides are easily solved, even those homicides that are not so easy, have significant investigative energy devoted to them. These crimes are given the highest priority. There is significant political and social pressure to solve homicides. The media also play a major role in many homicide investigations by contributing to the considerable pressure to solve the crime.

Often the first responder to a homicide crime scene is not the primary investigator; for this reason alone, it is of the utmost importance that all patrol officers are properly trained to secure and protect the crime scene. Because most homicides are very quickly solved, the first responder will frequently make an arrest—especially if the offender is at the scene or in the vicinity. In most instances there are ample witnesses who can identify the perpetrator, who in turn quickly confesses or enters into a plea agreement. In homicides, very little, if any, forensics is used, other than an autopsy. It is the rare exception that requires significant investigative input and forensics—although it is these rare exceptions that the public tends to hear about. This is especially the case in serial homicides. These crimes create considerable public fear.

The process of a homicide investigation does not differ significantly from that of other crimes. The investigation must still be conducted in a systematic manner. The homicide scene must be protected and preserved. It must be thoroughly documented. All evidence must be handled properly, paying particular attention to chain of custody. The key difference in a homicide investigation is that the body is the most significant piece of evidence. The body must be properly handled and an autopsy conducted.

AT THE SCENE A homicide investigation consists of two parts. The first portion of the investigation takes place at the scene, whereas the second portion of the homicide investigation is the autopsy. At the crime scene, the body will be the most significant piece of evidence. Not only will much of the evidence be located on the body, but the majority of the ancillary evidence will be located in close proximity to the body. As such, it is essential to the investigation that the body be protected. As the distance from the body increases, the amount of useful evidence found generally decreases.

The normal investigative procedures should be followed at the crime scene: a wide perimeter should be established; all personnel should wear gloves; the crime scene search should focus on the area immediately surrounding the body, the location of which should be photographed and diagrammed from a variety of angles and distances with extra attention focused on any visible wounds. The hands and feet of the victim should be covered with paper bags prior to the body being removed from the scene by the medical examiner. In many cases, a victim would have made an attempt to fend off attack and may have evidence such as the perpetrator's skin cells or blood under his or her fingernails. Securing paper bags to the victim's wrists and ankles will prevent the loss of this evidence.

When the lead investigator is ready to release the body to the medical examiner's office, the body should be wrapped in a clean white sheet and then placed in a body bag. Proper procedure dictates that all body bags should be cleaned prior to each use; if there is a breakdown in this procedure—or if the bag was not thoroughly cleaned—the sheet will prevent cross-contamination of the body with products from other deceased individuals. It will also serve to catch any evidence that may become dislodged from the body during transit, such as hair and fibers. The majority of the evidence derived from the body will be obtained during the course of the formal autopsy.

THE AUTOPSY As discussed previously, some jurisdictions still have coroners, but most have switched to a medical examiner system. Coroners, being elected officials, may or may not have a medical background; conversely, all medical examiners are medical doctors. Counties that have coroners either have coroners that do have medical degrees, or the services of a pathologist will be retained to perform autopsies. The office of the medical examiner (coroner) is charged with the investigation of all suspicious or violent deaths; the medical examiner will determine the cause, manner, and time of death. Of course, part of this investigation will include conducting an autopsy.

The autopsy is a physical examination of a cadaver with the goal of determining the cause of death. An autopsy can also be referred to as a *postmortem examination* or a *necropsy*, though the term *necropsy* is generally used for the examination of animals. The autopsy is performed by a forensic pathologist, and generally one or two assistants are present for the examination.

An autopsy may be conducted for a number of reasons, both medical and legal. Medically, autopsies may be performed at hospitals to study why a person died and to increase knowledge about disease mechanisms. This is especially the case in teaching hospitals. Legally, autopsies are performed on all individuals whose deaths are not attributed to natural causes, or if the family requests an autopsy to investigate possible medical product liability or medical malpractice.

THE AUTOPSY PROCESS   The autopsy consists of three distinct phases. First, the body will be inspected as it was received, usually clothed. The pathologist will then conduct an external study of the body without clothing. Finally—and most lengthy—an internal examination will be conducted.

Once the body arrives at the medical examiner's office, it may be stored in a refrigerated unit prior to autopsy. Storing the body in a refrigerated unit will significantly halt deterioration of the body, as bacteria will not grow in the cold, and decomposition will almost cease. Because of this, it is absolutely necessary that all determinations regarding time of death be made prior to storing the body. The body is stored in cold to allow the pathologist to inspect the body in as close to the same state as it was discovered in. The clothed body will be examined and any unusual circumstances will be noted, such as cuts or tears in clothing made from a knife or gunshot wounds. The pathologist will expect that cuts and tears evidenced on clothing will indicate underlying injuries to the body. If there is a considerable mismatch, such as knife wounds to the chest, but no cuts in the clothing, this is noted and it is likely that the body was redressed after death. Once the clothing has been removed, it should be retained. The clothing will be examined further for trace evidence, such as semen stains, microscopic blood, dirt, hair, fibers, pollens, and so forth. The examination of the clothing will not be conducted by the forensic pathologist. It will generally be sent to the forensic laboratory.

Once the clothing has been removed, the body is then inspected without clothing. Particular attention is paid to all visible wounds (e.g., puncture wounds, knife wounds, gunshot wounds) and distinguishing marks (e.g., birthmarks, tattoos). At this time, photographs will be taken; and the body will be both weighed and measured (Figure 8.7).

The bulk of the autopsy consists of the detailed internal analysis of the body. At all times the pathologist is looking for any abnormalities. The first incision that is made is a Y-incision that opens

Y-Incision

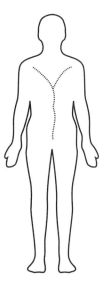

FIGURE 8.7   The autopsy Y-incision.

the chest and abdomen. The ribs are then cut away and removed to allow all of the internal organs to be removed. Each organ is weighed and examined, and samples may be taken to be sent to the laboratory for chemical analysis. Small sections of each organ are taken and preserved; thin slivers of the organs may be affixed to slides for microscopic examination. The stomach must be cut open and examined; its contents can be very important in establishing time of death because of the variable rates at which certain foods are digested. The heart is examined, the coronary arteries are sectioned, and all major blood vessels are also cut open and examined.

The brain is removed from the skull for inspection. First the top of the skull is removed, and then the brain is freed by cutting the brainstem. In some cases, the whole brain may be retained for future study, such as when there is significant brain pathology. In other cases, thin slices will be fixed to microscope slides for future analysis.

Time, Manner, and Cause of Death

Prior to autopsy, the time, manner, and cause of death may be estimated; the goal of the autopsy is to confirm this estimation. During the investigation of a suspected suicide or homicide, determining the time of death can be vitally important. Once the time of death is established forensically, it can support or contradict a suspect's statement and all of the other factual evidence being assembled during the investigation.

When a death is not witnessed—as most are—the medical examiner must initially determine the time of death. This determination is usually an estimate, it is often not possible to determine the *exact* time of death. The medical examiner's estimation is based on several factors: the time the deceased was last seen alive, compared to the time the body was found (referred to as the *death interval*), and the condition of the body when found. A body that evidences significant *rigor mortis*—under normal climatic conditions—may have been dead for about eight to twelve hours.

To estimate the time of death, the medical examiner will also take into account the temperature of the body. Normal body temperature is 98.6 degrees F (37 degrees C). A core body temperature will be taken in the liver—or just under the liver—shortly after the body is discovered; with the aim of estimating time of death. It used to be assumed that bodies cool to room temperature at an even rate of approximately 1.5 degrees an hour. However, this is not a fail-safe method for pinpointing the time of death as a variety of factors are known to affect cooling; such as the temperature of the room or the outside temperature, disease within the body prior to death (especially infection which tends to cause body temperature to rise after death), the environmental temperature around the body, and how the body was clothed or covered. Also, regardless of these other factors, many experts have varying opinions concerning what the *normal* rate of cooling for a body might be. Therefore, core body temperature can only serve as a rough estimation of how long the victim has been dead.

The *manner of death* is the circumstances surrounding death, and will be classified as one of the following: homicide, suicide, accident, natural causes, or undetermined causes. The majority of deaths are ruled natural causes, and the medical examiner is concerned only with those others such as homicide, suicide, undetermined, and some accidental deaths.

The *cause of death* is the injury or disease that began the sequence of events that ultimately results in death. A distinction is made between the proximal cause of death and the ultimate cause of death, with the proximal cause of death being the final condition that led to death.

Identification of the Dead

Unidentified bodies may come to light in various ways. Some are newly dead, some are long dead. Bodies may be found in water. When homeless people or runaways die, they frequently are not carrying identification—or may have had it stolen. Of course, the first priority when a dead body is found is to identify the deceased individual.

There are two types of identification, presumptive identification and positive identification. Presumptive identification is not a definite identification; it is based on assumptions. These

> ### Common Terms Surrounding Death
>
> *Rigor mortis* is the stiffening of the joints after death. This is created by a build up of the chemicals that cause muscle contractions. It begins within hours after death and continues until all joints are immovable, about 8 to 12 hours after death. It then subsides until the joints are again moveable 24 to 36 hours after death.
>
> *Livor mortis*, also referred to as *postmortem lividity*, refers to the settling of the blood into the lowest portions of the body after death. This results in a purplish red discoloration where the blood settles, much like bruising. The pattern of discoloration can be used to determine if the body has been moved after death. Each time the body is moved the blood will resettle and create a different bruising pattern.
>
> *Algor mortis* is the cooling of the body after death. It is estimated that the body cools approximately 1.5 degrees per hour until the body reaches room temperature.
>
> *Pallor mortis* is a paleness which appears almost immediately after death. Normal coloring in the human body is due to the blood that circulates just below the skin. Once blood stops circulating, the body becomes pale.

assumptions may be based upon physical features (birthmarks, scars, tattoos, organs that have been removed, and surgeries), clothing, personal items, circumstances surrounding death, and skeletal remains. If the investigators find a wallet on the victim, often the assumption is made that the wallet belongs to that person. However, wallets can be stolen. Likewise, the deceased may be wearing someone else's clothing, especially if the individual was a runaway. Often more certainty can be given to a presumptive identification when it is based upon a number of factors (birthmarks, clothing, and scars, for example).

Positive identification is definitive and generally is based upon one or more of the following: visual identification, X-rays, medical devices, fingerprints, dental records, and DNA analysis. Although the visual identification of a body is common, it presents significant problems. Accidents, fire, trauma, and length of time since death can change the facial appearance of the deceased considerably. Identification is easier if the body has not been dead for very long and if there has not been significant destruction to the facial features (through violence, fire, animals, or insects). Visual identification can also be very traumatic for relatives.

Postmortem X-rays can be compared to antemortem X-rays, unfortunately, many X-rays because of quality or age can only help with a presumptive identification. However X-rays of the skull and pelvis are very useful because of individual variation (Dix and Graham 1999). It has been noted that X-rays of the sinus region of the skull are highly individual (Kantarci et al. 2004). Although this was originally noted for applications during sinus surgery, it has application to forensic identification.

In cases where the individual has had a pacemaker inserted or another permanent medical device, an individual identification can be made. These medical devices have unique serial numbers on them that can be traced. The manufacturer of the device will have information regarding who had the device implanted, when the device was implanted, and where the device was implanted (Dix and Graham 1999).

Fingerprints, dental records, and DNA analysis are frequently used to identify bodies and will be discussed in significant detail elsewhere. Usually, deceased individuals are easily identified because they die in a hospital under the care of a doctor. Although estimates vary, about 40 percent of Americans die in a hospital and many others die in hospice care—either at home or in a facility.

FINGERPRINTING THE DEAD   The deceased is always fingerprinted during an investigation. This will help eliminate latent print evidence. If the deceased has not been positively identified, fingerprints may be needed to make identification. How long the individual has been dead and the overall condition of the fingers will impact how fingerprinting is done.

Normal inking, the same way fingerprints are taken from live individuals, can be done in the newly dead and after rigor mortis has left the body. If rigor mortis has set in, the fingers may have to be straightened. Another technique is to apply fingerprint powder to the deceased person's fingertips and use tape to lift the prints. Computer imaging, super glue fuming, and magnetic fingerprint powder can be used to obtain prints.

Fingerprinting becomes more and more complex as decomposition progresses. In cases where the skin has begun to slough off of the body, the individual taking the fingerprints can wear the skin like a glove and take the fingerprints that way.

COMMON CAUSES OF FATAL AND NONFATAL INJURIES

According to the CDC, the leading cause of fatal unintentional injury in the United States in 2004 was from motor vehicle accidents (43,432) and the leading cause of violent deaths in 2004 was from firearm suicide (16,750), followed by firearm homicide (11,624). This section will discuss the following causes of injuries: gunshot wound, puncture and incised wounds, blunt-force trauma, burning, drowning, asphyxiation, and strangulation.

Gunshot Wound

Firearms are used in the commission of a variety of offenses. DeForest et al. (1983) note that ". . . firearms are used in more than 60% of all homicides, more than 20% of all assaults, more than 35% of all robberies, and in almost half of all suicides" (p. 388). Even 25 years later, the CDC confirms that these figures are still accurate. Gunshot wounds can present in a variety of ways on autopsy depending upon where the individual was shot and the caliber of the weapon. Higher-caliber weapons cause greater destruction and automatic weapons are highly destructive. The pathologist will look for entrance and exit wounds and determine the path the projectile took as it moved through the body. If there is no exit wound, the pathologist will locate and remove the projectile from the body.

BALLISTICS Since the Saint Valentine's Day Massacre, law enforcement has recognized the importance of ballistics. The area of ballistics includes comparison and identification of weapons, bullets, cartridge cases, and projectiles. Ballistics experts are often called upon to testify regarding gunshot residue. At the scene of a homicide, bullets may be found not only in the victim but in objects at the scene, and the ballistics expert will determine the caliber of the weapon that fired the bullets while examining the discharged bullets for possible individual characteristics. The caliber of the bullet indicates the type of gun that could have fired the projectile, but it cannot prove what specific gun fired the bullet. However, the ballistics expert may examine the grooves on the spent bullet, which are made when the bullet passes through the gun barrel. When the gun is new, the markings that the barrel makes on the bullet are the same as the markings made by all similar type weapons (i.e., class evidence). Over time, with repeated firings, these markings will become individualized. This is one way in which the ballistics expert may match a bullet to the gun from which it was fired.

If the suspect is located shortly after the gun has been fired, gunshot residue may remain on his or her hands and clothing. This residue can be detected by laboratory analysis using a scanning electron microscope. Unfortunately, gunshot residue is easily removed from hands—through wiping, washing, or simply by engaging in activities that require the use of the hands. Also, the presence of gunshot residue does not necessarily indicate that the individual has fired a weapon merely that they have been around a weapon that has been fired.

The use of ballistics fingerprinting and firearms databases is somewhat controversial. The name *ballistics fingerprinting* is somewhat misleading because ballistic fingerprinting cannot be likened to normal fingerprinting. While all handguns have rifled barrels that create markings on bullets as they pass through the barrel, these markings will change over time and with repeated firings of the gun, whereas fingerprints will maintain their unique configuration throughout a person's life. The older the firearm, and the more often it has been fired, the more the markings will deviate from their original patterns. While some advocates have touted these databases as necessary in the fight against gun crime, detractors have noted that since a gun's fingerprint changes over time, these databases can be of limited use.

The Bureau of Alcohol, Tobacco, and Firearms maintains the National Integrated Ballistics Identification Network (NIBIN). NIBIN maintains a large database of markings made by firearms on both bullets and cartridge casings. Individual law enforcement agencies can compare evidence from their own cases to information that is stored in the database. Since the inception of the database, 12,500 "hits" assisting local law enforcement in their investigations (http://www.nibin.gov/nibin.pdf) have occurred.

Puncture and Incised Wounds

Puncture and incised wounds can be inflicted with a wide array of objects, including knives, ice picks, broken glass, and razors. A puncture wound, or stabbing wound, is made by trying to force entry into a body with a pointed instrument. This makes an injury that on the surface is small and round, but may extend deep into the body. The instrument does not have to be sharp—an individual can be stabbed with a pen—although sharp instruments will, of course, enter the body more readily. An individual who is stabbed with an ice pick has a puncture wound, as does the individual who steps on a rusty nail.

When a cut has smooth edges, it is referred to as an incision. Cutting and slashing wounds are made across an area. These wounds are generally made very quickly across an area, usually with a knife, razor, scalpel, or any other sharp implement, although surgeons also perform incisions when they operate, these are certainly done in a slow and deliberate manner.

The pathologist may note hesitation wounds and defensive wounds on the body. Hesitation wounds occur during a suicide when the individual makes several smaller and more shallow cuts (generally on the wrists) prior to making the deeper, fatal cuts. Hesitation wounds are very common in suicides where the wrists are cut. Defensive wounds will be found (usually on the hands and forearms) on an individual if they attempted to protect their face or body from an attack with a sharp object. The absence of defensive wounds may indicate that the victim was unconscious or dead when the knife attack occurred. It can also indicate that the individual was surprised by a quick and very violent attack—or that the victim knew and trusted the perpetrator.

Bloodspatter Analysis

Blood may be found at many different crime scenes, including homicides, suicides, assaults, and rapes. Less often, blood may be found at a robbery scene, although the perpetrator may be cut while entering or exiting the scene, or during the commission of the crime. Blood is analyzed for several reasons. Primarily, it will contain DNA—possibly the DNA of the perpetrator—secondarily, the patterns of blood on floors, walls, or other objects will be analyzed because it can reveal significant facts about how the injuries were inflicted; like distance, direction, repetition, and force and angle of strike. Categories of bloodstains include passive, transfer, and projected. A passive bloodstain occurs through gravity. Blood may drip onto a surface, flow from a wound, or pool under the victim. A transfer bloodstain occurs when one bloodstain object comes into contact with another surface. Projected bloodstains occur when the victim is injured through a strike of considerable force.

During an in-depth analysis of blood at the crime scene, investigators will examine the shapes, amounts, and the locations of blood. The investigator wants to determine how the stains were created, the origin and direction of travel of the blood, and the object used in the attack. A careful analysis can reveal the number of blows made with a weapon, the number of individuals at the scene, the sequence of events during the criminal act, and the positions of victim/perpetrator/and objects in the crime scene.

FIGURE 8.8 Bloodsmear on wall.

There may be blood spatter and blood smears at the crime scene. Blood spatter indicates that droplets of blood fell or were projected. Blood smears are created by a bloody object, such as a shoe, contacting another surface. Blood spatter analysis can tell the investigator the way in which the droplet was traveling and the angle of impact. Blood smears indicate that a bloody object contacted another object. This may have been accidental, or might have occurred when the perpetrator attempted to clean up the blood. Latent blood at the crime scene can be visualized through luminal techniques (Figure 8.8).

The angle of impact is the internal angle at which blood strikes a particular surface. If the angle of impact is 90 degrees, the blood impacts from directly above the surface and the resulting blood spatter is a circle. At all other angles, the blood spatter is an oval. Investigators may also determine a point of convergence, which is a common point that several bloodstains can be traced back to. The point of origin is the location at which investigators determine that the bloodstain came from.

Blunt-Force Trauma

Blunt-force trauma includes any physical trauma that was caused by any blunt object. This broad term covers lacerations (cuts), contusions (bruises), abrasions (scrapes), and bone fractures. These sorts of injuries are common in homicides, assaults, and rapes. A laceration is a tearing of the skin. A contusion is caused when the blunt-force trauma causes small blood vessels to rupture under the skin. An abrasion is caused by an object sliding across the skin. A fracture is a broken bone. A fracture may break the skin, which is an open fracture, or it may remain contained underneath the skin, which is a closed fracture. Such trauma may be inflicted by many items—such as bricks, rocks, statuary, candlesticks, or even an automobile.

The pathologist will look for indications of blunt-force trauma during the autopsy. For example, the presence of a bruise on the scalp and an underlying bone fracture may indicate that the victim was rendered unconscious by a blow prior to other damage being done by the attack—this could explain a lack of defensive injuries to the forearms and hands. At the emergency room, a living victim of an assault or rape will frequently evidence blunt-force trauma. Photographs of any injuries should be taken, because this evidence will fade long before trial.

Burning

Individuals generally do not burn to death, although certainly many people are injured by fire each year. Individuals who die in fires usually die as a result of smoke inhalation and lack of oxygen, the fire itself does not kill them. According to the CDC, in 2003, 3,145 people died in fires and many others were injured (http://www.cdc.gov/ncipc/factsheets/fire.htm).

In some cases, an arson fire may be an attempt to cover up a homicide. The perpetrator may hope to destroy all evidence of the circumstances surrounding the death. While it may be easy to burn fiber evidence and hair evidence, the human body is much more resilient. The exterior of the body may suffer extensive damage when exposed to fire, yet the interior often remains intact. Lungs, which should be black from smoke inhalation if the individual died because of the fire, are pink and clear, if the individual died prior to the start of the fire. While external injuries can be difficult to discern, the entry point of a bullet wound may be difficult to locate, but the bullet will remain intact and lodged within muscle tissue, untouched by the external fire, waiting to be found upon autopsy.

Burning is also a common nonfatal injury. In some cases of child abuse, the child may be burnt. The emergency room physician will examine the pattern of the injury on the child to determine if the burn was intentionally inflicted. Children may be intentionally burned with curling irons or other hot implements. They may also have their hands (or other body parts) forced onto hot stoves or radiators. The use of hot liquids (water, oil) is also common. Intentional burning is often evidenced by a clean outline of the object that was used to inflict the injury. Since the child is often forced to not pull away (the normal reaction) the burn will be equally severe across the entire wound.

Drowning

Drowning is a form of suffocation. Accidental drowning is common among young children who are unable to swim—or even among those who are able to swim, but panic. Finding a body in water is not necessarily indicative of an accidental drowning. A murderer may attempt to cover the crime by dumping the body into water. Determining whether the death was an accident, a suicide, or a homicide, is often dependent upon examining other circumstances. First, a drowned individual will have water in the lungs from attempting to breathe in water. If there is no water in the lungs, the victim was dead prior to entering the water—an almost definite indication of an attempt to cover up a homicide. If water is found within the lungs, it can be difficult to differentiate an accidental death from a suicide from a homicide. Suicidal deaths by drowning tend to be uncommon. Often, the presence of other injuries can indicate a homicide as opposed to an accidental drowning.

Asphyxiation and Strangulation

Asphyxiation is a loss of consciousness resulting from either too little oxygen or too much carbon dioxide in the blood. Death results if normal breathing cannot be restored. Asphyxiation may be the result of drowning, suffocation, heart failure, electric shock, or poisoning.

Suffocation is caused by obstructing the intake of air at the external respiratory openings (mouth and nose). Individuals are commonly suffocated with items like plastic bags and pillows. Asphyxiation may also result from choking. This is known as upper airway obstruction. Adults who die from choking are often incapacitated in some way—from drugs or alcohol or from a medical cause—that makes swallowing difficult. Children who choke often choke on small objects, toys, or food. Upon autopsy, the object responsible for the choking may still be lodged in the back of the throat. Strangulation can be manual (when hands are used) or ligature (when an instrument like a belt is used around a person's neck). In both cases, marks will be evidenced on the victim. In some cases, ligature marks will be so deep that the neck will be lacerated.

Autoerotic and erotic asphyxiation are both forms of asphyxiation that occur during sexual activity. Autoerotic asphyxiation occurs when an individual accidentally asphyxiates him or herself the act of masturbation or sex. Practitioners of autoerotic or erotic asphyxiation allege that the decreased

---

Working as a Forensic Pathologist

A forensic pathologist may work in the office of the medical examiner. Qualifications for this position include graduation from a recognized medical school; completion of an ACGME (Accreditation Council for Graduate Medical Education)-accredited anatomic or anatomic and clinical pathology residency with training in forensic pathology; certification in forensic pathology and anatomic or anatomic and clinical pathology by the American Board of Pathology; and possession of a license or eligibility to receive a license to practice medicine. A minimum of one year of experience in forensic pathology is required. The pathologist must be able to travel to death scenes when requested and perform medicolegal examinations, including autopsies and external examinations. Duties include the review of medical records, investigative reports, and microscopic slides, assisting in the identification of unknown remains, and providing cause and manner of death for cases that fall under the medical examiner's jurisdiction. The pathologist will assist in the administration of the office and supervision of staff; provide expert testimony before the grand jury and in criminal proceedings; consult with physicians, attorneys, coroners, medical examiners, law enforcement, and other investigators. The pathologist may also by asked to conduct or participate in service training as needed for law enforcement and associated agencies. The annual salary of a forensic pathologist can range anywhere from $100,000 to $250,000 depending upon the jurisdiction and the individual's experience and qualifications.

---

oxygen supply heightens the sexual pleasure. Erotic asphyxiation occurs when two or more partners engage in this practice as a part of their sexual activities, and one of them accidentally dies. Autoerotic asphyxiation is usually easy to determine at the scene because of the presence of sexual materials. There may be objects inserted into the anus or vagina of the victim. Pornography may also be present. In some cases, the scene may have been altered if the victim was found by a family member. This is often done more from embarrassment than from criminal intent. Erotic asphyxiation can be more difficult to determine. Because the death occurs during a sexual encounter, it can sometimes be mistaken for an intentional homicide.

BURIED BODIES

Although buried bodies decompose more slowly than exposed bodies, buried bodies present numerous challenges to investigators. The first challenge, naturally, is *finding* the body. Once a body has been buried, it may be years before it is found—if ever. The majority of buried bodies that are found have been located accidentally when the burial area is excavated for other purposes. Generally, if a body is not found, it is impossible to prosecute an individual for murder. The victim simply remains *missing*. Yet it is very difficult to successfully bury a body so that it is not found. If it is suspected that a perpetrator has buried a murder victim, there are three common methods that can be used. The body can be located through the use of investigative skill, technology, and/or cadaver canines.

Investigative Skill

Investigators frequently will locate bodies using only their knowledge of good investigative techniques. They will begin looking for a body if they have a general idea of where the perpetrator hid the body, perhaps because a witness saw someone digging in the woods, or the investigator can make an educated guess as to where the perpetrator could have quickly hidden the body. Bodies tend to be large, cumbersome, and difficult to move stealthfully. To bury a body, the perpetrator must have enough time to find a location, dig a hole large enough, place the body into it, and refill the hole. There is also a significant amount of displaced soil that must be accounted for. In many cases, digging a hole large enough to accommodate an adult would attract attention, so the burial site must be located somewhere that is isolated or where digging might occur unnoticed. The act of placing a body into a hole will also cause breakage of smaller plants around a site. Once a body is buried, the flora around a burial site will continue to look different for a period of time that can vary drastically depending upon the growing conditions. Additionally, the ground will settle over time, and what was once a level grave will eventually sink as decomposition progresses and the chest collapses.

If the perpetrator did not have much time to dispose of the body following the murder, then it likely will be located in the vicinity of the kill site. If there is no likely burial site near where the murder happened—and the perpetrator had more time—the body may have been transported by vehicle to another site and evidence to that effect may be located in the perpetrator's vehicle, such as: fibers from the victim's clothing, blood from the victim, or a shovel used to dig the grave.

Use of Technology

A buried body can be located through the use of sonar. The sonar machine emits sound waves that create a visual image of the density of the ground and can thereby be used to locate solid items like bodies, concrete walls, metal vaults, and large tanks. A buried body is denser than soil and will show up on the screen as such. Also, soil becomes progressively denser the deeper you go underground. The ground is disrupted when a body is buried, and also the ground is not as densely packed as it had once been; the sonar machine will depict that the ground has been disturbed and a dense object lies within.

Unfortunately, current sonar technology is not developed to the point where it is convenient to use over a large area. Investigators must have a general idea of where the body is located—either through witness statements or by facts revealed in the investigation; they can then use the machine to pinpoint the location of the body.

Cadaver Dogs

A dog's sense of smell is far more advanced and sensitive than that of a human being, and a dog will easily pick up scents where humans cannot—this is a prime reason for the use of canines to detect drugs, money, contraband agricultural products, and cadavers. Cadaver dogs are trained to pick up the scent of a decomposing body. They are trained using a simulated decomposition smell. Cadaver dogs are trained to track the scent of a decomposing body that is located in an open area, buried underground, or submerged in water. Over the past 15 years, the use of cadaver dogs has become more and more common in law enforcement.

FORENSIC ANTHROPOLOGY

Anthropology, the study of humankind, is broken down into four subareas: cultural anthropology, archaeology, anthropological linguistics, and physical anthropology. Some scholars also acknowledge applied anthropology, a fifth subdivision; that is the use of anthropology to solve current problems. Forensic anthropology fits into both physical anthropology and applied anthropology because it applies physical anthropology to current legal questions, usually involving the identification of skeletonized remains. Forensic anthropologists study bones and how bones relate to the appearance of the living person. Because of the highly specialized nature of this area, most forensic laboratories do not employ a full-time forensic anthropologist. Generally, a forensic anthropologist is called upon when skeletonized remains are found and identification is needed. Less frequently, a forensic anthropologist may be called upon to estimate a person's height from only a leg bone, such as a femur or a tibia, or to make a determination regarding gender from only a pelvis.

The forensic anthropologist has perhaps the most difficult job of all the professionals working in death investigation. Once the body has skeletonized, identification becomes much more difficult and the cause of death may be impossible to determine because tissues are gone and cannot be analyzed for toxins any longer.

Making a positive identification from skeletonized remains can be very difficult. If the body was buried in a container, clothing or other personal effects may be discovered with the skeleton and assist with the identification. If the skeleton was discovered outside, there may be no personal effects. The forensic anthropologist may note that while the individual was alive, a bone had been broken and set or surgeries occurred and may try to make an identification based upon these features. Such specifics, however, can be very difficult to trace; as there is not a central repository for medical records in the United States. If the surgery occurred many years ago in another location, it may be difficult to find the record, or, if the surgery is very common, it may not provide enough information. Poor or homeless victims are especially likely to have neither medical nor dental records. Be mindful that broken bones or dental work are only helpful in establishing a positive identification if a record of these were made while the person was alive *and investigators can access that record* (in many cases, simply accessing the record presents a major hurdle to law enforcement).

Forensic anthropologists are generally faced with one of two questions: remains are accidentally located and the forensic anthropologist is asked to make identification from those remains, or a person has been missing when remains are found, and the forensic anthropologist is asked to determine if the remains are that *specific* person. By far, the second question is easier to answer; frequently there will be medical records and a good physical description from which the forensic anthropologist can work. When human remains are stumbled upon, the forensic anthropologist will attempt to determine the age of the victim, estimate height and weight, and reconstruct the face, with identification progressing from there in hopes that the reconstructed face will match a missing person.

The most basic details a forensic anthropologist can provide regarding a particular individual are gender, age, height, and weight. A forensic anthropologist usually cannot provide an exact age, height, or weight of a victim, but only a general estimate. The bones of an elderly person may exhibit multiple fractures or evidence of loss of bone density. Children's bones are naturally smaller than adult bones. On a child's skeleton, the femur (thigh bone) is the most useful in making an estimation of age. If a child is close to 18, the top of the femur will be fully calcified. Height can also be estimated from the femur bone; it is the largest bone in the body and comprises a specific proportion of the total height. Weight is more difficult to estimate only from a skeleton. Gender can usually be determined if there is a pelvis bone with the skeleton. The pelvis of an adult female is wider to allow for a baby to pass through the birth canal during childbirth. There are general skeletal differences among the three races of physical anthropology—mongoloid, caucasoid, negroid—but the presence of any single difference cannot assure a positive racial identification.

Computer Models for Age Regression and Progression

Facial software also makes it possible to age-advance photographs by significant spans of time—5, 10, or even 20 years and has proven extremely useful in the continued investigation of cases involving long-term missing persons. Forensic anthropologists can use similar software to extrapolate what the face of an individual might look like based only upon a skull.

The basic premise of the software is to use data and expert knowledge of facial and teeth structures of racial and ethnic groups worldwide and formulate a natural age progression or regression to skull teeth and facial features. This technique has wide application and can be used in assisting police in identifying partial skull remains, burn victims, missing children, and adults. The resultant image can then be transformed into a plastic or rubber skull/face which can be finished by forensic artists to use in media presentations to enlist the public's assistance in the identification process.

FORENSIC ODONTOLOGY

Forensic odontologists, or forensic dentists, are generally called upon to testify in two areas: identification of a perpetrator through bite marks left at the scene or on a victim, and identification of remains through dentition (set of teeth).

Identification of Perpetrator Through Bite Marks

Bite marks may be found on many items at the crime scene: on partially eaten food, in chewing gum, or on either a live or deceased victim. If the perpetrator was at or near the scene for a substantial amount of time, the crime scene search should pay attention to any food that the perpetrator may have bitten into and discarded.

Prior to the commission of the crime, the perpetrator may have waited outside of the victim's residence. In some cases, a perpetrator may have visited the scene repeatedly prior to committing the crime. Investigators may find half-eaten food, cigarettes, soda cans, and other things that the perpetrator inadvertently left behind. Some of these items may be useful for teeth identification as well as for fingerprints and DNA. During the commission of rape and other sexually motivated crimes, bite marks may be found on living or dead victims. If the victim is alive, the bite mark, as evidence, can only be collected for a limited period of time before the body's natural healing process will obliterate any traces of the bite.

There are a variety of computer programs that forensic odontologists can use to assist in identification (McNamee et al. 2005). It has been noted in the literature that bite mark comparison on human skin can be difficult when the bite occurred in an area with complex curves (West et al. 1990). There have been cases where two suspects had similar bite marks and, therefore, bite mark evidence was less useful in determining the identity of the perpetrator (Pretty and Turnbull 2001).

Upon arriving at the scene, the first thing the forensic odontologist must do is obtain saliva swabs of the area of the bite mark; then photographs will be taken. Special care must be taken when positioning the camera, evidence, and the measurement reference scale. Any of these can distort the picture (Bowers and Johansen 2002). The camera must be on the same plane as the evidence and scale, or size will be distorted. Bites and bruises, because of the way the body heals itself, may become more visible 12 to 24 hours after the wound was inflicted. For this reason, investigators may want to obtain pictures during this time frame as well.

The forensic odontologist will classify the bite mark into one of seven types, depending upon the damage done to the victim: hemorrhage (small bleeding spot), abrasion (undamaged mark), contusion (bruise), laceration (punctured or torn skin), incision, avulsion (removal of skin), or artifact (bitten off piece of body).

The Oral Autopsy

The forensic odontologist will examine the teeth during an oral autopsy. This oral autopsy will be performed in different manners depending upon the condition of the remains. Skeletonized remains are easy to examine because all tissue is gone and therefore does not impede the odontologists view, the taking of X-rays, or photography. In this case, however, teeth that are dry, may be brittle and cracking, splintering, and breakage can be a problem. Teeth may also fall out of their sockets, for this reason, when skeletal remains are found, particular attention should be focused on an examination of the immediate area for possible dislodged teeth. Decomposing remains are difficult to examine; the process of decomposition fills the mouth with debris. In order to examine the teeth properly, the jaws should be removed. Charred remains are also very difficult to examine due to the shrinkage of the body during exposure to high heat; while the heat can cause considerable damage to teeth, it is not likely to completely destroy them. However, burned bone is fragile and must be handled with care. When examining mutilated remains, it is important to document any oral and facial trauma prior to removing the jaw for examination because its removal will obliterate much of the evidence of trauma. When an oral autopsy must be performed on a body that may need to be viewed in a funeral ceremony, care must be taken not to damage the face; this can make oral examination more difficult. While it is still possible to remove the jaws for examination and replace them, it is significantly more difficult than permanently removing them (Bernstein 1997).

Odontological Identification of Remains

The forensic examination of dentition as a means of identifying unknown remains has a long history, dating back at least to the Revolutionary War. It is a frequent means of identifying victims of mass casualties and fires because the teeth are very resistant to destruction. Even during the cremation process, remnants of teeth survive. It is not until long after skeletonization has taken place that the skull may begin to lose teeth because there is no longer any tissue to hold them in place (Bernstein 1997).

In the United States, a universal numbering system is used in dental records that assigns a number to each tooth in the adult mouth (1–32) and takes into account filings, extractions, surface structure, root configuration, adjacent teeth, and twisted/tilted teeth. Because this system is so detailed and used throughout the entire United States, it can be very useful in identifying remains—as long as the deceased individual's dental records can be accessed.

Teeth, like the long bones of the body, are another good indicator of the age when the deceased individual is a child. Teeth develop and erupt in a regular pattern until the appearance of the second molars between the ages of 14 and 16. By looking at which teeth have erupted, a good estimate of a child's age can be made. The third molars (wisdom teeth) appear between the ages of 15 and 22. After 22, the forensic odontologist will focus more on degenerative changes to estimate age, such as wear on the teeth and the transparency of the roots of the teeth. It should be noted that degenerative changes, unlike the eruption pattern of teeth, are extremely variable and produce only estimates (Bernstein 1997).

It is more difficult to positively determine gender through dentition alone. In general, males have longer root lengths than females, but this is just a general rule. If dental pulp remains, DNA can be extracted from it and the remains can be positively identified as either male or female. There are some racial differences in teeth, however a definite determination cannot be made using any one factor—but several should be present before race is tentatively established (Bernstein 1997).

FORENSIC ENTOMOLOGY

Forensic entomology is the study of how insects invade and colonize a dead body (forensic entomology also has applications in abuse cases and some automobile accidents). Forensic entomology has a long-documented history, having been mentioned in a thirteenth-century writing in China where a killer confessed to a crime because insects were attracted to the blade of his sickle—presumably because it still had remnants of human flesh on it that had not been washed away (http://www.research.missouri.edu/entomology/chapter1.html).

Knowledge of the invasion and succession of insects can help to determine the time of death, where death occurred, and if the body has been moved. Time of death can be determined because different stages of decomposition will attract different types of insects. Some flies prefer the outdoors and the presence of these insects in a body found inside may indicate that the body has been moved after death. Some insects live in certain geographic locations; the presence of these insects in bodies discovered in locations where the insects usually aren't found can also indicate that a body has been moved. The succession of insects that will colonize a body after death will also vary according to the time of year, so their presence (even as corpses) in a body can also tell a forensic entomologist how long a body has been dead.

Immediately After Death

Insects grow and develop at a steady rate, through examination of the insects' stages of growth; time of death can be estimated. Immediately after death, blowflies, flesh flies, and houseflies will be attracted to the body. They will begin to feed off of the body within the first 24 hours if death has not occurred during winter or in a very cold location. These insects will lay their eggs in an available moist area of the body, preferably an open wound, but any orifice will suffice.

COLONIZATION DURING THE FIRST DAYS   During the first days and weeks after death, the forensic entomologist can also use the presence and development of maggots to determine time of death. It takes seven days for the maggot to become an adult, and during that time it progresses through specific stages. After one week, there will be multiple generations of adults, so this method will no longer be useful in determining time of death (Anderson 1998).

Collection and Preservation of Entomology Evidence

Ideally, a forensic entomologist should be called to the scene of the homicide to collect insect evidence. If that is not possible, then evidence technicians must be specially trained or valuable insect evidence might be lost and results could be misleading.

Insects should be collected from all parts of the body where they are found. If there are several types of insects, then all types should be collected. It is important that insects from different parts of the body be packaged in different containers. From each area, two samples of the same insect should be collected. One should be placed into a vial containing preservative. This will allow the forensic entomologist to estimate time of death. The other sample should be kept alive for analysis of the maturation process of the insect.

Glossary

Antemortem—prior to death.

Adipocere—a body submerged in water will often become waxy.

Carnivore—an animal that eats meat.

Cause of death—the injury or disease that began the sequence of events that ultimately results in death.

Dentition—set of teeth.

Humidity—moisture in the air.

Manner of death—circumstances surrounding death: homicide, suicide, accident, natural, or undetermined causes.

Midwife—an individual, not a medical doctor, who assists women during childbirth. Many modern midwives are nurses.

Mummification—a process of drying and preserving a body. It may occur naturally under hot and dry conditions. Some cultures, like the Ancient Egyptians, used an artificial mummification process for their dead.

Positive identification—a definite identification.

Postmortem—after death.

Presumptive identification—identification based upon assumptions.

Radiograph—X-ray.

Serology—the study of blood serum.

Webliography

Forensic Dentistry Online.
(http://www.forensicdentistry online.org/)
Forensic Entomology.
(http://www.forensic-entomology.com/)

(http://www.deathonline.net/what_happens/autopsy/autopsy_steps.cfm)
This site deals with autopsies and even includes an interactive autopsy.

References

American Board of Forensic Entomology. Accessed on June 29, 2006, from http://www.research.missouri.edu/entomology/chapter1.html

Anderson, G. S. (1998). Forensic entomology: the use of insects in death investigations. Accessed on June 29, 2006, from http://www.rcmp-learning.org/docs/ecdd0030.htm.

Bernstein, M. "Forensic Odontology." In *Introduction to Forensic Sciences*, Edited by Eckert, W. G., 295–342. New York: CRC Press, 1997.

Bowers, C. M., and R. J. Johansen. "Photographic Evidence Protocol: The Use of Digital Imaging Methods to Rectify Angular Distortion and Create Life Size Reproductions of Bite Mark Evidence." *Journal of Forensic Science* 47, no. 1 (2002): 178–85.

Bureau of Alcohol, Tobacco, and Firearms. ATF's NIBIN Program. Accessed on June 22, 2006, from http://www.nibin.gov/nibin.pdf.

Centers for Disease Control and Prevention. Deaths-Leading Causes. Accessed on June 19, 2006, from http://www.cdc.gov/nchs/fastats/lcod.htm.

Centers for Disease Control and Prevention. Leading Causes of Death, 1900–1998. Accessed on November 27, 2006, from http://www.cdc.gov/nchs/data/dvs/lead1900_98.pdf.

Centers for Disease Control and Prevention. March 30, 2006. Fire Deaths and Injuries: Fact Sheet. Accessed on June 21, 2006, from http://www.cdc.gov/ncipc/factsheets/fire.htm.

Centers for Disease Control and Prevention. National Vital Statistics Report. Deaths: Leading Causes for 2002. March 7, 2005. Vol 53 (17). Accessed on June 19, 2006, from http://www.cdc.gov/nchs/data/nvsr/nvsr53/nvsr53_17.pdf.

DeForest, P., R. Gaensslen, and H. Lee. *Forensic Science: An Introduction to Criminalistics.* NY: McGraw-Hill, 1983.

Dix and Calaluce. *Guide to Forensic Pathology.* Boca Raton, FL: CRC Press, 1999.

Dix, J., and M. Graham. *Time of Death, Decomposition, and Identification: An Atlas.* Boca Raton, FL: CRC Press, 1999.

Federal Bureau of Investigation. September 2006. *Crime in the United States 2005.* Accessed on March 31, 2007, from http://www.fbi.gov/ucr/05cius/offenses/clearances/index.html#figure.

Kantarci, M., R. M. Karasen, F. Alper, O. Onbas, A. Okur, and A. Karaman. "Remarkable Anatomic Variations in Paranasal Sinus Region and Their Clinical Importance." *European Journal of Radiology* 50, no. 3 (June 2004): 296–302.

McNamee, A. H., D. Sweet, and I. Pretty. "A Comparative Reliability Analysis of Computer-Generated Bitemark Overlays." *Journal of Forensic Science* 50, no. 2 (2005): 400–5.

Pretty, I. A., and M. D. Turnbull. "Lack of Dental Uniqueness Between Two Bite Mark Suspects." *Journal of Forensic Science* 46, no. 6 (2001): 1487–91.

West, M. H., R. E. Barsley, J. Frair, and M. D. Seal. "The Use of Human Skin in the Fabrication of a Bite Mark Template: Two Case Reports." *Journal of Forensic Science* 35, no. 6 (1990): 1477–85.

Review Questions

1. Why is the homicide clearance rate so high?
2. What is the difference between presumptive identification and positive identification?
3. Under what condition is a body most likely to quickly skeletonize?
4. How can technology be helpful in locating buried bodies?
5. Why are specially trained canines helpful in locating buried bodies or bodies submerged in water?
6. Which two subdivisions of anthropology does forensic anthropology fit under?
7. Define forensic entomology.
8. Why is the time of death so difficult to estimate?
9. Explain some of the drawbacks to ballistics fingerprinting.
10. Why is the body the most significant piece of evidence at a homicide scene?

Some Things to Think About

1. Why is it that the longer a body has been dead the more difficult it is to determine the exact time of death?
2. What sorts of factors would make a body difficult to identify?
3. If heart disease is the leading cause of death, why do individuals tend to fear homicide more than a poor diet, which is more likely to kill them?

DNA

CHAPTER OUTLINE

Although most of the chapters in this text revolve around several crimes and the types of evidence that they may produce, this chapter is devoted entirely to a type of evidence—DNA, which has revolutionized the field of forensics. DNA is found in every cell of the body, in skin, in semen, in saliva, and it cannot be purposefully altered. As evidence, DNA provides greater certainty of conviction or exoneration than many other forms of evidence because it can, when handled properly, provide a genetic blueprint of the individual who committed the crime. Everyone, except identical twins, has DNA that is unique. DNA testing can also be misleading in the event of chimerism, in which a single individual has more than one cell line (Figure 9.1).

It is not uncommon for researchers and practitioners in many fields to employ techniques that originated within other disciplines, if such methods can be useful. Forensics is no exception. In fact, throughout its long history, forensics has borrowed many techniques from the sciences—blood-typing for instance. Perhaps the most obvious and most revolutionary of these techniques has been DNA analysis. DNA was not initially investigated because scientists believed that it would be useful in determining guilt at a crime scene. Scientists originally became interested in chromosomes and DNA because it was believed that these were essential to genetic inheritance. Once this connection was confirmed, chromosomes and DNA were examined for the role they play in disease mechanisms. It was not until much later, during the middle of the 1980s, that the possibility of using DNA for identification was explored. This exploration began with paternity testing and evolved into a means of criminal identification. During the past 10 years, the field has advanced significantly to allow analysis and reanalysis of previously useless evidence. Smaller and older samples now provide useful information. This has resulted in the exoneration of a number of wrongfully convicted

FIGURE 9.1   The DNA double helix.

Chimerism

Chimerism is a rare condition in which more than one cell line develops within an individual. This condition is found in a variety of animals. In human beings, chimerism can result from the fusion of fraternal twins early in development, so that the one remaining fetus has two different cell lines. It can also result from fraternal twins sharing a blood supply in the uterus. Although fraternal twins each develop their own placenta, if the placentas lie next to each other in the uterus, they can fuse and cause the sharing of blood. Cells from each twin can be transferred to the other via the blood. In vitro fertilization increases the chances of chimerism simply because multiple embryos are implanted and the mother is more likely to carry twins. Chimerism can result from a blood transfusion, from organ transplantation, or from fetal cells remaining in the mother after birth.

---

individuals. This has also resulted in successful prosecution of many cases that before would have lacked adequate evidence to move forward.

WHAT IS DNA?

Almost everyone has heard about DNA, but not everyone understands what DNA is and how important it is to science and forensics. DNA is the common shorthand name for deoxyribonucleic acid. It is the hereditary material in humans that is contained in almost every cell in the human body, but DNA is not alone in the story of heredity, there are also genes and chromosomes.

DNA is responsible for passing on genetic traits. While DNA does not determine everything about us (our environment also influences us), it is responsible for much of our makeup. Each parent contributes half of the child's DNA information in the form of 23 chromosomes, for a total of 46 chromosomes. The mother also contributes mitochondrial DNA (mtDNA), which has become increasingly important as techniques have developed for analyzing this type of DNA.

DNA is contained in the nucleus of each cell in the human body except for red blood cells—which have no nucleus. During cell division the DNA replicates. The strands separate and then create new copies of the opposing strand. This results in two strands that are exactly alike.

Chromosomes

Chromosomes were first visualized in 1842 in plant cells. Chromosomes are DNA wrapped around proteins. Each animal has a distinct number of chromosomes. Human beings have 23 pairs of chromosomes. Twenty-two are pairs of autosomes, which are nonsex chromosomes and are the same for both the mother and father. The remaining pair is sex chromosomes. Each parent contributes 23 chromosomes to the baby. The mother has two sex chromosomes (X, X). She always contributes an X chromosome to the child. The father has two sex chromosomes as well (X, Y). He contributes either an X or a Y to the child. If he contributes an X, the child will be a girl. If he contributes a Y, the child will be a boy. Interestingly, having two X chromosomes contributes to the fact that in many instances the female is more robust. Just like they have 22 pairs of identical chromosomes, their sex chromosomes are also identical. If there is something wrong on one of the X chromosomes they receive, the other X can make up for it. On the other hand, males have only one X chromosome and if it is damaged they will often evidence a specific abnormality—like color blindness, hemophilia, Duchenne muscular dystrophy, or fragile-X syndrome; there are also a variety of immunodeficiencies that can occur.

Genes are hereditary units consisting of a sequence of DNA that is located on a chromosome. Genes usually are responsible for producing a specific protein. Genes range in size from 1,000 base pairs to several hundred thousand base pairs. In some instances a single gene is located on more than one chromosome. All of our genes together are known as the human genome. Each individual has a

---

XYY Syndrome, Criminality, and Psychiatric Disorders

XYY Syndrome is a genetic defect. It is referred to as a trisomy—a condition in which, rather than having a pair of one of the chromosomes, there is an extra chromosome. Common trisomies include trisomy 21 (often referred to as Down syndrome) and trisomy 18 (or Edwards syndrome). During the 1970s and 1980s, there was a common misconception that males who had the XYY chromosomal abnormality had higher levels of testosterone, were taller, had lower intelligence, and were prone to violence. It was thought that they were overrepresented in the prison population (Schroder et al. 1981), were more impulsive, and had more temper tantrums as children (Money et al. 1975). Literally dozens of articles were published examining the connection between XYY and criminality and psychiatric disorders. Later research, however, revealed flaws in the earlier studies and has shown that XYY males are usually taller, but testosterone levels are normal. The XYY males are at increased risk of learning difficulties, but intelligence levels are within normal range.

---

unique genome except for identical twins. The Human Genome Project has sequenced the majority of the human genome. The project began in 1990 and was finished in 2006. Interestingly, as scientists have mapped more and more of the human genome, the estimated number of base pairs and the estimated number of genes in the human genome has decreased.

Composition of DNA

The DNA double helix is made up of four chemical bases: adenine (A), guanine (G), cytosine (C), and thymine (T). (RNA has three of the same chemical bases; it does not have thymine, but instead has uracil.) These four bases form pairs. Adenine always pairs with thymine, and cytosine always pairs with guanine. These bases form the rungs of the double-helix ladder. The edges of the ladder are comprised of phosphate and sugar molecules, which alternate. Human DNA is comprised of about 3 billion base pairs. How these bases are arranged determines the information that they will pass on during reproduction. Each base also attaches to a sugar molecule and a phosphate molecule to form a nucleotide. There is an almost infinite combination possible, making DNA a very individual identifier. The nucleotides are arranged in such a way that they resemble a twisted ladder, or double helix. This structure was discovered by James Watson and Francis Crick in 1953. The double helix gives the DNA strand considerable strength.

Base pairs group together in sets of three to form one of 64 codons. Codons, in turn, determine the production of one of twenty amino acids. Several codons will code for each one of the amino acids. Cells then use the amino acids to produce proteins. DNA will replicate itself by splitting itself in two pieces (in the middle of the ladder strands). Free-floating nucleotides bond with the ends of the half-ladders; this creates two new strands identical to the old strands. There are approximately three billion nucleotides in each cell and 30,000 genes.

One nucleotide that is very important in forensics is ATP, which provides energy to cells. It also regulates biochemical pathways; is used in the synthesis of RNA; and is used in anabolic reactions like the synthesis of polysaccharides and fats, active transport of molecules and ions, nerve impulses, and muscle contraction. It is the lack of ATP following death that causes rigor mortis.

DNA Analysis

The majority of DNA does not vary considerably even from species to species, let alone from one person to another. DNA testing concentrates on those portions of DNA that vary the most among human beings—a very small proportion of our DNA. These variations are called *polymorphisms*. Rather than analyze the entire DNA sequence, probes are used to seek out exactly those portions, or markers, that vary most among humans. While the odds of any two people having one marker in common is fairly high, when five or six markers are analyzed, the odds of two people being alike becomes astronomically high. The more markers that are analyzed, the greater the odds become of any two individuals' DNA samples being alike. The statistical likelihood of a random individual matching a sample taken at a crime scene should always be clarified for a jury. The most likely types of physical evidence to yield significant amounts of DNA at crime scenes are semen and blood. However, with advances in the analysis of mitochondrial DNA (mtDNA), DNA can also be extracted from hair, saliva, vaginal secretions, and tooth pulp.

Genetic Markers

There are both conventional markers and DNA-based markers. Conventional markers consist of cellular antigens and serum proteins. DNA-based markers consist of RFLP (restriction fragment length polymorphism), STRs (short tandem repeats), PCR (Polymerase Chain Reaction), and mtDNA (mitochondrial DNA) analysis.

RESTRICTION FRAGMENT LENGTH POLYMORPHISM   RFLP is one of the original techniques used in forensic DNA analysis. It is costly, very time-consuming, and requires a substantial sample of DNA. RFLP consists of the following steps:

1. Extraction and purification of the DNA sample.
2. An enzyme, called a restriction polymerase, is used to cut the DNA into pieces. These pieces are a variety of sizes.
3. Gel electrophoresis uses an electrical charge to separate the fragments based upon size, electrical charge, and other physical properties—the molecules are forced to move across the gel by the electric charge they carry.
4. The fragments are then hybridized with DNA probes that bind to particular areas of a sample that allow for analysis.

SHORT TANDEM REPEATS   STRs are short sequences of DNA that are repeated many times. Generally sequences that are repeated four or five times are used for forensic analysis. Specific regions of extracted DNA are amplified using PCR. Then they are separated by using either gel or capillary electrophoresis. Finally the DNA is stained using a variety of fluorescent dyes. The Combined DNA Index System (CODIS) database uses 13 STR loci to build individual genetic profiles.

POLYMERASE CHAIN REACTION   PCR is a useful technique because it can be performed on only a very small sample of DNA. It copies, or amplifies DNA using enzymatic replication. PCR is used to detect hereditary and infectious diseases, to clone genes, and to perform paternity testing and genetic fingerprinting. PCR consists of the following steps:

1. The DNA sample is denatured, which causes it to break apart.
2. The DNA is annealed and primers attach to the desired strand of DNA, which is then synthesized. Annealing is a process that allows the DNA to pair.
3. After annealing, the DNA is extended, which creates two DNA molecules.
4. Gel electrophoresis is used to separate out the PCR products.

One of the downsides to PCR is that it is very sensitive to contamination because it uses small amounts of DNA. Any contamination that is present will be amplified along with the desired DNA. DNA can be contaminated through a variety of means, including a dirty work surface that was not cleaned after the previous use. After PCR is completed, RFLP can be performed.

Genetic Fingerprinting and Animal Populations

Genetic fingerprinting is widely used in forensics to compare a suspect's DNA sample to a sample taken from a crime scene or victim. The sample may be derived from blood, hair, saliva, or semen. Genetic fingerprinting also has a variety of other applications, including paternity testing, matching organ donors, and studying animal populations.

Through the collection of DNA from animals, scientists can track population size. They can track the numbers of males and females in the population and construct family trees. They can also construct a species history. The Snow Leopard Trust uses genetics to study snow leopard lineage in different areas of the world (http://www.snowleopard.org/programs/science/genetics).

Genetic fingerprinting has been used to compare current lion and tiger populations to populations of 50–125 years ago through the testing of skins in museums. Through the analysis, it has been discovered that current inbred populations are similar to the populations of 50–125 years ago indicating that the population has not become more inbred (Shankaranarayanan et al. 1997).

Genetic fingerprinting is used to assess the needs of captive breeding programs. More genetically mixed males and females can be brought together to help broaden a species. Scientists in Britain are using genetic fingerprinting to study a rare kind of snake. The population is so small they hope to be able to track all of the snakes and learn how isolated the population is and how all of the snakes are related to each other (http://www.ceh.ac.uk/sections/pce/PopConsEcol_ConsMan_Snakes.html).

Mitochondrial DNA

The advent of the use of mtDNA has allowed forensic evaluations to be conducted on evidence that could not be analyzed using older DNA analysis techniques. Although this has been very beneficial, mtDNA is very sensitive to contamination and must be handled with considerable care. In the future it may be possible to use older and smaller samples of DNA and obtain more accurate results. This can be useful in missing-person cases because, while DNA degrades over time, mtDNA can be extracted from bones and teeth long after remains have skeletonized (Koblinsky et al. 2005).

First used in 1996, mtDNA has been used to differentiate between trace evidence left by the offender and the DNA of the victim. It has been used in high profile cases, such as the Boston Strangler and Laci Peterson homicides. Mitochondrial DNA has been used to identify brain tissue that was thousands of years old. It was used to examine the cremated remains of Anna Anderson, who had claimed to be Anastasia Romanov, daughter of the last Russian tzar. It was determined that she was not related to the Romanovs.

Mitochondrial DNA, as the name suggests, is found in mitochondria, not in the nucleus, which is where DNA is located. Also, unlike other DNA, mtDNA does not change from generation to generation but has a high rate of mutation. There are two regions of mtDNA that are often looked at: HVR1 and HVR2. Through the use of mtDNA, all living humans have been traced back to a single female ancestor who lived in Africa 200,000 years ago, this is because mtDNA is passed directly from mother to child without changing (http://www.pbs.org/wgbh/nova/neanderthals/mtdna.html).

Increasing Reliability of DNA Evidence

One major concern has been the reliability of DNA evidence. Although DNA has proven to be a very powerful tool, it is not flawless. The RFLP procedure was especially prone to problems and the PCR technique represents a significant improvement. Training for laboratory technicians has also been improved. However, better DNA analysis techniques are of little use if DNA samples are improperly handled prior to being received at the laboratory.

Poor handling of DNA evidence and poor laboratory procedures have lead to wrongful convictions (Telsavaara and Arrigo 2006). Proper handling of DNA evidence begins at the scene with technicians who are properly trained and who exercise caution during the evidence collection phase. Training for individuals who collect DNA for rape kits in hospitals has been standardized (e.g., Sexual Assault Nurse Examiner Programs).

The FBI Laboratory

The FBI operates two DNA Analysis Units. Unit 1 uses the standard techniques of RFLP and PCR to examine bodily fluids found at crime scenes. Unit 2 uses mtDNA to analyze small or degraded samples taken from hair, bones, teeth, and bodily fluids. This second unit analyzes samples that were previously useless (http://www.fbi.gov/hq/lab/html/mdnau1.htm).

EXONERATING THE WRONGFULLY CONVICTED

It is an unfortunate fact that the U.S. criminal justice system convicts innocent individuals every day. Some of these individuals accept plea bargains, often through the urging of their public defender who convinces them that they will be convicted anyway and that plea bargaining is the best way to get less time, even though they have not committed the crime. Some are wrongfully convicted by juries. There are many reasons why innocent individuals are convicted in the criminal justice system, including police and prosecutorial misconduct, inadequate defense counsel, racial biases, use of jail-house informants, poor eyewitness identification, and false confessions. Gross (1996, 1998) states that public pressure for arrests, absence of a living victim, decreased plea bargaining, and conviction-prone juries increase the likelihood of wrongful conviction. Warden (2005) noted that the following factors were influential in wrongful convictions in Illinois capital cases: cooperating witnesses (for example, accomplices who may gain from their testimony), false confessions, erroneous identification, ineffective assistance of counsel, junk science or pseudoscience (phrenology, astrology, or tarot card reading), and official misconduct (for example, a prosecutor failing to reveal evidence that may exonerate the defendant).

Since 1990, hundreds have been exonerated through DNA analysis. While the sources of wrongful conviction must be addressed, DNA analysis has been the single most important technique used for exoneration. Convicted offenders are increasingly requesting DNA testing for wrongful convictions (Telsavaara and Arrigo 2006). The first exoneration due to examination of DNA evidence occurred in Virginia in 1989. The wrongfully convicted David Vasquez, a mentally retarded young man, had confessed to avoid the death penalty after he was pressured by police to do so. As Vasquez sat in prison, the actual killer committed three more rape-murders. The second exoneration occurred later that same year. Gary Dotson was convicted based upon a concocted rape story, an alleged victim who was encouraged to identify him by police, and false testimony from a forensic scientist (Warden 2005). These two exonerations helped to create a public policy issue of wrongful convictions (Zalman 2006).

In 2000, Illinois Governor George Ryan placed a temporary moratorium on the death penalty because of errors at trials resulting in resentencing or retrial as ordered by appellate court. Perhaps the most salient reasons for the appellate court reversals were prosecutors at the original trials using jailhouse informants, coercing witnesses to lie, accomplices or codefendants testifying against the defendant as the sole means to convict, forensic fraud, prosecutorial and police misconduct, and faulty eyewitness testimony. In 2003, Governor Ryan emptied the Illinois death row, granted a blanket clemency to inmates, and placed a moratorium on the death penalty until the process was examined and laws revamped, as suggested by Warden in 2005. The most recent legislation allows pretrial hearings on jailhouse informants, protocol to scrutinize eyewitness testimony for probative value, and for judges to bar a death conviction in cases that rest on a single eyewitness or informant. Furthermore, jury instructions for capital cases were simplified, law enforcement officers were required to record interrogations, and police officers engaged in misconduct were fired (Warden 2005).

Innocence Projects

Once wrongful conviction became a public policy issue, DNA evidence and its reanalysis has led to convictions being overturned. The Innocence Project (www.innocenceproject.org) examines cases in which postconviction analysis of DNA evidence can yield proof of innocence. The Innocence Project focuses on poor inmates who have exhausted all other appeals. It has spawned similar organizations across the United States that highlight many of the shortcomings of the criminal justice system. Since 1992, The Innocence Project has helped exonerate 183 convicted individuals through the use of DNA. One hallmark of the integrity of The Innocence Project is that it doesn't take for granted that convicted individuals who claim to be innocent *are* innocent. The Innocence Project relies upon analysis of available DNA evidence and allows that evidence to speak. It should be noted that when DNA evidence affirms an inmate's guilt, that also becomes a matter of public record.

Unlike The Innocence Project, which focuses only on cases in which DNA evidence can yield proof of innocence, some state projects will examine *any* claims to innocence. Some convicted individuals may claim their trial was flawed by prosecutorial misconduct, junk science in the courtroom, or lying witnesses. However, in the absence of conclusive DNA evidence, it may be difficult to obtain a new trial or to have a conviction overturned.

There are many benefits to the advances in DNA technology. One is that DNA can now be analyzed from biological trace evidence, including minute samples of blood, semen, hair, and even sweat. Another is that now this technology can be applied to cases prosecuted prior to the advent of DNA technology. A considerable portion of the exonerated defendants were first tried and convicted prior to the widespread use of DNA in the courtroom.

The Justice for All Act (H.R. 5107, Public Law 108-405) was signed into law by President George W. Bush on October 30, 2004. The Act increases protections of victims' rights, but it also has as one of its major goals the elimination of a considerable backlog of DNA samples that have been collected from crime scenes and convicted offenders that should be entered into the CODIS database. The demand for the database has far outpaced the ability of the government to keep the database current. The Act also aims at improving procedures used in DNA testing to help eliminate laboratory failures due to poor handling of evidence. The Act provides funding for training programs for everyone involved in the process of handling DNA evidence, from law enforcement, to prosecutors, to laboratory staff. The Act seeks to expand and improve DNA testing capacity at federal, state, and local crime laboratories.

DNA DATABASES

The FBI maintains the CODIS database that contains DNA profiles from crime scenes and DNA profiles of convicted sex offenders and other violent offenders. CODIS currently contains over 4.5 million DNA profiles. The United Kingdom National DNA Database (NDNAD) was established in

---

The Problem of the Unknown Soldier

The Tomb of the Unknowns is in Arlington National Cemetery. It contains the remains of unidentified American soldiers from World War I, World War II, and the Korean Conflict. Many countries have similar monuments to fallen soldiers who cannot be identified. In the case of the Tomb of the Unknowns, the remains of the soldiers were believed to be unidentifiable. Previously the tomb included the remains of a Vietnam War soldier, but they were subsequently identified. In 1998, a DNA test was performed on the remains and First Lieutenant Michael J. Blassie was identified. He was disinterred and reinterred in a cemetery near his hometown. Because of rapidly advancing DNA technology, it is unlikely that remains will remain unidentified. Even remains that are now unknown will at some point in the future be identified due to this technology.

Working in DNA Analysis

The bulk of DNA work is done in the laboratory. The average advanced DNA analyst position requires a bachelor's degree in biology, chemistry, forensic science, or a closely related field. Specific coursework in genetics and molecular biology is generally required. Experience in DNA analysis and laboratory techniques and standards is required. Experience with CODIS is valuable. Individuals in this position will be required to train others in collection and analysis methods, as well as provide expert testimony in a courtroom. Starting salary, depending upon the jurisdiction, will be in the mid-to-high $50,000 range.

1995. It is run by the Forensic Science Service, which is part of the United Kingdom Home Office. Initially samples were taken only from convicted criminals or individuals awaiting trial. Now anyone who has been arrested is included in the database. NDNAD contains DNA profiles of over 3.5 million people. Over a half a million of those DNA profiles are from children. Just like the FBI database, the NDNAD contains a disproportionate number of DNA profiles from black individuals.

SEROLOGY-BLOOD ANALYSIS

Serology is the analysis of blood. It includes the use of the ABO and Rhesus (RH) blood groups—although it should be noted that there are numerous other ways to group blood. There are also numerous proteins and enzymes in blood. Forensic serologists individualize a blood sample based on these. The forensic serologist can identify whether a sample is blood and, if so, whether the blood is from a human or some other animal. Now blood can also be analyzed for DNA. Even with the advent of DNA analysis, blood and semen were the most likely fluids to create enough of a sample for analysis—until the more recent innovation of mtDNA.

Blood Composition

Blood is very important to the human body. It is responsible for many functions, supplying oxygen to tissues, and supplying nutrients such as glucose and amino acids. It also removes waste, such as carbon dioxide, urea, and lactic acid. It has immunological functions. It is responsible for coagulation. It transports hormones. It regulates pH in the body. It regulates core body temperature. It has hydraulic functions.

New blood is always being made in the bone marrow in a process called hematopoiesis. Red blood cells live for up to 120 days. In young children, all bones manufacture blood. As we age, not all bones are involved in blood manufacture. Blood manufacture becomes limited to the spine, breastbone, ribs, pelvis, and the upper arm and upper leg.

The circulatory system is comprised of the heart, blood, and blood vessels. Arteries carry oxygenated blood away from the heart to all parts of the body. The further the arteries are from the heart the smaller they become, until they are capillaries, which go into tissues and pick up waste and carbon dioxide. These small capillaries connect to small veins that carry deoxygenated blood back to the heart. The veins become larger and larger as they get closer to the heart. The blood enters the heart and exchanges carbon dioxide for oxygen and begins the process all over. Carbon monoxide can also bind to hemoglobin, which reduces the oxygen content in the body and quickly causes suffocation. Individuals who commit suicide by breathing in fumes from car exhaust die from suffocation.

Blood is made up of cells and plasma. Plasma constitutes about 55 percent of blood. The adult body contains about 5 liters of blood that account for about 7 percent of total body weight. Plasma is the liquid portion of blood. Plasma contains blood cells, white blood cells, and platelets, electrolytes, nutrients, vitamins, hormones, clotting factors, and proteins (some of which are antibodies). Red blood cells are the most abundant in the blood. Blood is red due to hemoglobin, which is an iron-containing protein. White blood cells are also called leukocytes; their main purpose is to help fight infection. There are six main types of white blood cells: neutrophils, eosinophils, basophils, bands, monocytes, and lymphocytes. Each of these white blood cells has a special function. Neutrophils make up about 58 percent of all white blood cells. They kill bacteria by ingesting them. Eosinophils make up about 2 percent. They kill parasites and have a role in allergic reactions. Basophils make up about 1 percent and also have a role in allergic reactions. Bands make up about 3 percent and are immature neutrophils. Monocytes make up about 4 percent; it is their job to destroy old, damaged, and dead cells in the body. Lymphocytes make up about 4 percent. There are T lymphocytes and B lymphocytes, both of which work with the body's immune system. Platelets are formed in the bone marrow and assist in blood clotting.

Prior to the advent of DNA, blood was primarily categorized using one or both of the common blood group systems; the ABO blood group system and the Rh blood group system. Karl Landsteiner identified the four human blood types (the ABO system) A, B, AB, and O. Blood type is determined by antigens on the surface of red blood cells. There are two antigens, A and B. Individuals with antigen A have blood type A, individuals with antigen B have blood type B. If both antigens are present, the blood type is AB. If neither is present, the blood type is O. The ABO system was discovered by Karl Landsteiner in 1901. Prior to Landsteiner's work, many individuals who received blood transfusions died because they received the wrong blood type.

If an individual receives an incompatible blood type during a transfusion, the blood can clump, which in turn can release toxins into the body, resulting in death. Individuals with the O blood type can give blood to all other blood types, but receive blood only from a person with O blood. Individuals with the A blood type can give blood to individuals with either A or AB blood types and can receive blood from A or O blood types. Individuals with the B blood type can give blood to either B or AB blood types and can receive blood from B and O blood types. Individuals with the AB blood type can give blood only to individuals with the AB blood type but can receive blood from all other blood types.

When an individual leaves blood at the scene of a crime, it always reveals their blood type. However, 80 percent of the population secretes their ABO blood group antigens into their bodily fluids. These individuals are referred to as secretors. Prior to the advent of DNA technology, knowing the blood type of the perpetrator could narrow down the suspect pool, although blood type cannot point to one specific individual.

The Rh antigen is either positive or negative. This fact has been useful in both paternity testing and forensics, but now DNA is used. The ABO system is still used when dealing with blood transfusions. Of all the blood types, O− ("O negative") is considered to be a *universal donor*; this blood type can be transfused into persons of all other blood types without difficulties. AB can receive all blood types during transfusion. Receiving the wrong type of blood during a transfusion can be deadly; the transfused blood may cause the recipient's blood to produce antibodies that bind to the transfused blood and cause clumping. These clumps, also known as agglutination, can block blood vessels and lead to death.

There is also an Rh blood group system, which is represented by either a + or a −. Eighty-five percent of the U.S. population is Rh+ ("Rh positive"). The Rh factor is a protein on the surface of the blood. If you are Rh+, you have that protein on your blood, if you are Rh− ("Rh negative"), you do not have that protein. Even when the ABO blood group and the Rh blood group match, an individual can have an adverse reaction to a transfusion. Rh incompatibility can also be a problem when a pregnant woman has a different Rh group than her fetus. Shots of Rh immune-globulin are given to the mother during the pregnancy and right after giving birth to prevent harm to the fetus and to any future fetuses.

Blood Analysis for Drugs

The presence of drugs in the human body can be measured by analyzing blood. When a subject is deceased, postmortem blood or tissue samples may be analyzed for the presence of drugs or poisons. Blood is often drawn from one of the two major veins of the leg, the femoral vein or iliac vein.

It makes a considerable difference where postmortem blood is drawn. Some areas of the body tend to concentrate toxins. Blood near the heart may be altered by postmortem cellular changes. If the individual is alive, blood can be drawn normally.

SEMEN ANALYSIS

Semen is frequently found at sexual offense crime scenes. In fact, other than drug evidence, semen is probably the most frequently submitted sample to forensic laboratories. It first became useful for forensic analysis when it was discovered that approximately 80 percent of individuals secrete their blood type into bodily products—this was, of course, long before DNA analysis.

Semen Composition

Semen, or seminal fluid, is comprised of fluids from four glands: the testes, the seminal vesicle, the prostate, and the bulbourethral glands. The testes contribute sperm. The seminal vesicle contributes amino acids, fructose, enzymes, and proteins, among components. The prostate contributes citric acid, prostate specific antigen, and zinc, among others. The bulbourethral glands contribute galactose, mucus, pre-ejaculate, and sialic acid.

The sperm contains the male's contribution during reproduction. Each sperm will contain 22 chromosomes and 1 sex chromosome. The father contributes either an X (making a girl) or a Y (making a boy) to the chromosomal complement of the child. The mother always contributes an X. Of course, semen contains the DNA complement of the male who ejaculated it.

Locating Semen at a Crime Scene

Semen is most frequently found at sexual assault crime scenes. However, this is not the only crime scene that may contain semen; burglaries, homicides, and arson crime scenes may also have semen evidence. It is, as always, important not to rule out any particular form of evidence just because of the type of crime. Likewise, an absence of semen at a crime scene does not mean that a sexual assault did not take place.

While it is most likely that semen will be located near where a victim was attacked, there are many other places where it can be located. It may be found on bedsheets, on clothing, in the victim, or on the victim. With a burglary, semen may be found on unusual items, including floors, furniture, or walls. It is important for investigators to know how to visually identify both wet and dried semen at the scene. Wet semen may appear whitish, grayish, or yellowish, and may contain globules. Dried semen often has a glistening appearance. Fluorescent techniques, like ultraviolet light, can be used to locate semen at the crime scene, although in some instances semen will not fluoresce. If a dried stain resembles semen, it should be collected and sent to the laboratory anyway.

Collecting Semen from a Victim

Semen may be present in or on a living or dead victim. In a deceased victim, semen will be collectable for some time. If a body is located within a few days after death, all semen within its orifices should be collectable. Also, semen located on the skin of a victim will be collectable unless the body has been submerged in water or exposed to severe environmental circumstances, for example, very heavy rains. The longer a body remains unprotected, the more likely semen and other evidence will degrade.

Semen collected from a victim is an important piece of evidence that should be collected by an appropriately trained individual, for example, a nurse who has been through sexual assault nurse examiner training. Semen evidence is often collected using a rape kit. Swabs should be taken of any orifice where there was penile contact. Even if a victim believes the perpetrator did not ejaculate, there may still be semen present. A victim who is alive should not shower or douche after the attack because these actions will decrease the likelihood that useable evidence can be collected. It should be noted on the collection kit if the victim bathed after the assault. It should also be noted if the victim had voluntary sexual intercourse within 72 hours of the assault. Semen from a deceased victim will be collected in the same manner, with swabs. Because of the possibility of cross contamination, gloves should be changed often during the collection phase. If samples are collected from the mouth, vagina, and anus, gloves should be changed after each location is examined.

Semen can also be located on a victim near the vagina, anus, and mouth; these likely areas also should be swabbed. A victim should also be asked if it is possible that there are any other areas on her body that may have come into contact with semen. Again, an alternate light source can be used to detect semen on the victim. Also, the characteristic dried and glistening presentation of semen can assist in locating semen.

Collecting Semen from a Crime Scene

Whenever possible the entire object on which evidence is found should be submitted to the laboratory. If semen or blood is found on a shirt, the entire shirt should be sent to the laboratory. However, that is not always feasible.

During a rape or attempted rape, it is likely that semen will be found on the victim's clothing. If the victim wears this clothing to the hospital, it should be retained along with the rape kit for evidence. The victim should bring a change of clothing to the hospital. If the perpetrator ejaculated into the victim's vagina or anus, semen will likely be present in the victim's underwear. Semen can also be found in clothing at the scene of a burglary. In some cases a burglar may masturbate into underwear or other articles of clothing at the scene.

Semen may be located on bedsheets, blankets, or pillowcases. If possible, the entirety of these objects should be taken as evidence. When this is not possible, smaller sections may be cut from them and submitted to the laboratory. All items that have been stained with bodily secretions should be allowed to air dry and then be packaged in a breathable container, such as a paper bag. This is to discourage the growth of bacteria that can render a sample useless in the laboratory.

In some instances semen will be found on other objects at a crime scene that cannot be submitted in whole or part to the laboratory. Semen may be located on carpeting or floors, for example. Wet semen can be collected with a swab. Dried semen can be moistened with distilled water and collected with a swab.

Even with old RFLP techniques, DNA analysis with an appropriately sized semen sample was very accurate, about 95 percent. Newer techniques, like STR, have increased this accuracy, even with much smaller samples.

SALIVA ANALYSIS

Saliva is secreted by our salivary glands. It consists mostly of water, but it also contains electrolytes (sodium, potassium, calcium, magnesium, bicarbonate, and phosphate), antibacterial proteins, mucus, and enzymes. Saliva serves a variety of functions, including aiding digestion, facilitating speech, destroying bacteria, and healing.

Not long ago, saliva was not terribly useful for forensic analysis, except for detecting a blood group if the individual happened to be a secretor. It was not until DNA analysis that saliva became far more useful in the forensic arena. At the crime scene, saliva may be found on cigarette butts, glasses, silverware, leftover food, gum, and bite marks. Saliva, like all bodily products, fluoresces under alternate light sources. At a crime scene, wet saliva can be collected with a piece of filter paper or a dry swab. Dried saliva can be moistened with distilled water and then collected with a dry swab.

When saliva is collected from a suspect, or from a potential father for a paternity test, it is collected using a buccal smear; this technique requires only a gentle scrape of the inside of the cheek with a swab. The swab is then submitted to the laboratory for full analysis.

Drug Testing with Saliva

Saliva can be tested for the presence of drugs. This method has some advantages over urine or blood testing. It is a far less invasive method and the mouth can be quickly swabbed. Most importantly, there really aren't any ways that an individual can attempt to change the results of a saliva drug test. Also, many drugs can be detected immediately after use. The downside of saliva testing is that drugs may be detectible for as little as only a few hours post-ingestion and almost all drugs are no longer detectable after three days. Saliva can also be observed under a microscope to detect the presence of hormones and can indicate when a woman who is trying to conceive is ovulating.

FECES ANALYSIS

Feces are comprised mainly of water. Other components include undigested food matter and living and dead bacteria, Feces are not terribly useful for genetic analysis, though they may contain some cells from the digestive tract. Only if there are no other possible sources for DNA would feces prove useful. A sample would be collected with a moistened swab that would be allowed to air dry. Feces are also not used for drug testing.

VAGINAL SECRETIONS

Unlike semen, vaginal secretions are not as plentiful at crime scenes. Also, the quantity of vaginal secretions is generally considerably less than normal semen output. Vaginal secretions are not as well understood and have not been studied in significant detail—to the point that there is disagreement regarding what constitutes *normal* vaginal secretions. Vaginal secretions contain a variety of substances, including some epithelial cells that originate in the walls of the vagina. Vaginal secretions may also contain mucous and blood. Because vaginal secretions are not usually found at crime scenes, they have limited forensic value, except for differentiation from the semen of an attacker.

TOOTH PULP

Tooth pulp or dental pulp is contained in the center of the tooth. It is valuable for DNA analysis because it contains soft tissue and nerve endings and because it will often survive when all other soft tissue has been destroyed. Tooth pulp is useful for DNA analysis when a skeletonized body is found. It can also be useful for reanalysis long after blood and tissues are no longer available. It is useful with badly burned bodies, because the back teeth are generally intact due to the protective tooth enamel that is highly resistant to heat and fire. Analysis of tooth pulp has confirmed the presence of plague in France at the end of the sixteenth century.

URINE ANALYSIS

Urine is comprised of water and other substances that are being flushed from the body. Blood may also be found in urine. It is common for urine to be analyzed for the presence of drugs. Urinalysis works because certain toxic substances are metabolized by the kidneys and passed into the urine. Urine that is used for drug testing is collected in a sterile cup. The analysis is first done macroscopically. The color and clarity of the urine is noted; normal urine should be clear and range in color from a light yellow to amber. The urine is later analyzed under a microscope.

Masking and Faking Urinalysis Results

Individuals who are tested through urinalysis may attempt a number of maneuvers to pass a drug test. One common method is to drink copious amounts of water. It is true that water will dilute whatever substances are present in the urine; however, this method is also easily detectable. Diluted urine will appear very light yellow or even clear in color. Samples that have obviously been diluted will often be flagged and tested further . A routine search on the Internet will yield a variety of marked methods of fooling a urine test. For example, caffeine, which is a diuretic, may be used to cause an increase in urination.

SWEAT

On the human body there are two kinds of sweat glands, eccrine glands, which are found on the entire body and are used for collection of samples for drug analysis, and apocrine glands, which are found in the armpits and the groin area and produce odor. The purpose of the eccrine sweat glands is body temperature regulation. These glands emit a fluid that is mostly water and some salt.

In some cases, sweat may be useful for drug analysis. A patch that collects perspiration can be worn for a two-week period and then analyzed. These are generally used for individuals on probation or parole. Sweat analysis is expensive when compared to other methods of drug analysis and the accuracy varies considerably because the patches detect only a limited number of substances. Sweat analysis does, however, have the benefit of requiring no further processing.

HAIR ANALYSIS

Hair may be analyzed for several reasons in a forensic setting. Hair found at a scene may be analyzed and DNA extracted. This can help to link the suspect to a crime scene. Hair is a fairly common find at crime scenes. Hair evidence can be found at any crime scene since hair loss and regrowth is constant for everyone. However, hair evidence is most likely to be a factor in crimes in which victim and perpetrator have close contact, such as rape, assault, or murder.

The perpetrator's hair may be found on the victim or at a crime scene; likewise, a victim's hair may be found on a perpetrator and at a crime scene, or at some other intermediary scene. Short of extracting DNA from hair, which has been difficult because hair is dead, it is very difficult to associate a particular hair with a particular individual.

Hair Collection

At the scene, most hair evidence will not be readily visible to the naked eye. Generally, hair evidence is collected by using a small vacuum fitted with a special micro-collection filter. This is used to vacuum areas that are most likely to contain hair evidence, for example, around and under the body in a homicide. Each area that is vacuumed should be vacuumed using a separate filter to prevent contamination of possible evidence.

Hair evidence is also collected from a victim. If a victim is deceased, the clothing and body will be closely examined for minute hair evidence prior to being unclothed during the autopsy examination. If a victim is alive, and was involved in a sexual assault, their clothing will be retained and turned over to law enforcement with the rape kit. The body of a victim is also examined for hair evidence during the course of a physical exam. Because of the intimate contact that occurs during sexual assault, a victim's pubic hair is also combed and examined for hair from the perpetrator. All combings from the pubic region are sealed in evidence envelopes and placed in the rape kit.

Hair evidence can be collected from a suspect as well. If a suspect is quickly located, his clothing can be examined for hair. If he is a rape suspect, his pubic hair can be combed and examined for hair that matches the victim.

Hair Laboratory Analysis

During a forensic analysis of hair, it is determined whether the hair is animal or human. If it is animal, an examiner is interested in what sort of animal a hair belonged to. If it is determined that a hair is of human origin, then an examiner is interested in what part of the body it originated from, the race of the individual, and how the hair was removed. The examiner is also interested in whether the hair had been chemically altered. With the advent of mitochondrial DNA analysis, hair can now be analyzed for DNA. This has made hair evidence much more useful in forensics.

SPECIES ORIGIN   The first determination made during hair analysis is whether a hair sample is of human or animal origin. To the trained analyst, this is a fairly easy determination. All animal hair, like human hair, has morphology that is specific to that species. Animal hair should not be disregarded as evidence at a crime scene. Deer hair found on a victim can indicate that the crime was committed outside, or perhaps that the body was transported in a trunk that also held hunting clothing. Domestic animal hair can be particularly useful, considering the number of dogs and cats that are owned by individuals not only in the United States, but in almost every country in the world. Perpetrators can be identified not by their own hair but by the hair of their dogs or cats. Dog hair, like human hair, varies considerably. Dog hair varies from breed to breed, from location to location on a single dog, and over time as a dog ages. In some dogs, hair may vary from puppies and adults. Work is ongoing to create a DNA database of cat and dog hair.

MORPHOLOGY OF HUMAN HAIR   Scanning electron microscopy can be used to visualize hair morphology. Hair is made up primarily of keratin. The external structure is comprised of the shaft and the root. The shaft is the visible portion of the hair and the root lies beneath the scalp. The internal structure is comprised of the medulla, cortex, and the cuticle. The medulla is the center of the hair. The cortex surrounds the medulla and contains the pigment which determines hair color. The cuticle is the outer portion of the hair.

BODY REGION   If a hair is determined to be human hair, further analysis will attempt to determine the bodily origin of the hair. Almost the entirety of the human body is covered with hair, except for the soles of the feet, the palms of the hand, and the tip of the penis. Most body hair is of little use in forensic analysis. Arm and leg hair, for example is not typically found at crime scenes. However, head hair and pubic hair are often very useful. To determine the origin of a particular hair, the forensic analyst focuses on structure. Hair varies in texture and structure based upon where it originates on the body. Head hairs tend to be the longest hairs, and almost always evidence cutting. Pubic hairs tend to be short and curly. Eyebrow and eyelash hairs are short and curved. Beard hair is coarse. Underarm hair is similar to pubic hair, although not as thick. Generally, hair evidence is class evidence; it can become individual evidence depending upon a variety of factors. This is especially the case for head hair, which may be chemically altered in a variety of ways and is also likely to be exposed to environmental toxins.

RACIAL DETERMINATION   There are racial differences in hair; however there is too much overlap among the races in these characteristics to be able to make a definitive racial identification in all cases. There is also considerable variation among the races and, because of intermarriage; many individuals have mixtures of more than one race in their genetic makeup. There are three racial groups as far as the analysis of hair is concerned: Caucasoid (European ancestry), Mongoloid (Asian ancestry), and Negroid (African ancestry). The races vary on the coarseness, appearance, color, shaft shape, pigment distribution.

Race	Caucasoid	Mongoloid	Negroid
Coarseness	Fine–medium	Medium	Very
Appearance	Straight or wavy	Straight	Curly or kinky
Color	Blonde to brown to black	May appear reddish	Dark
Shaft shape	Round to oval	Round	Twisted
Pigment distribution	Fine–medium granules; evenly distributed	Large granules; patchy distribution	Large granules; arranged in clumps

http://www.fbi.gov/hq/lab/fsc/backissu/july2000/deedric1.htm#Racial%20Determination

AGE DETERMINATION   It is not possible to make an exact determination regarding the age of a person based upon a hair sample. However, there are differences in the hair of an infant, child, adult, or elderly individual. Infants have very fine hair. Infant hair can always be positively identified. As the child ages, the hair becomes thicker. There is not a specific rate at which this change occurs. Elderly individuals may lose most or all of the pigment from their hair, yet loss of pigmentation can begin when individuals are in their twenties.

HOW WAS THE HAIR REMOVED?   Hair can be lost because it naturally falls out, or it can be forcibly removed. Human beings are constantly going through cycles of loss and regrowth of hair. Everyday we lose hair and everyday our hair grows. For an individual, hair will grow at a fairly steady rate, although that rate can vary from person to person. It can even vary across the scalp of a single individual. It has been noted that Negroid hair tends to grow more slowly than Caucasoid or Mongoloid hair.

When hair is lost naturally, the root of the hair will not be attached to the scalp any longer. This hair will have undamaged roots. Hair that is violently removed is damaged at the root. It may contain pieces of scalp attached to the root end. Hair that was pulled may also be broken or stretched. Prior to the advent of mitochondrial DNA analysis, it was only hair that had a portion of the scalp attached that might be useful in DNA analysis.

CHEMICAL ALTERATION   Frequently, the chemical treatments and alterations that are commonly used on head hair will give hair evidence its individual characteristics. Head hair may show evidence of chemical dyes, straighteners, or perms. Hair can also be treated with chemicals like hairsprays, mousses, shampoos, and gels.

Hair can also be altered by environment and biological factors. Toxins in the environment may be revealed upon analysis. Hair from individuals with a poor diet or who have been exposed to chemicals like mercury will also be apparent upon analysis.

Drug Analysis of Hair

Drug use can be detected by examining hair; however it is not possible to tell how much of a substance has been used, how often, or even when a substance was last used. Different individuals' hair grows at different speeds—even in one person, hair in various places on the scalp will grow at different speeds. It is possible for drug residue to remain within hair until that portion of the hair is removed, which can be quite a long time. Some individuals with long hair may have hair growth of several years, but the majority of forensic laboratories use only about 4 centimeters of hair growth closest to the scalp. Forensic examination of hair produces very accurate results but it is also costly and time consuming. Some substances are not detectable in hair—for example, alcohol.

More frequently, hair is taken from a living or dead individual to forensically examine for the presence of lead and other heavy metals to determine if the individual was poisoned or otherwise contaminated. The lead within the hair will remain intact after death and will not be affected by chemicals used for embalming. This certainly cannot be said for blood—which is removed during the embalming process.

ETHICAL ISSUES AND DNA

The brave new world of DNA has presented scientists and theologians with many ethical issues. Some of these questions are philosophical in nature: Should we decode our genetic code? What will we do with that information? The medical community knows that genetic counseling can lead to abortions of fetuses who may be predisposed to certain conditions. In China, many couples have an ultrasound to detect the sex of an unborn child and selectively abort female babies because they want a boy and the government allows families to have only one child. This practice has skewed the gender balance of the population so that in the current generation that is of age to marry, there are many more men than women.

Initially, the United States required DNA samples to be taken from all felony offenders and many sex offenders, however, many states are now collecting DNA profiles on individuals who have committed misdemeanor offenses and some are even contemplating establishing a DNA database of the general population and doing so-called *familial searches*.

In a familial search, the DNA database is searched and when a near-match is located, the investigation focuses on relatives of that offender because those individuals will have DNA profiles close to that of the offender. This makes an individual a suspect based upon being related to an offender. However, this technique has significant racial implications. Because African-Americans are overrepresented in the prison population, their relatives will be subject to a familial search more frequently than nonminorities. And this type of database searching does not require a search warrant or any form of consent, so millions of individuals can be invasively searched without consent.

The possibility of creating a database of the general population has also been considered. Ethical arguments have been raised against maintaining a DNA database of the general population because of privacy violation concerns. Every time the database is searched, the entire population would become a suspect. There is also a concern that the information could be used for purposes other than criminal investigations. While the government has maintained that they will not misuse this data, it is easy to examine DNA and use the information to exclude individuals from obtaining health insurance or life insurance because of their genetic code. While the DNA database can be a powerful tool for investigating crimes and capturing offenders, it also has the potential to be misused. As with any new technology, these ethical questions should be seriously considered and guidelines should be established for the use of DNA databases and the protection of the privacy of the general population.

Glossary

Autosomes—nonsex chromosomes.

Bands—white blood cells, immature neutrophils.

Basophils—white blood cells.

Chimerism—a rare condition in which an animal or human has more than one cell line.

Coagulation—clotting.

Eosinophils—white blood cells that kill parasites.

Fraternal twins—twins that are the result of two separate sperms fertilizing two separate eggs.

Hematopoiesis—the process of new blood being made in the bone marrow.

Mitochondrial DNA—DNA that is derived from the mitochondria and is passed only through the female line.

Monocytes—white blood cells that destroy damaged cells in the body.

Neutrophils—white blood cells that kill bacteria.

Polymorphism—variation in DNA.

Secretor— an individual that secretes his or her blood type into all bodily secretions.

Webliography

www.dnai.org
DNA Interactive web site.

www.dnalc.org
The Dolan DNA learning center.

References

Centre for Ecology & Hydrology. Smooth Snake. Accessed on April 15, 2007, from http://www.ceh.ac.uk/sections/pce/PopConsEcol_ConsMan_Snakes.html.

Deedrick, D. "Hairs, Fibers, Crime, and Evidence: Part 1: Hair Evidence." *Forensic Science Communications* 2, no. 3 (July 2000). Accessed on April 15, 2007, from http://www.fbi.gov/hq/lab/fsc/backissu/july2000/deedric1.htm#Racial%20Determination.

Gross, S. "The Risks of Death: Why Erroneous Convictions Are Common in Capital Cases. *Buffalo Law Review* 44 (1996): 469–500.

———. "Lost Lives: Miscarriages of Justice in Capital Cases." *Law and Contemporary Problems* 61 (1998): 125–152.

Justice for All Act of 2004. H.R. 5107, Public Law 108–405.

Koblinsky, L., T. Liotti, and J. Oeser-Sweat. *DNA: Forensic and Legal Applications.* New Jersey: John Wiley and Sons Inc. Publishing, 2005.

Money, J., A. Franzke, and D. Borgaonkar. "XYY Syndrome, Stigmatization, Social Class, and Aggression: Study of 15 Cases." *Southern Medical Journal* 68, no. 12 (1975): 1536–42.

Schroder, J., A. de la Chapelle, P. Hakola, and M. Virkkunen. "The Frequency of XYY and XXY Men Among Criminal Offenders." *Acta Psychiatrica Scandinavica* 63, no. 3 (1981): 272–6.

Shankaranarayanan, P., M. Banerjee, R. Kacker, R., Aggarwal, and L. Singh. "Genetic Variation in Asiatic Lions and Indian Tigers." *Electrophoresis* 18, no. 9 (1997): 1693–1700.

Snow Leopard Trust. 2007. *Genetic Research.* Accessed on April 15, 2007, from http://www.snowleopard.org/programs/science/genetics.

Telsavaara, T., and B. Arrigo. "DNA Evidence in Rape Cases and the Debbie Smith Act: Forensic Practice and Criminal Justice Applications." *International Journal of Offender Therapy and Comparative Criminology* 50, no. 5 (2006): 487–505.

Warden, R. "Illinois Death Penalty Reform: How It Happened, What It Promises." *Journal of Criminal Law & Criminology* 95, no. 2 (2005): 381–426.

Zalman. "Criminal Justice System Reform and Wrongful Conviction: A Research Agenda." *Criminal Justice Policy Review* 17, no. 4 (2006): 468–492.

Review Questions

1. What is DNA?
2. What is an autosome?
3. Describe the process of RFLP.
4. What are some of the ways in which genetic fingerprinting can be utilized?
5. What are the two major ways to group blood types?
6. What types of crimes are most likely to yield DNA samples?
7. How is hair analyzed?
8. Why aren't feces terribly useful for forensic analysis?
9. Of all of the bodily substances that can be analyzed for the presence of illicit drugs, which seems to be the most useful?
10. Can blood be analyzed from deceased persons after they have been embalmed?

Some Things to Think About

1. How has DNA revolutionized the field of forensics?
2. What are some of the ethical considerations in collecting DNA from the general population?
3. In what ways has mtDNA analysis proven to be beneficial to forensics?

CHAPTER 10

Assault, Abuse, and Sexual Crimes

CHAPTER OUTLINE

This chapter covers the violent crimes of assault, abuse, and sexual crimes. While these crimes and others that are related to them vary considerably, they also share many traits. These crimes are some of the most devastating to the victim. This is why this chapter also covers victimology—the study of the victim. While many of these offenses leave considerable forensic evidence in the form of bruises, contusions, and other physical signs, some leave little forensic evidence—and some are frequently not reported until years after the crime has taken place.

ASSAULT

Assaults vary in severity and they generally involve some form of person-to-person contact that results in injury. Definitions of assault also vary. California Penal Code section 240 defines assault as: ". . . an unlawful attempt, coupled with a present ability, to commit a violent injury on the person of another." California Penal Code section 242 defines battery as: ". . . any willful and unlawful use of force or violence upon the person of another." Some states differentiate simple assault and aggravated assault. Simple assault is an attempt to cause bodily injury. Aggravated assault causes serious bodily injury or is committed with a weapon. Some states also use the term *battery*.

Although more whites than blacks were arrested for assault in 2005, considering that African-Americans represent about 13 percent of the total population of the United States, they are overrepresented in arrest statistics for assault. In 2005, there were 329,247 arrests for aggravated assault. Of those, two-thirds were white (208,253) and one-third was black (113,062). There were 944,820 arrests in the category of *other assaults*. Of those, again two-thirds were white (615,268) and one-third was black (305,268) (www.fbi.gov/ucr/05cius/data/table_43.html).

The rates for female perpetrator aggravated assault were just over one-quarter of the rate for males. There were 57,923 females arrested for aggravated assault compared with 224,080 arrests of males. However, it should be noted that there has been an overall increase in aggravated assault arrests of women from 1996 to 2005, up 5.4 percent, whereas the male rate fell 14 percent from 260,469 to 224,080 (www.fbi.gov/ucr/05cius/data/table_33.html).

Gottfredson and Hirschi (1990) in their *General Theory of Crime* note that assault, like most of the other categories of crimes in the UCR tends to be committed by young males, many of whom are minorities. Interestingly, victims also tend to be young, minority males. Almost 20 years after the publication of Gottfredson and Hirschi's work, this is still the case.

Forensic Evidence in Assault Cases

Assaults that are not sexual in nature are most likely to result in injuries to the victim and often injuries to the perpetrator as well. One of the most common assault scenarios is when two young males become involved in a bar fight. In fact, this accounts for about 15 percent of all male-to-male assaults (Young and Douglass 2003). In many altercations, it is difficult to determine which individual is the perpetrator and which individual is the victim because both parties will suffer injuries.

Common injuries include bruises, contusions, lacerations, puncture wounds, and gunshot wounds. At the emergency room, the physician will document the extent of the injuries in writing and often emergency department personnel will also photograph the injuries. In the case of assaults that occur in public places, like a bar or at a sporting event, there are usually plenty of witnesses. Officers who respond to the scene will take statements from these individuals.

Photographing Injuries

If a victim is alive, it is important to photographically document any injuries that he or she has sustained because they will heal long before a case can be brought to trial. Injuries can be photographed at the scene if the victim remains there or at the emergency room when the victim seeks medical treatment. Injury photographs should be taken in a series. The first photograph should be either a head-and-shoulders shot or a full length shot of the victim to establish identity. If the injury is not linked to the particular victim when the photographs are taken, it may not be possible to do so later. Many bruises look the same as do arms, legs, and torsos. A jury will require proof that the injuries in the photographs belong to the victim in the case. Multiple photographs of each injury should be taken. The first photograph should establish the location of the injury on the body in general. The second photograph should be a close-up and illustrate the details of the injury. A measuring device, referred to as a *scale,* should be used in the second photograph to document the exact size of the injury. Portable crime scene kits will usually have a variety of small rulers made of cardboard, heavy paper, or plastic that can be used. Some injuries will require additional photographs. It may be beneficial to photograph a bruise on the torso, for example, from both the front of the body and the side.

PHOTOGRAPHING BRUISES   The proper photographing of bruises, also referred to as *contusions,* requires a number of photographs. It is important to photograph bruises using color film, even though most crime scene photography is done with black and white film, because the exact coloration of the bruise is an important indicator of the age of the bruise. A day after the impact occurs, the area will darken. In a week or so the area will become red. After that the color will fade to purple, black, or blue. Finally the bruise will become yellow before it fades completely. A light bruise can fade in a week. More severe bruises can take weeks. The color changes that are normal in bruising can be used to establish that a bruise occurred during an assault and not before. In cases of suspected child abuse, the particular coloration of bruises can indicate multiple injuries of different ages. Because it takes time for the full extent of bruising to appear on a body, bruises should be photographed a day or so following the injury. Ultraviolet technology can be used to photograph bruises that are weeks old and no longer visible to the naked eye. Again, in cases of child abuse, this technique can be useful to show repeated bruising over time. Another benefit of this technology is that it can photograph bruises even where tattoos exist. The ink of the tattoo will not be visible. Because there is considerable individual variation in how severe bruising is and how quickly bruises heal, bruise coloration cannot be used to definitively determine when bruising occurred. The coloration is used more as a general guideline, for example, a bruise that was inflicted hours before officers arrived on the scene will not have faded to yellow.

ABUSE AND SEXUAL CRIMES

A common theme among many of the crimes discussed in this chapter is how very difficult it can be to accurately define them. The definitions of these crimes—domestic violence, child maltreatment, and rape—have changed considerably both geographically and over time. By comparison the definition of murder has been relatively stable. Historically speaking, it is a relatively new phenomenon that a husband can be charged with raping his wife, or that a male could be raped. The term *domestic violence* is also of recent origin—and it is even more recent to consider assaults between same-sex partners to be domestic violence. Traditionally, it was more likely that law enforcement would view what happened within a home as a personal matter, or view same-sex partner abuse simply as assault. The field of forensics tends to use statutory definitions. This keeps confusion to a minimum because it allows the action in question to be defined by the law. The forensic professional who testifies in court must keep this in mind as well. It is the statute that defines the crime—not theory or personal feelings.

Victimology—The Importance of the Victim in Forensics

While it seems odd that the criminal justice system should mostly ignore the victim during an investigation, for much of the twentieth century that is exactly what the criminal justice system seemed to do—distance itself from involvement with victims. After all, it is a *criminal justice system*, not a *victim justice system.* Although early policing focused on service to the community, as policing became increasingly professional it also became increasingly focused on crime and not victims—as if, somehow, the two were not connected. Not only had policing turned its focus away from victims, but it often regarded victims with some degree of mistrust—their statements might be intentionally or unintentionally false. Victims could not be trusted to show up at trial. Victims could not be trusted not to withdraw their complaints—especially victims of domestic violence. Many police officers developed an *us vs. them* mentality and *them* included both the victims and the public in general. In many minority communities significant mistrust of the police developed due to police abuse of power. The police were seen not so much as wanting to protect the people but wanting to abuse the minority population.

The disjunction between police and victims caused many difficulties. Some victims preferred neither to report crimes to the police nor to testify in court. Unfortunately, without the cooperation of victims, the criminal justice system does not work well. Testimony and cooperation of victims and witnesses are necessary to the prosecution of most crimes. Communities that grew to distrust the police often grew hostile to the police as well. It is impossible to function as a police officer within a community that regards the police not as public servants but as the enemy.

Victimology is the study of the victim and the role the victim plays in the criminal act. Early victimology, dating back to the origins of criminology in the 1880s, looked at crime from the victim's perspective, rather than from the perpetrator's perspective. The early work in this field somewhat resembles criminal personality profiling and contributed to the development of that area of forensics.

Victim Precipitation

Victimology, as a more focused academic endeavor and subdiscipline of criminology, emerged in the 1930s and 1940s. In 1937, Mendelsohn originated what he termed *victim precipitation.* In his typology of victims, he created six categories: completely innocent victims, victims with minor guilt, voluntary victims, victims more guilty than the offender, victims who alone are guilty, and the imaginary victims. Interestingly, he saw only the first category of victims as bearing no responsibility for their own victimization.

Research during the 1940s focused on the role that victims play in the criminal act: how victims often contributed to their own victimization. Wolfgang (1958) found this to be especially true for homicide. Considerable research has shown that in male-to-male homicides very often whoever becomes the eventual victim is a matter of luck (or lack of luck); the other individual could have just as easily died. Research has also shown that frequently individuals who end up in the criminal justice system as perpetrators also have been victims. The criminal justice system tends to see the same individuals over and over—sometimes as victims, sometimes as perpetrators.

Unfortunately, early victimization studies that focused on the crime of rape often amounted to little more than blaming the victim for the attack that took place. It was a long time before the criminal justice system could get past focusing on what the victim wore, how late she was out, whether she had been drinking, and whether she was married to or had previously dated the perpetrator, to finally view rape as a crime comparable to other serious offenses. Largely because of the skewed view of rape that came out of victim precipitation, it fell out of favor for many years and the role of the victim in the criminal act came to be largely ignored. Because of the association with blaming the victim, questions like *why this victim?* were asked less frequently. It would not be until the 1980s and 1990s that the role of the victim would again become a central focus in criminal justice.

GENERAL VICTIMOLOGY   In an attempt to move away from its subordinate position to criminology, victimology has attempted to become a discipline in its own right. Researchers in general victimology have moved away from a preoccupation with victim precipitation.

Those who are in the field of general victimology investigate the relationship between victim and offender, the causes of victimization, and the search for solutions to various aspects of *the crime problem.* General victimology has given rise to *routine activity theory* and other theories that examine the environmental factors that may contribute to crime—an approach that is sometimes referred to as *environmental criminology.* Routine activity theory (Cohen and Felson 1979) states that in order for a crime to occur, three factors must come together: a suitable target(s), a motivated offender(s), and an absence of guardians to defend the target(s). This theory does not focus only on the offender—as the majority of criminological theories do—or focus only on the victim, as much of victimology traditionally has—but brings together three elements necessary for a crime to occur. This has given rise to an approach in crime prevention that focuses on making crime targets less attractive, referred to as *target hardening.* Target hardening can vary from installing steel doors at entrypoints to designing neighborhoods with cul-de-sacs. Just like it sounds, target hardening is anything that can be done to make it more difficult for an offender to access a particular target; for example, locking doors, installing burglar alarms, and installing lighting.

CRITICAL VICTIMOLOGY   Most recently, under the influence of radical theory and feminist theory in criminology, some victimologists have turned toward critical victimology. Critical victimology looks beyond the causes and remedies of victimization and questions how and why certain actions are deemed to be criminal while others are not. It questions why the criminal justice system has been quick to criminalize the greed of the poor (theft) and slow to criminalize the greed of the wealthy (white-collar crime), and why beating up a stranger (assault) is a serious crime, whereas beating up your spouse or child (domestic violence) has only recently begun to receive criminal sanction. Critical victimology looks at the relationships among power, wealth, and criminal definitions.

In the legal arena, blaming the victim can be very dangerous. Victimology is not about blaming the victim but rather about understanding what role the victim's behavior played in attracting the type of offender who committed the crime and the particular crime that was committed.

RESTORATIVE JUSTICE   Restorative justice is an approach to criminal justice that acknowledges the importance of the victim. Restorative justice views crime and the criminal act as a breaking down of society. Crime represents a break that exists among the criminal, the victim, and society. Restorative justice acknowledges that the crime problem cannot simply be addressed by longer prison sentences—the approach that is most common in the criminal justice system and is most often called for by the public and by politicians. Restorative justice holds that to the contrary, longer prison terms often make the problem worse, rather than better. Sending offenders, (especially petty, nonviolent offenders) to prison makes the break with society worse rather than better. In prison, the offender interacts with other more violent offenders. Rather than being rehabilitated, he emerges from prison a better criminal than when he entered. Prison also does nothing to repair the damage done to society. Rarely does a prison term repair the damage done to the victim. Rather than approach crime in a retributive way, restorative justice approaches crime in a restorative way and asks: how can the damage that is done be repaired?

Restorative justice programs can be used in prisons, with juvenile offenders, in schools, and in the workplace. Unlike traditional criminal justice approaches, restorative justice can be used in any setting when a perceived wrong has occurred. In prisons restorative justice techniques encourage prisoners to take responsibility for their actions. Victim–offender mediation can be used. Restorative approaches can be used to resolve complaints in prisons. Of course, conflict resolution techniques can be taught. Restorative approaches are particularly useful for juvenile offenders. Family group conferencing is often used with juveniles because the juvenile's family has a significant role in whether the juvenile will reoffend.

Restorative justice in a school setting can be used to help resolve disputes. Rather than view conflict as bad, restorative justice looks at conflict as inevitable. Not only is conflict inevitable, but it can be handled in positive ways and used as a learning tool. Restorative justice encourages young people to take responsibility for their behavior. Conflict resolution can be taught and peer mediation techniques can be utilized. Restorative justice in the workplace, like the school setting, can be used to resolve, rather than ignore, conflict. Conflict resolution and mediation techniques are the most frequently used in the workplace.

Not all offenders and crimes are amenable to restorative justice. Offenders who do not take responsibility for their actions are not good candidates for a restorative technique. Crimes that do not have clearly identifiable victims, like smoking marijuana, are not necessarily amenable to restorative approaches.

Who Are the Victims?

In criminal justice the rate of victimization is measured in three primary ways: the Uniform Crime Reports (UCR), victimization surveys, and self-report surveys. Of these three methods, the most widely cited and used for research in the field of criminal justice is the UCR. The UCR consists of data collected by local police departments concerning known offenses and persons arrested. Each local police department submits their data to the FBI. This data presents a general picture of crime in the United States; it has several significant limitations. First and foremost, it focuses only on offense categories, not on victims. While it is assumed that the reported crimes have associated victims, it does not in any way account for the victims of unreported crimes. This incomplete snapshot of victimization rates is a serious flaw in the UCR data. Second, participation by law enforcement agencies is voluntary; the FBI actually holds no jurisdiction over local law enforcement and cannot force them to participate. Some agencies choose not to submit their data because it takes too much time or because they do not want to. Third, although the FBI makes an instructional handbook available to law enforcement for completing the UCR, reporting errors are made. Some jurisdictions may also inflate their reports of crimes. This may be done to secure more funding. In one jurisdiction this was done simply by creating an official report of every instance of law-breaking that came to the attention of law enforcement—that jurisdiction's crime rate doubled during that year.

The second common way of measuring the extent of victimization is through the use of victimization surveys. Victimization surveys were created in response to the underreporting of victimization in the UCR. Rather than rely on police reports, victimization surveys are completed by contacting representative households and questioning individuals about their victimization experiences during the previous year. Since these surveys focus on crime from the perspective of the victim, they directly address one of the shortcomings of the UCR. Unfortunately, victimization surveys have limitations of their own. First and foremost is the fact that individuals who are contacted to participate may not correctly remember when victimization occurred or may not want to disclose their experiences with victimization. Victimization surveys generally report the level of victimization as being higher than the figures in the UCR. Although, oddly enough, the rate tends to co-vary with the UCR, so while the victimization surveys will show that there is more crime than the UCR shows, it also shows that over the past decade the crime rate has been dropping, a statistic also found in the UCR.

A third approach to measuring victimization is through self-report surveys. In self-report surveys, researchers conduct research on specific forms of victimization, such as rape. Again, this method is subject to its limitations, many of which are common to the victimization surveys: individuals may incorrectly report when victimization occurred, or they may not wish to discuss their experiences with victimization at all. In some cases, such as with self-report surveys dealing with drug use or juvenile crime, respondents may have significant impetus to overreport or underreport their experiences with victimization or criminal activity.

Each of these approaches reveals a slightly different picture of who is being victimized and what sorts of victimizations occur. As expected, UCR presents the lowest rate of victimization overall, because it focuses on the crime itself and not on the victim. Victimization surveys present a higher rate of victimization, and self-report surveys tend to present the highest rate of victimization. According to the UCR, the average victim is a young, minority male, mirroring the average perpetrator. Those individuals who are at the greatest risk for victimization are young, minority, males from lower socioeconomic groups. Conversely, those who are at the least risk for victimization are older, nonminority, females from higher socioeconomic groups. The only type of crime for which women are at greater risk than men is sexual assault. Even among domestic violence crimes, the risk tends to be fairly equal, although men are far less likely to report abuse when they are the victims. This may happen for several reasons. They may fear that they will not be believed. They may fear that they will be looked upon with scorn. They may fear that rather than be looked upon as a victim; they will be perceived as a perpetrator.

EYEWITNESS TESTIMONY

Historically, the court system favors direct evidence. Eyewitness testimony has been considered to be the best direct evidence; and is frequently used to convict. In fact, research has shown that adding eyewitness testimony to any case greatly increases the chance for conviction (Loftus 1996) yet eyewitness testimony is frequently in error. Research in the field of psychology has shown that eyewitness statements are often very inaccurate.

In *The People v. Lee* (NY, 2001), the appellate court in New York State held that it is up to the trial judge whether or not to admit expert testimony on the reliability of eyewitness testimony. This decision echoes the move in the courts to allow the judge to be the gatekeeper of what scientific evidence can and cannot be admitted to court.

In a court of law, direct evidence has traditionally been given the most weight during the trial process. Direct evidence consists of everything that a witness can state that he or she saw, heard, or personally did. This is contrasted with indirect evidence—otherwise known as circumstantial evidence—which is evidence that leads the jury to draw certain conclusions, but is not directly related to the fact in question. For example, finding a fingerprint on a gun does not mean that the individual fired the gun, but it does mean that the individual touched the gun; such evidence, along with other evidence, can lead the jury to conclude that the suspect fired the gun. All forensic evidence is indirect. In fact, the vast majority of all evidence in a criminal case is indirect evidence.

In *Holland v. United States* (348 U.S. 121, 1954), the Supreme Court found:

> Circumstantial evidence in this respect is intrinsically no different from testimonial evidence. Admittedly, circumstantial evidence may in some cases point to a wholly incorrect result. Yet this is equally true of testimonial evidence. In both instances, a jury is asked to weigh the chances that the evidence correctly points to guilt against the possibility of inaccuracy or ambiguous inference. In both, the jury must use its experience with people and events in weighing the probabilities. If the jury is convinced beyond a reasonable doubt, we can require no more.

While it seems as though *Holland* is telling the court to consider direct and indirect evidence equally, this has not been the case. If a witness gives his or her testimony in court and is a credible witness, then juries are likely to convict, even though psychological research has repeatedly demonstrated that eyewitness testimony is likely to be wrong.

Rattner (1988) found that 52 percent of wrongful convictions were based upon false eyewitness identification. The majority of individuals that have been exonerated through modern DNA techniques were originally convicted on the strength of eyewitness testimony.

Wells and Olsen (2001) point out that individuals are less likely to misidentify someone of their own race than they are to misidentify someone of another race. This can be significant, considering the racial disparity that exists within the correctional system; more jurors are white than black and a significant portion of defendants are black.

Research in the field of psychology also supports the ease with which eyewitness testimony can be corrupted. It can be corrupted because of racial biases. It can be corrupted from overhearing other witnesses discuss their perceptions. It can be corrupted through how police questioned the individual—through suggestions by police or even word choice. In traffic accidents, research has shown that if officers use words that seem to indicate higher speeds (for example, "smashed" versus "collided"), witnesses will make statements that the cars were traveling faster than when the cars "collided."

Juries will give more weight to the testimony of witnesses who seem confident of their recollections (Penrod and Cutler 1995). Unfortunately, confidence is not necessarily related to accuracy of recollections. It is possible to be highly confident of your own recollection, yet be incorrect. In fact, in some instances, the surer you are of a recollection, the more likely you are to ignore any cues that you are incorrect.

The credibility of lineups can be improved. Photographs should be presented sequentially. Witnesses should not be allowed to view a photograph more than once. The officer in charge should not confirm or disaffirm any choice. When possible, the officer in charge should not know the identity of the suspect so as to avoid influencing the witnesses' choice (Wells and Olsen 2001).

In 1999 (www.ncjrs.gov/pdffiles1/nij/178240.pdf), the Technical Working Group for Eyewitness Evidence published *Eyewitness Evidence: A Guide for Law Enforcement*. This paper was published in an acknowledgment of convictions based upon eyewitness evidence that were overturned based upon newer DNA evidence. The aim of the guide was to provide sound guidelines for eyewitness evidence. The guide recommended sequential presentation of lineup photographs, rather than simultaneous. The guide acknowledges that unintentional cues from officers can impact choice in a lineup but also acknowledge that blind procedures may be impractical.

The guide recommends separating witnesses at the scene to prevent contamination. The officer should always ask open-ended questions. Photos in mug books should not be suggestive. Photographs should all be the same format (color, black and white, Polaroid, 35mm, digital). Lineups should be created in such a way that the suspect does not stand out. It is a good idea to construct some lineups without the suspect being present in them (www.ncjrs.gov/pdffiles1/nij/178240.pdf).

DOMESTIC VIOLENCE

Domestic violence is broadly defined as any violent interaction that occurs between members of a household. The definition of domestic violence has historically been applied to violence that occurs between a man and woman in a marital or cohabiting relationship, with the male as the perpetrator of violence. The current definition of domestic violence has been expanded to include any violence that occurs within a household. This applies to violence among same-sex partners, violence among siblings, violence directed at older individuals who live in the home, and parental violence against children. It is no longer automatically assumed that the male is always the perpetrator and the female is always the victim—both males and females are perpetrators and victims.

Same-Sex Partner Violence

An often overlooked area of domestic violence is same-sex partner violence. Violence that occurs between a man and a man or a woman and a woman who are involved in an intimate relationship is more likely to be looked upon as a traditional assault than as an act of domestic violence; not only does this skew domestic violence statistics toward being lower than they actually are, this can lead to the victim being treated as a perpetrator.

Part of the difficulty has been the reluctance of law enforcement to deal with homosexual individuals. There is considerable bias. In some cases, officers may see victims as deserving of abuse and may contribute to the continued perpetrating of abuse by discouraging reporting. It is often at an officer's discretion whether same-sex partner violence is reported as domestic violence or as an assault.

Oddly enough, feminist views of domestic violence have discouraged the reporting of female–female partner violence. If only men are perpetrators, then a female–female partnership should not be subject to partner violence. In same-sex partner violence, there is a greater chance of both individuals being treated as perpetrators. So the victim may be looked upon as a perpetrator—adding to the trauma of the victimization. Because society has historically looked down upon both homosexuals and victims, these individuals have a double stigma.

Traditional victim services are often not appropriate for this segment of the victim population. This gap has been filled in some areas by GLBT centers (Gay-Lesbian-Bisexual-Transgender centers). These centers are staffed by the same population that they serve and have more of an understanding of the needs of the population.

Sibling Abuse

Traditional discussions of abuse often do not touch upon sibling abuse. Sibling abuse is the physical, emotional, or sexual abuse of one sibling by another. It is perhaps the most often overlooked form of abuse and even today, many forms of sibling abuse, are dismissed as *normal.*

Certainly conflict between siblings is normal and children will engage in physical conflict. It is difficult to determine how much violence between siblings is normal. Certainly, sexual contact is not normal. Abuse that results in hospital and doctor visits is not normal.

While Adult Protective Services serves the needs of abused elders, women's shelters serve the needs of abused women, and GLBT centers serve the needs of the GLBT community who are abused by their partners, there is no specific social service agency for sibling abuse. Law enforcement is often not contacted during instances of sibling abuse unless it is severe.

Elder Abuse

The problem of elder abuse is only just beginning to be studied, understood, and addressed. Elder abuse stretches far beyond violence committed by family members to encompass abuse by caregivers and abuse in nursing homes. Elder abuse may be physical, sexual, emotional, abandonment, self-neglect, or financial. All states have agencies that deal with Adult Protective Services; these agencies serve older adults and often disabled adults. They also provide assistance in instances of self-neglect.

A survey conducted by The National Center on Elder Abuse indicated that about half of all victims of reported elder abuse were women. Almost half of reported victims were over 80. Perpetrators are usually family members, almost a third were partners of the abused person. Sadly, the most frequently reported form of abuse was self-neglect, almost double the next most frequently reported category—physical abuse. Elders often pose risks to themselves. Very few reports of abuse originate from institutions. Just over half of all perpetrators were male.

Men as Victims

Men have been overlooked as victims of domestic violence. Many of the early philosophical underpinnings of the violence against women movement were directly opposed to any acknowledgment of men as victims. Because it was a women's empowerment movement, it was difficult for the movement to acknowledge that women could be perpetrators of abuse and not just victims. In fact, more recent research has shown that both men and women are equally likely to instigate a violent altercation, although women are likely to be more severely injured because of the size differential between men and women.

There are not clear statistics on male victims of violence and male victims of rape. We know that men are far less likely to report violence or rape. Rape within a prison setting affects a significant portion of inmates. Some researchers have estimated that if it were possible to track prison rape, the incidence of rape among men and women would be about equal.

There is considerable impetus for men not to report violence or rape. Even when a man reports abuse he is unlikely to be taken seriously. He may even experience ridicule for being victimized by a woman. There are few places that offer services to male victims of violence unless the victim is a child.

Men are also more likely to be the victims of false reports of sexual abuse. During divorce and custody disputes it is more frequent for women to fabricate allegations of physical or sexual abuse against their former partners.

Investigating and Collecting Evidence in Domestic Violence Cases

Historically, law enforcement often has been reluctant to view incidents of domestic violence as matters of criminal justice. Prior to the women's movement and the domestic violence movement of the 1960s and 1970s, officers viewed all but the most serious cases of domestic violence as a "private matter." Through the aforementioned women's movement and the domestic violence movements, the problem of domestic violence was researched and pressure was brought upon law enforcement to view domestic violence as a crime, and to arrest a perpetrator when called to a residence for a domestic disturbance. While mandatory arrest practices have had varied success, law enforcement has been made aware of the serious problem of domestic violence and has fashioned a response. It is rare that a police department does not have some form of written policy for handling cases of domestic violence.

During the initial contact between a victim of domestic violence and law enforcement, the first priority is assuring the victim's immediate safety and the safety of any children who may be in the residence. If medical treatment is necessary, medical personnel should be notified.

The law enforcement officer should fully document what he or she sees at the scene. Particular note should be given to: broken doors or windows; smashed furniture; broken objects; the presence or absence of weapons; individuals who are loud or abusive while the officer is present; injuries to the victim; the physical condition of any children present; if one or both parties is under the influence of alcohol, drugs, or other controlled substances; who has had the most physical damage done to them and the nature of that damage; and the emotional state of the individuals at the scene. Law enforcement will also determine if there are any outstanding warrants for any of the individuals involved.

First responders should separate the victim, suspect, and child witnesses/victims. The victim and perpetrator should be interviewed separately. When the victim is identified and interviewed, questions should be asked about previous domestic incidents or threats, and an inquiry should be made regarding any current court orders against the perpetrator. It is important to diagram and photograph the scene. The victim should indicate on the diagram where the incident occurred, and should also indicate the location of bodily injuries on an anatomical diagram.

Officers will collect evidence from the scene. Photographs should be taken of the scene in general, of damage at the scene, and victims' injuries. Weapons that were used either on victims or on property should be collected. If there is documentation of previous abuse, that should be collected as well. It must be determined if one or both individuals require transport to the hospital for their injuries. If there are children present at the scene, their needs must be attended to as well. In some cases, they may also require medical attention and in some circumstances children and family services will become involved.

Some jurisdictions will require that an arrest be made when there is a domestic violence call. In other cases, a determination must be made as to which party was the primary aggressor and which party was acting in self-defense. Officers must consider the relative degree of injury; history of domestic incidents between the parties; differences in age, size, weight, and strength; offensive and defensive wounds; severity of wounds; credibility of each party; use of substances; presence of power and controlling behavior; and the criminal history of each party.

In some cases, an arrest will be made at the scene. Whether or not an arrest is made can depend upon many factors: is one party seriously injured, did one party violate a protective order, and does one party exhibit evidence of having used drugs or alcohol recently. Twenty-five years ago, arrests were made infrequently in domestic violence cases unless injuries were severe. Police officers often considered domestic violence to be a private matter. The victim's and women's movements pushed to have mandatory arrest policies in many jurisdictions. It was reasoned that not arresting perpetrators of domestic violence made reoccurrence more likely. However, research has shown that mandatory arrest policies are not always the best response to domestic violence. Domestic violence is not a problem that can be solved with a one-size-fits-all solution. More recent research has focused on assessing which batterers are most likely to continue to batter and should receive the most intensive treatment and interventions (Goodman, Dutton, and Bennett 2000).

Law enforcement must also consider children at the scene. Law enforcement must always be concerned with the welfare of children who are living in a home where domestic violence is a problem. If both parents are arrested, a responsible friend or relative may take the children with them for a night or several days. If there is no friend or relation to do this, the children may be taken into custody by protective services. Protective services may also become involved if the officers on the scene feel that the children are in danger.

CHILD MALTREATMENT

The broad category of child maltreatment includes neglect, child endangerment, emotional/psychological abuse, physical abuse, and sexual abuse. It is difficult to estimate the actual scope of child maltreatment because child abuse is believed to be generally underreported. The Child Abuse Prevention and Treatment Act of 1974 (Public Law 93-247) found that approximately one million children are the victims of maltreatment each year. This number has remained unchanged over the past 30 years.

Child Neglect

Child neglect consists of not providing for the needs of a child. This may encompass food, shelter, clothing, education, or medical needs. Because children who are neglected are often not given adequate food, many public school systems now provide both free breakfast and lunch for students. Children who are neglected may not be given adequate shelter: they may not have a place to stay at night that affords protection from the elements. In some cases, it can be difficult to distinguish between this type of neglect and extreme poverty. If a child and parent are homeless, it is difficult to construe this as purposeful neglect. Children who are neglected may not have appropriate clothing; they may dress in shorts and tee-shirts even in cold weather because they have no other clothes or their clothes may be filthy. Children who are neglected may not attend school on a regular basis—or at all. This should not be confused, however, with children who are homeschooled in a nurturing environment. Educational neglect may take the form of an older child being kept home from school to look after younger children, or a child may simply not go because he or she does not want to go, and the parents do not provide adequate monitoring. Children who are neglected may not be given adequate medical care. They may not be taken to a pediatrician or dentist on a regular basis. Children who seriously injure themselves may not be taken to the hospital. Neglect must be distinguished from those cases in which parents do not seek medical attention for religious reasons. Neglect must also be distinguished from poverty. To alleviate this lack of medical care, many parents who cannot afford health insurance for their children can now obtain coverage through their state at little or no cost. Child neglect is the most common form of child maltreatment and comprises approximately 60 percent of substantiated cases of child abuse (www.preventchildabuse.com/neglect.htm).

Child Endangerment

Child endangerment occurs when adults who are responsible for the care of a child expose that child to potential or actual dangerous situations. This can range from leaving a child unattended in a car while running an errand, to allowing a child to stay at home without supervision for an extended period of time. Some states have specific statutes that outline how old a child must be before he or she may be left alone; in other states this age limit is nonstandardized and is reached through a "weighing of factors," such as the child's emotional maturity, general intelligence, and ability to cope with emergency situations, coupled with the time span over which the child will be alone, while factoring in the availability of adults.

Emotional Abuse

Emotional abuse interferes with a child's psychological, emotional, or social development. This abuse may consist of a variety of behaviors including criticism, belittling, name-calling, threatening, rejecting, ignoring, demanding too much of a child, or allowing children to participate in harmful or criminal acts. Emotional abuse is the hardest form of abuse to detect and prosecute. Although many children who are emotionally abused exhibit behavioral indicators—such as shyness or aggression toward others—others show no signs of abuse at all. Society has often condoned emotionally abusive behavior toward children. While law enforcement may be called when one adult repeatedly berates another adult in public, not much is done if the victim is that young. It is a sad double standard that our society will allow parents to treat their children in ways that they could not treat a stranger.

Physical Abuse

Physical abuse involves physical contact and there is often a pattern of repeated physical contact. Physical abuse includes hitting, slapping, punching, kicking, beating, striking with objects, stabbing, cutting, choking, and burning among other actions. Victims of physical abuse are more likely to be placed into foster care than victims of sexual abuse. Physical abuse is easier to visually document—black eyes and broken bones are more obvious to others than sexual fondling, even intercourse may only be evident upon a physical exam by a trained medical practitioner.

Sexual Abuse

Sexual abuse includes all forms of sexual contact between minors and other children, animals, or adults. It can also include sexual contact between two minors when a significant age difference exists between the two (in some jurisdictions three or four years) and sexual contact between minors where a significant age difference does not exist if it is reported to the authorities for investigation.

Sexual abuse may encompass activities such as encouraging minors to view or be involved in pornography, make obscene phone calls, and engage in sexual gestures or behaviors for an adult's pleasure or the sexual pleasure of others (including other kids). Other forms of sexual abuse include sexual conversation between adults and children or between children.

History of Child Maltreatment

Throughout history, most societies have viewed children as the property of their parents, usually the father. The father could generally do what he wanted with his children, including selling them into servitude, apprenticing them, marrying them off, or physically punishing them; in many societies, this parental prerogative extended to practices of infanticide. Even today, infanticide—especially female infanticide—is practiced in some parts of the world. For example, in some parts of rural India, female babies may be killed when they are born. Christianity, Judaism, and Islam all support a patriarchic family with the father as head of the home and endow him with the ability to do whatever he sees fit with his children (and wife).

The outlook for children began to change during the 1800s. In the United States, movements such as ChildSavers sought to improve how children were treated. In 1875, the New York Society for the Prevention of Cruelty to Children was formed. The juvenile court system was founded in Chicago in 1899. By 1918, all states had compulsory schooling laws. During the 1800s, many children worked in factories, on farms, in mines, and in other positions. They often worked 12-hour days for wages that were lower than adult wages. It was generally encouraged that poor children go to work as soon as possible. It was not until the 1930s that child labor laws were instituted across the United States.

Statute Definitions of Child Abuse

Pennsylvania statute (Chapter 63, Subsection 6303):

1. The term "child abuse" shall mean any of the following:

    i. Any recent act or failure to act by a perpetrator which causes nonaccidental serious physical injury to a child under 18 years of age.

    ii. An act or failure to act by a perpetrator which causes nonaccidental serious mental injury to or sexual abuse or sexual exploitation of a child under 18 years of age.

    iii. Any recent act, failure to act or series of such acts or failures to act by a perpetrator which creates an imminent risk of serious physical injury to or sexual abuse or sexual exploitation of a child under 18 years of age.

    iv. Serious physical neglect by a perpetrator constituting prolonged or repeated lack of supervision or the failure to provide essentials of life, including adequate medical care, which endangers a child's life or development or impairs the child's functioning.

Alabama Code (Subsection 26-14-1):

For the purposes of this chapter, the following terms shall have the meanings respectively ascribed to them by this section:

1. ***Abuse.*** Harm or threatened harm to a child's health or welfare. Harm or threatened harm to a child's health or welfare can occur through nonaccidental physical or mental injury, sexual abuse or attempted sexual abuse or sexual exploitation or attempted sexual exploitation. "Sexual abuse" includes the employment, use, persuasion, inducement, enticement, or coercion of any child to engage in, or having a child assist any other person to engage in any sexually explicit conduct or any simulation of the conduct for the purpose of producing any visual depiction of the conduct; or the rape, molestation, prostitution, or other form of sexual exploitation of children, or incest with children as those acts are defined by Alabama law. "Sexual exploitation" includes allowing, permitting, or encouraging a child to engage in prostitution and allowing, permitting, encouraging or engaging in the obscene or pornographic photographing, filming, or depicting of a child for commercial purposes.

2. ***Neglect.*** Negligent treatment or maltreatment of a child, including the failure to provide adequate food, medical treatment, supervision, clothing, or shelter.

Factors That Increase the Likelihood of Child Victimization

While any one factor does not predict that a child will be victimized, there are many factors that increase the likelihood that a child will be victimized. Younger children are more likely to be victimized and more likely to die as a result of victimization, following the general rule that the younger the child, the greater the risk of abuse and the greater the risk of death. Disabled children are at a greater risk for abuse. Children who have had contact with child protective services are more likely than other children to be seen on future occasions. African-American children are overrepresented among substantiated victims of child maltreatment. This may mean that there is a higher rate of abuse among African-Americans; however, it is more likely that this means that the abuse of African-American children is more likely to come to the attention of authorities and is more likely to be prosecuted.

Contrary to the popular belief that strangers pose the greatest risk to children, the reality is that children are most likely to be injured, abused or killed by their own parents or parent-substitutes. In fact, it is a rarity for a stranger to abduct and kill a child. Approximately 75 percent of perpetrators are parents. Parents who abuse alcohol or other substances are more likely to abuse their children. This is due not only to the fact that alcohol lessens the individual's ability to make good choices, but those who abuse substances are already likely to be living under a great deal of stress.

Investigation of Child Maltreatment

Any investigation into an instance of child maltreatment begins with a report from the parents, school, police, or other mandated reporter such as a doctor or therapist. In some states, anyone who suspects child abuse or neglect is required to report it, whereas in other states, only those individuals who work with children are required to report. Individuals reporting child abuse can remain anonymous (except for mandated reporters such as school officials, doctors, and therapists). The state's child protective services agency will conduct an initial investigation of all reports that they receive.

During the investigation, the child protective worker (CPW) will visually examine the child. The worker will also talk with the child. The CPW may obtain criminal and mental health records on anyone who is alleged to have abused or neglected a child. Medical and psychological examinations may be required to determine if abuse has occurred or if there is a risk of it occurring. Additionally, the CPW may visit the child's home to evaluate the living conditions and environment.

A determination will be made as to whether abuse has occurred or is at risk of occurring. The child may be removed from the home for safety reasons or in some cases the suspected abuser will be removed from the home and the child remains with the nonoffending parent or caregiver when long-term treatment is a possibility. A further decision must be made regarding whether the case should be turned over to law enforcement for criminal prosecution; this is most likely in cases of sexual abuse and physical abuse.

RAPE

There is no one definition of rape. It has been defined in a variety of ways over time, and the statutory definition varies from state to state (Figure 10.1).

Collecting Evidence in a Sexual Assault

If the sexual assault has just occurred *and* the victim goes to a hospital, physical evidence for use in court will be collected in a sexual assault kit, also referred to as a "rape kit." The rape kit contains all of the cotton swabs, urine and blood collection containers, a speculum, sterile sample containers, slides and envelopes necessary to collect enough evidence to prosecute the case. The victim will be given a complete physical examination and all injuries will be documented both in writing and in photographs. A blood sample will be taken to test for pregnancy and a variety of sexually transmitted diseases, including HIV. The hospital can also test for commonly used "rape drugs" such as royphenol, which can make victimization easier by impairing or incapacitating the victim. Scrapings will be taken from underneath the victim's fingernails because the victim may have scratched the perpetrator during the attack. The victim's pubic hair will also be combed to loosen hair and fiber evidence that may be in the area. Additionally, a number of pubic hairs will be plucked from the victim. Damage to her (or his) clothing will be documented and it will be saved as evidence. The nurse will collect swabs from the victim's mouth, vagina, and anus (depending upon where sexual contact occurred). The nurse will also examine other areas of the victim's body and clothing for semen.

Because the purpose of the rape kit is for the prosecution of the offender, chain of custody is important. Much of the evidence collected in the rape kit will fall into the following areas: serology, fiber and fragments, and hair. Once all evidence has been collected from the victim, the kit will be sealed and placed in a controlled area until the police can arrive and take it into their custody. While still at the hospital, the police will interview the victim for the first time. Follow up interviews may be conducted elsewhere. This initial interview will include the victim's account of what happened during the attack, where the attack occurred, and, if possible, a description or the identity of the perpetrator. Investigators will need to go to the scene to collect any evidence that is there.

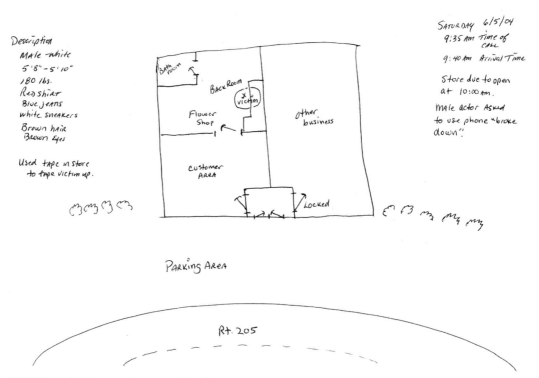

FIGURE 10.1 A rape crime scene sketch.

Rape Statutes

In Pennsylvania rape is defined as:

Subsection 3121. Rape.

a. ***Offense defined.***—A person commits a felony of the first degree when he or she engages in sexual intercourse with a complainant:

   i. By forcible compulsion
   ii. By threat of forcible compulsion that would prevent resistance by a person of reasonable resolution.
   iii. Who is unconscious or where the person knows that the complainant is unaware that the sexual intercourse is occurring.
   iv. Where the person has substantially impaired the complainant's power to appraise or control his or her conduct by administering or employing, without the knowledge of the complainant, drugs, intoxicants or other means for the purpose of preventing resistance.
   v. Who suffers from a mental disability which renders the complainant incapable of consent.
   vi. Who is less than 13 years of age.

FORENSIC NURSING

Forensic nursing is an emerging subdiscipline of nursing. Forensic nurses may provide care to victims, identify and collect forensic evidence, assist medical examiners, and work in psychiatric facilities or correctional settings. Victims and offenders are routinely brought to emergency rooms, but they are also seen in primary care settings and the appropriate training of forensic nurses can assist in the identification of victims who do not self identify.

When rape victims are seen in the emergency room, forensic evidence must be collected from them using a rape kit. If the evidence is not collected, sterilized, and packaged correctly, it can damage the chances for successful prosecution.

Forensic nurses may assist medical examiners during autopsies, which is a new area for nurses to work in. Forensic nurses have long worked in psychiatric facilities and correctional settings.

Glossary

Battery—a synonym for assault.

Contusions—bruises.

Victimology—the study of the victim.

Victim precipitation—the theory that many victims are partly responsible for their own victimization.

Webliography

American Society of Victimology.
www.american-society-victimology.us
International Victimology web site
www.victimology.nl

Restorative justice online
www.restorativejustice.org
World Society of Victimology.
www.world-society-victimology.de/wsv/index.aspx

References

Cohen, L., and M. Felson. "Social Change and Crime Rate Trends: A Routine Activity Approach." *American Sociological Review* 44 (1979): 588–605.

FBI. September 2006. Crime in the United States 2005. *Table 33: Ten-Year Arrest Trends by Sex, 1996–2005.* Accessed on November 27, 2006, from www.fbi.gov/ucr/05cius/data/table_33.html.

FBI. September 2006. Crime in the United States 2005. *Table 43: Arrests by Race, 2005.* Accessed on November 27, 2006, from www.fbi.gov/ucr/05cius/data/table_43.html

FBI Laboratory: DNA Analysis. Accessed on August 24, 2006, from http://www.fbi.gov/hq/lab/html/dnau1.htm (http:// www.preventchildabuse.com/neglect.htm).

Goodman, L., M. Dutton, and L. Bennett. "Predicting Repeat Abuse Among Arrested Batterers." *Journal of Interpersonal Violence* 15, no. 1 (2000): 63–74.

Gottfredson, M., and T. Hirschi. *A General Theory of Crime.* Stanford: Stanford University Press, 1990.

Groleau, R. (January, 2002). *Tracing Ancestry with MtDNA.* Accessed on August 29, 2006, from www.pbs.org/wgbh/nova/neanderthals/mtdna.html.

Holland v. United States (348 U.S. 121, 1954).

Loftus, E. *Eyewitness Testimony.* Cambridge, MA: Harvard University Press, 1996.

National Institute of Justice. 1999. *Eyewitness Evidence: A Guide for Law Enforcement.* Accessed on November 27, 2006, from www.ncjrs.gov/pdffiles1/nij/178240.pdf.

Penrod, S. and B. Cutler. "Witness confidence and witness accuracy: Assessing their forensic relation." *Psychology, Public Policy, and Law* 1 (1995): 817–845.

Rattner, A. "Convicted But Innocent: Wrongful Conviction and the Criminal Justice System." *Psychology, Public Policy, and Law* 1 (1988): 817–45.

Wells, G., and E. Olson. "The Other-Race Effect in Eyewitness Identification: What Do We Do About It?" *Psychology, Public Policy, and Law* 7, no. 1 (2001): 230–46.

Wolfgang, M. *Patterns of Criminal Homicide.* Philadelphia, PA: University of Pennsylvania Press, 1958.

Young, C., and J. Douglass. "Use of, and Outputs from, an Assault Patient Questionnaire Within Accident and Emergency Departments on Merseyside." *Emergency Medicine Journal* 20 (2003): 232–37.

Review Questions

1. Why have abuse and sexual crimes been defined in a variety of ways in the past?
2. How does the victim relate to the criminal act?
3. What are some of the pitfalls of eyewitness testimony?
4. What is the purpose of the "rape kit"?
5. How does the microscope assist in the analysis of fiber evidence?
6. Describe the steps that should be followed when collecting evidence at a domestic violence crime scene.
7. Discuss some of the forms of child neglect.
8. Why is sibling abuse not generally recognized as abuse?
9. List and discuss the different types of elder abuse.
10. What are some of the activities that a forensic nurse might perform?

Some Things to Think About

1. If eyewitness testimony has been proven to be frequently incorrect, why do you think the criminal justice system still relies upon it so frequently to convict?
2. How does victimology as we employ it today differ from "victim blaming"?
3. From a philosophical standpoint, how does restorative justice differ from the more traditional view of justice?

Very Large Crime Scenes; Forensic Mental Health

Section V is comprised of Chapters 11 and 12. Chapter 11 covers fires, arsons, explosions, and mass casualties. These crime scenes are typically much larger than the average crime scene. Although an arson crime scene may be limited to a car or other small area, these scenes frequently encompass an entire building. Explosions create an even larger crime scene, with debris and evidence scattered far away from the center of the explosion. Mass casualties—airplane crashes, bombings, and explosions, involve many people and are often spread out over a significantly large area. These much larger crime scenes present unique problems to forensics teams. They are more difficult to secure and because evidence is scattered over a much larger geographic area, evidence may be harder to identify and collect. Chapter 12 presents forensic mental health. Not long ago, the only scientists who were routinely permitted to testify as experts in a court of law were medical doctors. If an expert opinion was needed regarding a person's mental state, perhaps while that person was making out a will or committing a crime, the individual who testified would be a forensic psychiatrist—a medical doctor who specialized in psychiatry—although he (and it was almost always a man) would probably not have called himself a forensic psychiatrist but perhaps a criminal psychiatrist or simply a psychiatrist. The modern courtroom allows a variety of mental health professionals with different types of training, education, and experience to testify in court. Forensic mental health deals with the interface of behavioral science and the law. This chapter discusses topics ranging from police selection and training, to insanity and competency evaluations, to prediction of dangerousness, to treating offenders and mandated counseling. Unlike most forensic science professionals who do the majority of their work prior to a case going to court, the average forensic mental health professional can be involved in all aspects of the criminal justice process, from training police officers, to evaluating offenders prior to trial, to treating individuals in correctional settings and after they have been released back into society.

CHAPTER 11

Arson, Explosives, and Mass Casualties

CHAPTER OUTLINE

This chapter addresses the investigation of arson (fires), explosions, and mass casualties. All three of these types of investigations share a number of similar challenges and approaches. Although some arson fires involve only a small area, generally all three of these types of investigations encompass larger areas than most other crimes. An explosion scene may encompass entire city blocks. Each of these crime scenes presents significant challenges to the investigator in terms of protection, recognition, and collection of evidence. The more a crime scene is spread out, the more difficult it can be to determine what is and is not evidence. It is also much easier for evidence to be overlooked or obliterated. Finally, each of these crime scenes is highly dangerous, not only to victims, but also to crime scene personnel as well, and *the unknown* is a significant factor in the early stages of the investigation.

ARSON AND FIRE INVESTIGATION

From an investigative standpoint, there are many similarities between a fire investigation and an arson investigation. They will both begin with determining the point of origin of the fire. From carefully analyzing this area, it can often be determined whether or not a fire is the result of an accident or if it was intentionally set. Both types of fires pose similar hazards to rescue workers and investigators. Evidence from both is handled similarly (Figure 11.1).

The FBI defines arson as "any willful or malicious burning or attempt to burn, with or without intent to defraud, a dwelling house, public building, motor vehicle or aircraft, personal property of another, etc." (www.fbi.gov/ucr/cius_04/offenses_reported/property_crime/arson.html). The majority of all arsons involve structures. From an investigative standpoint, it is much more difficult to investigate and successfully prosecute arsons involving motor vehicles; whereas there is a significantly higher rate of successful structural arson prosecutions. Arsons involving motor vehicles will leave a lot less evidence for investigators to find than arsons involving structures. There is a greater chance that the evidence contained in the vehicle will be completely destroyed. The vehicle can even be moved and all evidence lost completely.

FIGURE 11.1   Any fire can be the result of arson.

The good news is that the rate of arson has fallen steadily over the past 10 years; in fact, an article from the March 2005 issue of *Fire Chief* was entitled: "Arson fires reach historic low" (West 2005). According to the FBI's Uniform Crime Reports, the arson rate was 44.8 per 100,000 in 1995 (www .fbi.gov/ucr/Cius_97/95CRIME/95crime2.pdf); whereas in 2004 it had fallen to 28.2 per 100,000 (www.fbi.gov/ucr/cius_04/offenses_reported/property_crime/arson.html). The rate quoted in the Uniform Crime Reports may not be accurate because arson is not tracked as thoroughly by the FBI as the other index offenses (homicide, rape, robbery, assault, burglary, larceny, and car theft). The Uniform Crime Reports include only crimes clearly ruled as arson, not suspicious fires where arson is suspected but not proven. Further complicating the statistical picture, some agencies do not report all or some of their arson data to the FBI.

Yet, there is good reason to believe that there actually has been a decrease in arsons. Data from the United States Fire Administration reflects an even more dramatic decrease than the Uniform Crime Reports. In 1995, 90,500 arson fires were reported, with a total of 740 deaths. In 2004, the number of fires reported had fallen to 36,500, with a total of 320 deaths. The number of fires and deaths has decreased by more than half—and although the number of deaths in 1995 was inflated by including the 168 casualties from the bombing of the Federal Building in Oklahoma City, even when these deaths are removed from the statistics, the number of deaths still has declined sharply (www .usfa.dhs.gov/statistics/arson/).

Compared to other index offenses, arson is a crime of the young, which has significant implications for investigations, as juveniles are more likely to target schools for arson or vandalism than other structures. About half of all arson fires are set by juveniles and more than 40 percent of all arson arrests involve only juvenile offenders.

Protecting a Crime Scene

When firefighters respond to a fire, rescuing victims and extinguishing the fire are their top priorities. Firefighters do not approach a fire thinking of how the scene can best be preserved for later crime scene processing. In some jurisdictions there is disagreement regarding whether the investigation of arson is the responsibility of law enforcement or fire services (Figure 11.2).

FIGURE 11.2 Smoke from fire.

The action of extinguishing a fire is inherently destructive to almost all types of forensic evidence; bodily fluids, fiber evidence, hairs, and fragments can easily be washed away—if the fire itself does not destroy them. This destructiveness is why some perpetrators use arson in an attempt to disguise other crimes, such as homicide or fraud. This is also the reason investigators must be especially systematic and careful in their evidence collection. Arson investigation focuses on cause and origin: what started the fire and where the fire started.

COLLECTION AND PRESERVATION OF ARSON EVIDENCE   Once the fire has been fully extinguished, the lead firefighter will make a determination as to when non-firefighters can enter the scene. In some cases, a hazardous materials professional will be involved in this determination. Until this determination is made, all crime scene personnel should maintain a safe distance from the scene. Fire scenes pose numerous hazards to everyone; portions of the structure may be unstable; the structure might contain chemical and biological hazards among other possible hazards. Like all crime scenes, as few individuals as possible should enter, to avoid evidence destruction and contamination.

During the investigation, the arson investigators will first determine the point of origin of the fire—where it began—and then examine the burn patterns from the fire, collect physical evidence, and—finally—the scene will be reconstructed. When arson evidence is collected—just as when any other type of evidence is collected—proper chain of custody must be followed.

Most of the evidence will be found near the point of origin of the fire. The investigators focus on lower portions of the fire, where more evidence is likely to be located. Ash samples should be collected in this area and from areas extending away from the point of origin; this will assist investigators in determining how the fire spread.

All evidence that is collected must be packaged in separate, plastic, airtight containers and marked with identifying information, including the initials of the investigator who collected the evidence, the time it was collected, and the location from which it was collected. Photographs of the scene should be taken both before and after evidence is collected.

Arson evidence is preserved differently from other types of evidence. In general, wet evidence from other types of crime scenes is allowed to air-dry and is packaged in a breathable container. This is not the case with wet arson evidence—and much arson evidence is usually wet because of the water used to extinguish fires. Wet arson evidence is packaged immediately in an airtight container. This is done to prevent trace vapors from evaporating from the evidence. These vapors, especially at the point of origin, are most likely to contain residues from any accelerant that may have been used.

PHOTOGRAPHING AN ARSON CRIME SCENE   An arson crime scene presents unique challenges to a crime scene photographer. Although all crime scenes have the potential to be dangerous, arson crime scenes have a greater potential to cause injury or even death. Structures that have been the target of arson may be significantly weakened. Walls may crumble, ceilings may collapse. Shards of glass and metal are potential hazards. There may also be hazardous chemicals and chemical residues in the environment. If electrical power and gas have not been turned off, these represent other dangers. The first concern for a photographer is personal safety. Although a crime scene should first be declared safe to enter before it is photographed, even when it is declared *safe,* there are still hazards. A photographer should wear safety gear and be wary of the environment at all times.

The second concern for a crime scene photographer is protecting their camera and all of the equipment needed to photograph the crime scene. All of this equipment is very expensive and can be damaged by water. In some instances, it may be necessary to tent the camera with plastic to prevent damage.

A crime scene photographer will also run into some technical issues when photographing arson scenes. Lighting can be a significant issue. The burnt areas of the arson are very dark, often black, making it difficult to photograph even when there is adequate lighting as photographs will be improperly exposed (a similar problem occurs when photographing outdoor scenes with snow).

Even when photographing areas that are not black from being charred, adequate lighting is often lacking. Additionally, evidence at an arson crime scene is often difficult to locate and may be burned beyond recognition. The lead investigator will point out what should be photographed.

Point of Origin

At the outset of an investigation, an arson investigator will determine where the fire started, its *point of origin;* generally, this is not difficult for a trained investigator or seasoned firefighter to determine. Since most of the valuable evidence will be found in the immediate area of the point of origin, this determination is very important and the investigation will follow the path that the fire followed as it burned. It is at the point of origin that a fire will burn hottest—unless it comes into contact with fuel elsewhere. This will be true of any fire—not just fires that have been intentionally set.

A point of origin will also contain tell-tale signs of arson: if accelerant was used to start or maintain the fire, residue is most likely to be found there; there also may be remnants of an incendiary device, which may contain prints or other evidence. When multiple points of origin are determined, it is often a definite indicator of arson.

Burn Patterns and Spread of Fire

A number of factors affect how fire spreads. First, fire moves toward fuel. When accelerant is spread over a floor, a fire will follow along this path. Generally, a fire will burn upward and outward; if accelerant is poured down a flight of stairs, however, the fire will follow the accelerant. This sort of fire path would be a tell-tale sign that a fire was set purposefully.

Fire always burns in a predictable pattern unless it encounters a new fuel source. Fire spreads in a circular pattern, moving out evenly from the source, in concentric circles. Fire burns upward and outward, creating what is referred to as *an inverted cone burn pattern.* Fire burns hottest at its base and cooler further away from the base. The expected pattern will be altered if a fire meets a new fuel source, or is suddenly robbed of fuel by encountering an obstacle such as a wall. In a structural fire, burn patterns will also be altered. Ceilings cause the fire to spread wider than it would otherwise because they present a barrier to the fire; stairwells cause rapid upward spread because suddenly the fire encounters a new means of moving upward and more oxygen. Fire burns with air flow. Fire travels toward oxygen.

The investigator will look for both backdrafts and flashovers, which will alter normal burn patterns. Backdrafts occur when a fire occurs in a closed area. Once all of the oxygen is used up, the fire will continue to smolder. The smoldering creates superheated carbon monoxide gas that continues to fill the room. If a door or window is opened or broken or melts, the new oxygen causes an explosive fire. Unlike normal fires, that have a burn pattern that is worst at floor level, backdrafts create a burn pattern that is worst at the top of the room. A flashover will occur when objects within a room reach their ignition point and burst into flames. Neither backdrafts nor flashover will have accelerant residue present.

Once investigators locate the point of origin, they will look to see how much has burnt and how quickly. A fire that burned very rapidly can be suspect. The investigators look at how much was burnt and the fuels that should have been present at the scene. A fire that has burned rapidly and consumed more matter in a manner than cannot be contributed to the fuels that should have been present in the area is very likely arson. The investigator will also look for areas in which the fire may have come into contact with more accelerant which aided in keeping the fire burning longer and faster than it naturally would have. Of course the use of accelerant is also indicative of arson.

ACCELERANTS   The detection and analysis of accelerant residue found at an arson scene is an important part of an investigation. An accelerant is any substance that is used to speed up a fire. Commonly used accelerants include liquids such as gasoline, kerosene, lighter fluid, oils, nail polish remover, and alcohol (Figure 11.3). The investigators will collect ash and debris from around the

FIGURE 11.3   Every household contains a variety of possible accelerants.

point of origin and from other areas where it seems likely that an accelerant was used. Chemical tests may be used to detect accelerant residues at the scene. It's a good idea to also collect substances that are absorbent—such as wood and cloth—because of their porous nature they take in and hold chemicals from a fire. The investigator should obtain samples from many areas in an attempt to determine how and where the accelerant was used. In the laboratory, accelerants can be analyzed through gas chromatography and infrared spectrophotometry.

CANINE USE FOR ACCELERANT DETECTION   According to federal case law, accelerant canine evidence is admissible in court. Dogs are trained by daily exposure to various accelerants. Through exposure to five basic explosive groups canines are trained to detect chemical compounds that are used in over 19,000 explosives (http://atf.treas.gov/explarson/canine.htm). The ATF (Bureau of Alcohol, Tobacco, Firearms and Explosives) provides training to explosive and accelerant detection canines not only to federal, state, and local law enforcement here in the United States, but around the world. The ATF trains canines to recognize explosives, explosive residue, and postblast evidence. These dogs can also detect firearm residue. Because of their superior sense of smell, these dogs can detect very minute traces of residue long after the fire has been extinguished.

Incendiary Devices

An incendiary device is designed to start a fire. It can be electric or something as simple as a candle. There are solid chemical incendiary devices that are sometimes used to ignite a fire, including both candles and flares. A variety of chemicals can also be used—either alone or in conjunction with other chemicals to create an incendiary device. These devices very often will leave chemical residue that will be found at the scene. Mechanical and electrical portions of incendiary devices are also generally recovered from the fire. These include batteries, relays, wires, ropes, timers, and so forth. Any of these may be found and matched to objects that a suspect has in his or her possession, and may include items found with a search warrant at the suspect's apartment, garage, or house.

FIGURE 11.4 This Molotov cocktail was seized as evidence.

Specific device patterns can be indicative of a serial arsonist, and such evidence may link multiple arsons. Each arsonist tends to set fires in a particular way, becoming better and better at setting fires as time goes on. The incendiary device that they use or create will be unique, like their signature (Figure 11.4).

INFORMATION FROM FIRST RESPONDERS   Investigators must talk with the first firefighters who responded to the fire. These firefighters will be able to tell investigators about the behavior of the fire as they found it—including smoke color, odor, and size of flames. Investigators also want to obtain information regarding wind direction and speed, and other meteorological conditions (rain, snow, sunshine). This sort of information can be helpful in determining the accelerants that may have been used to ignite the fire. First responders will also have observed the behavior of individuals at the scene; it is not uncommon for an arsonist to remain at the scene to watch the results of his or her efforts. Like a burglary photographer who takes photographs of the street in front of and behind where a burglary occurred because the perpetrator may have left a car behind, an arson photographer should always photograph the crowd that gathers to watch a fire burn.

Reconstruction of the Crime Scene

Reconstruction of the arson crime scene follows the fire from its point of origin, by way of its burn patterns, through all the fuel sources and accounts for changes in the behavior of the fire dictated by the layout, the structure, and finally, to extinguishment. In this way the investigator can determine if the fire behaved as it should have, and if it did not, what accounts for the discrepancy.

Likely Targets for Arson

Arson fires disproportionately occur in poorer neighborhoods where there are more likely to be abandoned buildings. These fires may be set just for the excitement of watching a fire burn. Churches have also been targeted. In 1996, after an increase in arson fires involving predominately

African-American churches in the southern United States, President Clinton formed the National Church Arson Task Force. This task force helped local, state, and federal agencies deal with the problem of church arson and the number of church arsons has decreased steadily since 1996 (www.usfa .dhs.gov/downloads/pdf/tfrs/v1i8.pdf).

Typology of Arsonists

A typology answers two key questions about arsonists: who commits arson and why. Approximately half of all arson fires are set by juveniles. Of the remaining fires, the majority are motivated by insurance fraud. Only a small percentage of arson fires are committed to cover another crime, or for revenge. Some arsonists, both adult and juvenile, commit their crimes repeatedly and are labeled *serial arsonists.*

CHILDHOOD FIRESETTERS A typology of childhood firesetters has developed in the literature, although the typology is thought to be most beneficial for assessment of a child's problem with fire. Childhood firesetters generally fall into one of five categories that vary in their level of pathology and social skills: curiosity, accidental, cry for help, delinquent, and severely disturbed firesetters. Curiosity firesetters are young children, usually between the ages of three and six who engage in firesetting to experiment with fire (Figure 11.5). These children exhibit low levels of pathology and low levels of social skills. They are more interested in fire than other types of firesetters, and their fires tend to lead to greater damage and destructiveness (Barreto et al. 2004; Kolko and Kazdin 1991).

Accidental firesetters are children under the age of 11. They exhibit low levels of delinquency and pathology. These children have few problems socializing or expressing emotions. They would not be labeled as different or troublesome by either teachers or peers. As the name of this subtype suggests, the fires these children set are accidental. In some cases, these children may be so young as to have only a limited knowledge of the danger of fire. These children may simply be exploring fire. The best prevention for these types of fires is to keep matches and lighters out of the child's reach. The child should be educated both about the danger of fire and the proper use of matches and lighters (Barreto et al. 2004; Kolko and Kazdin 1991).

FIGURE 11.5 Many children exhibit curiosity toward fire.

The cry-for-help firesetter exhibits low levels of pathology, has little trouble socializing or expressing emotions, and is more likely to be female and Caucasian. The delinquent firesetter exhibits a developmental trend. Delinquent tendencies are found during preadolescence and increase during adolescence. While they show empathy for others during preadolescence, this is not the case during adolescence, when they exhibit the greatest amount of deviancy and behavioral dysfunction and low levels of both pathology and social skills. They engage in firesetting because of an inability to express anger. The severely disturbed firesetter exhibits low levels of delinquency but high levels of pathology. They show warning signs of pathology often during elementary school years. Neglect and parental dysfunction are likely to be correlated with this type of firesetting (Barreto et al. 2004; Kolko and Kazdin 1991).

INSURANCE FRAUD   The largest category of arson crimes attributed to adults is insurance fraud. The motive is clear: get money fast on a business or property that is losing money. The perpetrator has a clear and obvious need for cash on the targeted property; statistically, this category is gender nonspecific. The building is vacant during the fire. Some arsonists will even have increased insurance premiums on the target property not long before setting the fire. Others may remove expensive equipment in an attempt to get more money by selling it separately. When the target is a high-end property, the owner will most likely hire another individual to set the fire. They will often attempt to set the contract into motion anonymously to avoid detection. Because insurance companies have been investigating suspicious fires more aggressively to limit insurance fraud, fewer claims are being paid out. Because of this, insurance fraud is less of a motivator for arson now than it has been in the past.

ARSON TO COVER ANOTHER CRIME   Arson may be a secondary offense, committed to try to mask a primary offense, such as homicide or fraud. Some perpetrators may think that by burning the evidence of their crime, the investigators will focus on the fire rather than the primary offense. It is generally fairly obvious to investigators when arson fire is used to attempt to cover a homicide. Rarely does a fire burn hot enough to destroy a body. The average fire burns around 800 degrees F. An arson fire, because of accelerant use may burn as hot as 1,200 degrees F, this is not hot enough to destroy the human body—for example, bodies are cremated at between 1,400 and 1,800 degrees F. Of course there will be significant damage to the exterior of the body, but the internal organs generally remain intact and the teeth, especially back teeth, are also intact. When the body is recovered it can still be autopsied, and the absence of smoke in the lungs will indicate that the individual was dead prior to the start of the fire.

REVENGE FIRES   Statistically, only a small number of arson fires are motivated by revenge. Revenge fires are usually set impulsively and in instances where one has perceived a wrong inflicted upon them by another. The arsonists are not focused on killing others but instead on destroying property. In larger cities, the focus of revenge arson is generally on smaller vacant properties such as cars, smaller buildings, and similar structures. In more rural areas, barns and other outbuildings are likely targets.

Setting a revenge fire is usually an impulsive act that leaves clear trace evidence. Psychologically, these fires are better viewed as acts of severe vandalism. The perpetrator knows the owner of the property, has had an ongoing dispute with the individual, and generally lives in very close proximity to the targeted property. This criminal act tends to be committed by males under the influence of controlled substances, who have a long history of complaining about how they have been wronged by the other party.

SERIAL ARSONISTS   A serial arsonist is an individual who sets two or more fires that are separated by both time and space. While individuals may engage in serial arson to collect on insurance or for revenge, the typical serial arsonist loves fire and becomes sexually aroused by the fire. When serial arsonists are clinically interviewed, many will report sexual excitement associated with their criminal conduct. In fact, many report that they become sexually excited before, during, and after the fire to the point of orgasm. This is also true for a portion of juvenile arsons as well.

The serial arsonist will often desire to assist in the rescue of the building or the occupants, hence the reason why many serial arsonists are also volunteer fire fighters. Unlike many other arsonists who target vacant buildings, serial arsonists, in general, do not care if the building is occupied or empty. Their motive is to attract attention by way of the chaos that the fire creates. This individual may have a long history of low grade offenses such as vandalism, indecent exposure, peeping, and so forth. The perpetrator usually has a sexually frustrated lifestyle, and is psychosexually stunted in the teen-year range. There is usually evidence upon capture of more serious mental health disorders, such as delusional beliefs associated with grandeur and persecution by others.

EXPLOSIVE INVESTIGATION

In general, explosive investigations are very similar to arson investigations. Evidence is collected in the same manner, and packaged in the same manner to preserve residues for laboratory analysis. Both types of crime scenes are challenging because of their size. However, most explosive investigation scenes will cover a much wider area than the usual arson investigation scene. The World Trade Center scene covered many city blocks, and when the space shuttles *Challenger* and *Columbia* exploded, debris was located across several states. These much larger scenes present considerable challenges to investigators, and there are many opportunities for evidence to be missed entirely.

As if the sheer scale of the crime scene does not make it difficult enough to locate evidence, it is also difficult to locate forensic evidence at the explosion crime scene due to the destructive nature of explosions, which is why the investigation will necessarily focus on the *blast seat*—the center of the explosion. Just as most of the evidence in a fire investigation is collected at the point of origin, most of the evidence from an explosive event will be located in the vicinity of the blast seat.

The perimeter of large explosive scenes is difficult to determine and hard to protect. Technically, the boundary of the crime scene should be the furthest point at which debris is found. The example of the *Columbia* and *Challenger* explosions clearly illustrates the problem with having the crime scene extend to the furthest reaches of the debris. Investigators are left to make a reasonable determination regarding the boundaries of the crime scene, and as to whether the case warrants establishing secondary crime scenes. The larger the area that the crime scene covers, the more difficult it is to protect not only from people, but also from the elements. Because of the nature of explosions, almost all of these crime scenes are exposed to the elements.

Accidental and Intentional Explosions

Whether an explosion is accidental or intentional, the first responders will behave in a similar way. Neither an accidental nor an intentional explosion is inherently more dangerous than the other; both scenes are full of unknowns. Any explosion scene is dangerous: there may be multiple explosions, and the structures involved may become unstable.

Any investigation revolves around answering the question "how did this happen?" Of course, an intentional explosion will be investigated differently than an accidental explosion, and although both investigations may assign fault, the fault in the case of the accident may be negligence. An intentional explosion may be an act of domestic or international terrorism, or a criminal action. Once it is known how the explosion occurred, the focus of the investigation will diverge.

Types of Explosives

Explosions are classified as either *diffuse* or *concentrated*. A diffuse explosion occurs when gas or vapor is ignited; these create a uniformly distributed pattern of damage. A concentrated explosion, such as one caused by the use of dynamite creates most of its damage near the blast seat. A series of events occurs when dynamite, is ignited: energy flows from the igniter to the detonator to the main charge (sometimes with a booster charge), and then the explosion occurs (DeForest et al. 1983).

The explosives themselves are classified as either low explosives or high explosives. Low explosives deflagrate, which means they burn slowly and create less pressure than a high explosive; black powder (gun powder) and smokeless powder are low explosives. Low explosives actually do not explode and they create much less damage than a high explosive. High explosives burn quickly and create high pressure; both nitroglycerine and dynamite fall into the category of high explosives. High explosives explode violently and cause significant damage. Interestingly, a low explosive is often used to ignite a high explosive.

Improvised Explosive Devices

An improvised explosive device (IED) is any device that is made from materials that are either at hand or are easy to acquire. IEDs can be detonated with normal household items such as garage door openers, cell phones, and pagers. IEDs have been frequently encountered in the war in Iraq, and have been responsible for a significant proportion of troop and civilian deaths. In Iraq, IEDs are commonly made of unexploded land mines, mortar, and artillery projectiles; the bomber combines these found items with a household detonator, plants the device, waits for a suitable target, and detonates the device. In some cases, after the IED has been detonated, troops will be engaged by the enemy with gunfire.

Signature Devices

The explosive device created by any bomber, serial or not, will tell the investigators a lot about that individual bomber. In many ways, it can be compared to a signature. Investigators will consider the sophistication of the device. Could the components be obtained anywhere, or would the bomber need access to components that are found in certain industries or the military? Does the construction evidence reflect considerable experience with explosives, or is it a very simple construction? Does the bomber leave a note? Is it likely that the device would have caused a lot of destruction, or not? The answers to these questions shape the investigation.

A sophisticated device can indicate a bomber who has received specialized training (perhaps in the military), it can also indicate a bomber who has exploded numerous devices. If the bomb components can only be obtained by an individual who has access to certain industries (a chemical plant, for example) or the military, the investigation will be focused in these areas. A device that exhibits a more sophisticated level of construction is likely to indicate a more experienced bomber. A bomber who leaves a note is trying to attract attention or send a message. Of course, the content of the note will be very important. Is it sent prior to the bombing as a warning? Is it sent afterward to gloat? Does it talk about revenge? A bomb that would be unlikely to cause significant damage may indicate that the bomber really doesn't want to kill someone but does want to create fear.

Analysis of Explosives

There are a variety of spot tests that can be performed to locate and identify explosive residue. When employing microcrystal tests, reagent is added to the questioned residue and, if a certain accelerant is present, crystals will form. In the laboratory, thin-layer chromatography and infrared spectrophotometry can be used to identify the substance used. Canines can also be used for explosive residue detection.

Serial Bombers

Perhaps the most famous case of serial bombing was the Mad Bomber in New York. This case is famous not only because it is an instance of serial bombing, but because it is one of the first cases that employed criminal personality profiling. The Mad Bomber, George Metesky, planted his first bomb at the Consolidated Edison building in November 1940. This first bomb did not explode—perhaps intentionally—because there was a note with the bomb that read: "Con Edison Crooks, This Is For You." The incident was forgotten until a year later, when a second unexploded bomb was found several blocks from another Con Ed office; there was no note with this bomb. After the second bomb was found, the bomber began to communicate via notes with the police, Con Edison, movie theatres, and private citizens. Some of his notes were handwritten; others were comprised of letters cut from the newspaper. Because of World War II, he wrote, he would take a hiatus from constructing bombs (Brussel 1968).

In March 1950, a third bomb was found. During the intervening years, Metesky had honed his bomb construction skills. Like the others before, this bomb also did not detonate. Everything changed, however, with the fourth bomb; it detonated in front of the New York Public Library. Metesky went on to detonate more than 30 bombs in all—many in public places such as Grand Central Station—and he also sent bombs via the mail, and targeted movie theaters (Brussel 1968).

When a bomb exploded in a theater in December 1956, Inspector Howard Finney of the New York City crime laboratory decided to employ an unconventional method in hopes of solving the case. He contacted criminal psychiatrist James Brussel who read the case file and constructed an uncannily accurate criminal profile of the bomber. Brussel predicted that the bomber would be unmarried and live with female relatives; a classic paranoid, intelligent but not formally educated; of Eastern European descent (based upon his awkward and out-dated use of English); carrying a grudge against Con Edison; and wearing a double-breasted suit, buttoned, when he was caught by the police. And Brussel was sure he would be caught. When George Metesky was arrested, he was indeed wearing a double-breasted suit—buttoned (Brussel 1968).

Serial Bombers are a fascinating group, in that they often share the following characteristics: they desire to create mass destruction to areas where they often can watch the trauma unfold (a trait they share with serial arsonists); they are usually of higher intelligence, and skilled in a profession involving use of their hands; they are alienated from others in terms of intimacy; and they are either sexually inactive or sexually defective. The power motivator for them is obviously through the size, complexity, and extent of the explosion. They are not so much interested in killing people, but are motivated by a desire to cause property destruction on a large scale, and to be able to witness the destruction and its aftermath. Emotionally they are like children who have never socially matured past the teen years. Serial bombers tend to be very similar psychologically, and their trigger mechanism is usually associated with frustration and rejection. This frustration tends to arise from a social or political system—such as the social security system, postal service, or the United States government in general, as opposed to arising from an unsatisfying interaction with a singular emotionally significant person. They see their rejection/frustration as part of their inadequacy and thus as part of a larger conspiracy by a vague system which they tend to believe is focused upon them as an individual. They further reason that the system must be made to pay attention to the "little guy" and that their criminal actions take on a fight for the majority of others who—like them—are not being heard. For them the massive explosion embodies a powerful social/political statement. The targets they choose reveal not only the bombers' twisted justification, but also an explosive need for recognition.

Suicide Bombers

Suicide bombers are usually associated with extreme religious, social, or political reform movements or groups. Even those who do not belong to a zealot group can join in this game of insanity by claiming a mission to die for a *pure and just* cause. Suicide bombers tend to go through months of preparation before the suicide explosion; during this time, they sink into a deeper agitated depression with the delusional belief that through their death they will be able to make both a statement and a difference that will affect change on the target or the broader social system in which the target lives and functions.

Because a suicide bomber cannot achieve recognition for their criminal conduct after the event has occurred, they must achieve recognition from their *group* for their impending sacrifice in advance of the bombing. This may come in the form of adoration from the group and their family. It may also come in the form of the group promising to take care of the bomber's family after the bombing. There are also a few suicide bombers with a psychotic belief that they are being commanded by a higher power to blow themselves up to right a wrong in the world. They are far less common than the mainstream group of suicide bombers cited above and often do not belong to any organized group.

MASS DISASTERS

A mass disaster is any incident in which a number of people are killed or injured at the same time. A mass casualty incident may be the result of an accident (1984 gas leak at a Union Carbide Corporation plant in Bhopal, India), a natural disaster (hurricane Katrina), or a terrorist attack (crash of Pan Am flight 103 over Lockerbie, Scotland). Mass casualties occur during war and in incidents of mass murder. Of these, only terrorist attacks and mass murder are criminal offenses.

Space Shuttle *Challenger* Disaster

The space shuttle *Challenger* did not explode, but rather it broke apart. Seventy-three seconds after liftoff, a faulty O-ring caused the main fuel tank to tear apart, stopping the engines, and creating a fireball at 46,000 feet. The pieces of the shuttle continued upward, carried by their own momentum to a top altitude of 65,000 feet. The shuttle debris then began a downward descent and hit the water at a speed in excess of 200 miles per hour; the intensity of the impact destroyed everything (Oberg 2006).

The main wreckage was found 18 miles northeast of the launch pad at Cape Canaveral, Florida (Harwood n.d.). Forensic analysis indicated that the crew was alive—and perhaps conscious—throughout their descent into the ocean off the coast of Florida. The total flight time was 207 seconds (Oberg 2006).

NTSB and the ValuJet Flight 592 Crash in the Florida Everglades

The National Transportation Safety Board (NTSB) investigates civil aviation accidents and major accidents involving other forms of transportation. It was formed in 1967 to conduct independent investigations that focus on increasing safety, although it has no regulatory or enforcement powers. When the cause of a major accident is deemed to be criminal, the FBI will be called in to be the lead investigative agency (www.ntsb.gov/Abt_NTSB/invest.htm#criminal).

The NTSB begins its investigation at the accident scene. A team of investigators respond to the scene as quickly as possible and individual investigators oversee inquiries in each of the following areas: operations, structures, engines, systems, air traffic control, weather, human performance, and survival factors. At major accident scenes, psychologists and social workers are also sent to work with surviving family members to facilitate debriefing, focusing on emerging stress reaction. As time wears on, many survivors may also experience posttraumatic stress disorder.

Captain Russell Fischer, who supervised operations at the forward command post during the ValuJet 592 recovery effort, discussed the experience in a candid article he wrote for the *FBI Law Enforcement Bulletin* (Fischer 1997).

BACKGROUND INFORMATION FLIGHT 592   At 2:02 P.M., May 11, 1996, Flight 592 was cleared for takeoff out of Miami-Dade International Airport. Within minutes, however, smoke filled the cabin and cockpit, and Pilot Kubeck informed controllers that she needed to return to the airport. Eleven minutes after takeoff, Flight 592 crashed into the Florida Everglades killing all 110 passengers and crew members.

The crash site was 17 miles northwest of Miami International Airport, and fell within the jurisdiction of the Metro-Dade Police and Fire Rescue departments. These agencies bore responsibility for the search and recovery of Flight 592 and worked alongside numerous local, state, and federal agencies.

By the end of the day, federal, state, local, and private agencies were meeting to discuss long-term plans with the NTSB acting in the capacity of lead investigative agency. A plan was outlined for the recovery of human remains and plane wreckage; the recovery process eventually lasted 29 days.

The Valujet recovery provides an excellent example of the process: a recovery plan was quickly put into place, provisions were made for establishing and maintaining a recovery effort in an isolated location, safety hazards were taken into account and addressed, and record-keeping was thorough and accurate.

ESTABLISHING A RECOVERY PLAN   In order to facilitate recovery, the Valujet crash site was divided into four quadrants, much the same way that any other crime scene might be searched in quadrants.

Each search group consisted of two teams of 12, with each person tasked with specific responsibilities. Members of each team included:

1. Two homicide detectives, who supervised the recovery, packaging, and documentation of all items
2. One crime scene technician, who photographed and documented all recovered items
3. One medical examiner, who provided on-site review and further documentation of human remains
4. One dive supervisor, who coordinated search patterns for the team's six divers
5. One safety officer, who scanned the terrain for any hazards, including snakes, alligators, or any other visible environmental dangers. (Fischer 1997)

Problems Associated with the Remote Crash Site

Any response to a mass disaster is fraught with problems. In the case of the crash of Flight 592, even the establishment of a command post was difficult because the plane had crashed into swampland. The primary command post was 13 miles from the actual crash site. A second command post was established within 300 yards of the actual crash on a small area of coral rock. It took more than an hour to commute between the command posts, and eventually helicopters had to be used.

Having a large number of people in an area that usually has very few people in it presented other challenges. Not only did food and water have to be brought in for rescue workers, but waste from the packaging containers—along with human waste—had to be removed.

SCENE SAFETY ISSUES   The scene of Flight 592 presented a variety of unique safety hazards: aircraft fuel spilled into the Everglades, and the bodies of the crash victims were rapidly decaying in the heat and humidity, workers at the disaster scene wore disposable bio-hazard suits to protect themselves from these hazards. After working, the garments were removed and disposed of in biohazard containers.

Temperatures generally reached 85–90 degrees F during the day; these temperatures placed recovery workers at risk of both dehydration and exhaustion. Workers were warned to hydrate properly and shifts were rotated. Because the crash happened during Florida's rainy season, lightning storms were a further hazard workers contended with during the entire recovery process, and in particular slowed work during the first 72 hours. While the spilled fuel kept alligators and snakes away from the crash site, they still approached from adjacent areas. Wildlife that lingered too long or ventured too close was removed by state wildlife officers. The mental health of recovery workers was also at risk due to the extreme danger. Crisis counselors were on-site and available for everyone. Shifts were rotated and rest was enforced.

RECORDKEEPING During a rescue and recovery operation as large as that of the ValuJet crash, accurate recordkeeping is essential. A database was developed to store all information related to the crash and recovery. This assisted with accurate report writing and tracking of expenditures. This also facilitates the tracking of both physical remains and human remains recovered at the crash site.

THE MEDIA Within minutes of the crash, the media sought information, and made their way to the command post. The Metro-Dade Police Department had a staff to handle the media. While it may not always be necessary to devote an entire staff to handling media issues, a plan must be in place for handling legitimate media inquiries, while maintaining the integrity of the site. The NTSB held daily press briefings to keep the media and the public informed.

COST Responding to any type of mass disaster is a costly proposition. In the case of the ValuJet crash, the metro-Dade Police Department absorbed many of the costs. Depending upon where a disaster occurs, very small jurisdictions may become responsible for very large recovery and clean-up costs. Cost should not be a factor in responding to a disaster. States and the federal government should be prepared to assist local authorities not only with recovery effort but also with recovery cost.

DETERMINING CAUSE The final report of the NTSB regarding the crash of ValuJet 592 attributed the cause of the crash to several concurrent factors. ValuJet did not properly oversee its contractor, SabreTech, which was responsible for ValuJet maintenance. Additionally, ValuJet did not enforce its own *no-carry* policy for hazardous materials. SabreTech failed to properly prepare, package, and identify the potentially hazardous oxygen generators, and the Federal Aviation Administration (FAA) did not require fire suppression systems in the cargo compartments of this type of plane. The FAA also had not responded strongly enough to previous oxygen generator fires in airplanes.

Forensic Engineering and The World Trade Center Collapse

Forensic engineering is the study of why structures behave the way they do when subjected to extreme stress. This also encompasses the reconstruction of structures to analyze why they behaved as they did during a particular incident.

Generally, individuals do not specialize in "forensic engineering," but instead are engineers who will analyze how structures respond to damage or destruction when the need arises. They will usually be involved in designing structures and they study how materials respond to stresses with the aim of designing better structures. Buildings must be built to withstand loads—the weight and stresses placed upon a building or upon the supports of a building. In earthquake-prone areas, bridges, roads, and buildings are built to withstand the stresses that earthquakes can generate. Structures in flood-prone areas can be built to allow water flow through or around them. To build better structures, forensic engineers study how structures that have sustained damage—or been destroyed—react to particular incidents of physical or structural stress.

The North and South World Trade Towers did not collapse because each was struck by an airplane. Each tower would have been more than able to withstand the impact of a plane, even a Boeing 767. The towers were designed to withstand significant stress from wind, and while the initial impact of the planes destroyed several of the outer columns in each tower, the load was transferred to other columns (Eager and Musso 2001).

After the initial impact of the planes, the jet fuel carried by each plane—about 90,000 gallons of fuel—ignited. While many have speculated that the fire further damaged the structures by melting the metal columns of the building, this is not the case. The World Trade Center fire was fuel-rich and diffuse. Fuel-rich fires create black smoke, as was evidenced that day; diffuse flames burn at relatively low heat and could not reach the temperatures necessary to melt steel. What the flames did, however, was distort the steel, and because the fire burned hotter in some places than in others, the steel distorted unevenly. This, in turn, caused the load of the building to shift unevenly and weaken the structure enough to initiate collapse. This collapse occurred, because the most fire-damaged floors could no longer support their own weight and the weight of the floors above them. Each collapsing floor in turn initiated the collapse of the one below it by exceeding the amount of weight (load) that floor could support. Once the collapse cascade began, it took approximately 10 seconds for each tower to completely fall, hitting the ground at about 125 miles per hour (Eagar and Musso 2001).

Another question that is commonly asked about the collapse of the World Trade Center revolves around why the buildings did not fall onto surrounding buildings, like dominoes, but instead, collapsed in on themselves. It should be noted that because any building is mostly air and not solid, it will tend to collapse in on itself. When buildings are purposefully demolished, this fact is taken advantage of with charges set to facilitate this type of implosion (Eagar and Musso 2001).

Effects on Disaster Scene Workers

The principal effects experienced by disaster scene workers focus around fatigue—both physical and emotional. Post-traumatic stress disorder is quite common, and critical incident stress de-briefing teams must be used. Workers may be overwhelmed with the scope of the disaster and—regardless of how well they are trained—they can and often are impacted by the nature of the disaster. Frequent staff rotations must occur with at least 12 hours of rest elapsing before return to duty. The response to the destruction of the World Trade Center provides an example of some mistakes that can be made when running a disaster scene—wherein workers were present before the scene was determined to be stable, and staff worked in 20-plus hour shifts, often to the point of exhaustion.

Disaster Planning

There is an old saying in crisis intervention: "prepare for the worst, hope for the best." Ideally, this should guide all disaster planning. We have become painfully aware of the need to prepare for any eventuality since the events of September 11, 2001. It is better to create a disaster plan before a disaster occurs, rather than trying to create the plan during the middle of a crisis. Planning is much easier when there isn't a crisis. When planning for a disaster, all stakeholders should be involved. In other words, everyone who might be involved in responding to a disaster should be involved, along with members of the community, and community government.

It is important to assess vulnerabilities, whether the plan is for a building, a city, or an entire state. The following questions should be considered: Are there bridges, tunnels? Is it a port town? Are there power plants? While it is impossible to prepare for everything, it is possible to determine where a city is vulnerable and prepare for those disasters. Likewise, a building will be most vulnerable at its entrances. And certain buildings are more likely to be targeted than others—federal buildings, for example.

Being prepared can make a considerable difference in the outcome of the situation. This can be seen in the way Florida responded to multiple hurricane threats during the 2004 hurricane season—very successful responses. And the way Louisiana responded to Hurricane Katrina—a very unsuccessful response. Florida responds better because the state has frequently been threatened by hurricanes and the state has learned from the mistakes made during Hurricane Andrew in 1992. This Category 5 hurricane that made landfall south of Miami caused significant damage and is ranked as one of the most damaging hurricanes in U.S. history. It caused the building codes in Florida to be significantly revised. The initial federal response to Andrew, like Katrina, was slow; Florida created a better state response system as a result. The claims filed with insurance companies caused numerous insurance companies to close and led to the creation of new agencies to deal with catastrophic insurance claims in the state of Florida.

It is important to have disaster service providers assess their level of preparedness. It is better to address shortcomings when the services are not immediately needed. Disaster drills are recommended to assess plans.

Glossary

Accelerant—a fuel used to encourage a fire to burn faster than it otherwise would.

Backdraft—occurs in a closed area when all oxygen has been used and suddenly new oxygen causes an explosive fire.

Blast seat—the origin of the explosion.

Burn pattern—the typical pattern that a fire makes as it burns through a room or building.

Flashover—when objects within a room reach their ignition point and burst into flames.

Ignition point—the temperature at which a substance will ignite.

Incendiary device—a device that is designed to start a fire.

Inverted cone—the normal burn pattern of a fire. It burns narrow at the base and wide at the top.

Point of origin—where the fire started.

Radiation—transfers heat via energy waves in space.

Webliography

Federal Bureau of Investigation Uniform Crime Reports. (www.fbi.gov/ucr/ucr.htm)

International Society of Explosives Engineers. (www.isee.org/)

References

Barreto, S., J. Boekamp, L., Armstrong, and P. Gillen. "Community-Based Interventions for Juvenile Firesetters: A Brief Family-Centered Model." *Psychological Services* 1, no. 2 (2004): 158–68.

Brussel, J. A. *The Casebook of a Crime Psychiatrist.* New York: Bernard Geis Associates, 1968.

Bureau of Alcohol, Tobacco, Firearms and Explosives. Arson & Explosives: Canine. Accessed on November 27, 2006, from http://atf.treas.gov/explarson/canine.htm

DeForest, P., R. Gaensslen, and H. Lee. *Forensic Science: An Introduction to Criminalistics.* NY: McGraw-Hill, 1983.

Eagar, T. W., and C. Musso. "Why Did the World Trade Center Collapse? Science, Engineering, and Speculation." *JOM* 53, no. 12 (2001): 8–11. Accessed on June 28, 2006, from www.tms.org/pubs/journals/JOM/0112/Eagar/Eagar-0112.html

Federal Bureau of Investigation. Crime in the United States 2004: Arson. Accessed on June 28, 2006, from www.fbi.gov/ucr/cius_04/offenses_reported/property_crime/arson.html

Federal Bureau of Investigation. Section II: Crime Index Offenses Reported. Accessed on June 28, 2006, from www.fbi.gov/ucr/Cius_97/95CRIME/95crime2.pdf

Fischer, R. "Emergency in the Everglades: The Recovery of ValuJet Flight 592." *FBI Law Enforcement Bulletin.* Accessed on June 28, 2006, from www.fbi.gov/publications/leb/1997/sept397.htm

Harwood, W. The Fate of Challenger's Crew. Accessed on June 28, 2006, from www.space-shuttle.com/challenger1.htm

Kolko, D., and A. Kazdin. "Motives of Child Firesetters: Firesetting Characteristics and Psychological Correlates." *Journal of Child Psychology and Psychiatry and Allied Disciplines* 32 (1991): 535–50.

Oberg, J. 7 myths about the Challenger shuttle disaster. MSNBC. Accessed on June 28, 2006, from www.msnbc .msn.com/id/11031097/

U.S. Fire Administration. USFA Arson Fire Statistics. Accessed on June 28, 2006, from www.usfa.dhs.gov/statistics/arson/

U.S. Fire Administration. (2001). Topical Fire Research Series: Arson in the United States. Vol 1(8). Accessed on June 28, 2006, from www.usfa.dhs.gov/downloads/pdf/tfrs/ v1i8.pdf

West, P. (March 3, 2005). Fire Chief. Arson Fires Reach Historic Low. Accessed on June 28, 2006, from http://firechief .com/awareness/arson-fires-reachlow87653/

Review Questions

1. What are some of the similarities between arson and explosive investigations?
2. Statistically, what is the profile of the individual most likely to commit arson?
3. What are the similarities and differences between accidental and intentional explosions?
4. How are canine arson dogs trained?
5. Where are arson fires most likely to occur?
6. How does the "average" suicide bomber differ from the "average" serial bomber?
7. How is accelerant residue analyzed in the laboratory?
8. What is the difference between a high and low explosive?
9. What is the purpose of the NTSB?
10. What are some of the challenges associated with a mass disaster scene in a remote location?

Some Things to Think About

1. The crash of ValuJet Flight 592 was not a criminal action, why is it included in this text?
2. How might the overworking and exhaustion of rescue workers at the World Trade Center site have compromised the scene and recovery efforts?
3. Postulate what clues may have led James Brussel to the traits identified in his profile of George Metesky, the Mad Bomber.

Forensic Mental Health

Not long ago, this chapter would have been entitled *Forensic Psychology* and it would have focused on the juxtaposition of psychology and the law. But this would not reflect the current work that is going on in the field. Today, Forensic mental health is inclusive of all those individuals who are in mental health and developing their expertise to testify in court. The differences among the experts are established in court during the process of expert qualifications. Anyone in any mental health subfield can practice under the term *forensic mental health* provided that their experience, training, and education qualifies them. If we were to limit the discussion to forensic psychiatry or forensic psychology, this would create the false impression that only those individuals who have MDs and PhDs can practice in the special area of forensics. Individuals in this field hold a variety of degrees, including BA, BS, MSW, MA, MS, Ph.D., and MDs. Currently there is a movement in forensic mental health for both state licensure and board certifications, but ultimately judges decide who is and who is not an expert in the area of forensic mental health.

HISTORY OF THE FIELD

Forensic mental health is an emerging discipline that brings together all professionals who work in the mental health field as it intersects with the law. It brings together the history of forensic psychiatry, forensic psychology, and forensic social work. This section will briefly discuss a few of the historical figures in each of these disciplines.

Forensic Psychiatry

Forensic psychiatry is a division of legal medicine, which was discussed in Chapter 2. As we know, medical doctors have been testifying regarding *state of mind* since ancient times, however, this was more of an exception, rather than a rule. In the early portion of the twentieth century, it became more common to call upon a psychiatrist to testify in court. There are many important individuals in forensic psychiatry; we discuss only Kraepelin and Freud here.

Emil Kraepelin is acknowledged as the father of psychiatry. He believed that psychiatric diseases were the result of biological and genetic disorders, and he grouped mental disorders according to patterns of symptoms, creating syndromes. Kraepelin broke psychosis down into two forms: manic depression and dementia praecox (schizophrenia). Although he was often overlooked in his day, his work is the basis for much of modern psychiatric research. He believed, as many do now, that one day we would be able to trace all psychiatric disorders to brain abnormalities.

Sigmund Freud, in direct opposition to Kraepelin, believed that psychiatric disorders were the result of psychological factors. His theory focused on psychosexual development. Although Freud's theory is untestable and is now largely relegated to historical value only, he is responsible for popularizing the concept of *the unconscious*. He used the techniques of free association, where a doctor reads a list of unrelated words to a patient who responds with the first thing that comes into their head. He also pioneered dream analysis, believing that dreams indicate what is in the unconscious.

Keep in mind, however, that although psychiatrists have long been testifying in court, it was only in 1992 that the subspecialty of forensic psychiatry was recognized by the American Board of Medical Specialties.

Forensic Psychology

Hugo Munsterberg is credited with being the father of forensic psychology. In 1908, he wrote *On the Witness Stand,* in which he addressed the areas of memory and eyewitness accuracy, confessions, hypnosis, crime detection, and suggestibility. It was not until the middle of the twentieth century that forensic psychology began to gain wide acceptance, first for its applications in civil court, and later in criminal court. Although it would be another half century before the profession of forensic psychology gained widespread popularity, Munsterberg set the stage for later developments.

William Healy founded the Juvenile Psychopathic Institute in 1909, which worked in conjunction with the then newly founded juvenile court system in Chicago. He wrote *Pathological Lying, Accusation, and Swindling—A Study in Forensic Psychology*, which was an early typology of juvenile offenders.

Intelligence and personality testing figure strongly into the history of forensic psychology. Intelligence has long been linked to crime. Even today, the average IQ of inmates in state prison systems is about 15 points below the average IQ of non-inmates. In 1901, Charles Henderson wrote *The Dependent, Defective, and Delinquent Classes*. Hans Eysenck worked in both intelligence and personality. He created a theory of personality with three main factors: neuroticism, extraversion, and psychosis. He also developed scales to test personality.

Research on intelligence had a significant downside and created momentum for eugenics movements both in the United States and in Europe. Eugenics is a science that attempts to create a better human race by sterilizing individuals who are deemed unfit to reproduce. In its most horrific form, those who are deemed *unfit* are euthanized. The American Eugenics Movement lasted from the very early years of the twentieth century until 1939. In America this was done through forced sterilizations of many types of people, including criminals, mentally retarded individuals, welfare mothers, epileptics, and immigrants. In Europe, the Eugenics movement saw a horrific culmination in the Holocaust and the killing of Jewish, handicapped, homosexual, and Eastern European individuals. It is estimated that approximately 12 million individuals died as the Nazis tried to create a "master race."

Forensic Social Work

Social work as a discipline emerged from two driving forces: first from the academic discipline of sociology during the end of the nineteenth century; second, from the charity movement, which started around the end of the Civil War. The first class in social work was offered in 1898 at Columbia University. Social work was also strongly influenced by sociologists in Chicago who desired not to remain in academia but to go out into the field, work with people, and try to make a difference. Social workers established settlement houses, one of the earliest and perhaps the most famous of which was Hull House, founded by Jane Addams in Chicago.

Early social workers and social activists lived at the settlement houses in order to be among the people they served. They dealt with poverty, crime, and mental health issues. Unlike earlier charity movements, social workers looked at societal causes of social ills. Previously, individuals who were poor and unemployed were often seen as lazy or morally lacking. Also, unlike earlier charity movements that often helped break attempts to unionize, Hull House was an active supporter of labor unions.

Social work and the settlement house movement adapted the concept of *the visitor* that had been used in the earlier charity movements when wealthy women would visit the poor and decide who was worthy of services and who was not. Later, visitors, who were trained in social work, visited children in their homes, visited schools, and visited the sick. Early social workers were very much reformers of society; they were involved in the labor movement. They fought against racism. They worked for peace. They were active in both the suffrage and prohibition movements.

During the Progressive Era—which lasted from 1900 to 1917—social work expanded and grew. Social workers turned their attention to the plight of poor children, many of whom worked long hours and received little schooling. Infant and maternal mortality rates were very high. Social workers advocated that poor children not be removed from their homes but rather, cared for at home, and widows given money to raise their children. In 1912, the government formed the Children's Bureau to help address these issues.

As psychiatric departments in hospitals were created at the turn of the century, social workers became involved in providing psychiatric services. Post–World War I services were initially focused on veterans and their families. Soon they were expanded to provide services to children. Psychiatric social workers worked in clinics, with in-patients, and in juvenile courts. With the rise of Freudian theory, social workers linked themselves to this approach. This association with Freud helped to professionalize social work, yet it also cast social work in a subservient position to psychiatrists and took social workers away from reform. In 1920, the Psychiatric Social Workers Club was formed.

The field of social work also originated the casework approach, which focuses not so much on reform but more on individuals and their needs. In modern social work, this is still the common approach—linking individuals to services.

SCOPE OF FORENSIC MENTAL HEALTH

Forensic mental health is the application of the behavioral sciences to legal issues. It differs from most of the other subdivisions of forensics, like ballistics or forensic pathology, that are covered in this text, because psychology is a behavioral science, not a physical or biological science. Forensic psychology is broader than *criminal psychology*, which is limited to criminal applications; forensic psychologists work on both criminal and civil issues. The bulk of the work of a forensic psychologist is in civil court.

Forensic mental health is practiced in court to assist the fact finder—judge or jury—in the ultimate pursuit of the truth in a criminal or civil case. All court jurisdictions have the ultimate responsibility in executing the Constitution of the United States to examine any and all evidence in legal matters in order to effectively argue a case to shake out the truth.

Because forensic mental health is the intersection of mental health and the law, professionals in this field can work in any area that deals with legal issues. Forensic mental health professionals are found working on both the criminal and civil side of the law. They may assess, evaluate, and testify in their area of specialization. They can work in conjunction with attorneys as trial consultants. They may work with police officers and police departments. Forensic mental health professionals may conduct assessments and oversee treatment in correctional settings and mental health settings. In criminal court they can be called upon to assess sanity and competency, criminal responsibility, and assess and treat individuals who are at an elevated risk for aggressive, violent behavior—especially sexually aggressive behavior. They may also work in civil court answering questions regarding custody and divorce and in tort, personal injury, and malpractice litigation. Forensic mental health professionals may assess the presence or absence of psychological disorders. They may also work in educational settings, assessing the presence or absence of learning disabilities.

THE TRIAL CONSULTANT

The phrase *trial consultant* encompasses a variety of roles. Trial consultants may offer many before-, during-, and after-trial services. Before-trial services include case evaluation and risk assessment, alternative dispute resolution, development and testing of case themes and strategies, witness evaluation and preparation, competency and sanity determinations, development of jury profiles and questionnaires, change of venue issues, and practice sessions for attorneys (Hess and Weiner 1999; Wrightsman 2001).

The during-trial services may consist of assistance with jury selection, impaneled jury communication, jury motivation, attorney trial skills training, helping attorneys to communicate with the jury, evaluating eyewitness testimony, trial monitoring, shadow juries, witness preparation, and assistance with opening statements and closing arguments (Hess and Weiner 1999; Wrightsman 2001).

After-trial services consist of post-jury interviews, determining how positively or negatively a shadow jury or real jury perceived the speaker's statements post-trial analysis, and interviews (Hess and Weiner 1999; Wrightsman 2001).

INSANITY AND COMPETENCY   Insanity and competency issues revolve around the question of whether an individual is aware of his or her actions and the results of those actions, either in the present or at some point in the past. Our legal system assumes that an individual is competent/sane; therefore, the party that questions competency/sanity bears the burden of proof to provide evidence to the contrary.

Competency in the Criminal Court   Competency is measured by a defendant's ability to assist counsel in mounting a defense in the courtroom. This is usually tested by having the defendant explain, in detail, how the judicial system works. A competent defendant should be able to explain the system to the same degree that an average individual would. Competency to stand trial is the most common criminal referral to forensic psychologists. Approximately 60,000 competency evaluations are completed each year (Grisso 1986). In order to be competent to enter a plea, the defendant must be able to demonstrate operant knowledge that by entering a plea of guilty, he or she has eliminated the right to a trial; the individual must also understand the obvious consequences of the waiver of those rights under law as applied to infringement upon his or her freedom.

***Dusky:* The Legal Standard for Competency**   The legal standard for whether a defendant is competent to stand trial was established in *Dusky v. U.S.* (1960): "It is not enough . . . to find that 'the defendant is oriented to time and place and has some recollection of events,' but that the test must be whether he has sufficient present ability to consult with his lawyer with a reasonable degree of rational understanding—and whether he has a rational as well as factual understanding of the proceedings against him." The defendant must also be able to demonstrate an operational understanding of the fundamental elements of the legal/court process, for example, the respective roles of the judge, the prosecutor, the defense attorney, and the jury.

Competency Assessment Instruments   There is no single means for assessing competency. In all cases, a forensic interview should be done with the individual. Competency assessment instruments may be administered, along with other psychological measures, such as the Minnesota Multiphasic Personality Inventory-2 (MMPI-2), the Personality Assessment Inventory (PAI), and the Wechsler Adult Intelligence Scale-III (WAIS III) (Lally 2003). When organic brain damage is suspected, neuropsychological tests may be administered, such as the Luria-Nebraska that is made up of 269 questions and 11 scales that measure specific cognitive functioning. While neuropsychological tests are very accurate, they are both time-consuming and expensive. It is also very seldom that a defendant has neurological issues that impair his or her ability to be judged competent.

The basic elements needed for competency are the ability to understand the judicial process and everyone's role in the judicial process, the ability to cooperate with the defense in mounting a defense aimed at the defendant's best interests, the ability to know right from wrong and understand consequential actions to behavior and of course not suffer from any mental health disorder, such as psychosis, that would render him or her incompetent. However, even if psychosis does in fact exist at the time of the competency exam that does not mean that it existed at the time of the offense.

Competency Assessment Instruments

The Competency Screening Test (CST). This test is a 22-item sentence completion instrument and is useful as a quick screening device, although its reliability is questionable (Ackerman 1999).

The Competency to Stand Trial Assessment Instrument (CAI). This instrument was developed as a companion test to the CST. When used as an interview alone, it appears to have face validity but lacks empirical support (Ackerman 1999).

The Interdisciplinary Fitness Interview (IFI). This device was designed to assess various legal and psychopathological characteristics of competency to stand trial. There is little reliability and validity data available.

The Interdisciplinary Fitness Interview-Revised (IFI-R). This instrument was designed to reflect changes in constitutional law and the adoption by many states of "articulated" competency standards (Ackerman 1999).

The Georgia Court Competency Test (GCCT) and the Revised Georgia Court Competency Test-Mississippi State Hospital (GCCT-MSH). These tests assess knowledge of the charge, knowledge of possible penalties, some understanding of courtroom procedure, and ability to communicate with an attorney to prepare a defense. This instrument was designed to identify clearly competent defendants (Bartol and Bartol 2004; Ackerman 1999).

The MacArthur Competence Assessment Tool-Criminal Adjudication. This instrument consists of seven measures that assess issues related to competence to assist counsel and decisional competence (Bartol and Bartol 2004; Ackerman 1999).

The Evaluation of Competency to Stand Trial-Revised (ECST-R). This tool is designed to assess both competency to stand trial and feigned incompetency (Rogers et al. 2004).

Competency to Be Executed In order to be deemed competent to be executed, the defendant must be able to demonstrate that he (almost all individuals under sentence of death are male) is not suffering from a mental health disease that renders him out of touch with reality—and, consequently, unaware of what is about to happen during execution. The premise here is that it is not humane to execute a person if he is not aware, because of a mental illness, that he is going to be executed.

Insanity Insanity is defined as being unaware of what one has done criminally, or what occurred during one's criminal behavior as a result of a mental illness that effectively renders the defendant out of touch with reality (usually psychotic). It should be stressed that *insanity* is a *legal* term and neither a medical nor a psychiatric term. There is no psychiatric illness called *insanity*. In many states, the plea that is entered in the courtroom is *not guilty by reason of insanity* (NGRI).

The defendant can be temporarily insane both before and during the offense. This determination depends upon the ability of the defendant to premeditate the offense and act in a way that substantiates being cognizant of his or her behavior prior to, during, or immediately after the crime. The difficulty here is that most insanity defenses require an expert to opine as to the mental capacity of the offender at the time of the offense, while the assessment occurs long afterwards. Hence the assessment is driven by an analysis of the offender's recorded behaviors prior to, during, and after the offense to look for evidence to support—or rule out—a state of mental illness (psychotic break) or a long-term preexistent mental illness that had been recorded previously (e.g., through a psychiatric hospital admission, or by having been under the care of a psychiatrist for a mental illness of which psychosis is a feature).

Guilty But Mentally Ill The guilty but mentally ill (GBMI) verdict applies to those cases in which the prosecution stipulates that the defendant is mentally ill but is still guilty of the crime. This verdict often results in a special placement in a prison or a forensic hospital—depending upon the power of the evidence to indicate that there is a mental illness and what type it is and of course the nature of the offense itself. Rarely does a GBMI verdict result in a reduced sentence. The plea of guilty but mentally ill came about because it is extraordinarily difficult to prove NGRI. NGRI requires clear and convincing evidence to prove that the defendant was insane (psychotic) and incapable of exercising free will at the time of the crime. This, in turn, requires the expert to prove that at the exact time of the crime the defendant was insane; because the exams for sanity are completed after-the-fact it makes it very difficult to prove. The GBMI plea also arose because of general dissatisfaction with the plea of NGRI. This was a result of public outrage at the NGRI verdict in the *Hinkley* case (John Hinckley Jr. attempted to shoot President Reagan on March 30, 1981 to impress actress Jodi Foster). Shortly after the verdict, changes were made to the NGRI guidelines in many states' statutes, and several states have since eliminated this plea option altogether.

GBMI is still somewhat of a compromise. The verdict acknowledges that the defendant is ill, while at the same time finds that the defendant does bear responsibility for the criminal act. In many cases, the defendant who is found GBMI is sent to a forensic hospital until such time that a determination can be made that he or she is no longer mentally ill. At that time, the individual is transferred to a prison. It is sometimes erroneously believed that even a GBMI is a cop-out—a way for a defendant to "get off easy." However, the reality is that most individuals who are found GBMI actually serve *more* time than if they had plead (or been found) guilty. Because they are generally remanded to a forensic hospital until they "no longer pose a threat to self or other," they generally remain at that hospital for a period of time exceeding their actual criminal sentence. Their sentence is dependent upon their behavior. A hospital stay does not automatically extend their sentence beyond the maximum but it can.

Competency–Civil Court Issues The test for competency in civil court is much the same as in the criminal court. An attorney who is drafting a will and executing it may challenge the competency of the client; however, this generally only happens if the client is blatantly out of touch with reality. If the challenge arises afterwards by a family member who is convinced that the testator was incompetent at the time the will was executed, then the burden of proof is upon the person raising the challenge. This same scenario is true for civil contracts, with the provision that the person must be of adult age. Again it is incumbent upon the attorney executing the contract to ensure that the person signing the contract is not flagrantly out of touch with reality. In general, it is assumed that an adult individual is competent to write up a will, enter into contracts, and so forth.

Police Psychology

The purpose of police psychology is to help officers perform their jobs better and help police departments to better serve the public. The forensic mental health professional may assist with preemployment screening and officer training. They can provide counseling to officers (and family members) who have been involved in stressful work-related incidents in addition to debriefing entire departments after significant events. Forensic mental health professionals can also assist in the criminal investigation process in numerous ways: helping officers to better understand the criminal mind, constructing criminal personality profiles, administering lie detector tests, conducting interviews and interrogations, advising during hostage negotiations, and assisting with community relations.

Forensic mental health professionals may conduct preemployment mental health assessments on aspiring police officers. The applicant's emotional stability in a variety of police situations must be evaluated to ensure the protection of the public while in control of lethal force weaponry. All applicants should display firm, fair, and reasonable responses even under extreme stress.

Forensic mental health specialists may also provide counseling to officers (and their families) associated specifically with the stressors of law enforcement. The services of these individuals may be used in critical incident stress debriefing when a police officer is involved in a shooting or has been shot, or in any other unusually stressful incident. The protection here is not only for the officer but also for both the department—in terms of liability—and the community at large. These types of mental health services can help officers return to work faster after their involvement in a critical incident and to function at a higher level, while reducing workers' compensation and medical claims. Such services also decrease the likelihood that the trauma of an incident will reduce the officer's ability to function over the long term under stress and during normal duty.

CRIMINAL PERSONALITY PROFILING   Criminal personality profiling is a method of identifying the perpetrator of a crime based on an analysis of the nature of the offense, the victim, and the manner in which the crime was committed. In Chapter 11, we discussed James Brussel's criminal personality profile of the Mad Bomber. Brussel was the first modern criminal personality profiler. He also constructed a profile of the Boston Strangler.

Since the days of Dr. Brussel, criminal personality profiling has developed considerably. During the 1970s and 1980s, the technique gained popularity and was heralded as a panacea. Unfortunately, it was often poorly applied by untrained profilers, and the general result was that many people—law enforcement included—lost faith in the technique. Law enforcement has been disappointed because most profiles that are created are too general and do not assist in the isolation of a particular suspect. Profiles often apply to such a broad category of possible suspects that their usefulness is rendered dubious: "the suspect is a white male, between the ages of 25–35, probably unmarried, either not working or in an unstable work situation, with a possible criminal record." It is easy to see why law enforcement would rather not waste the time and money on having a criminal personality profile constructed if this is all that is forthcoming. In point of fact, this is not an example of what criminal personality profiling *should* be.

Part of the problem stems from profiles constructed by improperly trained personnel. It is unwise to think that just anyone can produce a worthwhile criminal personality profile. The profiler must be trained in the areas of psychology and abnormal psychology, crime-scene investigative procedures, and forensic medicine. He or she must review countless cases before awareness of the underlying relationships between the perpetrator's psychological status, needs, and the details of the criminal act become apparent.

Criminal personality profiling, when done thoroughly and properly, should begin at the crime scene. Like any other forensic technique, criminal personality profiling cannot make up for improper handling of the crime scene. The criminal personality profile should narrow the suspect pool, assist in the creation of an interview/interrogation schedule, and facilitate the arrest of the perpetrator. A good profile consists of the following eight specific analytic elements: an analysis of the crime scene, a demographic analysis of the community, an autopsy review (when the crime is homicide) or review of medical records (when the crime is rape) development of victimology, cross-referencing how the murder (or crime) was committed, projective needs analysis, cross-referencing the projective needs analysis with known convicted felons, and production of a specific factor analysis. This will result in a suspect interview and interrogation form.

Use of Computer Modeling for Criminal Personality Profiling Criminal personality profiling systems began in early 1970s and focuses on the analysis of specific behavioral and personality factors of known convicted felons sorted by offense category. The objective is to identify common

---

Analytical Elements of the Criminal Personality Profile

1. **Analysis of the Crime Scene**   While the typical crime-scene investigation simply seeks to gather physical evidence that will link a suspect to a crime scene, the profiler's analysis seeks to answer questions such as: Why this crime? Why this community? Why this victim? The profiler's analysis examines all of the subtle signs left behind by the offender at the crime scene.
2. **Demographic Analysis of the Community**   This portion of the profile will take into account how the crime and the victim fit into the wider community.
3. **Autopsy and Medical Records Review**   This contains details of specific body conditions and outlines how the victim was violated or destroyed. The profiler uses this information to determine what type of an offender would carry out this kind of destruction of a victim.
4. **Development of Victimology**   In offender profiling, much more attention is given to who the victim was and what the victim represented to self and others. The end goal of the victimology is to understand the victim's life and to detail what the victim was doing up until the point of death (victimization), as well as how the victim interacted with others personally, sexually, and professionally, because more than likely the offender chose this particular victim for very specific psychological-need-reduction reasons.
5. **Cross-Referencing of How Murder Was Committed**   This cross-referencing highlights the fact that the various factors involved in creation of the profile are interrelated and must be considered together—not just individually. This macro-analysis seeks to understand the crime as well as the victim's role in the crime.
6. **Projective Needs Analysis**   The projective needs analysis (PNA) determines how the psychological needs of the perpetrator were satisfied during the commission of the crime. This is accomplished by looking at who the victim was, how the victim was destroyed, what was done during the offense, and who the victim was within the greater community.
7. **Cross-Reference PNA with Known Convicted Felons**   Offenders who have committed similar actions, of course, are of particular interest. This data comes from law enforcement, including probation and parole agents, and offender databases.
8. **Specific Factor Analysis**   All factors of the profile are brought together. A personality profile is then generated that includes race, age, interests, vocational developmental history, sexual preferences, hobbies, IQ, temperament, style of interactions, social skills, living preferences, disabilities, and location among others.
9. **Design Suspect Interview and Interrogation Form**   The desired end result of the profiling process is the creation of a suspect interview and interrogation form that will lead to a confession and arrest.

behavioral and personality factors within each offense category across the population. Objective testing is often used when studying offender groups. The assumption behind this approach is that all convicted felons within a specific offender group are, in fact, guilty of the offense. Caution is warranted here because of plea bargaining. The offense that was committed can be quite different from the offense that an offender is convicted of. Details of each crime within each offense group are studied, and the details are assigned values based upon how prevalent those details are among the groups. The focus is upon avoiding generic trait analysis—which has been the downfall of many criminal personality profiles created by the FBI—and attempting to obtain specific behavioral personality factors.

The premise behind criminal personality profiling is that all crimes are committed because of motivational factors driven by attempts to reduce certain needs (like a need for control or dominance). Criminals who repeatedly commit specific types of crimes are attempting to reduce specific physical and/or psychological needs. The resultant profile is then applied to the police suspect pool to assist law enforcement in narrowing the suspects to specific suspects for more intense investigation. This saves both time and money. The profile is also used during the interview and interrogation development process because each offender group has odd elements of their personality based upon their needs demonstrated during the commission of the offense. Once a specific suspect is isolated for more intensive analysis, additional details can then be developed about the suspect. These details will facilitate the investigation and encourage the suspect to reveal critical crime-specific information, leading to arrest and conviction. The overall development of the profile is based upon specific mathematical laws of statistical probability for rates of occurrence of the crime and not subjective intuition. This increases the accuracy of the prediction of behavioral patterns.

POLYGRAPH   Cesare Lombroso (1835–1909), father of the positivist school of criminology, did extensive work on the physical attributes of criminals and used the first polygraph machine in 1895. The modern polygraph machine measures an individual's respiration, electrodermal skin response, blood volume, and pulse rate. These physiological responses are measured while the individual answers a series of questions.

The polygraph was the first instrument developed to assist law enforcement in the detection of deception. The original polygraph used the ink chart method of operation. Modern machines utilize the personal computer (PC). A test subject is connected to several mechanical devices to measure physiological changes in such areas as GSR (Galvanic Skin Response), blood pressure, and rates of respiration. The premise is the same as mentioned earlier. The machine detects significant physiological changes when an individual tells a lie and realizes that their response is in fact not true. The baseline questions to establish normative reference responses are established prior to the actual test questions and then the responses are compared for variance within definitive statistical parameters. The newer models now use a PC with specifically designed software to accomplish the same objective without the use of ink charts. The validity and test–retest reliability of the polygraph has steadily increased over time and is still considered to be the best deception-detection instrument on the market. Of course it is important to realize that all truth detection instruments are not admitted into court but instead are used by law enforcement to assist in their investigations and must be voluntarily submitted to by the accused and or the victim in some cases. In some cases victims of alleged crimes with questionable motives have been offered the polygraph to assist the investigator in the investigation. Keep in mind, the polygraph doesn't actually measure fact. If the individual who is connected to the polygraph believes that a statement is true—whether or not it actually is true—then the polygraph will, most often, register that statement as true.

The polygraph can also be used outside the courtroom in a treatment setting. Sexual offenders who are in treatment should also be administered a therapeutic polygraph when being questioned about past and present sexual behavior or offenses. This facilitates the individual's desire to tell the truth and dramatically assists treatment specialists in redirecting treatment plans as well as to increase the intensity of therapeutic surveillance.

VOICE STRESS ANALYSIS—A TRUTH DETECTION DEVICE The voice stress analysis instrument was developed as an alternative to the conventional (ink chart) polygraph for detecting deception in individuals during the course of a structured interview. It has also been used in industrial settings in the preemployment risk assessment of *job candidates*. It does not require any intrusive wires or connections. It is small in size and can be and has been used during telephonic communications to assist in determining deception. The examiner essentially establishes a baseline audio pitch and range frequency for a subject's voice during a benign conversation, and when critical questions are asked of the subject, the computerized analysis digitally scans the audio pitch and range of an individual's voice responses and cross compares the data from baseline to actual responses to the critical questions. The system is based upon the research that during acts of deception an individual's physiological responses change significantly in many forms and can be detected with sensitive instruments. This specific instrument measures the changes in pitch, tone, range, etc., on the basis of stress commonly experienced during a willful act of deception. An individual's voice will reflect the stress and that will be reflected by digital comparison. This assumes, just like the polygraph, that the subject actually realizes that he or she is engaged in deception. It also assumes that the subject knows the difference between a truth and a lie, and realizes that there are social, cultural, and legal consequences for deception. As with any sensitive deception detection devices they are only as effective as the quality of the instrument, the operator, and the environment in which they are administered. Although this instrument has been and is being used by various law enforcement agencies and corporations, like all truth and deception detection devices, it has a limited range of applicability as to validity and test–retest reliability. The research has shown that it ranks lower on the scales of accuracy than other lie detection instruments but of course can be used quite covertly because it does not require any intrusive physiological connections to the subject.

INTERVIEWS AND INTERROGATIONS Interview designs are different from interrogation designs. Interviews do not focus on establishing innocence versus guilt; instead they focus on gathering useful information. Any information that is learned when the suspect is interviewed can later be used in an

---

Forensic Interviews with Children[1]

Very often the concept of a *balanced forensic interview* is misunderstood. It is often confused with either a *clinical interview* or an *interrogation*. Yet a forensic interview is neither of these. It has very different approaches and goals. A clinical interview, one that would be used by a therapist, strives to understand a child's psychological/mental state. The client, in this case, is the child/parent. The interviewer is in the role of the advocate and the stance is pro-child. Complete confidentiality is given. An interrogation is very different from an interview. An interrogation is dominated by the interrogator and is agenda-driven. The tone is intentionally accusatory in nature and design. The questioning is closed and highly directive. The purpose of the interrogation is to gain a confession.

Police officers and CYS (Children and Youth Services) personnel are typically the first professionals to have contact with a child when there is a report of suspected sexual or physical abuse. Once a report of suspected abuse is open for investigation, a mistake either way is very serious. On the one hand, you don't want to put an innocent person into prison. On the other hand, you don't want to allow an abuser to remain with a child. One of the common problems with traditional interview techniques used by law enforcement and child protective service workers is that they begin with the assumption that *something* happened. Even worse, they begin with the assumption that *something*

---

[1]Material for this section contributed by Carol Hughes.

bad happened. When working with children, especially regarding the possibility of child sexual abuse, they abandon the normal presumption of innocence of the accused. Very often interviews are agenda-driven. Techniques used can introduce information from the interviewer that was not there in the first place that can be incorporated by the child. Often, the interviewer is not objective.

In their guidelines for practice, the American Professional Society on the Abuse of Children (2002) notes that properly conducted forensic interviews are key to making good decisions regarding both the safety of the child and prosecution of offenders. When forensic interviews with children are done regarding allegations of abuse, the standards of the American Professional Society on the Abuse of Children should be adhered to—yet often this is not the case. Upon review of transcripts of expert testimony of police officers and child protective services personnel, it is clear that many lack the specific interview skills needed to interview child victims. They often conduct interviews with children in a haphazard manner. They do not maintain the integrity of the interview, and therefore they are not maintaining the integrity of the child's statements. Many interviewers also seem to enter an interview with the goal of validating the allegation, rather than with the goal of collecting data. In many jurisdictions, the nature and extent of training that police officers and child protective services personnel receive on forensic interviewing of child witnesses either is not adequate or is not being put into practice in the field.

A forensic interview with a potential child victim is not an interrogation. It is not a therapy session. The forensic interviewer must strive to minimize stress to the child and lift the burden of proof off of the child. The critical task becomes eliciting details for corroboration purposes. During the forensic interview there is no confidentiality. The client of forensic interview is the judicial system, and the interview is conducted to provide the court with information. The interviewer is neither an investigator nor a therapist. A technique referred to as the *balanced forensic interview* is recommended.

The balanced forensic interview is a fact-finding tool. It strives to obtain uncontaminated data which necessitates that the evaluator be neutral and objective—considering all reasonable explanations for any allegation. The forensic interview process seeks to elicit as complete and accurate a report from the alleged victim as possible. The interviewer collects information to corroborate or refute the allegation by asking questions and listening to answers. This creates a conversational exchange of information that is non-accusatory in design. The balanced forensic interview maximizes the amount and accuracy of information obtained, and it maintains the integrity of the investigative process. (When you maintain the integrity of the interview process, you maintain the integrity of the child's message/statement—whatever the statements might be.)

In the forensic interview, it is important to have a rationale for what is asked, why it is asked, and when it is asked. The interview should not be haphazard. It is important for an interviewer to remain aware of and understand his or her underlying attitudes and beliefs to remain as free from bias as possible. There should be a balanced exploration of a range of abuse-related topics. The interviewer should begin with more open-ended questions that allow the subject to respond however he or she sees fit and progress to more specific, close-ended questions that limit responses to only a few answers, they may be "yes or no," or multiple choice. In all forensic interviews the interviewer must have good child skills (to interact with children), interview skills, and clinical skills. The interviewer needs to both master and continually fine-tune forensic interview skills.

---

interrogation. Collateral subjects are interviewed who may have useful data about the primary suspect or the crime. Interrogations use data obtained during interviews in a structured format to determine innocence versus guilt pertinent to the crime being investigated. It is important to remember that both interviews and interrogations require the Miranda warnings when conducted with a primary suspect.

CRISIS INTERVENTION The type of crisis must first be identified and an intervention strategy applied. Three rings of containment should be created. The first ring is the center of the crisis. Operatives are staged from this point and all operations emanate from this point. The second ring contains the tactical team who are ready to respond. The third ring contains support personnel. Medical personnel, fire fighters, and the media will all be in this area.

Each category of crisis requires a different method of handling. A suicide is handled differently from a hostage situation, which in turn is handled differently from a bomber. A hostage-taking requires at least two teams of primary and secondary negotiators. The tactics team follow the directions of the command center. The command center, in turn, follows the directions of the primary interventionist. Under no circumstances should anyone make a move without the consent of the command-post leader.

Time is on the side of the negotiating team and not on the side of the perpetrator. Time should be stretched out as much as possible unless a tactical assault is needed. The primary interventionist should create the illusion that the perpetrator is in control at all times. This illusion of control is created through specialized intervention. The needs of the perpetrator should be identified and those needs should be used to constructively manipulate the crisis. If the perpetrator is hungry, food can be provided in exchange for taking a step toward resolution of the crisis. It is important to collect as much data on the perpetrator as possible prior to the intervention. Again, this information will be used to successfully manipulate the outcome of the crisis.

During the crisis situation, the safety of the team is the first concern. The safety of the people involved in the crisis is the second concern. Physical assault should always be the last option in a hostage-taking or a barricade situation—remember it is a rare perpetrator who wants to die.

Hostage Negotiation In any hostage situation, there are two goals of negotiation: that no one gets hurt and that the situation is resolved without assault. The four common types of hostage-takers are criminals, mentally ill individuals, unorganized groups, and terrorist groups. Negotiations may also be used to deal with individuals who are threatening to commit suicide. The criminal hostage-taker is typified by the armed offender who is caught in the act by quick police response, and who takes a hostage in order to facilitate escape. Of the four types of hostage-takers, those who suffer from mental health or mental retardation issues commonly present the most challenging issues for negotiators and law enforcement. It is important for the team to obtain as much information as possible about the perpetrator. A situation in which an unorganized group takes hostages is usually the result of a spontaneous riot or jail break, and a quick response is necessary, because once the group gains cohesion and a leader, negotiations will be more difficult. Local law enforcement would rarely be involved with negotiations with terrorists. Of course, the strategy for each situation will change depending upon the type of incident, where it occurs, what types of weapons are involved, and how many hostage-takers and hostages are involved.

The successful resolution of any hostage situation requires that the negotiation team progress through a three-phase process of containment, control, and diffusion. When the team arrives at the scene, only the basics are known about the situation and anything can happen. During the *containment* phase, the team should approach with caution and immediately establish multiple secure perimeters. Contact should be initiated with the perpetrator by primary and secondary negotiators. The primary negotiator conducts all communication with the perpetrator, and the secondary negotiator acts as an on-site advisor to the primary negotiator. The secondary negotiator is also responsible for coordinating the intelligence data on the perpetrator as provided by the technical staff as it is developed.

The second phase in the negotiation process is *control*. This is accomplished by interaction with the hostage-taker. Through talking, the negotiator determines the perpetrator's level of stability and the intent to harm self or others. The negotiator also determines the perpetrator's needs. Finally, talking will slow down the sense of pressure created by the uncertainty of the situation and build trust between the negotiator and the perpetrator. The longer the crisis continues the more likely it will be successfully resolved.

The final phase in the negotiation process is *diffusion*, during which terms are agreed upon for the surrender of hostages, weapons, and self to law enforcement. Because most hostage-takers do not want to die, diffusion is usually the likely result. Once the situation has been resolved, debriefing occurs. By examining how the team responded in this situation, its responses can be improved for future crises.

IMPROVING COMMUNITY RELATIONS   Forensic mental health professionals can also assist law enforcement in improving their relationships within the community. This is invaluable because law enforcement relies heavily upon the public's assistance to solve crimes. The public can provide leads, information, suspect names, and testimony. If law enforcement consistently interacts in a positive manner with the public, this will encourage a two-way flow of service and information; police provide service to the public and the public provide information to the police.

Grass roots educational programs for schools, churches, and community groups that raise awareness of the police process of investigation, their staff, and the financial limitations of law enforcement can be built. These programs can also be used to effectively address concerns that the public have regarding law enforcement. Forensic mental health professionals can also assist with the effective and positive use of the media.

Correctional Settings

In a correctional setting, forensic mental health professionals may assess prisoners during the intake process, develop treatment plans, and administer treatment to a variety of offenders (sexual offenders, drug offenders, offenders with a wide range of mental health disorders and substance abuse issues) on an ongoing basis. They are also involved in conducting security risk ratings for internal placements within the prison setting and reviews for community release programs, parole reviews, disciplinary reviews, and commutation reviews.

TREATING OFFENDERS AND MANDATED COUNSELING   In correctional settings, including community corrections, counseling is often mandated for offenders who have committed crimes involving the use of drugs or alcohol, and for those who have committed sexual offenses. For each offender, an individual treatment plan pertinent to his or her pathology and criminal behavior pattern should be put into place. This treatment plan needs to be developed with built-in measurements and goals that can be used to evaluate if the treatment is working; some examples include therapeutic treatment polygraphs, structured partial release programs, and standardized testing as well as drug and alcohol testing.

Mandated treatment has often been viewed as ineffective because of noncompliance. Many offenders do not want to be in treatment and are not truly motivated to change. However, attaching punitive sanctions for failure to comply with treatment can be effective as a treatment-surveillance model (such as return to confinement). For sexual offenders, treatment is mandated over the long term. This serves as yet another vehicle for supervision of the offender, while at the same time addressing the pathological thinking and behavior that triggers repeat offending.

MENTAL HEALTH SETTINGS   Forensic mental health professionals work in a variety of mental health settings including state hospitals, forensic treatment centers, private and public clinics, and victim advocacy centers and programs. Forensic mental health professionals are employed in mental health settings that specialize in the assessment and treatment of individuals who have committed a crime or who have been accused of committing a crime. Many state hospitals have wards that are specifically designed to house and treat individuals who have broken the law and suffer from mental illness and or substance abuse. Most conventional hospitals and community mental health facilities do not have the staff or facility to provide forensic assessment and treatment services because of the risk these patients pose.

THERAPEUTIC JURISPRUDENCE   Therapeutic jurisprudence is a newer approach in criminal justice that acknowledges that the law can be used as a therapeutic tool to encourage people to seek and receive treatment. Two common approaches in therapeutic jurisprudence are drug courts and mental health courts.

Drug Court   The first drug court was established in Miami in 1995. While the implementation of the drug court philosophy can vary widely, at its best, it is a focus on rehabilitation rather than retribution. And while some drug courts amount to little more than having a dedicated judge to hear all drug cases; many courts have implemented very innovative treatment options.

In a drug court, the level of supervision is generally much higher than in a traditional court, which may not have much involvement with an offender on probation unless there has been a violation of probation. Treatment is mandatory for an offender who has gone through drug court. Treatment may not even be a part of the more traditional approach to drug crimes. The best drug courts in the country focus on long-term recovery and the person as a whole. Many drug offenders have deficits in educational and job skills. Addressing these can, in turn, lead to greater success for the former offender.

In the traditional courtroom the approach is very adversarial. Often, the prosecution presents a plea bargain that is accepted by the defendant. In a drug court, everyone works together. Not only are the judge, attorneys, and the defendant present, but also, very often, there will be a therapist involved in the process.

Drug courts boast two key benefits over the traditional system: lower recidivism rates and lower cost. While initial reports on drug courts boasted considerable success, over the long term, shortcomings have been noted. However, overall, the recidivism rate for an offender who has been through a drug court is lower than that of offenders who have been charged with drug offenses through the traditional system. The cost savings is dramatic. An incarcerated offender can cost a state anywhere from $35,000 to $70,000 per year to house. The cost of an offender going through a drug court is about $5,000.

Mental Health Court   Each state's prisons and jails seem to be repositories for individuals who are poor, and who suffer from a variety of mental health problems. Prison clearly is not a place for offenders with mental disabilities. Many jurisdictions have turned to establishing mental health courts, along the lines of drug courts. Reactions to mental health courts have been mixed. They have only been in existence since 2000, so long-term data is not available and while everyone agrees that prison is not a good place for mentally disordered individuals, many fear that mental health courts will only increase the stigmatization and incarceration of these individuals.

Predicting Dangerousness/Risk

In some cases a forensic mental health professional may be called upon to make a determination regarding whether an individual poses a risk to the community. Although this was once done through clinical interviewing, this is actually a fairly poor way of assessing risk. There are a wide range of tests available that are used to predict dangerous behavior; these tests are driven by static and fluid variable analysis and are all focused upon an individual's history of actual dangerous behavior. In court, the only true risk predictor is past behavior; however, most judges are now beginning to admit testimony from experts based on actuarial risk assessment instruments that focus upon recidivistic violent behavior.

Actuarial risk assessment is a growing subspecialty in forensic mental health. When actuarial risk instruments are administered by a properly trained professional, they can provide valid and reliable statistical risk ratings that are associated with short, medium, and long-term risk to re-offend over the course of five-, ten-, and fifteen-year periods. The power of actuarial risk prediction rests upon the huge volume of actual cases studied over the course of 15 years that are statistically sorted by offender typology and rates of re-offending.

DUTY-TO-WARN   Therapists must warn others if their client threatens to physically harm another person or has a plan in place to do so. This warning can be to the intended target or to the police about the intended target or to both. Prior to the beginning of treatment, the therapist must disclose this duty-to-warn along with an explanation of treatment limits of confidentiality. The client must also sign a form stating that he or she has been told of these limitations. While for many clients this never becomes an issue, it is an absolute necessity that the client be aware of the duty to warn in cases that are mandated into treatment, are violent in nature, or are sexual offenders. There are limits to confidentiality. A therapist cannot guarantee confidentiality if prior crimes are revealed that law enforcement does not already know of. Therapists are also mandated reporters regarding child abuse.

Family Court Issues

In family court, forensic psychologists are most frequently involved in custody evaluations. These cases require macro- and micro-analytic interviews of all parties involved, in addition to collateral, objective, authoritative sources of case file input (e.g., schools, doctors, and police). Assessment interviews are completed with the adults as well as the children alone and then interactively, to analyze the interactions and sort through family dynamics. The guiding principles for child custody recommendations rest upon the "best interests" of the child concept, which states that rather than custody always being given to the mother because mothers are more nurturing than fathers, which had previously been the guiding principle of custody decisions, the ultimate concern is whatever may be the greatest good for the minor child. There is also a continuing drive to preserve the rights of both parents to be actively involved in the child's life. The concept of "best interests of the child" can be overridden when a child is over 14. The child then has more of a voice in court as to where he or she wants to live, and the judge can then take the child's wishes under advisement.

PARENTAL ALIENATION SYNDROME   Domestic disputes of all sorts—divorce, custody disagreements, arguments over failure to pay child support—foster the environment for the false abuse allegations that are the hallmark of Parental Alienation Syndrome (PAS)—referred to in court as *taint* (Gardner 1992).

It is believed that a significant portion of abuse allegations without physical evidence that arise during the course of a divorce or custody battle are false. These allegations are created by one parent against the other as a means of vengeance or an attempt to try to secure custody by poisoning the child against the targeted parent. The younger the child is, the more susceptible the child is for PAS. The courts are also likely to believe a young child, especially when the child has been well tutored by the parent.

PAS is a newer area of expertise for forensic mental health experts. It is slowly gaining acceptance as more and more research is conducted. When evaluating children and their parents to differentiate between possible PAS and possible abuse, it is important for the expert to differentiate between symptoms of PAS that are most likely to present and the symptoms likely to present themselves in cases where actual abuse has occurred. In PAS, the symptoms the child exhibits focus on the alienated parent (e.g., support of the alienating parent and absence of guilt over cruelty to the alienated parent), whereas when abuse has occurred, the symptoms focus on the abuse (preoccupation with the trauma, flashbacks, dissociation) (Gardner 1999). Although PAS is not currently in the *DSM-IV-TR*, it is being considered as an entry in the *DSM-V*.

Tort, Personal Injury, and Malpractice Litigation

Although it is not the focus of this text, much work that is done in forensic mental health is done in the area of tort law, personal injury litigation, and malpractice litigation.

Assessing Psychological Disorders

Forensic mental health professionals are often called upon, not only in criminal court, but also in civil court, to assess the presence or absence of psychological disorders.

THE *DSM-IV-TR*   The *DSM-IV-TR* is the *Diagnostic and Statistical Manual of Mental Disorders-Fourth Edition-Text Revision*. Clinicians use it for diagnosing mental disorders. It is important to utilize the *DSM-IV-TR* in forensic settings because it standardizes diagnoses and takes much of the subjectivity out of the diagnosis process. Mental health issues are by their very nature often nebulous, using the *DSM* minimizes this softness in description and prediction of criminal behavior. In the courtroom, it provides a recognized, research-based clinical standard for the issue being discussed. The *DSM-IV-TR* meets the standard of "widely accepted within the scientific community" criteria set forth for the acceptance of scientific testimony in the courtroom. The use of the *DSM* also facilitates the assessment and development of a structured treatment plan that is meaningful and measurable. This is now required by all insurance companies in order to reimburse for treatment.

Forensic mental health specialists conduct evaluations and testify in court regarding the presence or absence of psychological disorders such as post traumatic stress disorder, battered woman syndrome, rape trauma syndrome, antisocial personality disorder, mood disorders, and postpartum Depression.

Personality disorders are commonly found in many forensic mental health settings. In an incarcerated population, there are many individuals who suffer from antisocial personality disorder.

Educational Settings

In educational settings, mental health experts have long been assessing children for specialized services. They may administer intelligence tests to determine if a child should be placed in gifted or special education classes. They can assess for the presence of learning disabilities.

Glossary

Dementia praecox—original term for schizophrenia.

Guilty but mentally ill—a plea that acknowledges that the defendant committed the offense but there is the presence of a mental illness that interferes with culpability.

Unconscious—part of the mind that we cannot access.

Webliography

Megan's Law by State
(www.klaaskids.org/pg-legmeg.htm)
American Board of Forensic Psychology
(www.abfp.com/)

Forensic Psychology Programs at PsychWeb
(www.psywww.com/careers/forensic.htm)

References

Ackerman, M. *Essentials of Forensic Psychological Assessment.* NY: John Wiley & Sons, 1999.

American Professional Society on the Abuse of Children (APSAC). *Practice Guidelines, Investigative Interviewing in Cases of Alleged Child Abuse,* 2002.

Bartol, C., and A. Bartol. *Psychology and Law,* 3rd ed. Belmont, CA: Wadsworth/Thompson Learning. 2004.

Dusky v. United States, 362 U.S. 402 (1960).

Gardner, R. A. "Differentiating Between Parental Alienation Syndrome and Bona Fide Abuse-Neglect." *The American Journal of Family Therapy* 27, no. 2 (1999): 97–107.

Gardner, R. A. *The Parental Alienation Syndrome,* 2nd ed. Cresskill, NJ: Creative Therapeutics, 1992.

Grisso, T. *Evaluating Competencies: Forensic Assessments and Instruments.* New York: Plenum, p. 545, 1986.

Healy, W. and M. Healy. "Pathological Lying, Accusation, and Swindling—A Study in Forensic Psychology." *Criminal Science Monograph No. 1 Supplement to the Journal of The American Institute of Criminal Law and Criminology.* Boston: Little, Brown, and Company, 1915.

Henderson, C. 1906. Introduction to the Study of the Dependent, Defective, and Delinquent Classes—and of the Social Treatment, 2nd edition. Boston: D.C. Heath and Co.

Hess, A., and I. Weiner. *The Handbook of Forensic Psychology,* 2nd ed. New York: John Wiley & Sons, Inc. 1999.

Lally, S. "What Tests Are Acceptable for Use in Forensic Evaluations?: A Survey of Experts." *Professional Psychology: Research and Practice* 34, no. 5 (2003).

Rogers, R., C. E. Tillbrook, and K. W. Sewell. *Evaluation of Competency to Stand Trial-Revised (ECST-R) and Professional Manual.* Odessa, FL: Psychological Assessment Resources, Inc. 2004.

Wrightsman, L. *Forensic Psychology.* Belmont, CA: Wadsworth/ Thompson Learning, 2001.

Review Questions

1. Define forensic mental health.
2. How might a trial consultant assist an attorney?
3. What is the question that insanity and competency issues revolve around?
4. What is the purpose of police psychology?
5. What is criminal personality profiling?
6. What is the purpose of "development of victimology" in criminal personality profiling?
7. What is the "duty to warn"?
8. How can mandated treatment be made to be more effective?
9. What is actuarial risk assessment?
10. What are some of the major differences between drug courts and the traditional court approach to drug offenses?

Some Things to Think About

1. If it is not considered humane to execute a person who, because of mental illness, is unaware he/she is going to die, why is it humane to execute a person who knows he/she is going to die?
2. Why is the *DSM-IV-TR* such a useful tool for the forensic psychologist?
3. Why are we using the term *forensic mental health* instead of *forensic psychology* in this chapter?

In the Courtroom and the Future of Forensics

This final section is comprised of Chapter 13, *In the Courtroom,* and Chapter 14, *An International Perspective and a Look Toward the Future.* Chapter 13 moves away from the crime scene and into the courtroom, focusing on the functioning of the expert witness on the stand. All of the preparation from the previous chapters results in a case being ready to be presented in court. If forensic science is to be a useful tool within the criminal justice system, the expert witness must present findings to the jury in a clear, concise, and easily understandable manner. The forensic work that has taken place up until this point, from the crime scene to the laboratory, can be useless if the information is not presented well to the jury. Although many forensic scientists are reluctant to admit it, forensic science really is science in the service of the law. Chapter 14 presents forensics in an international light and also looks at the future of forensic science. The majority of this text has examined forensics from a U.S. point of view; but there is much to be gained from stepping back and using a more global perspective. Finally, we will look to the future. We can expect continued rapid progress in DNA analysis and in computer applications, but there are also many areas that will hold surprises for us.

In the Courtroom

There is not one U.S. judicial system. The U.S. judicial system is comprised of a complex variety of courts. These courts were created over a time span of 225+ years to respond to the needs of a growing and changing country. There are both federal and state courts. State courts have both criminal and civil divisions. There is also a juvenile court system within each state's civil court system. In addition to these more common courts, there is a variety of military courts, tribal courts, drug courts, tax courts, bankruptcy courts, and appeals courts within the United States.

Federal Court Structure

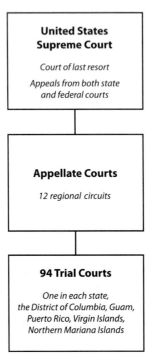

United States Supreme Court

Court of last resort

Appeals from both state and federal courts

Appellate Courts

12 regional circuits

94 Trial Courts

One in each state, the District of Columbia, Guam, Puerto Rico, Virgin Islands, Northern Mariana Islands

FIGURE 13.1 Federal court structure.

FEDERAL COURTS

The federal court system is comprised of the Supreme Court, the U.S. Court of Appeals, the U.S. District Court, the bankruptcy courts, and a number of special courts. These special courts include the U.S. Court of International Trade, and the U.S. Court of Federal Claims, the Court of Appeals for Veterans' Claims, and the U.S. Court of Appeals for the Armed Forces (Figure 13.1).

Jurisdiction of the Federal Courts

The word *jurisdiction* refers to whether or not a court has the appropriate power to hear a case. Jurisdiction limits courts to certain types of cases. If all courts could hear all cases, the court system would be a hopeless mess and some cases might never be resolved. The jurisdiction of the federal courts was established in Article III, Section II of the U.S. Constitution:

> The judicial power shall extend to all cases . . . arising under this Constitution, the laws of the United States, and treaties made, or which shall be made, under their authority;—to all cases affecting ambassadors, other public ministers and consuls;—to all cases of admiralty and maritime jurisdiction;—to controversies to which the United States shall be a party;—to controversies between two or more states;—between a state and citizens of another state;—between citizens of different states;—between citizens of the same state claiming lands under grants of different states, and between a state, or the citizens thereof, and foreign states, citizens or subjects.

Generally, there are two types of jurisdiction to consider when determining if a court has jurisdiction over a case. The first type is *geographical jurisdiction*. This limits the types of cases a court can hear to those that are in a particular area. For example, each state court has the geographical jurisdiction of those cases that fall within its borders. West Virginia has geographical jurisdiction over cases that occurred in West Virginia. West Virginia does not have jurisdiction over cases that occurred in Georgia. Courts also have what is known as *subject matter jurisdiction*. Federal courts do not have jurisdiction over divorce cases or probate cases. State courts never have jurisdiction over the military or over bankruptcy cases.

Federal courts have jurisdiction over three basic types of cases: those that involve a *federal question*, those that involve *diversity jurisdiction*, and those that involve *supplemental jurisdiction*. Cases that involve federal questions deal with constitutional matters or other federal laws, for example, if an individual has experienced discrimination in a work setting. Cases that involve diversity jurisdiction are cases in which the parties involved are citizens of different states, for example, if the plaintiff is from Delaware and the defendant is from Ohio. Cases that involve supplemental jurisdiction refer to the ability of the federal court to hear a case that would normally be a state matter: if the case that would normally fall under the state's jurisdiction is substantially related to a case and forms part of the same case that the federal court is already hearing, then the federal court will have supplemental jurisdiction over that case as well.

The U.S. Supreme Court

The U.S. Constitution established the Supreme Court in Article III, Section I. It also allows for Congress to establish any inferior—or lower—courts that it deems necessary. It states: "The judicial Power of the United States, shall be vested in one supreme Court, and in such inferior Courts as the Congress may from time to time ordain and establish."

The federal court system is hierarchical; with the Supreme Court being the highest court in the United States. The Supreme Court sits atop not only the federal system of courts, but all state systems as well. For this reason it is sometimes referred to as *the court of last resort*. And while the Supreme Court is the highest court in the United States, there are many cases that could never be appealed to the Supreme Court because the Supreme Court does not have jurisdiction—a divorce case, for example. The Supreme Court is comprised of nine justices who are appointed by the president of the United States (as per Article II of the Constitution) and confirmed by the Senate; these justices are appointed for the remainder of their lives—or until they decide to retire. The Supreme Court has discretionary control over the cases that come before it, except for a very few cases in which it has original jurisdiction and will serve as the trial court. Only cases that involve significant national or constitutional matters are heard by the Court and while more than 1,000 cases are presented to the Court for possible consideration every term, only about 80 will receive a full review by the Court.

The U.S. Courts of Appeals

Directly beneath the Supreme Court there are 12 U.S. courts of appeals; the U.S. Court of Appeals for the Armed Forces is also at this level. These courts hear all of the appeals from all of the federal courts throughout the United States and its territories and possessions. In 2006, there were 66,618 appeals filed, down from 68,473 the previous year, but up from 57,464 in 2001. From 2001 to 2005 there was an upward trend in appellate filings (http://www.uscourts.gov/cgi-bin/cmsa2006.pl).

These courts are sometimes referred to as *circuit courts*. When the United States was a young country, the Supreme Court justices were expected to travel to various courts throughout the states hearing cases on a regular basis. Long before plane travel or even a transcontinental railroad, this meant travel by horses and was a difficult process. This was called *riding the circuit*. It took quite some time to ride from Washington, D.C. to the farthest states, yet the justices did just that for many years. It was not until 1891, with the creation of the circuit courts of appeal, which eventually became known as the U.S. courts of appeal, that Supreme Court justices no longer had to ride the circuit.

The Circuit Courts

The First Circuit Court of Appeals is comprised of Maine, Massachusetts, New Hampshire, Rhode Island, and added in 1915, Puerto Rico. The court has six authorized judgeships. This court is based in Boston, but as a circuit court should, the judges sit in Puerto Rico each year and may travel to other parts of the circuit.

The Second Circuit Court of Appeals is comprised of Connecticut, Vermont, and the four (eastern, northern, southern, and western) districts of New York. This court has 13 authorized judgeships and sits in New York City.

The Third Circuit Court of Appeals is comprised of Delaware, New Jersey, the Virgin Islands, and the three districts in Pennsylvania (eastern, middle, and western). The Third Circuit Court has 14 authorized judgeships and sits in Philadelphia.

The Fourth Circuit Court of Appeals is comprised of Maryland, North Carolina (eastern, middle, and western districts), South Carolina, Virginia (eastern and western districts), and West Virginia (northern and southern districts). The court has 15 authorized judgeships and sits in Richmond, Virginia.

The Fifth Circuit Court of Appeals is comprised of Louisiana (eastern, middle, and western), Mississippi (northern and southern), and Texas (eastern, northern, southern, and western). The court has 17 authorized judgeships and sits in New Orleans. Originally, this circuit also covered Florida, Georgia, and Alabama. At one point in time it also had jurisdiction over the Panama Canal zone. The Fifth Circuit was responsible for many key civil rights decisions.

The Sixth Circuit Court of Appeals sits in Cincinnati, Ohio, and is comprised of Kentucky (eastern and western), Michigan (eastern and western), Ohio (northern and southern), and Tennessee (eastern, middle, and western). The court has 16 authorized judgeships.

The Seventh Circuit Court of Appeals sits in Chicago and is comprised of Illinois (central, northern, and southern), Indiana (northern and southern), and Wisconsin (eastern and western). The court has 11 authorized judgeships.

The Eighth Circuit Court of Appeals is comprised of Arkansas (eastern and western), Iowa (northern and southern), Minnesota, Missouri (eastern and western), Nebraska, North Dakota, and South Dakota. The court sits in St. Louis, Missouri and has 11 authorized judgeships.

The Ninth Circuit Court of Appeals is comprised of Alaska, California (central, eastern, northern, and southern), Hawaii, Idaho, Montana, Nevada, Oregon, and Washington (eastern and western). This court also has jurisdiction over Guam and the Northern Mariana Islands. With 28 authorized judgeships it is the largest court of appeals. This is truly a circuit court, with cases regularly heard in Seattle, Portland, San Francisco, and Pasadena. On occasion, the court will also hear cases in other locations. The size, in terms of both geography and population, has caused considerable difficulties for this court. The Ninth Circuit has traditionally been known as a liberal circuit and has been responsible for numerous decisions limiting the power of government.

The Tenth Circuit Court of Appeals is comprised of Colorado, Kansas, New Mexico, Oklahoma (eastern, northern, and western), Utah, and Wyoming. It was created by dividing the Eighth Circuit into two circuits. The court has 12 authorized judgeships and is based in Denver, Colorado.

The Eleventh Circuit Court of Appeals is comprised of Alabama (middle, northern, and southern), Georgia (middle, northern, and southern), and Florida (middle, northern, and southern). It was created in 1981 by dividing the Fifth Circuit Court into two circuits. The court has 12 authorized judgeships and sits in Atlanta, Georgia.

The U.S. Court of Appeals for the District of Columbia Circuit is the Twelfth Circuit Court of Appeals and is comprised of the District of Columbia and has 12 authorized judgeships. Many individuals who have served on this court go on to serve on the Supreme Court.

U.S. District Courts

Almost every federal case has its beginnings in a federal district court. These are the major trial courts of the federal system. Federal cases are tried at this level and then may proceed to the appellate or Supreme Court level. At the federal level, fewer than 2 percent of cases will go to trial; all others are settled prior to the trial stage.

In 2006, there were 326,401 cases filed in U.S. district courts. Of those, 259,541 were civil cases and 66,860 were criminal cases. Just over one-fifth of cases in the federal system were criminal cases. Of the criminal filings, drug filings have been declining steadily over the past five years. Prior to the mid-1980s, there were far fewer criminal cases heard in federal court. Once the federal drug laws began to change, more criminal drug cases were processed through federal court. Of the civil filings, which include social security cases, civil rights cases, labor law cases, personal injury/product liability cases, and prisoner petitions, prisoner petitions are the most common type of case. Because of recent changes in bankruptcy laws, bankruptcy filings fell by almost 40 percent from 2005 to 2006 (http://www.uscourts.gov/judbus2006/completejudicialbusiness.pdf).

Since the ratification of the Constitution in 1789, a great number of federal courts have been added. In fact, there is at least one federal court district in each state, territory, and the District of Columbia. Areas with smaller populations have only one (for example, Alaska, Virgin Islands, Vermont). California, has four districts; Guam has a single authorized federal judgeship, while California, has 55. Beneath the courts of appeals are 94 U.S. district courts. There are also several specialized courts at this level—such as the tax court, the court of federal claims, the court of veteran appeals, and the court of international trade; these specialized courts are designed to hear only particular cases. All but a few federal cases originate in these trial courts. These trial courts conduct the majority of the day-to-day work of the federal court system.

U.S. Bankruptcy Courts, Tax Court, and Special Courts

All federal judicial districts hear bankruptcy cases. Bankruptcy is a way for individuals and businesses to be relieved of their debts, to repay creditors, and to reorganize. The U.S. Tax Court was created to allow individuals who dispute taxes to have a forum for disputing them. There are 19 members appointed by the president.

The federal special courts include the U.S. Court of International Trade, the U.S. Court of Federal Claims, the U.S. Court of Appeals for Veterans' Claims, and the U.S. Court of Appeals for the Armed Forces. The U.S. Court of International Trade was created by the Customs Courts Act of 1980. This court deals with disputes that arise when engaging in trade and customs issues. This court can settle disputes that involve nations, individuals, manufacturers, consumer groups, labor unions, and others that are involved in international trade. Nine judges, appointed for life by the president, preside over this court.

The U.S. Court of Federal Claims was established in 1855. The purpose of this court is to allow private citizens a court in which to sue the federal government. The court handles private property issues (when the government has taken private property), refunds of federal taxes, damages for breach of contract with the government, patent and copyright infringement against the United States, some cases transferred from Native American courts, and cases arising from vaccine lawsuits. Currently, the majority of cases involve vaccine cases. As of September 30, 2006, there were 5,347 vaccine compensation cases, 875 contract cases, 473 civilian pay cases, 434 tax cases, and 385 property taken cases pending in the court (http://www.uscourts.gov/judbus2006/completejudicialbusiness.pdf). The court is located in Washington, D.C. It is a jury-less court.

The U.S. Court of Appeals for Veterans' Claims has seven judges. This court was created in 1988 and has jurisdiction over the decisions of the Board of Veterans' Appeals. This court hears cases for veterans who have been denied benefits. Prior to the creation of this court, when the Veterans Administration denied benefits, there was no court in which a veteran could appeal such a decision.

The U.S. Court of Appeals for the Armed Forces is the final appellate court that reviews court-martial cases. This will be discussed along with military courts later in this chapter.

TRIBAL COURTS AND MILITARY COURTS

All Native American tribes are sovereign nations. As sovereign nations, each tribe has jurisdiction over everything within its territory. Each tribe has also codified its own laws. In some instances a federal or state court may have concurrent jurisdiction when certain criminal acts are committed and an individual is tried in federal/state court and tribal court.

The Uniform Code of Military Justice is the criminal laws that apply to all members of the United States military. This code differs from state or federal codes in two ways. First, whether or not the Uniform Code of Military Justice applies to an individual depends not upon that person's geographical location but rather on whether or not they are a member of the armed forces. Also, although there are many crimes within the Code that are similar to state or federal crimes, there are other crimes that are specific to this Code. Military personnel who commit crimes are subject to court martial. After a court martial, all convictions are subject to posttrial review to assure that the law has been applied correctly and there has not been a mistake of fact. Convictions for more serious crimes are automatically appealed to a service court of criminal appeals. If this court denies the appeal, the defendant may have the case reviewed by the U.S. Court of Appeals for the Armed Forces, although this is a discretionary court and does not hear all appeals. Above this court sits the U.S. Supreme Court.

STATE COURT SYSTEMS

The bulk of the court work in the United States takes place within the state court system and the majority of these cases, in every state, are either domestic cases or traffic cases. Under the doctrine of *states' rights,* each state has the power to set up and change its own court system. The federal government cannot interfere in this matter except in instances when a state's actions are unconstitutional. Each state's court system developed uniquely and was influenced by a number of factors, including population growth and colonial occupation. States with larger populations developed more courts

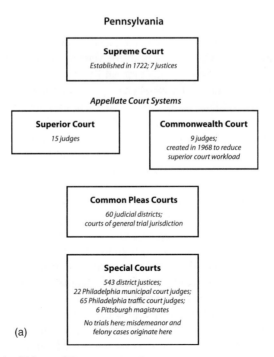

(a)

FIGURE 13.2   Pennsylvania, Ohio, and Texas court systems.

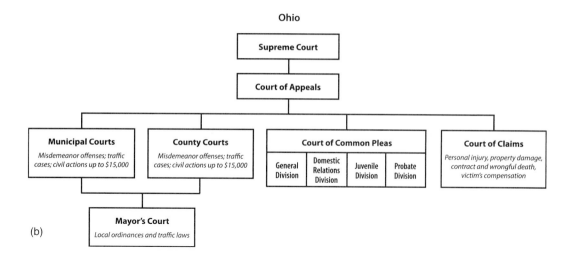

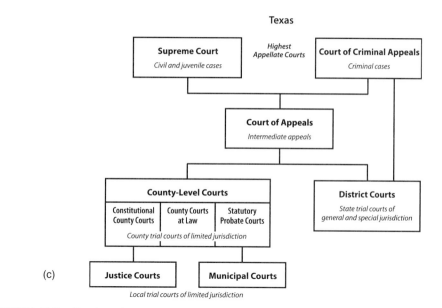

FIGURE 13.2 Continued

at a faster pace, for example, New York or California. Even today states with smaller populations have fewer courts, for example, Alaska or Montana. States that had been among the original 13 colonies were strongly influenced by the British legal system, while other states were influenced by other powers, including Mexico, Spain, and France (Figure 13.2).

Modern state courts, like the federal court system, have a hierarchical structure; however during the first 100 years of our country's existence, most states had little more than a state supreme court where all cases were heard. Today, most states have a supreme court, under which sits an appellate court. The appellate court will hear all appeals and only a select few cases from the appellate court will then be heard in the supreme court. Beneath the appellate courts are trial courts. The trial courts are divided into the courts of general jurisdiction and the lower courts. The courts of general jurisdiction hear felony cases and lower courts hear misdemeanor cases.

Pennsylvania's Courts

Like all of the original 13 colonies, Pennsylvania's early court system was modeled after the courts of England. Until 1727, there was no supreme court in Pennsylvania; all final appeals had to be heard by the Crown. The 1776 Constitution of Pennsylvania established the courts of sessions, courts of common pleas, and orphans' courts in each county. Further changes were made to the constitution and to the Pennsylvania court system in 1790, 1838, 1874, and 1850. The Pennsylvania Superior Court was created in 1895.

In the last 40 years, many states have made efforts to simplify and streamline their court systems by eliminating or combining redundant courts and creating specialized courts. In 1968, a series of major changes were made to the courts. The Commonwealth Court was created, which reduced the workload of the superior and supreme courts. More importantly, the Unified Judicial System was created; under this reorganization; the Pennsylvania Supreme Court is the court of last resort in Pennsylvania. Beneath the Pennsylvania Supreme Court, the Superior Court and Commonwealth Court are situated. The common pleas courts sit below these courts. At the lowest level are the magisterial district judges, Philadelphia Municipal Court, Philadelphia Traffic Court, and Pittsburgh Municipal Court (http://www.courts.state.pa.us/index/ujs/courthistory.asp).

State Supreme Court

All states have a state supreme court, although it may be called by different names. The state supreme courts function much like the U.S. Supreme Court. If the state also has an appellate court, the state supreme court will have discretion over the cases it hears. If a state does not have an appellate court, that state's supreme court will function as the appellate court and hear all appeals in the state.

State Appellate Court

Each individual who receives an unfavorable decision from a court is entitled to file an appeal. In most cases, that appeal is heard in the state appellate court. Just as in the federal court system, these appeals are filed based on a mistake in the application of the law during the trial process and not on a mistake of fact. An appeal may also be based upon ineffective assistance of counsel. The appellate court does not concern itself with the guilt or innocence of the individual but rather with appropriate application of the law. When a state does not have a separate appellate court, appeals are heard by the state supreme court.

Most appeals are denied. It is a rare occasion that a verdict is overturned; more often than not, a new trial results in a new guilty verdict. Generally, guilty verdicts are built upon many pieces of evidence. Appeals may be based on the particular way in which the law may have been misapplied in a case, or on the fact that faulty instructions were given to the jury. Only about one out of every sixteen appeals results in a different verdict from the initial verdict.

The Trial Courts

The state trial courts are responsible for doing the bulk of work of the court system. They are divided into upper and lower courts. The lower courts handle the initial stages for all cases. They also handle the majority of misdemeanor cases. The upper courts, sometimes called superior courts, will handle all felony cases after the initial stages.

CIVIL COURTS   Each state court system has both criminal and civil courts. Civil courts hear a tremendous variety of cases, including cases involving contract disputes, damage to property, injury, product liability, landlord/tenant cases, and small claims. All these cases involve one party suing another for damages. Civil courts also have jurisdiction over family cases (divorce, child support, and custody), juvenile cases, and probate cases (wills, trusts, guardianship, conservatorship, adoption, and name changes). The bulk of all state court cases are civil cases, and the majority of these cases involve family court issues—excluding traffic court cases. Forensic testimony is most likely to be heard in injury, product liability, family, and some juvenile cases.

Forensic testimony first became widely accepted in civil court in product liability cases. Expert witnesses testified regarding the safety of products, the chemical makeup of products, and the medical consequences of the use of products. Product liability cases generally involve an injured party having been harmed by use of a specific product—for example, a drug like thalidomide (which was prescribed to pregnant women in Canada and Europe as a treatment for severe morning sickness but caused major limb malformations in fetuses) or silicone breast implants (which may or may not cause connective tissue disease). Another area of significant forensic expert involvement—especially forensic mental health experts—is in family court. Family court resolves issues dealing with divorce, custody, and child support. A forensic mental health expert may testify regarding the fitness of each parent for custody, which home environment would be more beneficial for a child, or whether abuse has occurred—among other areas.

In civil cases the burden of proof is different than in criminal cases. In order for a manufacturer to be found liable, a preponderance of evidence must point to that liability; in other words, if it is more likely than not that the manufacturer caused the injury, the jury will generally find for the plaintiff. In a criminal case, the defendant must be found guilty *beyond a reasonable doubt*, which means that the defense has been able to cast enough doubt on the state's case against the defendant and that no *reasonable* individual could find the defendant guilty. One of the main reasons O. J. Simpson was found not guilty at his criminal trial but was found liable in his civil trial was the differences between the criminal court's much higher standard for burden of proof and the civil court's much lower standard for burden of proof. Criminal court maintains a higher burden of proof because the penalty for being found guilty may be a loss of personal freedom. This is much more valuable than the monetary damages that are common in the civil court.

CRIMINAL COURTS   Criminal court is for all matters in which a criminal law has been broken. In criminal court, the government is a party to all cases (for example, *The People of the State of NY v. Lee*). The government becomes the plaintiff, and if there are victims, they will be witnesses for the prosecution. This has benefits for victims because they do not have to pursue their own cases or hire an attorney, the state takes on that task. However, there is also a downside to this system because the victim is not central to the case and merely becomes another witness for the prosecution. It is the district attorney who will make the decision whether or not a case is prosecuted and not the individual victim.

SPECIALIZED COURTS   There are many specialized courts within the state courts of the United States; juvenile court, drug court, teen court, and mental health court. All states have established juvenile courts and many have established drug courts and mental health courts. Interestingly, there is sometimes overlap among these different types of courts. For example, many juvenile courts have juvenile drug courts within them or juvenile mental health courts

Juvenile Court   Although juvenile courts are encompassed within the civil court system of each state, juvenile cases are handled in a very different way from other civil cases that the court hears. Juvenile court does not levy fines or mediate between two individual parties. It is also a closed court—to mention a few differences. The first juvenile court was established in Cook County, Illinois in 1899. This court was founded largely because of the influence of movements like the Chicago Woman's Club, Hull House, and Child Savers. These groups, along with others like them sought to improve the plight of poor, mostly immigrant children who were often in trouble with the law.

Historically, children were viewed as miniature adults, with the same rights, responsibilities, and cognitive abilities as adults. Even in the Bible, the age of seven is considered to be the threshold for moral responsibility. Under the age of seven, the child does not know right from wrong. In 1850, the lives of poor children were neither long nor happy. The infant mortality rate was high. There were no vaccines against childhood illnesses; sanitation in the cities was poor, at birth, an infant had about a 50 percent chance of surviving to age 18. Life expectancy was about 50 years. Few children received formal schooling. Most went to work before the age of 10 either in factories or at home. During this time, increasing numbers of immigrants were coming to America. In 1880, the population of Chicago was under 5,000. By 1920, it was over 2 million. This influx of immigrants into Chicago had significant impact on everything in the city, from where and how people lived, to social services. In fact, there was perhaps no greater need for social services, which were almost nonexistent at this time, than in Chicago and other growing urban areas. It was in this environment that some middle class and wealthy women began to identify social problems and create a blueprint for change.

Prior to 1899, laws applied to everyone equally, regardless of age. A 10-year-old who stole was treated in the same manner as a 30-year-old who stole. Children were tried for adult crimes and were given adult sentences that they served in adult institutions. After 1899, children were viewed more as being in need of protection and training than in need of punishment. While children who broke the law were a concern of the juvenile court, so were children who had been abandoned by their parents, as were children who were being mistreated by parents or even employers. The juvenile court handled children who were in need of supervision (because they broke the law) and children who were in need of services (because they were abandoned or mistreated). Unlike the adult criminal system, which had as its goal to punish offenders, the goal of the juvenile justice system was to guide young people. There were both positive and negative outcomes to this new system.

For the first time in history, children began to be viewed as different from adults. They were not just small adults, they were completely different. Psychology, still very much in its infancy, was just beginning to look at issues of child development. Compulsory schooling laws were just beginning to be passed to ensure the education of children. Massachusetts passed the first such law in 1852. By 1918 all states then in the United States had compulsory schooling laws (Alaska enacted its compulsory schooling law in 1929, but it was not granted statehood until 1959). In 1850, many children had no possibility of education. And while many states had child labor laws even in the early 1800s, even a century later, many of these laws were still ignored. In many cases the laws didn't apply to immigrant children.

The driving philosophy behind the juvenile court system is the concept of *in loco parentis*—meaning, literally, in the place of the parent. Prior to this time, the government did not see that it was its job to interfere in children's lives. Children were the responsibility of their parents. In fact, they were the property of their parents. The inception of the juvenile justice system represented a significant step away from viewing children simply as the chattel of their parents. Children who could not be controlled by their parents were now viewed as needing the assistance of the state to step in and serve as their parents.

Because the juvenile justice system is not a criminal system but a civil system, it serves to keep children out of the criminal justice system. It keeps children away from adult courts and adult jails, even when the actions they commit would be criminal acts if committed by adults. The juvenile justice system, from its inception, has had rehabilitation at its core. Because juveniles are viewed as impressionable, the system believes that they can change for the better. Adults are not viewed as so malleable. The adult system's commitment to rehabilitation has waxed and waned over the years.

There are also negatives associated with the juvenile justice system. The juvenile court system was created by the middle and upper classes. It is a vehicle for their values. In 1899 Chicago, it served as a way to control the children of immigrants who were seen as needing to be controlled. Just like the adult system, there have been instances of significant racial inequalities in the juvenile justice system. The juvenile justice system is more often involved with racial and ethnic minorities and the poor.

This also marked the beginning of laws that applied only to children, and created the concept of the *status offense*. A status offense is an action that when engaged in by an adult is perfectly legal, but is not allowed for a juvenile, for example, not attending school, leaving home, drinking, smoking, and being out past curfew. The juvenile justice system put children under the control of the state who might not otherwise have come into contact with the system. Rather than just concentrate on those juveniles who have broken the law, juveniles may be brought under state control for other reasons.

For many years, the juvenile court system afforded juveniles no civil rights. Hearings were closed, which was done to protect the juvenile, but this also prevented oversight into what the system was doing. It was possible for judges, who were supposed to be looking out for the juveniles, to behave in a capricious manner and, in some cases; juveniles were punished far more severely than an adult would have been for the same offense.

Civil Rights and Due Process Movement During the civil rights era when the rights of the accused in the criminal courts were being expanded and solidified by the Supreme Court, civil rights for juveniles also began to become an issue. *In re Gault* (387 U.S. 1, 1967) granted juveniles the same constitutional and procedural rights enjoyed by adults when the matter in front of the juvenile court could result in incarceration (note, this is not extended to all proceedings in the juvenile court). This includes the right to have an attorney assist with the defense, the right to have counsel appointed if the child and parents cannot afford counsel, the right to have the child and the child's guardians informed of the court proceedings, the right against self-incrimination, and the right to confront witnesses,

In re Winship, (397 U.S. 358, 1970) changed the standard of proof in juvenile court from the lower *preponderance of the evidence* which is used in civil court to *beyond a reasonable doubt*, the standard used in the criminal court.

In *McKeiver v. Pennsylvania* (403 U.S. 528, 1971) the U.S. Supreme Court held that the Pennsylvania trial court did not err when it denied a juvenile the right to a jury trial. The Supreme Court contended that juveniles did not have all due process rights that adults have and that the protections of a nonjury, nonadversarial proceeding outweighed the due process protections of a jury trial.

The Modern Juvenile Justice System Much has changed over the years in the juvenile justice system. However, it should be stated that in juvenile court juveniles still do not have the same rights as adults. In fact, it is not uncommon for an attorney representing a juvenile to request that the case be waived to adult court so that the juvenile will have all of the rights that are afforded to adults in court.

The juvenile court system has always kept its focus on rehabilitation. Juvenile court systems apply many of the therapeutic jurisprudence approaches discussed in Chapter 12. Juvenile courts are encouraged to take a restorative justice approach, which regards a crime as a break with society and seeks to restore the relationship among the victim, offender, and society.

THE CRIMINAL COURT PROCESS

There is a formal criminal court process that begins with the arrest and ends with the sentencing of the offender. However it is more of an exception rather than a rule that an individual offender progresses through the entire criminal court process: most criminal cases are resolved through a quick admission of guilt, and the offender proceeds directly to sentencing. The admission of guilt is often the result of a plea bargain, with the most common sanction being the payment of a fine. Among felony offenders, one-third of offenders will serve probation, one-third will spend less than one year in prison, and the remaining third will serve more than one year in prison (Figure 13.3).

Although not part of the official criminal court process, a crime instigates the journey into the criminal justice system. Most crimes are unremarkable; property crime is much more common than

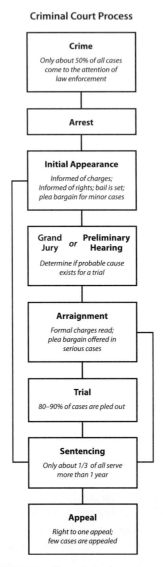

Criminal Court Process

Crime

Only about 50% of all cases come to the attention of law enforcement

Arrest

Initial Appearance

Informed of charges; Informed of rights; bail is set; plea bargain for minor cases

Grand Jury *or* **Preliminary Hearing**

Determine if probable cause exists for a trial

Arraignment

Formal charges read; plea bargain offered in serious cases

Trial

80–90% of cases are pled out

Sentencing

Only about 1/3 of all serve more than 1 year

Appeal

Right to one appeal; few cases are appealed

FIGURE 13.3 The criminal court process.

violent crime. It has been estimated that about half of all crimes do not come to the attention of law enforcement. This is commonly referred to as the *dark figure of crime.* Some crimes—like homicide—are much more likely to be noticed because of the inherent difficulties in disposing of bodies, whereas a crime such as rape is far less likely to be reported because victims often feel that within the criminal justice system they are treated more like the suspect than the actual perpetrator. Victims of abuse crimes often do not report their victimization to avoid interrogation by opposing counsel, to avoid having to retell their story repeatedly, and to avoid reliving the shame and the terror of the attack.

The official entry into the criminal justice court process is marked by an arrest. About half of all offenses that come to the attention of law enforcement result in an arrest. Some offenses have a higher clearance rate than others; homicide generally has the highest rate. In general, the "index offenses" listed in the Uniform Crime Reports have the highest clearance rates, far higher than property offenses.

Homicide Clearance Rate

The higher clearance rate for homicide is the result of many factors. First, the killing of a human being is considered to be the most serious crime that can be committed except possibly treason. Because of the serious nature of the crime, homicide is given top priority by law enforcement and considerable investigative effort—both in terms of dollars and work hours—is expended to solve open cases. Law enforcement also gives the crime of homicide top priority because of pressure from elected officials and the public to solve these types of crimes. Because there is no statute of limitations regarding homicide, these crimes can be prosecuted decades after the actual crime occurred.

An arrestee must appear before a magistrate within a designated amount of time after arrest—usually within 24 hours—although this period may be longer in some jurisdictions, especially if the arrest occurs over a weekend. The appearance before a magistrate takes place in a lower court. At this time the individual is officially booked and the charges are read. Even for a felony offense, the first contact that the suspect has with the court system is at the lower-court level. The accused must be informed of the right to remain silent, and the right to have representation.

Generally, at this point in the process, misdemeanor arrestees will be offered—and accept—a plea bargain. Approximately 90 percent of all misdemeanors are resolved through such means. Felony arrestees may not plea bargain at this point because the lower court does not hold jurisdiction for major felonies. They must wait until their case has been sent to the court of general jurisdiction.

The judge will also make a decision regarding bail. Bail is not a *right*, nor is it guaranteed by the Constitution. If an individual presents a significant flight risk, is deemed to be a significant threat to the public, or has numerous past offenses, bail may be denied. Generally, the judge will set a bail amount based on the charged offense, often factoring in the individual's prior record. The bail may be paid in full by a representative of the defendant (friend or family member). This amount will be returned to the defendant when the case goes to court. There are some jurisdictions that will accept property rather than money in exchange for being released on bail, but it is unwieldy for agencies to deal with these properties. Most defendants do not have enough money—or property—to pay the full bail amount and must utilize bail bond services. Through this service the defendant gives the bail bonds person a portion of the full bond—usually 10 percent. The bonds person, in turn, pays the full amount to the court, which will be returned when the defendant appears for the court date. The bonds person will retain as payment for services the amount given by the defendant. If the individual does not show up for court, the bonds agency will pursue the defendant and do whatever it takes to bring that person back.

The next step in the criminal justice system varies, although its aim is to determine whether or not there is probable cause to continue with a trial. The case will either go before a grand jury, or a preliminary hearing will be held. The federal court system employs a grand jury, as do some states. The grand jury carries out their work behind closed doors. It is very different from all other aspects of the criminal justice system, which are open for inspection. When an individual testifies before a grand jury, he or she may *not* have a lawyer present. The secrecy is necessary because not all cases that are presented to the grand jury are allowed to go forward to prosecution. In some jurisdictions, the grand jury is used to weed out cases where probable cause is weak, whereas in other jurisdictions, the grand jury functions more as a rubber stamp for approving the decision to prosecute.

The preliminary hearing, like the grand jury process, may function as a rubber stamp for the decision of the district attorney to prosecute in some jurisdictions. In other jurisdictions, the preliminary hearing is carried out almost like a mini-trial. In this case, it may have the effect of significantly reducing the number of trials that are held. Unlike grand jury proceedings, preliminary hearings are generally open to the public (in some cases the hearing may be closed based upon the

---

The Plea Bargain

The plea bargain is both highly controversial within the criminal justice court system and an intrinsic part of the system. There is no constitutional right to a plea bargain. It is up to the prosecutor to decide whether or not to offer the defendant a plea bargain. About 80 percent of all felony arrests and 90 percent of misdemeanor arrests are cleared through a plea agreement.

The plea bargain is controversial because it appears that offenders are *getting away with something* when they accept a plea and serve a lesser sentence. To many it seems as though justice is not best served through plea agreements. The plea bargain is an intrinsic part of our current criminal justice system. Without offenders accepting plea agreements, our courts, which are already backlogged with cases, would be deluged with cases. Rather than taking six months to two years to resolve the average felony case that goes to trial, it would probably take five to ten years. Offenders have considerable impetus to accept plea agreements because the possible sentence that an individual would receive if a guilty verdict is returned during a trial is generally much more severe than the sentenced offered with the plea.

Most plea agreements that are entered into are known as *blind plea agreements.* In a blind plea the defendant pleads guilty but there is no special agreement. In effect, the defendant is throwing himself on the mercy of the court. While this sounds risky, for most of the crimes committed, the plea agreement that is offered is pretty standard—it is the same for all offenders committing the same offense. In fact, when an offender agrees to *just pay the fine*, in effect, that is accepting a plea agreement.

There are three different types of plea agreements: charge bargaining, count bargaining, and sentence bargaining. Charge bargaining consists of pleading guilty to a less serious charge than the original charge. The less serious charge will carry a lighter sentence. In count bargaining, the prosecutor accepts a plea of guilty in exchange for dropping some or all but one of the counts against the offender. Very often when an individual is arrested it is not on one count, but several. The arresting officer will write up as many counts as possible to allow for the prosecution to drop several of them during count bargaining. Sentence bargaining, or "plea on the nose," consists of pleading guilty in exchange for a lesser sentence. The charge does not change but the sentence does.

In many cases, diversion can be considered to be a form of plea agreement. The defendant agrees to comply with certain terms, perhaps counseling or community service. In exchange for compliance with the terms of diversion, there will be no prison time served.

---

alleged crime, for example, sexual crimes involving children). Preliminary hearings—like the grand jury—are the first step in establishing whether or not a felony charge has merit to go forward from a lower court of limited jurisdiction to a court of general jurisdiction. Generally, at the preliminary hearing some of the charges are dropped or consolidated into lesser or fewer charges.

During the next step in the process, the arraignment, the felony offender is finally brought before a judge in the court that holds jurisdiction, the court of general jurisdiction. The formal charges against the defendant are read and a plea is entered.

The defendant who does not plead *guilty* has a choice of several other pleas and may enter a plea of *not guilty, not guilty by reason of insanity, guilty but mentally incompetent, double jeopardy,* and *nolo contendere.* Each of these pleas will impact the progression of the case in a different manner. A *not guilty* plea means that, unless the plea is changed at some point to *guilty,* a trial will occur.

Not all jurisdictions accept pleas of either *not guilty by reason of insanity,* or *guilty but mentally incompetent.* While both of these pleas admit that the defendant did commit the offense, they argue that the defendant is not responsible for his or her actions because of some form of mental incapacity. Defendants that are found *not guilty by reason of insanity* will be committed to forensic hospitals until they are deemed to no longer be a danger. At that time, they will be released. Defendants that are found *guilty but mentally incompetent* are confined to forensic hospitals until they are deemed to

---

Double Jeopardy

When a defendant enters a plea of *double jeopardy*, he is saying that he has already been tried and found *not guilty* of the crime. The burden of proof for this plea rests with the defendant. If he successfully proves double jeopardy, then constitutional protections guarantee that he may not be tried again for that crime. The protection against double jeopardy arises from the Fifth Amendment, which states "nor shall any person be subject for the same offense to be twice put in jeopardy of life or limb." It is designed to protect individuals from being repeatedly tried by a government that has limitless resources.

There are, however, numerous exceptions to double jeopardy—instances when it might seem as though an individual is being tried twice, but, when examined closer, that isn't the case at all. If an individual is retried after a mistrial, this is not considered to be double jeopardy because the mistrial means that in the eyes of the court the first trial never happened. An individual may also be tried on separate charges even though they resulted from the same criminal action—although generally an individual would be tried on all charges at once and the jury would return separate verdicts for each charge. A person can be retried after an appellate court has overturned a conviction. When the conviction is overturned, the appellate court is stating that the trial court's handling of the case was so flawed that it was not reliable—it is as if the trial never occurred. An individual may be tried in jurisdictions of *different sovereignty*—for the same crime, for example, in federal court and state court, in federal court and tribal court, or in both criminal court and civil court.

---

no longer be a danger, then they are sent to prison if any of their sentence remains to be served—although most of the time, offenders that are confined to forensic hospitals serve *more* time than if they had merely been found guilty because the forensic hospital must confine them until they are no longer a danger.

A plea of *nolo contendere* may be entered. With this plea, the defendant does not admit guilt, but also does not contest the charges. This plea is also referred to as *no contest.* The court finds the individual guilty and he or she is sentenced. This plea is not allowed in all jurisdictions. Richard Nixon's Vice-President Spiro Agnew famously resigned his office and pled *nolo contendere* to charges of tax evasion and money laundering for accepting bribes while he was governor of Maryland.

During the pretrial conference, the judge will set a date for the trial. The primary purpose of the pretrial conference is to get all parties *on the same page* regarding the plea, any special conditions that have been set, or other items of importance.

In the discovery phase, both the prosecution and the defense must present the evidence that supports their case to the other side. Contrary to how this process is portrayed in television and movies, there are few surprises in a real courtroom. Discovery may consist of formal depositions, or it may simply involve sharing a copy of the opposing side's witness list, or it may include talking with opposing counsel. This process allows both prosecution and defense to ascertain how strong a case exists for both sides and whether each could get a favorable verdict at trial. Generally, the prosecution will only go to trial with a case that they are confident of winning. This is partly for political and financial reasons. Prosecutors want to have high conviction rates. The government wants to spend money only on cases that it believes it can win.

When the criminal justice process has progressed to this point, jury selection will begin. Jurisdictions maintain lists of individuals who may be called to serve on juries. These lists are generally comprised of registered voters, registered drivers, and other government databases. Prospective jurors' names are obtained in a variety of ways, two of the most common being voter registration lists, and drivers' licenses. Prospective jurors are questioned in open court regarding their qualifications in a process called *voir dire.* Each attorney is allowed to excuse jurors for cause—because they believe

---

Why O. J. Was Tried Twice

On January 24, 1995, the criminal trial of Orenthal James Simpson began. Almost nine months later, on October 3, 1995, the jury returned the verdict of *not guilty*. A year later, on October 23, 1996, opening statements were heard in the civil trial of O. J. Simpson. On February 4, 1997, the jury found Simpson liable and awarded $8.5 million in damages. It seems as though O. J. was tried twice, but although there were two trials, one was a criminal trial and one was a civil trial. This is not double jeopardy. It would be possible for O. J. to be tried a third time if he were tried in federal court (remember O. J.'s criminal trial was a state trial). However, he cannot be tried in the state criminal court again—even if the prosecution made errors in their handling of the case—that would be double jeopardy.

---

there is some factor that will bias the juror. Each attorney is also allowed to excuse a limited number of jurors without cause. In some cases, the attorney may employ an expert in jury selection, but most attorneys pick jurors based on their past experiences and admitted perceptions.

In the opening statements, each side presents an overview of the case. Neither attorney is permitted to argue the case, but rather to tell the jury what points they will be making during the trial. A good opening statement sets the stage for what is to come; jurors better understand what is presented during a trial when they have been given a clear framework for that information.

The state presents its case first. The prosecutor will call all of the state's witnesses and the defense will have the opportunity to cross-examine the witnesses after each has provided his or her individual testimony. When the prosecution rests, the defense will present its case. The defense calls all of its witnesses and the prosecution then has the opportunity to cross-examine each, in turn. During cross examination, opposing counsel gets to ask questions of the other side's witnesses. The trial ends with closing statements, during which both prosecution and defense provide the jury with a summary of what was and, in some cases, was *not* proven during the trial. If the defendant is found guilty, sentencing will follow during the sentencing phase.

Every individual who is found guilty in a criminal court is entitled to one appeal. Appeals are made on the basis of a mistake of law—that the law was misapplied in the defendant's case. The appellate court does not *retry* the case, witnesses are not called, but rather the appellate court makes a decision as to whether or not the trial was correctly and fairly conducted. In all death penalty cases an appeal is automatically filed. This is done because of the seriousness and finality of the sanction.

Professionals in the Criminal Courtroom

The average expert witness spends relatively little time in the courtroom testifying. Even the average attorney rarely goes into a courtroom to try a case. This is because of the significant percentage of defendants who will accept a plea agreement. All forensic scientists (whether the individual is a forensic anthropologist, a laboratory supervisor, or a forensic psychologist) spend most of their time preparing for the possibility of going into court, but very little time actually testifying in court.

As an expert witness, the three professionals with whom you will have the most contact in the courtroom are the judge, the defense attorney, and the prosecutor. The judge is in charge of the courtroom and presides over the pretrial and trial process. It is often erroneously assumed that the judge is the most powerful person in the courtroom, but that is not the case; the judge's power lies in ensuring that the trial process is fair. It is the responsibility of the judge to intercede if either attorney behaves in a way that would compromise or endanger the fairness of the proceedings. While it has been traditional for the judge to be completely uninvolved in the process of questioning witnesses, some jurisdictions will allow the judge to ask a question or to ask for clarification.

Generally, most judges have previously been practicing attorneys. Assuming a judgeship is often looked at as the capstone of a legal career. The vast majority of judges at the appellate level were attorneys. However, in some jurisdictions, judges are elected officials who may or may not have previously been attorneys. It is not uncommon for local judges (or magistrates) to have been active in politics and served in an office such as city council member.

The defense attorney is the attorney who represents the individual who has been accused of a crime. In the criminal courts, most defendants are represented by attorneys who have been provided by the state. Most criminal defendants are poor and cannot afford an attorney. The right to counsel was first enumerated in the Sixth Amendment to the Constitution: "In all criminal prosecutions, the accused shall enjoy the right . . . to have the Assistance of Counsel for his defense." At that time, however, it only applied to federal cases where the individual was in jeopardy of losing his life. Since the ratification of the Bill of Rights in 1791, the right to counsel has been extended—through a number of Supreme Court decisions (see, in particular, *Gideon v. Wainwright*, 1963)—to extend to any case in which an individual may be in jeopardy of losing his or her freedom or having a significant fine imposed. In many jurisdictions, the right to counsel is extended to all defendants.

The prosecutor is the attorney who presents the state's case. The prosecutor has considerable power during the criminal justice process: charges are filed and the trial goes forward only with the approval of the prosecution. The prosecutor is also the author of any plea bargain that may be presented to the defendant. Although it may seem as though the job of the prosecutor is to secure a conviction, it is actually the goal of the prosecutor to ensure that justice is served. If it should come to light that the individual being prosecuted for a particular crime is not actually guilty of that crime, the prosecutor should no longer continue to pursue charges against that person. It is unfortunate that, in many jurisdictions, much emphasis is placed on a prosecutor's record of convictions.

These are by no means the only professionals in the courtroom. As an expert witness, you may interact with a host of other professionals, including bailiffs, police officers, social workers, clerks, and court reporters among them.

The Jury

The modern jury system developed from the system that the colonists brought with them from England. The individuals who make up the jury are the finders of fact. The use of 12 jurors has no special significance and has evolved out of convention; some courts use fewer jurors. In our modern courts, the jury is comprised of individuals who have no involvement in the case, and, in fact, often have no knowledge about the case or any special knowledge that may pertain to the case. Historically, however, this has not always been how the jury was constructed. In colonial times, jurors were often involved in the case in some way; they may have been family members or witnesses to the event. Even today, there is debate concerning whether juries comprised of individuals who know nothing of the case are the best individuals to make a decision regarding guilt. Some jurisdictions are even considering *professional juries*—comprised of individuals whose job it is to be the finders of fact during trials, much the same way the judge and the attorneys are professionals.

JURIES' UNDERSTANDING OF FORENSIC EVIDENCE There has been considerable research examining the ability of juries to understand forensic evidence that is presented to them. Almost all of this research has drawn the conclusion that not only do most jurors lack the scientific and technical background to understand the majority of forensic testimony, but the majority of judges and attorneys lack this expertise as well (it has only been very recently that courses in the understanding of scientific testimony have been offered in law schools). This has significant implications. If no one in the courtroom can understand the testimony of an expert, then the testimony may only confuse or mislead. In some instances, jurors may simply decide to ignore testimony that they do not fully comprehend. Most notably, this occurred during the criminal trail of O. J. Simpson regarding DNA evidence that was presented. Considering this, one of the most important jobs of the expert then becomes acting as a translator of the highly technical information that he or she possesses in relation to the case so that it may be useful during the trial process. This is especially true for experts in highly technical or newer areas of expertise, such as the DNA analysis in the Simpson case.

An added concern for many experts and attorneys is what may be called the *CSI effect*, discussed in detail in Chapter 1. Because forensics has become so popular and there are numerous television shows that deal with forensics on a weekly basis, the public often erroneously assumes that they are well informed regarding forensic science. In many cases, the public possesses information that—at best—is incomplete, and—at worst—completely false. There is a considerable difference between forensic science in the real world and forensic science in Hollywood!

BEING AN EXPERT WITNESS

Seventy years ago, expert witnesses were most likely to be medical doctors. Many different professionals now testify in court on a wide variety of topics. As long as a professional possesses knowledge that may be of use to the judge and jury, that person may be an expert witness.

Qualifications of an Expert

In many jurisdictions the Federal Rules of Evidence (FRE) guide expert qualifications. FRE 702 states:

> Expert witnesses may testify if they have scientific, technical, or specialized knowledge that will assist the trier of fact. The expert witness must be qualified by knowledge, skill, experience, training, or education. That expert's testimony must be based upon facts or data. It must be the result of reliable principles and methods. That expert must apply those reliable principles and methods to the facts of the case.

Although FRE 702 consists of only five sentences, it is a powerful guide to what sort of testimony can and cannot be heard and who may and may not testify in court. First, any expert who is called must "have scientific, technical, or specialized knowledge that will assist the trier of fact." Whereas 70 years ago, expert testimony was limited to medical doctors, FRE 702 acknowledges that "experts" may have scientific knowledge in a variety of disciplines (medicine, chemistry, biology, physics, psychology, etc.), but they may also have technical knowledge (like an auto mechanic or an engineer specializing in metal fatigue) or specialized knowledge (for example, an individual who installs pool filtration systems for many years would gain specialized knowledge about those systems).

Second, "[t]he expert witness must be qualified by knowledge, skill, experience, training, or education." Any of these four categories may qualify someone as an expert. Frequently in the courtroom, however, the opposing attorney will try to interpret this as knowledge *and* skill *and* experience *and* training *and* education.

All forensic experts are expected to have adequate experience in their specialization and to have obtained appropriate schooling. Many forensic experts are also expected to belong to professional organizations, attend and present at conferences, and—in some cases—publish in their field. Being published is especially important for establishing credibility in the courtroom. The expert must also be able to demonstrate that his or her knowledge is current, via professional trainings.

There is a wide variety of training and education that may qualify different experts. A police officer may be qualified by police academy training, working in the field, or having worked in a specialized area, such as homicide. A forensic anthropologist meanwhile may be qualified by having completed a Ph.D. in physical anthropology, and having worked in the area of forensic anthropology. A fingerprint examiner may be qualified by certification and by having completed an appropriate training program.

Third, the "expert's testimony must be based upon facts or data." Experts cannot testify regarding theories—although they may give opinions. Making theoretical statements, since they cannot be proven, are also used by opposing counsel to attack. Expert opinions must be based on facts tied directly to the evidence uncovered in the case. Their opinions must be based either upon the facts of the case, the physical evidence, or upon the results of tests that they have conducted on evidence. The tests performed must be deemed to be reliable and valid by the scientific community in which they are used and they must be relevant to the question at hand. It should be noted that good experts in the social and behavioral sciences avoid tests because they are rarely conclusive and can create reasonable doubt.

Fourth, the testimony "must be the result of reliable principles and methods." This is intended to rule out *junk science*, or methods that have not been widely tested or are not accepted in the field. There has been some debate as to whether this restriction also keeps new forms of legitimate science out of the courtroom, in addition to junk science. For example, in some jurisdictions, information obtained through the use of a lie detector is allowed as evidence, while in others, it is inadmissible.

Fifth, "expert[s] must apply those reliable principles and methods to the facts of the case." This must be done without prejudice and with complete objectivity regarding the facts both for and against their own points.

Presenting Yourself in Court

How you present yourself in court may make a considerable difference in whether the jury views you as trustworthy and credible, and whether the judge will view you in a positive or negative light. Because you will be seen even before you testify, your physical appearance is important. It may be a cliché to say that you only have one chance to make a first impression, but during your appearance in the courtroom, it is true and basically, all the jury will get is one impression of you. Courtrooms are professional and conservative places and your attire should reflect this. Judges, in particular, tend to be very conservative individuals. When you appear in court, business attire is appropriate; police officers should wear their uniforms; hair should be neat; and women should not wear excessive makeup or jewelry or provocative clothing.

Testifying

Even more important than how you *physically* present yourself, is how you *verbally* present yourself. While testifying in court, the vast majority of information you will convey to the jury will be spoken. However, you will have submitted a detailed and formal report of your findings. This report will serve as your platform from which you will provide your opinion. It is extremely important to make sure that your report is constructed for court to provide all data. The report will be entered as evidence as an exhibit. While testifying, it is important to try to stay within the confines of the report because the opposing attorney will attempt to get you to opine far away from the facts of the case to discredit you as an expert.

You should speak in a distinct voice, in a volume that is loud enough to be heard. Also, do not speak too quickly—which can be a natural tendency when an individual is nervous. If you do not speak well in public, of if you get nervous under pressure; it is a good idea to practice.

As an expert witness you will be required to "tell your story" multiple times, just like any other witness. During the trial process, you will be questioned multiple times. Prior to the start of the trial, both sides must submit to *discovery*. During discovery you will be required to give a deposition under oath, or, more frequently in criminal court, the report is submitted prior to the hearing or the trial and then the expert attends the hearing and presents his or her findings.

During trial, you will be questioned by the attorney who retained your services. This is referred to as direct examination. The purpose of direct examination is to allow the witness to fully present his or her findings in factual form—to tell his or her story. On direct examination, the attorney will ask questions for clarification. You will also be questioned by the opposing attorney, this is called cross examination.

Perhaps the most important thing any expert witness can do prior to testifying is to prepare. The trail will occur weeks—if not months—after you have completed your work on it. The information may no longer be fresh in your memory. Prior to testifying, it is essential that you review the case and go over your report and other notes.

You should also be prepared to testify regarding your own expertise in your area. Attorneys will often try to discredit experts on the opposing side. Do not take this personally—that's actually what they want you to do: they want you to get upset; become flustered and defensive and perhaps even overstate your qualifications or overstate or misrepresent the findings within your report. Under no circumstances should you *ever* argue with an attorney.

Another important part of testifying is knowing when to say "I don't know." As an expert, you are not expected to know everything. If you do not know the answer to a question, simply state that you do not know. Never guess or make up an answer. It is also appropriate to state that you would need to review the literature, or that what was asked is not in the area of your expertise. Never overstate your expertise, as this could come back to haunt you and once you are found out, you may damage your reputation and will also weaken your chances of being employed as an expert in future cases.

Presenting Exhibits in Court

Exhibits are physical demonstratives—in the courtroom these can range from foamboard charts to electronic slides to representative scale models. It is not necessary that every witness use exhibits in court. Exhibits are necessary when presenting complex information or when illustrating concepts that are best understood when presented visually. Exhibits should not be created for the mere sake of creating exhibits, but only for clarification of difficult-to-understand information. In the courtroom, an expert in tire impressions might present an exhibit showing photographs of tire impressions taken at the crime scene, alongside a photograph of the suspect's tire for comparison. This exhibit will allow the jury to clearly see whether or not the impressions match the tread of the tire. In the case of court-room exhibits, it is the task of the expert witness to ensure that the old saying: "a picture is worth a thousand words" proves to be true.

Ideally, exhibits should be used as an aid when testifying, not in place of well-spoken testimony. The expert should not simply show an exhibit, but rather use the exhibit to illustrate the findings or important points of testimony. Any exhibit should be clear and concise and avoid the use of jargon. The point of an exhibit is to clarify, not to dazzle the jury with the specialized knowledge that the expert has.

Glossary

Circuit courts—also known as the United States courts of appeal.

Dark figure of crime—the crimes that do not come to the attention of law enforcement.

Diversity jurisdiction—a court case in which the parties involved are citizens of different states.

Double jeopardy—being tried twice for the same crime.

Federal question—court cases that deal with constitutional matters or other federal laws.

Geographical jurisdiction—a court may hear cases that originate in a particular area.

In loco parentis—the juvenile court acting in place of the parents of a juvenile.

Jurisdiction—whether or not a court has the appropriate power to hear a case.

Nolo contendere—a plea that does not admit guilt but also does not contest the charges.

Preponderance of evidence—the lowest burden of proof in the court system, generally considered to be 51 percent.

Sovereign nation—the power of a Native American tribal nation to have jurisdiction over everything within its territory.

State's rights—each U.S. state possesses certain rights and powers in relation to the federal government and guaranteed to them by the Tenth Amendment to the Constitution.

Subject matter jurisidiction—whether or not a court hears a particular type of case (for example, tax court hears only tax cases).

Supplemental jurisdiction—the ability of a federal court to hear a case that is normally a state matter.

Voir dire—the process of selecting the jury.

Webliography

The web site for the federal judiciary
   www.uscourts.gov
The web site for the U.S. Supreme Court
   www.supremecourtus.gov

Tribal court clearinghouse web site
   www.tribal-institute.org

References

A History of Pennsylvania's Courts (1999). Accessed on June 28, 2006, from http://www.courts.state.pa.us/index/ujs/courthistory.asp

Cornell Law School. *Federal Rules of Evidence.* Accessed on August 28, 2006, from http://www.law.cornell.edu/rules/fre/

U.S. Courts. U.S. Court of Appeals-Judicial Caseload Profile. Accessed on June 1, 2007, from http://www.uscourts.gov/cgi-bin/cmsa2006.pl

U.S. Courts. *2006 Judicial Business of the United States Courts.* Accessed on June 1, 2007, from http://www.uscourts.gov/judbus2006/completejudicialbusiness.pdf

Review Questions

1. What is the only court created by the Constitution?
2. What sorts of cases fall under the jurisdiction of the federal court system?
3. Is most of the work of the courts done at the state or the federal level?
4. What is therapeutic jurisprudence?
5. Where and when was the first drug court formed?
6. How does the burden of proof differ in criminal and civil court?
7. If an individual is tried in criminal and civil court for the same activity, why doesn't that violate the protection against double jeopardy?
8. How did England influence the court system in the colonies?
9. What sort of power does a prosecutor hold in the criminal process?
10. Who can be an expert witness?

Some Things to Think About

1. The text mentions that requiring testimony "be the result of reliable principles and methods" can serve to keep out reliable science as well as junk science. Explain why.
2. Discuss some of the positives and negatives that have become apparent since the inception of drug courts.
3. If science relies upon theory to guide its research, why is it bad to base expert opinions that are shared in a courtroom on theory?

CHAPTER 14

An International Perspective and a Look Toward the Future

In the first 13 chapters of this text, we have explored the history and current status of forensic science in the United States. The purpose of this final chapter is to take a broader look at the field of forensic science. First we will examine the state of forensics around the world. Some countries—those in Europe, Australia, and Canada are almost indistinguishable from the United States in the types of forensic services that are offered. Other countries—developing nations and poor nations—lag behind in the forensic and police services that can be offered. Second, we will take a look into a crystal ball and see what we can predict for the future of forensics. While it is easy to predict that there will be continued significant advances in DNA and computers, as there have been during the past 20 years, it is not so easy to determine what the next major breakthrough in forensics will bring us. Science has the ability to surprise us and every day researchers in forensics are working to change the field dramatically. Finally, we will wrap up this chapter and this book with a discussion of some of the pressing ethical issues we are facing in forensics.

FORENSICS AROUND THE WORLD

Our studies in both criminal justice and forensics in the United States tends to be almost exclusively U.S.-centered. We study our own history, laws, methods, advances, and theories. Since the vast majority of criminal justice and forensic students will work within the United States, this seems to be a legitimate focus. However, it may not be the approach that benefits us the most.

As one of the leading nations in both technology and wealth, many practitioners feel that our focus should not be solely on ourselves but on the world in general. Our technology and talents can be used to benefit the greater good. While we are developing mitochondrial DNA technology to a more sophisticated degree, many nations lack even fair policing or basic technology. Some scientists believe that we have a duty to help other nations, especially developing nations. We also benefit from the wider perspective. By using DNA technology to solve different problems we learn to stretch the boundaries of the discipline. We will ask questions that might not be asked otherwise.

Forensics in the European Union

The state of the forensic sciences in the European Union (EU) is very much like forensic sciences in the United States. In many EU countries, the technology that is utilized is similar, and the training of scientists and investigators is similar.

European unification has helped investigations because of increased cooperation among member nations. Formerly, it was difficult for law enforcement to pursue a perpetrator once he or she crossed a border. Now member nations can better work together to respond to serious offenses. Of course, information is not always readily shared across borders even when a crime is very serious. This problem, known as *linkage blindness,* is frequently seen in the United States when various jurisdictions at the local, state, and federal levels do not share information. Of course, this openness has a downside: open borders have allowed criminals to more easily pass from nation to nation without being stopped at border crossings. In some respects, the cooperation among European nations can be likened to the cooperation among states within the United States.

While the EU is joined economically, and there is a constitution for the member states, there is not one set of laws that govern all of the member nations. Each country has developed its own set of laws and legislation and there is considerable variance in the legal framework among these nations. It is unlikely that the member nations of the EU would consent to one common set of laws or one common legal system.

Just as the EU member nations have worked hard to create one economic community, law enforcement within the EU is also working to establish one set of standards for forensic work. Information technology specialists have created standardized procedures for computer investigations which allow investigators to follow a step-by-step procedure in the gathering, preserving, and submitting evidence.

Yet there is still quite a long way to go. Forensic psychiatrists have not yet been successful at standardizing forensic assessment of mentally disordered offenders, and forensic psychiatry training

The European Union

Not long ago, all of the countries in the EU were separated by borders that required passport checks to cross. Unification very rapidly changed that. The Treaty on European Union went into force on November 1, 1993. This was the formal beginning of the EU. Although many of the European nations had worked closely together since the end of World War II, the treaty joined them in many ways. While the individual countries still retain their own national identities, economically they are all joined to create a more powerful economic presence than any of the individual nations could create. Monetarily, there is one currency, the Euro—except for the United Kingdom, which has retained the British pound.

In the Treaty of the European Union, which became effective on November 1, 1993, EU member nations sought to develop cooperation in criminal justice affairs. In 2004, the EU adopted a constitution. The constitution outlines the process for criminal proceedings and substantive criminal law, among other issues.

The European Law Enforcement Organization (Europol), an EU police force, has been established. Europol has the goal of facilitating cooperation among member nations regarding law enforcement issues. Europol addresses issues of terrorism, drug trafficking, international organized crime, forgery, and pornography, among other crimes that affect member nations and cross national borders.

The EU currently consists of 27 member states (Figure 14.1): Austria, Belgium, Bulgaria, Cyprus, Czech Republic, Denmark, Estonia, Finland, France, Germany, Greece, Hungary, Ireland, Italy, Latvia, Lithuania, Luxembourg, Malta, Netherlands, Poland, Portugal, Romania, Slovakia, Slovenia, Spain, Sweden, and the United Kingdom.

The European Union ("EU") – 2008

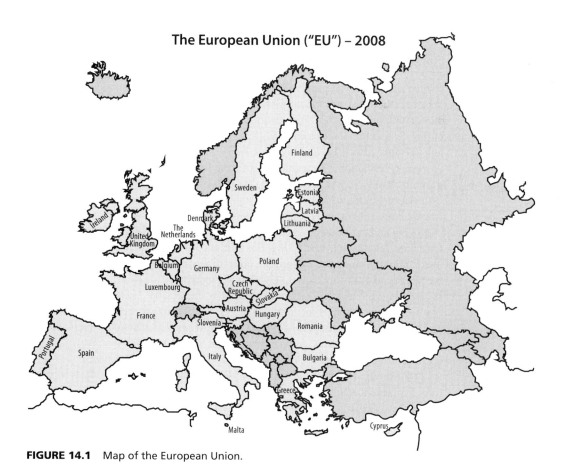

FIGURE 14.1 Map of the European Union.

standards vary considerably. Seamless integration of forensic psychiatry among member nations is unlikely. However, it is possible that forensic psychiatric education can become more standardized across the EU (Dressing and Salize 2006).

Many nations in the EU have forensic DNA databases (Asplen and Lane 2004). The United Kingdom's database was created first and is the most extensive. Just like in the United States, EU nations have concerns with maintaining DNA databases. There are privacy issues and fears that data will be misused. Some countries advocate that DNA should be taken from all offenders because serious offenders frequently commit less-serious offences prior to serious offences. Other nations wish to limit the database only to the most serious offenders. Any nation that maintains a DNA database seems to struggle with the same ethical issues.

The EU has worked together to assist other nations with forensics issues. After the war in Kosovo, teams of experts from Finland were sent to investigate allegations of mass graves and crimes against humanity on behalf of the EU. Skeletal remains were examined in locations including Racak, Klecka, Volujak, Glodjane, Gornje Obrinje, Orahovac, and Golubovac. The investigators brought together the fields of forensic pathology, forensic odontology, and forensic anthropology and utilized X-rays, photographs, videotape, and DNA to perform analyses. In some areas, the investigative teams ran into security issues and were prevented from gaining access. In Racak, the cause of death was determined to be gunshot wounds, which resulted in filings of charges of crimes against humanity against five Yugoslavian officials (Rainio et al. 2001).

One major difference between how forensics is handled in the United States and in the EU is the centralization of forensic services in European nations. In the United States, each state establishes its own system of forensic laboratories. This has led to a wide array of approaches to handling forensic laboratory work. Centralization generally ensures consistency of services. While the FBI does operate a forensic laboratory, there is no federal coordination of forensic laboratories. In the EU, each country has a federally coordinated system, allowing for an even distribution of resources. Poor and rural areas are not neglected, but can have the same forensic resources at their disposal as affluent metropolitan locations. Some have called for a coordination of laboratory services among all EU member nations. All forensic science laboratories across the EU need to be technologically competent and scientifically up-to-date, however, laboratory services vary widely from country to country across the EU, this is especially true as poorer and former Eastern Bloc nations have been admitted to the EU. Through cooperation among all of the member nations, criminals who cross borders within the EU can be better apprehended. This is not just the duty of on-site investigators, but forensic laboratories should also be more involved in the process. While national accreditation is a good first step, international laboratory standards and international accreditation of laboratories would assure an even standard of service across countries. Unfortunately, at this time, a significant percentage of EU forensic laboratories are not accredited. Even worse, about half have no quality assurance system in place (Malkoc and Neuteboom 2007).

England has a coroner system much like the one that is still in use in certain jurisdictions in the United States and death investigation is controlled by the state. On the continent of Europe, death investigations are not under governmental control and usually conducted by individuals employed at local universities. This has the benefit of separating death investigation and criminal prosecution. As more and more nations join the EU, they must conform to certain standards. For example, in preparation for joining the EU, Turkey has worked to change its autopsy procedures to make them more in line with autopsy procedures in other EU nations (Celbis et al. 2006).

A variety of forensic associations operate both within different European nations and across their borders. The International Society for Forensic Genetics consists not only of working groups from a variety of European countries but China and Japan as well. This society deals in the sharing of knowledge regarding genetic markers (www.isfg.org/). The European Network of Forensic Science Institutes formed to share knowledge among forensic science laboratories across Europe (www.enfsi.eu/).

In Europe, many countries offer forensic science education. Sir Alec Jeffreys, the inventor of genetic fingerprinting is at the University of Leicester at The Institute of Genetics. The University of Zurich houses an *Institut für Rechtsmedizin* (Institute of Forensic Medicine). Germany, where many pharmaceutical companies are based, is a significant producer of forensic equipment, including a wide variety of microscopes and other standard laboratory equipment.

Forensics in Former Eastern Bloc Nations

Prior to the fall of communism at the end of the 1980s, both policing and forensics faced challenges in Eastern bloc nations (Figure 14.2). Both areas were too politicized, underfunded, and understaffed. When the communist governments collapsed, former communist nations reached out to western nations for assistance in many ways. Western nations have responded by helping to modernize both policing and laboratories. Many of the nations that border Western Europe have had some success in modernization. Yet, they have struggled with modernizing their technology, which is often 40 or 50 years behind, and with attracting and retaining properly trained personnel because of lack of funding. Many Eastern European universities have established exchange programs with universities in the United States; this joint effort has benefits on both sides.

In closed cultures there are many problems facing law enforcement investigations. The cornerstone of all effective law enforcement investigations is cooperation between police agencies, the public, and the media. The strict control of information generally functions to work against investigations. In closed cultures, emphasis is placed on controlling information. Controlling information helps to control public perceptions and awareness of international events. Controlling information is often associated with public control and political self-protection. Closed cultures are sadly often more

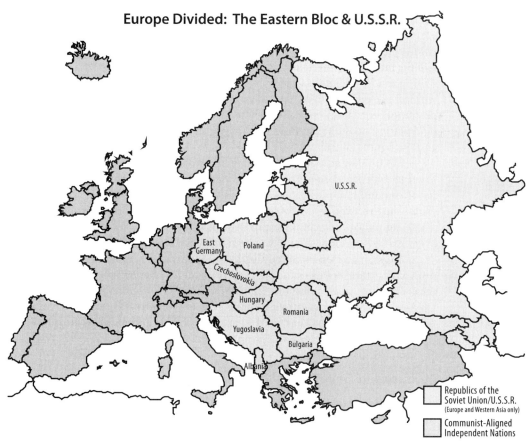

FIGURE 14.2   Map of the Eastern Bloc.

concerned with the public reputations of political officials rather than the pursuit of justice. In many cases, arrests made by police generally served the Communist political agenda and were not the result of police investigative work. In closed societies, policing serves mainly to bolster the status and political power of the high-ranking Communist party members and less to solve crimes that pose a threat to society. In closed societies, the sharing of criminal intelligence between borders is not a priority but rather is a last resort.

Prior to the end of communism, police organizations were strictly controlled by the state. A serial killer operated in Russia for many years with great ease because police were prohibited from warning the public in any way because the presence of a serial killer would have tarnished the nation's reputation. This form of information blackout is the perfect breeding ground for repetitive criminal behavior because the public cannot become the eyes and ears of law enforcement because they are not even aware that these crimes are being committed.

Closed cultures are rife with suspicion within law enforcement agencies stemming from the fact that the officials are not elected by the public, but rather appointed by other autocrats. Social control becomes more of a priority than public safety, and the protection of one's position is often more important than focusing upon public crime.

Canada

Canada has both a provincial and a federal system of forensic laboratories. There are very few formal forensic science programs in Canada, most are based in Ontario and almost all are undergraduate programs. Most Canadian forensic scientists with advanced degrees were educated in the United States. The educational system in the United States, because it is not under governmental control, has been quicker to respond to the market's demand for forensic education.

The Michigan–Ontario Identification Association is a joint effort of Canadian and U.S. law enforcement, involving mostly Michigan state police, Detroit local police, Ontario provincial police, and the metro Toronto police.

Canada, like the United States, has become aware of the problem of wrongful convictions within their justice system. Like our system in the United States, the Canadian justice system has a presumption of innocence and they use the more stringent standard of proof *beyond a reasonable doubt* just as we do. They afford the accused the same protections as we do; the right to an attorney, and the right to remain silent.

In Ontario, an effort has been made to lessen the rate of wrongful convictions regarding forensic evidence. Forensic opinions should always be in the form of a written report. The possibility of contamination of forensic evidence should be documented. An advisory board should be established to oversee evidence handling. Also, a quality assurance unit should be established. There should be a mechanism put into place for complaints regarding the Centre for Forensic Sciences. Staff training should be a high priority (Manishen 2006).

A Canadian Department of Justice study specifically examined the problem of miscarriages of justice. The study points out some of the difficulties of eyewitness identification and testimony, and the problems of false confessions. It makes recommendations regarding procedure for the handling of DNA evidence, and protocol for forensic evidence and expert testimony. It also recommends education for police, attorneys, and forensic scientists to help address all of the problems within the system (http://canada.justice.gc.ca/en/dept/pub/hop/).

Forensics in Developing Nations

Developing nations struggle in many ways to catch up to the standards of the developed nations. Many countries in Asia and Southeast Asia face challenges with health care, education, and providing shelter. When the basic needs of large portions of the population are not being met, it is difficult to develop advanced scientific techniques.

Mainland China has established a system of regional forensic laboratories in its provinces. These laboratories are equipped comparably to U.S. laboratories, yet because of the closed nature of China, scientists work to back up the findings of the government and not to question them. Forensic psychiatry in China has a long history of being an agent of political and social control.

Forensic science services in Hong Kong are comparable to any services offered in the United States. The government of the Hong Kong Special Administrative Region (The United Kingdom ceded control of Hong Kong to China in 1997) operates a federal system.

In Japan, forensics is under the direction of the National Research Institute of Police Science. There are four forensic science divisions: biology, physics (including fire, explosives, and mechanical), chemistry, and information science (www.nrips.go.jp/index-e.html). The Japanese Association of Forensic Science and Technology publishes the *Japanese Journal of Forensic Science and Technology*, which presents cutting-edge research across the spectrum of forensic science disciplines. The association also hosts an annual meeting that provides scientists with the opportunity to interact and give private-sector forensic businesses the opportunity to showcase their products (www.houkagaku.org/society_e.html).

Southeast Asia

One of the most recent forensic challenges happened on December 26, 2004, when a tsunami occurred in the Indian Ocean (Figure 14.3). Approximately 230,000 people died or remain missing from one of the deadliest modern disasters (Figure 14.4). The earthquake measured 9.3 on the Richter scale and the resulting tsunami devastated the coast of Sri Lanka, Thailand, and India. The number of DNA tests performed was staggering, far in excess of the over 100,000 performed after the World Trade Center disaster.

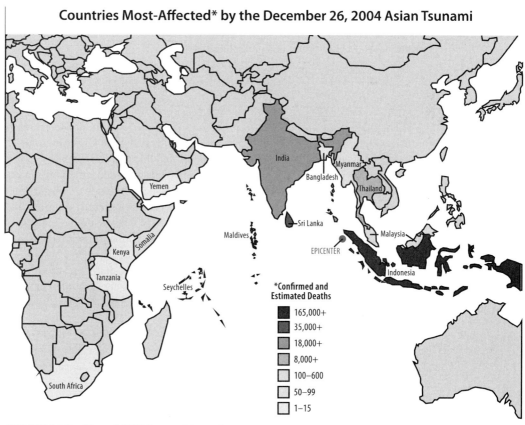

FIGURE 14.3 Map of 2004 tsunami impact.

Countries Most-Affected* by the December 26, 2004 Asian Tsunami

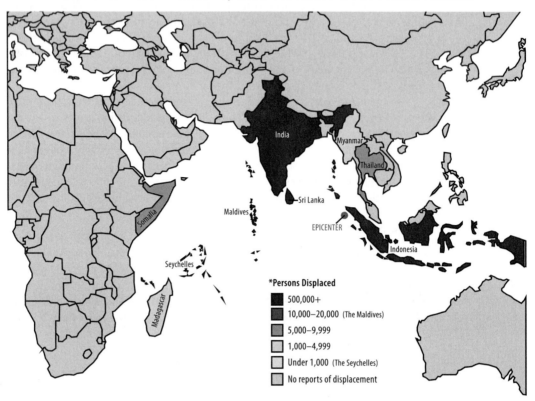

FIGURE 14.4 Map of 2004 tsunami displaced persons.

The magnitude and the geographic location of the tsunami created numerous challenges for forensics. First, the wave hit predominantly poor areas, where structures and entire villages were easily washed away. Second, identification is attempted through DNA, dental records, and fingerprints. Many poor individuals had never had their fingerprints recorded, and many had never visited a dentist. DNA analysis is only possible when a close relative can provide a comparison sample. Third, the nations most adversely affected by the tsunami were ill-prepared to mount rescue and recovery operations. Time was lost in the initial response. However, many nations around the world responded quickly to the need. Even with most of the world working together, because many bodies were lost at sea, over 40,000 people remain missing.

In 2004, the state forensic laboratory in Andhra Pradesh, India, received ISO-17025 certification, which is the international benchmark for guaranteeing the quality of laboratories. This is in an effort to increase technical excellence in the laboratory (www.hindu.com/2004/10/04/stories/2004100411800500.htm).

In India, although medical evidence is generally accepted in the courtroom, especially medical evidence relating to autopsy, there is no agreement on what other types of scientific evidence should always be allowed into the courtroom. India does have rules of evidence, but they are not as specific as the FRE in the United States, the Frye standard, or the *Daubert* ruling. India is still trying to establish guidelines for what constitutes appropriate scientific testimony.

The National Academy of Science in Washington, D.C., has established a joint program in Lahore, Pakistan, that is training law enforcement and medical personnel in evidence collection, analysis, and presentation. The program also has undertaken the training of a limited number of forensic students. The students traveled to the United States for training (www7.nationalacademies.org/dsc/Strand_CAMB_2005.html). The National Police Bureau of Pakistan established its first forensic laboratory with DNA capabilities early in 2006.

Central America

Since 1993, over three-hundred women have been murdered in Juarez, Mexico, a factory town close to the U.S. border. There was much speculation that a serial killer was responsible, although, in 1999, the FBI, who had agreed to assist in solving the murders, concluded that most of the killings were single homicides. Since frequently several bodies would appear during a week, this is astounding.

In 2004, however, Special Prosecutor Maria Lopez Urbina stated that many of the killings were not, in fact, the work of a serial killer, but rather the boyfriends or husbands of the victims (Weissert 2004). One reason this did not come to light sooner was due to poor policing. The police repeatedly announced success in arresting the killer, only to have the killings begin again soon after each arrest (Nieves 2002). Not only was policing poor, but one suspect stated that he was tortured until he confessed (Weissert 2004). In August of 2006 an arrest was made in Denver for 10 of the killings.

In Juarez, Mexico, numerous factors have come together to allow men who want to kill the impunity to do so. The deaths of women are not taken seriously. Many of these victims are poor and came to Juarez to work at the U.S.-owned factories. In Mexican society in general, women are valued less than men. Domestic violence and rape are not considered to be serious crimes. Even if these crimes were given the attention that they deserve, the police have proven themselves to be largely incompetent. Evidence has been overlooked and homicides have been haphazardly lumped together to create a prolific serial killer. When the police needed to make an arrest to subdue public outrage, they resorted to torture.

In Colombia, thousands of individuals have disappeared over the past decade in a war waged by militias. Now, in a period of calm, people are beginning to come forward to tell authorities where bodies are buried. In some cases, individuals can only be identified through the use of forensic techniques. More than 400 bodies have been unearthed. Colombia does not have the capacity to store or good processes in place to identify such a large number of victims. During the summer of 2006, there were only eight people in the technical investigations unit who were exhuming remains, but more were being trained to help deal with the problem (Bajak 2006).

The Middle East

Forensic services are available in several Middle Eastern nations. In the United Arab Emirates, there are three laboratories, two are police forensic laboratories and one is a corporate laboratory. A significant portion of forensic services in Middle Eastern nations deals with analyzing toxicology evidence for blood alcohol content. In many of these nations, alcohol consumption is illegal.

In Jordan, the toxicology laboratory is housed at the University of Jordan. It provides services in forensic pathology and forensic toxicology. Domestic violence is a significant problem in Jordan, where very few women seek services for the abuse that happens to them. Jordan is tracked by Amnesty International for possible human rights violations.

Africa

The continent of Africa contains great wealth but also great poverty. In wealthier, urban areas, forensic services are available. In poorer, rural areas, forensic services may be nonexistent. Africa tends to be concerned with providing rudimentary health care to much of its population, as opposed to utilizing forensics to solve crimes. It is even difficult to make statements regarding cause of death in sub-Saharan Africa due to poor record keeping. Often, cause of death is not even recorded (Garenne et al. 2000).

A recent study found that medical services to rape victims were very uneven. Many health care providers do not feel that rape victims are in need of medical care. Doctors were sometimes reluctant to provide services. Even when doctors were willing to provide medical services, only about one-third were trained to do so, and very few providers would refer a woman who has been raped for psychological counseling. Very few providers would send a victim's clothing for forensic analysis, thereby losing an opportunity to obtain good evidence. Many hospitals lacked a protocol for the collection of rape evidence, very few had rape kits. Some medical providers even made statements indicating that some rapes were the fault of the woman and some women might make false accusations (Christofides et al. 2005).

FORENSIC SCIENCE AND HUMAN RIGHTS INVESTIGATIONS

The twentieth century may become known as the century of genocide. Forensics has many applications in the prosecution of war criminals and in the investigation of possible genocide: DNA analysis can be conducted to identify victims; ballistics can help reconstruct shootings. Forensic experts have gathered forensic evidence in Kosovo, East Timor, and other nations where mass killings have occurred.

The International Forensic Centre of Excellence for the Investigation of Genocide investigates crimes against humanity, war crimes, and genocide. They utilize expertise in the areas of forensic archaeology, anthropology, pathology, and crime scene investigation (www.inforce.org.uk/about_us.htm).

INTERNATIONAL FORENSIC ORGANIZATIONS

Professional organizations provide an opportunity for individuals in various fields to exchange information. Most organizations host conferences where their members and others can meet to share information regarding developments in their respective fields. These occasions also provide an opportunity for members of a single field to get together and share information and ideas on both a formal and informal level. Professional organizations can provide educational opportunities for members. Some organizations also publish a newsletter or journal for the dissemination of research. Many organizations now also have web sites.

The International Association of Forensic Toxicologists (TIAFT) was founded more than 40 years ago to facilitate communication among toxicologists in many fields and toxicology research. TIAFT also sponsors a yearly conference that has been held all over the world (eastern and western Europe, Asia, Australia, and the United States) (www.tiaft.org/).

The International Association for Craniofacial Identification (IACI) developed out of the International Association of Forensic Sciences in 1987. Scientists in the IACI work in forensic odontology and anthropology, computer-based skull reconstruction, facial aging, facial mapping, and composite sketching (www.forensicartist.com/IACI/index.html). Closely related is the International Association for Identification (IAI), which was formed in California in 1915. Although it has the word *international* in its title, most of its members reside in the United States or Canada. The IAI offers six certification programs, publishes the *Journal of Forensic Identification,* and hosts educational conferences.

The International Association of Forensic Mental Health Services—a relatively new society—focuses on four separate areas: clinical forensic psychiatry and psychology; administrative and legal issues; research in forensic mental health, violence, and abuse; and training and education (www.iafmhs.org/iafmhs.asp?pg=about).

INTERFACE WITH INTERNATIONAL LAW

It is not uncommon to face jurisdictional issues within the United States when crossing state borders; this problem is magnified many times when dealing with international law and the laws of many countries. There are a variety of difficulties in prosecuting across borders. One difficulty in prosecuting crimes internationally is that nations have not agreed on definitions of what constitutes a crime. What is a terrorist? What is genocide? Nations with different ethnic groups, religious groups, and customs have clashing cultures that ultimately shape the laws which define criminal behavior. Different cultures view the world in very different ways.

Further complicating international cooperation is the view of various countries on the death penalty. Some nations will not cooperate or extradite suspects to nations in which capital punishment is practiced (the United States and India are the only democratic nations that still practice capital punishment).

FORENSICS AND THE FUTURE

It really is impossible to predict with any accuracy what the future holds for forensics. In science two types of advances are made: those that are predictable and those that are completely unpredictable. We can easily predict that DNA technology will continue to advance and be applied to the field of forensics. We cannot predict where the next breakthrough will occur. Science can be very surprising. We do know that the various fields will continue to advance at an extremely rapid rate. This rapid rate of advancement will necessitate frequent textbook revisions. It also means that when an individual completes a degree in forensics (or medicine, or computers, or many other disciplines), his or her knowledge is already out-of-date only a few years after graduation. This rapid rate of advancement creates a burden on you to constantly update your education. After graduation, you should attend workshops and conferences on a yearly basis. It is up to you to keep your training current—although it will also be required in many fields for you to do so.

Forensics is not a panacea—it will *not* solve all the problems in the criminal justice system, and, in fact, it may create new problems. Forensics does not currently, nor will it ever, make up for poor investigative technique. Forensic scientists are always searching for new types of physical evidence to examine. However, we must have realistic expectations for the future. We also need to keep in mind that as the technology to solve crimes advances, so does the technology to commit crimes.

Computer-Based Technologies and the Future

If you are an undergraduate now, you grew up in a world filled with computers. It is likely that your home always had a computer. You have been using computers since grade school, if not kindergarten. Now you may use a computer on a daily basis, to check e-mail, text your friends, download music and games, and interact in virtual worlds. It does not require a significant amount of foresight to predict that computers will continue to advance, and that those advances will continue to impact our lives. These advances will also allow analysis of data in ways that are currently unimaginable. Thirty years ago computers had no forensic applications. Thirty years from now, we may have seamless interface from crime scene to laboratory to courtroom.

Currently, artificial intelligence software is used to anticipate and identify criminal behavioral patterns. This uses statistical (actuarial) studies of known and captured criminals sorted by offender typologies. This application of artificial intelligence will continue to be utilized in criminal investigations.

Crime scene photography has been influenced by the development of digital photography. The crime scene photographer can assess the quality of photographs immediately after they are taken, so fewer photographs are missed. Advances in facial recognition software have made it easier to create drawings of suspects from descriptions provided by witnesses.

It is becoming increasingly common to see crime scene personnel with a variety of handheld computer devices at the scene that are utilized in logging and tracking evidence. Software assists expert witnesses to create drawings of rooms and buildings. During the trial process, a jury can be shown these drawings of the crime scene in three dimensions and be *walked through* the crime scene in a replication of how the lead investigator first approached the scene.

As computing power increases, so will the ability to create and use databases, such as the fingerprint and DNA databases maintained by the FBI. Greater computing power allows for more information to be stored. It also allows for easier retrieval and processing.

Scent Evidence

One area that researchers are looking into is scent evidence—the use of scent for identification. Rescue dogs have been used to track individuals by scent for many years. Cadaver dogs (as mentioned in Chapter 9) are specially trained to find human cadavers, even under many feet of water. The Drug Enforcement Administration (DEA) trains canines to detect a variety of drugs by scent; dogs are also trained to detect residue from chemical components of explosives, large amounts of currency, and other contraband (such as agricultural products). However, a newer application of canines' highly developed sense of smell is the identification of an offender's scent at the scene of a crime.

Tomaszewski and Girdwoyn (2006) reviewed the acceptance of scent identification in the United States, and in Western and Eastern Europe. In the United States, there has been some acceptance of scent identification, but it is by no means widely accepted. In Germany, there is more acceptance of scent identification than in the United States, but there is still some caution regarding this type of evidence whereas scent evidence is commonly accepted in the Netherlands and in Poland.

In their article, the authors suggest that scent identification methods need to be standardized—like all other forensic applications—and scent dogs need to be tested for accuracy in much the same way that a machine might be calibrated. The question remains whether human scent is undeniably an individual characteristic.

Global Positioning System Tracking of Criminals

In many respects, global positioning tracking systems have a promising future in the high-tech fight against crime. On an individual-offender level they have been and are being used as 24/7 electronic bracelet monitors in cases of low-level offenses that were plea bargained into a period of probation and/or home confinement. These systems essentially utilize global satellites that serve as a means to bounce electronic signals from a security monitoring station on the ground that can set physical parameters, or a zone within which the wearer of the bracelet can physically travel. If the offender travels outside of the preestablished zone, the monitoring station is electronically alerted to the violation and the police can be dispatched to apprehend the offender, who can lose his or her conditional release and be placed in jail. For such instances as attorney consultations, doctors' appointments, etc., the offender can, in advance, specifically request new parameters in which he or she can travel, and the system will permit these movements without a violation. The cost associated with the bracelets is minimal and often paid for by the offender on a monthly basis. The system is privately operated by a company that leases the equipment and service to the respective board of probation/parole and also provides monitoring services and daily reports about the offenders' movements. This method of plea bargaining is often used in low-level offenses that meet sentencing guidelines for probation consideration in lieu of confinement time. It is a cost-effective method of exercising justice by enabling the judicial system to provide oversight to an offender at considerably less expense when compared to the high tax-payer costs associated with jail time. It also allows an offender to demonstrate to the justice system that he or she is amenable to treatment and supervision and does not need to be locked up in prison.

The global positioning system (GPS) is being considered for skin implantation in sexually violent predators with a higher than average probability for re-offending. It will use the same principle of operation as the global positioning tracking system; however, the GPS will be implanted under the offender's skin along with all of the data relative to the offender, including offense history and other information. It could only be removed surgically. It is quite possible that skin implantation of

GPS may also be used with other offender groups who have been determined to be an ongoing threat to the community at large. This method of offender tracking would in effect be global. As a result no offender could possibly avoid law enforcement detection and monitoring. Also under consideration is voluntary GPS insertions for children (to assist in locating children if they are lost or abducted by an offender).

Satellite Photography

Law enforcement now uses satellites for many applications and also for photographs of crime scenes. These satellite photos can be requested from various vendors and government agencies. They can provide images of the approximate time and place of the crime scene that can be digitally enhanced to focus upon the specifics of the scene. Although not frequently used at present—but seen in television shows like *24*—it is anticipated that satellite photo use will increase over time. It is startling how accurate and how close-up video surveillance can be from a satellite thousands of miles away.

Satellite photos are being used by the military to identify the locations and movements of identified war targets with great success. *Spy planes* have also been used in drug wars to identify and locate drug traffic, shipments, and sales distributions. In addition, photographs taken from the vantage point of space can be used in large crime scenes for identifying suspicious traffic in and out of the area prior to and immediately after the criminal act has occurred. Another advantage to satellite photography is that photographs can be time-sequenced just like all other photo or video surveillance.

Cameras in Cities

Photo surveillance in cities has gained favor over the last few years The use of cameras in cities has proved to be both an effective means of deterring crime and an effective means of solving crime. Large cities have installed video cameras on buildings, utility poles, police cars, public transportation, and within businesses. Home security companies have completed independent research that has validated their findings that homes with security systems clearly show a significantly lower rate of home invasion when compared to homes without a system. When those homes are equipped with cameras the rate of home invasion drops even further. Cities that use wide-area public video surveillance have reported a significant drop in general crime rates. Banks, although equipped with videos, still are robbed, however it has been documented that banks with sophisticated surveillance equipment have a lower rate of robbery than do banks with older equipment. ATM machines are also now equipped with video cameras to digitally record all customers as they withdraw money, which has cased rates of ATM theft to go down. Profit-oriented criminals want to commit crimes with as little risk as possible and the biggest payoff possible. For many would-be criminals, just knowing that they are being watched is enough to deter them from committing a crime. Criminal behavior specialists have shown that in general criminals do not want to be caught and are more prone to avoid criminal behavior when they realize that they are being watched. There are of course always exceptions to the rule as in cases of mentally ill criminals, sexual offenders who are compulsively addicted to sexual crime, drug addicts who must feed their addiction at all costs, and other impulsive crimes.

Voice and Face Recognition Systems

Voice and face recognition technologies are currently gaining favor with law enforcement, especially since the terrorist attacks of September 11, 2001. Facial recognition systems are now in use at some airports. This technology takes pictures of customers and cross compares them against databases of watch lists or known convicted felons. Although the original intent of face recognition technology was to add security to airports for identifying terrorists, law enforcement now uses the technology for the identification of other convicted felons who have outstanding arrest warrants. The systems are efficient, cost effective, and provide results on the spot.

Voice recognition systems use a PC-based software program that digitally identifies individuals' voices. The software compares the voice sample in question to known voice samples. This technology can be used on access systems which use voice print recognition for gaining access to a building or an account. Also in use are eye, facial, and fingerprint scanning for the same purposes. Again the intent is to ensure proper identity to avoid identity theft, which is the fastest growing crime of all crime types.

Infrared Surveillance for Wireless Communications

Infrared and laser surveillance systems have been developed. These systems use infrared beams that bounce off a long-distance target. A conversation can be listened to by bouncing back sound waves from a target and then translating them into voice prints. A beam can be bounced off of a window that will pick up the sound vibrations from the occupants inside. The beam then bounces back to the transmitter for analysis and voice printing. This application can be used by police in order to hear conversations from a long distance without physically requiring anyone to be present at the scene of the conversation. It should be noted that this sort of eavesdropping does require a warrant for the information obtained to be admissible in a court.

Night-Vision Surveillance Systems

Night-vision technology was invented specifically to assist police and military to visualize targets in little to no light in both wartime and conventional police applications. The equipment can be fitted to small vision devices such as field glasses as well as to planes and helicopters. The night vision results can then be used to track and physically assault the target or the target can be videotaped for counter-intelligence purposes. This essentially allows lethal weapon destruction to occur 24/7 without regard to the environmental conditions for conventional sight recognition.

Chemical Enhancements for Interrogation Purposes

Chemical enhancements for interrogation purposes are also known as pharmacological enhancements/agents. In 1930s, it was realized that if a suspect was given various drugs that affect his or her ability to engage free will (for example, Sodium pentathol), he or she could be interviewed with maximum levels of cooperation. While these chemicals cannot be used by traditional police, they are frequently relied upon in nonconventional counter-intelligence applications.

ETHICAL CONSIDERATIONS

Forensics, like any science, has inherent ethical questions. Law enforcement, as a means of social control, also always brings up ethical considerations. When we bring science and law enforcement together, many ethical dilemmas are created. We will discuss two key ethical issues: privacy and being a hired gun.

Privacy

Privacy concerns abound in forensics, especially in the areas of DNA, surveillance technology, and electronic data. Since it became possible to work with DNA, questions were asked regarding how far the scientific community should go with DNA technology and what we should do with that technology. Now that many jurisdictions are requiring that DNA be taken from felony offenders, there is concern that this information could be misused. There are concerns that "familial DNA searching" will lead to further racial disparities in the criminal justice system.

In the fight against terrorists, how much freedom should we give up? Some have suggested that random searches should be conducted on private citizens' electronic data and computer usage to screen for possible terrorist or pornography use.

On the other hand, there are privacy issues that need to be considered. This leads to many social questions regarding the surveillance cameras and the right to privacy in the common public areas of our society, and many debates have resulted. However, it does not appear that anyone can raise a convincing argument that if a device is available to increase their safety that they would not use it. Of course this is all predicated upon the belief that the authorities will use surveillance for its intended purpose and not for the invasion of privacy and when a crime is not being committed.

The Battle of the Experts

There has been concern that as the courts allow more and more specialized testimony from experts that the court process will become a *battle of the experts*, during which the jury will determine guilt based more on the ability or personality of the expert, rather than on the facts of the case (although good attorneys will not allow this to happen). Many judges are very resistant to some experts coming into their courtrooms.

A serious ethical consideration is the danger of being a *hired gun*, or an expert who will skew his or her testimony to fit the theory of whoever is paying for the testimony. While it is legitimate for experts to be hired by and paid for by either the defense or the prosecution, it is not legitimate for the expert to ignore facts or present facts in a misleading light. Not only does functioning as a hired gun damage the justice system, but it serves to damage the reputation of the expert as well. Judges are very sensitive to the possibility of an expert being a hired gun and will often ask the expert leading questions in an attempt to solicit the expert into advocating for the party who is paying for his or her services even when it is obvious that the defendant has liabilities that need to be mentioned.

The expert should advocate neither for the prosecution nor the defense. Even though the expert has been hired by one side in a criminal case, under no circumstances should the expert tailor testimony to support that attorney's case. The expert should only testify as to what the evidence has revealed. If those revelations are damaging to the attorney's case, then the attorney has the option of whether or not to call the expert as a witness.

Glossary

Eastern Bloc—nations in Europe that were formerly communist.

European Union—a group of nations in Europe joined economically and by a constitution.

Genocide—the mass killing of a group of people.

Scent identification—identification by means of scent.

Sub-Saharan Africa—the portion of the continent of Africa that is south of the Sahara desert.

Webliography

American Civil Liberties Union
www.aclu.org

Explore satellite photographs of the world
www.google.earth

References

Asplen, C., and S. Lane. "International Perspectives on Forensic DNA Databases." *Forensic Science International* 146 (Suppl) (2004): 119–21.

Bajak, F. *More of Colombia's 'Disappeared' Found.* Accessed on August 1, 2006, from www.forbes.com/feeds/ap/2006/08/01/ap2919389.html

Celbis, O., N. Aydin, and A. Kok. "Amended Forensic Autopsy Legal Procedures in Turkey During Integration with the European Union." *The American Journal of Forensic Medicine and Pathology* 27, no.4 (2006): 345–46.

Christofides, N., R. Jewkes, N. Webster, and L. Penn-Kekana. "Other Patients Are Really in Need of Medical

Attention—The Quality of Health Services for Rape Survivors in South Africa." *Bulletin of the World Health Organization* 83, no.7 (2005): 495–502.

Department of Justice Canada. 2006. *Report on the Prevention of Miscarriages of Justice.* Accessed on May 12, 2007, from http://canada.justice.gc.ca/en/dept/pub/hop/

Dressing, H., and H. Salize. "Forensic Psychiatric Assessment in European Union Member States". *Acta Psychiatrica Scandinavica.* 114, no. 4 (2006): 282–89.

European Network of Forensic Science Institutes. www.enfsi.org/

Garenne, M., K. Kahn, S. Tollman, and J. Gear. "News from the Regions. Causes of Death in a Rural Area of South Africa: An International Perspective". *Journal of Tropical Pediatrics.* 43, no. 3 (2000): 183–90.

International Association for Craniofacial Identification. www.forensicartist.com/IACI/index.html.

International Association of Forensic Mental Health Services. Accessed on August 28, 2006, from www.iafmhs.org/iafmhs.asp?pg=about.

International Association of Forensic Toxicologists. Accessed on June 26, 2006, from www.tiaft.org/.

International Forensic Centre of Excellence for the Investigation of Genocide. www.inforce.org.uk/about_us.htm.

International Society for Forensic Genetics. www.isfg.org/.

Japanese Association of Forensic Science and Technology. www.houkagaku.org/society_e.html.

Malkoc, E., and Neuteboom, W. "The Current Status of Forensic Science Laboratory Accreditation in Europe, pp. 121–126, July 31, 2006," in "Selected Articles of the 4th European Academy of Forensic Science Conference (EAFS2006) June 13–16, 2006 Helsinki, Finland," ed. Pierre Margot. *Forensic Science International* 167, no. 2 (April 11, 2007): 93–262.

Manishen, J. "Wrongful Convictions, Lessons Learner: The Canadian Experience." *Journal of Clinical Forensic Medicine* 13, no. 6–8 (2006): 296–99.

The National Academies. (October 13, 2006) *Pakistan-US Science and Technology Cooperative Program 2005.* Accessed on October 13, 2006, from www7.nationalacademies.org/dsc/Strand_CAMB_2005.html.

National Research Institute of Police Sciences, Japan. www.nrips.go.jp/index-e.html.

Nieves, E. (May/June 2002). *To Work and Die in Juarez.* Accessed on August 26, 2006, from www.motherjones.com/news/feature/2002/05/juarez.html.

Rainio, J., K. Karkola, K. Lalu, H. Ranta, K. Takamaa, and A. Penttila. "Forensic Investigations in Kosovo: Experiences of the Europena Union Forensic Expert Team." *Journal of Clinical Forensic Medicine* 8 (2001): 218–21.

Reddy. K. S. The Hindu. "ISO-17025 certification for State Forensic Lab." Accessed: on June 28, 2006, from www.hindu.com/2004/10/04/stories/2004100411800500.htm.

Tomaszewski, T., and P. Girdwoyn. "Scent Identification Evidence in Jurisdiction (Drawing on the Example of Judicial Practice in Poland)." *Forensic Science International.* 162, no. 1–3 (October 16, 2006): 191–95.

Weissert, W. (June 4, 2004) *Report: No Serial Killer in Juarez.* Accessed on August 28, 2006, from www.phillyburbs.com/pb-dyn/news/88-06042004-311203.html.

Review Questions

1. Discuss some of the challenges that forensic science faces in developing nations.
2. How has the use of mitochondrial DNA changed the way DNA evidence is analyzed?
3. Why would a laboratory (like the state lab in India) seek ISO-17025 certification?
4. How does the centralization of laboratory services benefit countries in the EU?
5. How is policing adversely affected in a closed society?
6. How has poor policing contributed to the ongoing killings in Juarez, Mexico?
7. Discuss a few of the ways in which forensic science may assist in the prosecution of war criminals.
8. What are the four forensic science divisions at the National Research Institute of Police Science in Japan?
9. How can night-vision technology assist investigations?
10. How can cameras help to reduce crime in cities?

Some Things to Think About

1. Visual and auditory evidence is regularly presented in court. This chapter discussed advances in olfactory evidence. Postulate as to how the other "senses" may find their way into the courtroom as forensics continues to evolve.
2. Why shouldn't an expert witness be an advocate?
3. What do you feel is the most pressing ethical issue that forensics will face in the near future—why?

INDEX